A. Maclean (Alexander Maclean) Sinclair

The Clan Gillean

A. Maclean (Alexander Maclean) Sinclair

The Clan Gillean

ISBN/EAN: 9783743306486

Manufactured in Europe, USA, Canada, Australia, Japa

Cover: Foto ©ninafisch / pixelio.de

Manufactured and distributed by brebook publishing software (www.brebook.com)

A. Maclean (Alexander Maclean) Sinclair

The Clan Gillean

CONTENTS.

CHAPTER I.

	PAGE
Introduction	1

CHAPTER II.

Origin of the Clan Gillean	29

CHAPTER III.
The First Eight Chiefs.

I. Gillean of the Battle-Axe	40
II. Malise	41
III. Malcolm	42
IV. John Dubh	44
V. Lachlan Lùbanach	44
VI. Hector Roy of the Battles	53
VII. Lachlan Bronnach	55
VIII. Lachlan Og	58

CHAPTER IV.
Hector Odhar and Lachlan Cattanach.

IX. Hector Odhar	59
X. Lachlan Cattanach	61

CHAPTER V.

Hector Mor and Hector Og.

XI.	Hector Mor	90
XII.	Hector Og	106

CHAPTER VI.

XIII.	Sir Lachlan Mor	108

CHAPTER VII.

Hector Og and Hector Mor.

XIV.	Hector Og	159
XV.	Hector Mor	177

CHAPTER VIII.

Sir Lachlan and His Sons.

XVI.	Sir Lachlan, First Baronet	178
XVII.	Sir Hector Roy, Second Baronet	191
XVIII.	Sir Allan, Third Baronet	196

CHAPTER IX.

Sir John and Sir Hector.

XIX.	Sir John, Fourth Baronet	202
XX.	Sir Hector, Fifth Baronet	236

CHAPTER X.

Genealogy of the Macleans of Duart. 247

CHAPTER XI.

The Macleans and Maclaines of Lochbuie.

THE MACLEANS OF LOCHBUIE	254
THE MACLAINES OF LOCHBUIE	266

BRANCHES.

The Macleans of Scallasdale	272
The Macleans of Uisken	273
The Maclaines of Scallasdale	274

CONTENTS.

CHAPTER XII.
The Descendants of Terlach Mac Hector.

THE MACLEANS OF URCHART	276
BRANCHES.	
1. THE MACLEANS OF KINGERLOCH	279
The Macleans of Rochester	284
Captain John Maclean	285
2. THE MACLEANS OF DOCHGARROCH	286
The Macleans of Culbokie	295
The Macleans of Kaffraria	297
The Macleans of Pitmain	298
The Macleans of Lochgorm	300
3. THE MACLEANS OF KNOCK	303

CHAPTER XIII.
The Descendants of Donald of Ardgour.

THE MACLEANS OF ARDGOUR	305
BRANCHES.	
1. THE MACLEANS OF BORERAY	315
(1) Terlach Mac Neil Bàn	320
The Macleans of Scour	320
The Macleans of Princeton	322
The Macleans of Kilmoluaig	323
(2) The Macleans of Heisker	325
(3) The Macleans of Balliphetrish	327
2. THE MACLEANS OF TRESHNISH	330
The First Macleans of Blaaich	335
The Macleans of Achnadale	336
The Macleans of Hynish	337
The Macleans of Glenbard	339
3. THE MACLEANS OF INVERSCADALE	341
4. THE LATER MACLEANS OF BLAAICH	343
Major-General Francis Maclean	343

CHAPTER XIV.

The Descendants of Neil of Lehir.

THE MACLEANS OF LEHIR	346
The Macleans of Langamull	347
BRANCHES.	
1. THE MACLEANS OF ROSS	349
(1) Lachlan Odhar of Airdchraoishnish	349
The Macleans of Monachuich	352
Lachlan Bàn of Bunessan	352
(2) Ewen of Ormsaig	354
The Macleans of Killean	355
The Macleans of Ardfinaig	358
(3) John Odhar	360
2. THE MACLEANS OF SHUNA	360
The Macleans of Laggan, Islay	363

CHAPTER XV.

The Descendants of John Garbh of Coll.

THE MACLEANS OF COLL	367
BRANCHES.	
1. THE MACLEANS OF ARNABOST	384
NEIL MOR AND NEIL OG	386
2. THE MACLEANS OF CROSSAPOL	389
Rev. Donald Maclean	390
The Last Macleans of Giurdal	395
3. THE MACLEANS OF ACHNASAUL	396
Lachlan Maclean	400
Rory Maclean	401
4. THE FIRST MACLEANS OF GRISHIPOL	402
5. THE MACLEANS OF MUCK	404
Hugh Mac Hector	409
Lachlan Mac Hector	409
The Macleans of Haremere Hall	410

The Descendants of John Garbh of Coll.—(continued)

	PAGE
6. THE MACLEANS OF DRIMNACROSS	411
The Macleans of Germany	413
Dr. Neil Maclean, of Connecticut	414
Allan Maclean, of Connecticut	415
7. THE MACLEANS OF TOTARANALD	418
8. THE MACLEANS OF GALLANACH	419

CHAPTER XVI.
The Macleans of Gigha and Morvern.

	PAGE
THE MACLEANS OF GIGHA	424
John Diurach	432
THE MACLEANS OF MORVERN	433
1. ALLAN MAC IAN DUY	434
(1) THE MACLEANS OF KINLOCHALINE	435
(2) TERLACH MAC ALLAN	436
THE MACLEANS OF DRIMNIN	437
THE MACLEANS OF CALGARY	443
THE MACLEANS OF GRULIN	444
The Macleans of Killunaig	446
Hector of Torranbeg	447
The Macleans of Pennycross	448
The Macleans of Pennygoun	450
DONALD MAC TERLACH	452
HECTOR MAC TERLACH	453
EWEN MAC TERLACH	454
2. JOHN GARBH MAC IAN DUY	454
3. CHARLES MAC IAIN DUY	455

CHAPTER XVII.
The Macleans of Torloisk, Sweden, and Brolas.

THE MACLEANS OF TORLOISK	457
THE MACLEANS OF SWEDEN	463
THE MACLEANS OF BROLAS	465

Contents.

The Last Five Chiefs of the Clan Gillean.

		PAGE
XXI. Sir Allan of Brolas, Sixth Baronet	. .	468
XXII. Sir Hector Maclean, Seventh Baronet	.	470
XXIII. Sir Fitzroy J. G. Maclean, Eighth Baronet	.	471
XXIV. Sir Charles Fitzroy Maclean, Ninth Baronet		471
XXV. Sir Fitzroy Donald Maclean, Tenth Baronet	.	472

CHAPTER XVIII.

𝔘ntraced 𝔉amilies 477

CHAPTER XIX.

The Chiefship of the Clan Gillean.

General Facts with Regard to the Chiefship of Clans   493
The Claims of the Maclaines of Lochbuie to the Chiefship
  of the Clan Gillean 498
Proofs of the Chiefship of the Macleans of Duart . 500

ADDITIONS, REFERENCES, AND CORRECTIONS . . . 515
LIST OF SUBSCRIBERS 525

MACLEAN

MACLEAN (HUNTING)

THE CLAN GILLEAN.

CHAPTER I.

Introduction.

I. THE KINGS OF SCOTLAND FROM 1058 TO 1603.

MALCOLM III. ascended the Scottish throne in 1058 A.D. He was known as Gillecalum a chinn mhóir, or Malcolm of the big head. He married, first, Ingebiorg, widow of Thorfinn, Earl of Caithness and Orkney, by whom he had two sons, Duncan and Donald. He married, secondly, Margaret, daughter of Edward, son of Edmund Ironside, and had by her eight children, Edward, Ethelred, Edmund, Edgar, Alexander, David, Matilda, and another daughter. He was killed at Alnwick in 1093. Matilda was married in 1100 to Henry I., King of England. Malcolm Kenmore was succeeded by his brother, Donald Bàn, who, according to the Scottish law of succession, was the lawful heir. Duncan, the eldest son of Malcolm, procured from the King of England a large number of Anglo-Norman soldiers and deposed

Donald Bàn. Duncan was murdered after a reign of fifteen months, and Donald Ban restored. In 1097, Edgar, the sixth son of Malcolm Kenmore, obtained help from the King of England, and deposed Donald Bàn a second time. He deprived him of his eyesight, and threw him into prison. King Edgar removed the court from Scone to Edinburgh. He looked upon Scotland as his own property, and willed the kingdom to his brothers, Alexander and David. Alexander became King of Scotland in 1107. He was known as Alexander the Fierce. He crushed an insurrection of the men of the Mearns and Moray, in 1116. He was succeeded by his brother David, Earl of Cumbria, in 1124. David, known as David I., had a son named Henry, who had three sons, Malcolm the Maiden, William the Lion, and David, Earl of Huntingdon.

According to the tribal system of government the land belonged to the people who resided on it and used it for the purpose of making a living for themselves and their children. According to the feudal system the land belonged to the king, not by a fiction of law, but in reality. As the king was the owner of the land he had a right to divide it among his subjects as he pleased, and also a right to nominate his successor, and will the kingdom to him. This system was clearly in its nature a self-perpetuating despotism. The only limitation to the power given by it was the inability of the ruler to carry out his wishes in all cases.

According to the tribal system every tribe possessed a district of its own, the land being the property of the tribe as a whole. Every freeman had a right to a certain portion of arable land, whilst the pasture lands were held in common. The freemen consisted of the chief, the kinsmen of the chief, and those who were simply freemen. The serfs had no legal claim to a share of the land. The chief or head of the tribe was not a landlord. He had a right, like other freemen, to some of the land, but only to so much of it as he really needed as a means of supporting himself and his family. He had of course certain rights as the head ruler of the tribe, but the right to take possession of his neighbour's lands was not one of them. According to the feudal system the land belonged, not to the tribe, but to the person who had received it from the king, whether that person was the chief of the tribe or some Anglo-Norman adventurer. So far as the right to land was concerned the members of the tribe were, from a legal point of view, no better off than the serfs of the tribal system. The real difference between the tribal and the feudal systems was that the former took the family for its starting point, while the latter took the king for its starting point. The tribal system made regulations to suit a number of independent families living in the same district; the feudal system made regulations to suit the king, and to suit him as owner of the land and lord of the people.

The mode of introducing the feudal system into

a district was by no means of a complicated nature. The king gave the chief of the tribe, or some of his own favourites, a charter or deed of all the lands in the district, on condition of rendering to him, as owner of the lands, good, faithful, and gratuitous services. The people were now under a landlord, and a landlord who could depend upon the king to maintain him in his position. So long as the landlord flattered and pleased the king he was safe. If, however, he should be so unfortunate as to displease him by an act of disobedience, either in civil or religious matters, he might be deprived of his lands, and perhaps of his head.

The sons of Malcolm Kenmore were all thoroughly feudalistic in their conceptions of the mode of government and the ownership of land. It was as a feudal king that Edgar divided Scotland between his two brothers. But as Alexander's subjects were almost wholly Kelts, he was not in a position to extend feudalism, except on a small scale. David was in a better position, and was able to act with a firmer hand. He had a host of Anglo-Norman warriors under his control, and could always depend upon them to fight for the sake of getting an estate or an heiress. He planted quite a number of them as independent landlords among the old Keltic inhabitants. King Edgar introduced feudalism into Scotland; King David established it on a firm basis. The latter crushed out the Keltic spirit of personal independence—the same spirit as that of the ancient Greeks—to as great an extent as he possibly could. He was not a bad man ; he simply believed that he had a right to do as he liked with his own—with the hills and glens of Scotland as his property, and with the people as his servants.

Malcolm the Maiden succeeded his grandfather, David I., as King of Scotland in 1153. William the Lion succeeded Malcolm in 1165. Alexander II., only son of William the Lion succeeded his father in 1214. Alexander III., only son of Alexander II., was killed at Kinghorn by a fall from his horse in March, 1286. Margaret, granddaughter of Alexander, died in September, 1290. The legitimate descendants of William the Lion were now extinct. John Baliol, who, according to the feudal system, was the lawful heir to the throne, was crowned King of Scotland, as a vassal of Edward I. of England, in November, 1292. In 1296 Edward compelled Baliol to surrender his crown and kingdom to him, and reduced the whole of Scotland to subjection. In the spring of 1297 William Wallace, the great uncrowned king of Scots, raised the standard of freedom, attacked the English oppressors, and drove them, bag and baggage, beyond the Tweed. He could overcome the English, but he could not overcome the cupidity, vanity, folly, and treachery of his own countrymen. He was betrayed and delivered to Edward by Sir John Stewart, son of Walter Ballach Stewart, son of the High Steward of Scotland. He was put to death in London, with the most shocking barbarity and cruelty, on the 23rd of August, 1305. Robert Bruce was crowned King of Scots at Scone on March 25th, 1306. He defeated the English at Bannockburn on Monday, June 24th, 1314, and by this magnificent victory restored his country to its former state of independence. He died on June 7th, 1329, in the fifty-fifth year of his age and twenty-third of his reign. Of all the Scottish monarchs he was by far the greatest. David Bruce, known as David II., was only five years of age when his father died. He was crowned at Scone in November, 1331. Edward, son of John Baliol, was King of Scotland, off and on, from 1332 until 1338. David Bruce took the reins of government into his own hands in 1342. He was a prisoner in England from 1346 until 1357. He died childless in 1370.

Walter, High Steward of Scotland in the time of David I., was the ancestor of the Stewarts. He was succeeded by his son Allan, who was succeeded by his son Walter. Walter, the third High Steward, had two sons, Alexander and Walter Ballach. Alexander succeeded his father as High Steward. Walter Ballach obtained possession of the earldom of Menteith. He had two sons, both of whom changed their name to Menteith. John, his second son, was the Judas who sold Wallace to the English. Alexander, the fourth High Steward, married Jane, daughter of James, son of Angus, son of Somerled of Argyll. He had two sons by her, James and John. James was succeeded as

High Steward by his son Walter. Walter, the sixth High Steward, was one of the principal commanders at the battle of Bannockburn. He married Marjory, daughter of Robert Bruce, by whom he had one son, Robert. Robert, the seventh High Steward, was born in 1315. He had ten natural children—four sons and six daughters—by Elizabeth Moore. He married her in 1349, but had no issue by her after their marriage. He married in 1355, Euphemia, daughter of William, Earl of Ross, by whom he had two sons, David and Walter. He became King of Scotland, as Robert II., in 1370. He died in 1390. John, his eldest son, was born about 1335. John succeeded his father as King, but changed his name to Robert. He is consequently known in history as Robert III. Walter, second son of Robert II., died without issue in 1360. Robert, the third son, was created Duke of Albany in 1398. Alexander, the fourth son, became Earl of Buchan in 1371, and afterwards Earl of Ross. He was known as the Wolf of Badenoch. He died in 1394. He left four natural sons. Alexander, the eldest of his sons, became Earl of Mar in 1404. Alexander died in August, 1435. He left two natural children, Thomas and Janet. David, fifth son of Robert II., and his first son by Euphemia Ross, became Earl of Strathearn in 1371. Euphemia, his only child, was married to Sir Patrick Graham, who in her right became Earl of Strathearn. Walter, sixth son of Robert II., was created Earl of

Atholl in 1403. He had two sons, Robert and Allan. The latter was for a short time Earl of Caithness. Robert III. died in 1406. James I., his son and successor, was murdered at Perth in February, 1437. James I. was the ablest and best of the Stewarts. James II. was killed at Roxburgh, by the accidental bursting of a cannon, in August, 1460. James III. was slain at Sauchieburn in June, 1488. James IV. fell at the battle of Flodden on September 9th, 1513. James V. died in December, 1542, and was succeeded by his only child, Mary Queen of Scots. Queen Mary was deposed in July, 1567, and beheaded in England in February, 1587. James VI., Queen Mary's son, was born in Edinburgh in June, 1566, and crowned at Stirling in July, 1567. He was educated by the celebrated George Buchanan, and made rapid progress in learning. He began to govern the kingdom in 1578. He became King of England and Ireland in 1603. He was now King of all the Britons. He died in March, 1625.

II. THE MACDOUGALLS OF LORN.

In 1140, Somerled, Lord of Arregaithel, or Argyll, married Ragnhildis, daughter of Olave the Red, the Norwegian sub-king of Man, and had by her three sons, Dugald, Reginald, and Angus. He was either assassinated or slain in battle at Renfrew on the Clyde in 1164. Dugald, his eldest son by Ragnhildis, was the progenitor of the Macdougalls of Lorn. Dugald possessed the whole of Lorn—which extended from Loch Leven to the Point of Asknish—the districts of Morvern and Ardnamurchan, and the islands of Lismore, Kerrera, Seil, Luing, Shuna, Scarba, Jura, Mull, Iona, Ulva, and Tiree. He was succeeded by his son, Duncan, who was chief of the Macdougalls in 1244. Duncan had three sons, Ewen, Alexander, and Malcolm. Ewen held the castle of Cairnburgh and other strongholds for Haco, King of Norway, in 1249. He refused to support Haco in 1263. He was succeeded by his brother Alexander, who was the most powerful of all the Macdougall chiefs. Alexander fought against Robert Bruce, and was deprived of all his possessions. John Bacach, his son and successor, received a charter of the district of Lorn from David II. John Bacach, had four sons, John, Somerled, Allan, and Alexander Og. John succeeded his father. He was the sixth and last Macdougall of Lorn. He had two daughters, who inherited his estate, and found husbands among the Stewarts. Allan, his brother, succeeded him as chief of the Clan Dugall.

III. The Macrories of Uist and Garmoran.

Reginald, or Ranald, second son of Somerled and Ragnhildis, had two sons, Donald and Rory. Donald was the progenitor of the Clan Donald; Rory was the progenitor of the Clan Rory.

Rory, second son of Reginald, succeeded his

father in North Kintyre and other lands. He was a noted pirate. He fought under King Haco at the battle of Largs in 1263. He received from Alexander III. the islands of Rum, Eigg, Barra, and Uist, in 1266. He was succeeded by his son Dugald, who was succeeded by his brother Allan. Allan obtained possession of Garmoran, as the districts of Moydart, Arisaig, Morar, and Knoydart, were called. He left three natural sons, Roderick, Lachlan, and Dugald, and a legitimate daughter named Christina. Roderick succeeded his father as chief of the Clan Rory. He joined Bruce in 1307, and followed him faithfully until the independence of Scotland was secured on the field of Bannockburn. Bruce, in reward of his services, bestowed upon him the district of Lorn, and also some lands in Lochaber. He was married, and had two children, Ranald and Amie. Ranald was known as Raonall Fionn. He was murdered in 1346 by William, Earl of Ross. His possessions became the property of his sister Amie. The Macrories were now landless.

IV. THE LORDS OF THE ISLES.

Donald, son of Reginald, son of Somerled, was the progenitor and first chief of the Clan Donald. He held the lands of South Kintyre and Islay. He was succeeded by his son Angus Mor, who was succeeded by his son Alexander, who was succeeded by his brother, Angus Og. Angus Og was a faithful adherent of Robert Bruce, who bestowed upon him the islands of Tiree, Coll, Mull, and Jura, and the districts of Morvern, Ardnamurchan, Duror, Glencoe, and Lochaber. Bruce gave the Macdonald lands in Kintyre to Robert, son and heir of the High Steward, and placed the Castle of Tarbert in charge of a royal garrison. Angus Og was succeeded by his son John. John was the fifth chief of the Clan Donald. He married, about 1337, Amy, daughter of Allan Macrory of Garmoran. On the death of Ranald of Garmoran, Amy succeeded to his estates. The chief of the Clan Donald was now in possession of an extensive estate, and styled himself, as he had a perfect right to do, Lord of the Isles. About the year 1358 he discarded his wife, Amy Macrory, who was in every respect an excellent woman, and married Margaret, daughter of Robert, High Steward of Scotland. By his first wife, the amiable but ill-treated Amy Macrory, he had four children, John, Ranald, Godfrey, and Mary. By his second wife, Margaret Stewart, he had three sons, Donald, John Mor Tanaistear, and Alexander. He died at Ardtornish in 1386. John, his eldest son, had a son named Angus, who died without issue. Reginald was the progenitor of the Clan Ranald. Godfrey settled in North Uist. Donald succeeded his father as chief of the Clan Donald. John Mor Tanaistear was the progenitor of the Macdonalds of Islay and the Glens. Alexander, known as Alasdair Carrach, was the progenitor of the Macdonalds of Keppoch.

Donald, sixth chief of the Clan Donald, and second Lord of the Isles, was educated at Oxford. He married Margaret, daughter of Sir Walter Lesley, and in her right claimed the earldom of Ross. Robert, Duke of Albany, who was regent of Scotland, wanted the earldom for his own son, and with gross injustice refused to give it to Donald. In June, 1411, Donald raised his followers and sailed with a large fleet from Ardtornish to Strome, where he landed. He defeated Angus Dubh Mackay and Mackenzie of Kintail at Dingwall, and afterwards took possession of Inverness. He left Inverness with an army of 10,000 men and marched towards Aberdeen. He encountered the Earl of Mar at Harlaw on the 26th of July. Instead of renewing the battle the next day and utterly crushing his opponents, he began to retrace his steps. His fight at Harlaw was thus of no immediate benefit to him. He died about the year 1423. He was succeeded by his son, Alexander.

Alexander, seventh chief of the Clan Donald, and third Lord of the Isles, was seized by James I. at Inverness in 1427, and carried off a prisoner to Perth. He was released shortly afterwards. In 1429 he raised an army of 10,000 men, and attempted to obtain possession of the earldom of Ross. James I. collected a strong force and marched against him. The Camerons and the Mackintoshes deserted the Lord of the Isles and joined the King. James entered Lochaber about

the beginning of 1430 and inflicted a severe defeat
upon Alexander and his followers. Shortly afterwards the Lord of the Isles went to Edinburgh and
threw himself upon the mercy of the King. His
life was spared, but he was confined in Tantallon
Castle. The King planted a royal garrison at
Inverlochy, and placed Alexander Stewart, Earl of
Mar, and Allan Stewart, Earl of Caithness, in
charge of it. In 1431 Donald Ballach, son of
John Mor Tanaistear, sailed with a large fleet to
Lochaber, and disembarked at Inverskipnish, two
miles from Inverlochy. The Earls of Mar and
Caithness attacked the invaders, but suffered a
crushing defeat. The former was slain; the latter
succeeded in making his escape. Immediately
after this battle Donald Ballach plundered and
laid waste the lands of the Camerons and the
Mackintoshes, who had been supporting the King
against the Lord of the Isles. James led an army
to Dunstaffnage Castle, with the avowed intention
of pursuing and punishing his rebellious subjects.
The chiefs and chieftains of the Isles deemed it
prudent to go to meet him and throw themselves
on his mercy. Donald Ballach fled to Ireland.
Alexander of the Isles was set at liberty in October,
1431. Shortly after the death of James I., which
took place in February, 1437, the Lord of the Isles
received the much-coveted earldom of Ross. He
was at the same time appointed Justiciar of the
whole of Scotland north of the Forth. He drove
the chief of the Camerons out of Lochaber, and

gave a charter of their lands to John Garbh Maclean of Coll. Alexander had a natural son, named Gillespick or Celestine, by a daughter of Macphie in Lochaber. He had another natural son, named Hugh or Austin, by a daughter of Patrick Roy Obeolan. He married, about 1430, Elizabeth, daughter of Alexander Seton, Lord Gordon and Huntly, and had one son by her, John, his successor. He died in May, 1449.

John, eighth chief of the Clan Donald, fourth Lord of the Isles, and second Earl of Ross, was born about the year 1431. In 1462 James, ninth Earl of Douglas, the Earl of Ross, and Donald Ballach entered into a treaty with Edward IV. of England for the conquest and division of Scotland. This treaty was kept a profound secret until 1475. As soon as it came to light steps were taken to visit the Earl of Ross with the punishment which he so richly deserved. In December, 1475, the government of Scotland declared him a traitor, condemned him to death, and deprived him of all his possessions. In June, 1476, he went to Edinburgh, confessed his faults, and cast himself upon the royal mercy. The King pardoned him for his rebellious conduct, and also treated him in a very liberal manner. His possessions were all restored him, except the earldom of Ross and the lands of Kintyre and Knapdale. Angus Og and John, his natural sons, were at the same time acknowledged as his legal successors. He was still Lord of the Isles, and should have been profoundly thankful that he had escaped so well.

Shortly after the settlement of 1476, Angus Og, heir apparent of the Lord of the Isles, quarrelled with his father. This quarrel terminated in a war. About the year 1484 Angus Og defeated his father at the battle of Bloody Bay and inflicted a heavy loss on him. Angus was a hot-tempered and imprudent man, but brave, energetic, and generous. He was undoubtedly a very able commander. He was murdered at Inverness by a treacherous Irish harper, in 1490. In 1491 Alexander Macdonald of Lochalsh, apparently with the consent of his uncle, the Lord of the Isles, made an attempt to wrest the earldom of Ross from the government. He was utterly ignorant of the art of war, and apparently too full of conceit to take advice from any of the old warriors who served under him. He was attacked at Park, near the river Conan, by Kenneth Mackenzie of Kintail, a very able commander, and completely defeated. In 1493 Alexander of the Isles was deprived by the government of all his estates and titles. He died in a lodging-house at Dundee in 1498. His funeral expenses were paid by the government. From the battle of Harlaw in 1411 to the battle of Park in 1491 the earldom of Ross was only a curse to the Lords of the Isles. It would have been better for them if they had never claimed it. They were brave and generous men ; but they were too fond of land and power for their own good.

Alexander of the Isles had three children, Angus Og, John, and Margaret. John died without issue. Angus Og married, about 1478, Mary, daughter of Colin Campbell, first Earl of Argyll, and had by her one son, Donald Dubh, who, on the death of his grandfather in 1498, became chief of the Clan Donald.

V. THE MACDONALDS OF ISLAY AND THE GLENS.

John Mor Tanaistear, fifth son of the first Lord of the Isles, received from his father 120 marklands in Kintyre and 60 marklands in Islay, in all about 5,400 acres. He resided at Dun-Naomhaig or Dunniveg in Islay. He married, in 1399, Marjory Bisset, and obtained the Glens of Antrim with her as a dowry. He was murdered by a man named James Campbell, in 1426. He was succeeded by his son, the warlike Donald Ballach, who died about 1480. Donald Ballach was succeeded by his son John Mor, who was succeeded by his son, John Cathanach. John Cathanach was on very bad terms with John Macdonald of Ardnamurchan, with whom he had a dispute regarding the lands of Sunart. He seized the royal castle of Dunaverty in 1498, and put its defenders to death. James IV. commissioned Archibald, second Earl of Argyll, to bring him to account for his rebellious act. Argyll found a willing assistant in John of Ardnamurchan. The latter treacherously seized John Cathanach and two of his sons at Finlaggan Castle in Islay, and sent them to Edinburgh, where they were executed. John Cathanach was succeeded

by his son Alexander, who was known as Alasdair
Mac Iain Chathanaich. Alexander married Catherine, daughter of John of **Ardnamurchan**, his
father's enemy and captor. He had by his wife
nine children, James, Angus, Coll, Alexander Og,
Donald **Gorm, Sorley** Buie, **Mary, Meve,** and
another daughter. James succeeded his father.
Coll was the ancestor of the famous Alasdair Mac
Cholla, the supporter of Montrose. Sorley Buie
obtained possession of the Glens of **Antrim** in
1586, and had a son named Randal, who was
created Earl of Antrim in 1620.

James, sixth Macdonald of Islay and the Glens,
was educated in Edinburgh. He possessed an
extensive estate. It embraced 91 marklands and
1064 shilling lands in Islay ; the lands of **Kintyre,**
north and south, consisting of **294** marklands and
53 shilling lands ; the lands of **Ardnamurchan and
Sunart ;** 184 shilling lands in **Jura ;** certain lands
in Arran, Gigha, Colonsay, and **Uist ;** and the
Glens of Antrim. In 1565 he crossed over to
Ireland to assist his brothers against Shane O'Neill.
He was defeated, wounded, and taken prisoner at
the battle of Glentaise on the 2nd of May. He
was imprisoned in Castle Corcke near Strathbane,
where he died in the course of two months. He
was married to Agnes, daughter of **Colin,** sixth
Earl of Argyll. He left six sons, Archibald,
Angus, Coll, Ranald, Donald Gorm, and Alexander. Archibald died shortly after his father, and
was succeeded by his brother, Angus. In 1596

Angus sold the island of Gigha to Sir John Campbell of Calder for 3,000 marks. He married a daughter of Hector Og Maclean of Duart, by whom he had three children, James, Angus Og, and Margaret. James, Angus's son, was the ninth and last Macdonald of Islay.

VI. THE MACDONALDS OF SLEAT.

Hugh or Austin, first Macdonald of Sleat, was a son of Alexander, third Lord of the Isles. He was known as Uisdean Bàn, or fair-haired Hugh. He made a plundering expedition to Orkney, along with William Macleod of Dunvegan, in the year 1460. On his way back he remained for some time in Caithness. He received a charter of Sleat, Benbecula, and other lands, in 1469. He had three natural sons. He had Donald Gallach by a daughter of the chief of the Gunns, Donald Herrach by a daughter of Macleod of Dunvegan, and Gilleasbuig Dubh by some other woman. He married Finvola, daughter of John Macdonald of Ardnamurchan, and had by her a son named John. His wife was living in 1469. He died in 1498. John, second of Sleat, died without issue in 1502. Donald Gallach, third of Sleat, was born about 1461. He had one son, Donald Gruamach. Donald Herrach, his brother, had two sons, Ranald and Angus Fionn. Gilleasbuig Dubh murdered his two brothers, Donald Gallach and Donald Herrach, in 1506, and took possession of all the lands which had belonged to his father. Donald

Gruamach and Ranald, son of Donald Herrach, slew the murderer of their fathers, about the year 1514. Donald Gruamach became laird of Sleat. Ranald distinguished himself as a warrior in Ireland. Owing to a severe wound he was under the necessity of returning to Scotland. He was accompanied to Skye by Dr. Maclean, a native of Mull. Ranald settled at Griminish. Donald Gruamach, fourth of Sleat, was succeeded by his son Donald Gorm, who was succeeded by his son Donald, sixth of Sleat. Dòmhnall Mac Dhòmhnaill Ghuirm married Mary, daughter of Hector Mor Maclean of Duart, by whom he had three sons, Donald Gorm Mor, Gilleasbuig Cléireach, and Alexander. Donald Gorm Mor succeeded his father in 1585, and died without issue in 1616. Gilleasbuig Cléireach, or Archibald the Clerk, married Margaret, daughter of Angus Macdonald of Islay, and granddaughter of Hector Mor of Duart. He had three children by her, Donald Gorm Og, Hugh, and Sheela. Hugh, who was known as Uisdean Mac Ghilleasbuig Chléirich, was a man of enormous physical strength, but extremely treacherous and selfish. He was a great curse both to the Macdonalds and the Macleans. Sheela, Gilleasbuig Cléireach's daughter, was married to John Macleod of Minginish and Waternish, by whom she had Tormod, John Dubh and others. John Dubh was a worse man than even his uncle Hugh. Donald Gorm Og, eighth of Sleat, was created a baronet on July 14th, 1625. He died in 1643.

VII. The Macdonalds of Lochalsh.

Celestine, natural son of Alexander, third Lord of the Isles, was the first Macdonald of Lochalsh. He possessed, in addition to Lochalsh, the districts of Lochcarron and Lochbroom. He married, about 1462, Finvola, daughter of Lachlan Bronnach of Duart, by whom he had Alexander, and two or three daughters. Alexander, second of Lochalsh, married a daughter of Lord Lovat. He was assassinated at Orinsay in 1497 by John Macdonald of Ardnamurchan. He left three sons and two daughters. Margaret, the elder daughter, was married to Alexander Macdonald, fourth of Glengarry. Janet, the second daughter, was married to Dingwall of Kildun. Donald Gallda, eldest son of Alexander, was the third Macdonald of Lochalsh. He died in 1519, either at Cairnburgh or in the island of Tiree. He was the last of the family of Lochalsh in the male line. His estates were divided between his two sisters. Dingwall of Kildun sold his half to Mackenzie of Kintail. The Macdonalds of Glengarry and the Mackenzies were now neighbours.

VIII. The Macdonalds of Glengarry.

Alexander, sixth of Glengarry, married Margaret, daughter of Sir Alexander Macdonald of Lochalsh, and great-granddaughter of Lachlan Bronnach of Duart. He had by her an only son, Angus. Angus, seventh of Glengarry, married a daughter of Hector Mor Maclean of Duart, and had by her one son, Donald. Donald, eighth of Glengarry, married Margaret, daughter of Allan Macdonald of Moydart, by whom he had Angus Og, Alexander, Donald of Scotus, and others. Angus Og was killed in a feud with the Mackenzies in 1602. Alexander, known as Alasdair Dearg, married Jane, daughter of Allan Cameron of Lochiel, by whom he had Angus. Donald of Glengarry died in 1645, and was succeeded by his grandson, Angus. Angus, ninth of Glengarry, was raised to the peerage, in 1660, by the title of Lord Macdonell and Arros. He died, without issue, in 1682.

IX. THE MACLEODS OF DUNVEGAN.

Leod, the progenitor of the Macleods, had two sons, Tormod, who succeeded him in Dunvegan, and Torquil, who succeeded him in Lewis. Tormod had two sons, Malcolm and Murdoch. Malcolm was succeeded by his son John, and John by his son William, who was known as Uilleam Cléireach. William married a daughter of Murdoch, second Maclean of Lochbuie, by whom he had John Borb, his successor. John Borb was succeeded by his son William Dubh, who married a daughter of John Maclean, third of Lochbuie, and was succeeded by his son Alexander. Alexander, known as Alasdair Crotach, was succeeded by his son William, who was succeeded by his brother Donald, who was succeeded by his brother Tormod. Tormod obtained possession of his father's estate in 1580. He married Marion, daughter of Hector Mor of Duart, by whom he had William, Rory Mor, Alexander, and three daughters. William, twelfth of Dunvegan, was succeeded in 1590 by his brother Rory Mor, who was knighted in 1613. Sir Rory married Isabel, daughter of Donald Macdonald, eighth of Glengarry, by whom he had John Mor, Sir Roderick of Talisker, Sir Norman of Bernera, William of Hamer, Donald of Grishornish, Margaret, Mary, Janet, and Florence. John Mor succeeded his father in 1626. He married Sibella, daughter of Kenneth, first Lord Mackenzie of Kintail, and had by her seven children, Roderick, John Breac, Mary, Marion, Julian, Sibella, and Margaret. Roderick succeeded his father in 1649. John Breac succeeded Roderick in 1664. Mary was married, as his second wife, to Sir James Macdonald, ninth of Sleat, and had one son, John of Backney. Marion was the mother of Ailein Muideartach, Allan of Moydart, who fell at Sheriffmuir in 1715. Julian was the mother of Sir John Maclean of Duart; Sibella was the mother of Simon Fraser, Lord Lovat, who was beheaded in 1747.

X. The Camerons of Lochiel.

The history of the Camerons of Lochiel begins with Donald Dubh, who fought at the battle of Harlaw in 1411. He was the son of Allan, son of Paul, son of Patrick, son of Martin, son of Paul, son of Millony, son of Gilleroth, who is mentioned in 1222, and was then living. He had two sons, Ewen and Allan. Ewen succeeded him as chief. Allan was captain of the Clan Cameron in 1472. Ewen, son of Allan, married a daughter of Celestine of Lochalsh, and a granddaughter of Lachlan Bronnach of Duart. He had by her Donald, his successor. He received from Alexander of Lochalsh, in 1492, a charter of the thirty marklands of Lochiel, the lands of Kilmallie, and others. Donald, son of Ewen, married, in 1520, Agnes, daughter of Sir James Grant of Freuchy, by whom he had Ewen Beag, who died about 1553. Ewen Beag was succeeded by his brother Donald, who married a daughter of Hector Mor of Duart, but died without issue. Donald was succeeded by his nephew, Allan, son of John Dubh. Allan was brought up under the care and protection of Lachlan Mor of Duart, and took an active part in avenging the death of the latter. He married a daughter of Stewart of Appin, by whom he had John, Donald and Jane. John married, in 1626, Margaret, daughter of Robert Campbell of Glenfalloch, by whom he had Ewen Dubh—the famous Sir Ewen of Lochiel. Donald was the ancestor of the Camerons of Glendessary. Jane was the mother of Lord Macdonell and Arros. Allan of Lochiel died about 1647, and was succeeded by his grandson, Ewen Dubh. Sir Ewen of Lochiel married, first, a daughter of Sir Donald Macdonald, eighth of Sleat, but had no issue by her. He married, secondly, **Isabel**, eldest daughter of **Sir Lachlan Maclean of Duart**, by whom he had **three sons** and four daughters. **He** married, thirdly, a daughter of Colonel David Barclay of Urie, by whom he had one son and seven daughters. He died in February, 1719.

XI. THE MACKENZIES OF KINTAIL.

Colin, Cailein Cam, eleventh Mackenzie of Kintail, succeeded his father, Coinneach na Cuirce or Kenneth of the dirk, in 1568. He married Barbara, daughter of John Grant of Freuchy by his wife, Marjory, daughter of John Stewart, third Earl of Atholl. He had by his wife eight children, Kenneth, Roderick, Alexander, Colin, Murdoch, and three daughters. He died in 1594. Kenneth, his eldest son, succeeded him in Kintail. Kenneth was created **Lord Mackenzie of Kintail** in 1609. He was succeeded in 1611 by his son Colin Roy, Cailein Ruadh, who was created **Earl of Seaforth** in 1623. Roderick, second son of Cailein Cam, was a man of ability and determination. He was for some time tutor of Kintail. He obtained the lands of Coigeach and Assynt by his wife. He was knighted in 1609. He died in 1628. He was succeeded by his son **John,** who was succeeded by his son **George,** who was created Earl of Cromarty in 1703. Cailein Og's eldest daughter was married to Simon, eighth **Lord Lovat.** His second daughter was married to Hector Og Maclean of Duart, by whom she had Hector Mor and Sir

Lachlan. His third daughter was married to Sir Donald Macdonald of Sleat, Dòmhnall Gorm Og, by whom she had Sir James, ninth of Sleat, Donald of Castletown, and others.

XII. THE CAMPBELLS OF ARGYLL.

"Dubgall Cambél," or Dugald Campbell, was the progenitor of the Campbells and thus their first chief. He flourished about the year 1225. He was the son of Gillespick, son of Malcolm, son of Duibhne. It is impossible to trace him farther back. Neil, son of Colin Mor, son of Gillespick, son of Dugald, was the fourth chief. He was a loyal supporter of Robert Bruce. He was married twice. By his first wife he had Colin, his successor. By his second wife, Marjory, sister of Robert Bruce, he had at least one son. Duncan, Donnachadh an Aigh, son of Colin, son of Gillespick Mor, son of Colin, son of Neil, was the eighth chief. He married Margaret, daughter of Robert Stewart, Duke of Albany, and granddaughter of King Robert II. He had two sons by her, Gillespick Roy, Gilleasbuig Ruadh, and Colin of Glenurchy. He was created Lord Campbell in 1445. He was a member of the Privy Council, Justice-General of Scotland, and Lieutenant of Argyll. Gillespick Roy, his heir, married Elizabeth, daughter of Lord Sommerville, by whom he had Colin and other children. Gillespick Roy died before his father. Lord Campbell died in 1453, and was succeeded by his grandson Colin, a boy of fifteen or sixteen years of age. Colin was created Earl of Argyll in 1457. He married shortly afterwards Margaret, daughter and co-heiress of John Stewart, Lord Lorn, by whom he had two sons and seven daughters. He was for a long time Chancellor of Scotland. He was succeeded by his son Archibald in 1493. Archibald, second Earl of Argyll, married Elizabeth, daughter of John Stewart, Earl of Lennox, by whom he had ten children, Colin, Archibald of Skipnish, John, Donald, Margaret, Isabel, Mary, Jane, Ann, and Elizabeth. He was slain at Flodden in 1513. Colin, his eldest son, succeeded him. John married, in 1510, Muriel, daughter and heiress of Sir John Calder, and obtained possession of her father's estate. He is known in history as Sir John Campbell of Calder. Colin, third Earl of Argyll, married Janet, daughter of Alexander Gordon, or really Seton, third Earl of Huntly, son of George, second Earl of Huntly, by his wife, Annabella, daughter of King James I. Colin had by his wife four children, Archibald, John Gorm of Lochnell, Alexander, and Margaret. He died in 1542. Archibald, fourth Earl of Argyll, embraced the Protestant religion, and was an active supporter of it. He married, first, Helen, daughter of James Hamilton, Earl of Arran, by whom he had Archibald, his successor. He married, secondly, Mary, daughter of William Graham, Earl of Menteith, by whom he had Colin of Buchan, Margaret, and Janet. He married, thirdly, Catherine, daughter of Hector

Mor Maclean of Duart. He died in 1558. His widow held the lands of Craignish in life-rent. Margaret, his elder daughter, was married to James Stewart, Lord Down, by whom she had James, "the bonny Earl of Moray." Janet was married to Hector Og Maclean of Duart, by whom she had the celebrated Lachlan Mor. Archibald, fifth Earl of Argyll, died in 1575, and was succeeded by his brother, Colin of Buchan. Colin, sixth Earl of Argyll, had two sons, Archibald and Colin of Lundy. He died in 1584. Archibald, seventh Earl of Argyll, fought against the Roman Catholic earls, Huntly and Errol, at Glenlivet in 1594. He pursued and slaughtered the Macgregors without mercy in 1603. He persuaded their chief, Alexander Macgregor of Glenstrae, to surrender to him, by promising him that he would send him to England, whither he desired to go to plead with King James for pardon. Instead of carrying out his promise in an honest way, he sent Macgregor across the Tweed, and then took him back to Scotland, and conveyed him to Edinburgh to be put to death. Alexander of Glenstrae was executed on January 12th, 1604. Archibald of Argyll married, first, Ann, daughter of William Douglas, Earl of Morton, by whom he had Archibald, his successor. He married, secondly, Ann, daughter of Sir William Cornwallis of Brome. Through the influence of his second wife, he became a Roman Catholic. In 1618 he left Scotland, and entered the service of Philip II., King of Spain. He tried now to atone for his opposition to the Roman Catholic earls in 1594 by fighting, under the Duke of Alva, against the Protestants of Holland and killing as many of them as he could. He died in London in 1638.

Archibald, eighth Earl of Argyll, was born in 1698. He was known as Gilleasbuig Gruamach, or morose Archibald. He became practically chief of the Campbells when his father left Scotland in 1618. He received the family estates shortly afterwards. He succeeded his father as Earl in 1638, and was created Marquis of Argyll in 1641. He married Margaret, daughter of William Douglas, seventh Earl of Morton, by whom he had two sons, Archibald, his successor, and Neil of Ardmaddy. He was beheaded with the maiden at the Cross of Edinburgh on May 27th, 1661. Archibald, ninth Earl of Argyll, married Mary, daughter of James Stewart, Earl of Murray, by whom he had Archibald, his successor, John Campbell of Mamore, and others. He was executed in Edinburgh on June 30th, 1685. Archibald, tenth Earl of Argyll, came to Britain with the Prince of Orange in 1688, and received all the titles and possessions which had belonged to his father. He was created Duke of Argyll and Marquis of Lorn on July 23rd, 1701. The Campbells were now at the height of their power. He died in 1703, and was succeeded by his son John, Iain Ruadh, a man of ability and kindness of heart.

CHAPTER II.

Origin of the Clan Gillean.

THE Book of Ballymote, the Book of Leccan, the Skene Manuscript, and MacFirbis's Book of Genealogies are the oldest works that deal with the origin of the Highland Clans. The first was compiled in 1383 A.D., the second in 1416, the third in 1467, and the fourth between 1650 and 1666. The Skene MS., or as Skene himself calls it, the MS. of 1467, was written in Scotland; the others were written in Ireland; but they all agree in deriving the Highland Clans from the kings and kinglets of Ireland. The Macleans are traced back, first, to Lorn Mac Erc, and next through a long line of royal ancestors to the great Milesius. The other clans are honoured in the same way.

According to the early historians of Ireland, Eber and Eremon, the sons of Milesius, began to reign over Erin as joint-kings in the year 1699 B.C. Angus Tuirmeach, who was lineally descended from Eremon, became high-king of Ireland in the year 384 B.C. He was an excellent king, and reigned during the long period of sixty years. He died quietly in his bed at Tara. Two of his sons, Enna Aighneach and Fiachaidh Fearmara, were very eminent men. Enna was the ancestor of Conn Ceudchathach and the Macdonalds. Fiachaidh was the ancestor of the kings of Scotland, the Macleans, Macgregors, and other clans. As the word tuirmeach means having many children, we may take for granted that the good King Angus had a very large family. As he was a heathen, and a powerful king, it is possible that he did not deem it necessary to limit himself to one wife. Eidersgeol, a descendant of Angus, became high-king of Ireland in the year 130 B.C. He reigned five years. Conaire Mór, son of Eidersgeol, became high-king in 109 B.C. He had a prosperous reign of thirty years. Conaire, son of Mogh-Lamha, and a descendant of Conaire Mór, married a daughter of Conn Ceudchathach, and succeeded his father-in-law as high-king of Ireland in 158 A.D. He had by his wife three sons, Carbri Riada, Carbri Baschaoin, and Carbri Musg. Eochaidh Muinreamhair, or Eochy of the fat neck, was descended from Carbri Riada. He was King of Dalriada in Ulster, and had two sons, Erc and Eolchu. Erc, who succeeded his father, as King of Dalriada, had three sons, Fergus, Lorn, and Angus. About 497 A.D. the sons of Erc settled in Argyll, and founded the kingdom of Dalriada. In 844 A.D., Kenneth Mac Alpin, King of the Dalriadan Scots, succeeded in placing himself upon the Pictish throne. By uniting the Picts and Scots under his authority he laid the foundation of the kingdom of Alban, or Scotland.

As the Gaelic words **paipear,** peann, litir, leugh, and sgriobh, or paper, pen, letter, read, and write, are all of Latin origin, we may safely conclude that the Gaidels learned the art of reading and writing from the Romans. But the Romans did not settle in South Britain until the year 43 A.D. Patrick settled in Ireland about 425 A.D., and died about 469. There may have been some men in Ireland, before the time of Patrick, who could read and write, but they must have been extremely few. It is quite certain that the pious and zealous Patrick did not trouble his head with genealogies and histories. It is equally certain that the first converts to the Christian religion had nothing to do with these branches of knowledge. They had more important matters to attend to. It may be regarded as fairly certain, then, that there was not a single historical or genealogical work of Irish origin in existence prior to 450 A.D. As this is our belief, we attach very little importance to the history of pagan Ireland. It is certain that it contains elements of truth; but it is equally certain that it is to a very large extent a mass of fictions. So far as the genealogies are concerned, they are utterly untrustworthy. There may have been a man in Ireland who was known as Angus Tuirmeach of Tara, but to suppose that the Macleans, Macdonalds, or any other clan, could be traced back to him step by step, would be sheer hallucination.

The pedigrees of the Highland Clans as given by the Irish genealogists and the writer of the Skene MS. are fairly correct to the year 1150, or the time of Malcolm Kenmore. From that date back to the year 844 they are trustworthy only to a very small extent. Back of 844 A.D. they are utterly worthless for historical purposes. We know the names of the kings who flourished in Alban between the days of the sons of Erc and the time of Kenneth Mac Alpin; but with the names of the chiefs and chieftains who quarrelled and fought and fell during that period we are almost wholly unacquainted.

According to the genealogy of the Macleans as given in the MS. of 1467, Old Dugald of Scone was the son of Fearchar Abhraruaidh. Old Dugald must have been born about the year 1030. Fearchar Abhraruaidh was a young man, and probably fighting under his brother Fearchar Fada, in 678. How, then, could Old Dugald have been his son? The plain fact is that the writer of the MS. of 1467 knew nothing whatever about the ancestors of Old Dugald of Scone. Yet he was a good scholar, and as intimately acquainted with the genealogy of the Macleans as he was with that of any other clan. He would no doubt have given it correctly as far back as the time of the sons of Erc if he had the materials required. But the materials he had not. The presumption, then, is that they were not in existence.

Origin of the Clan.

It is held by some writers that the Macleans are of Norman origin. Gillean, it is affirmed, was a son of John Fitz-Thomas, chief of the Geraldines in Ireland, who was descended from a certain Otho that came over to England with William the Conqueror. We are also told that Gillean had a brother named Colin, that Colin had a son named Kenneth, and that Kenneth was the progenitor of the Mackenzies. The writer of the Ardgour MS. accepts the foregoing views in full. These are his words:—"Upon the whole the account of the Macleans being brothers to the Mackenzies from their first settlement in Scotland, together with their descent from the Fitzgeralds, is founded on undeniable facts and the unexceptionable testimonies of the best historians and public records, together with a constant tradition to the same purpose amongst the two clans."

The theory which maintains that the Macleans and the Mackenzies are of Norman descent is of comparatively recent origin. The earliest trace of it on record is to be found in a manuscript history of the Mackenzies, written by George, first Earl of Cromarty, in 1669. It has no foundation upon which to rest. It is based entirely on a forged charter and an ancient fragment of history, which was said to exist, but which no one has ever seen. Besides, it is contrary to well-known facts. It is simply the invention of those Highland genealogists who believed that it was more honourable to be descended from some Danish pirate, Norman knight, or Irish kingling, than from an honest farmer, hunter, or shepherd in their own glens. It stands upon a level with the absurd notion that the Gaidels of Scotland and Ireland are descended from Gathelus and his wife, Scota, daughter of Pharaoh, King of Egypt. Kenneth, the progenitor of the Mackenzies, was not the son either of Colin Fitzgerald or of any other Colin. He was the son of Angus, son of Gilchrist, son of Kenneth, son of Gilleain Og, son of Gilleain na h-Airde, or Gillean of the Aird. While the Macleans and the Mackenzies were invariably good friends, we have no ground for supposing that their progenitors were related. Gillean of the battle-axe lived in Argyleshire, while Gillean of the Aird lived in Ross-shire.

About the year 1160, Malcolm IV., King of Scotland, removed some of the inhabitants of the province of Moray from their old homes, and planted strangers from the Lowlands in their place. Skene, in his "Highlanders of Scotland," started the theory that among the men who were removed by King Malcolm were the Macleans. He considered it "not unlikely that Glenurchart was their original settlement," and regarded the district of Lorn as their oldest seat in Argyleshire —the place to which they had been removed by King Malcolm. "The Highlanders of Scotland" is a valuable work. At the same time it is the production of a young man, and contains a number of erroneous statements. In reading it, however, we should do justice to its distinguished author. We have no right to make extracts from it and call them Skene's views, when we find that the statements in these extracts are not in accordance with statements in Skene's last work, " Keltic Scotland, a History of Ancient Alban." In his " Keltic Scotland," Skene traces the Macleans back to Scone, not to the province of Moray. In justice to Skene we should also bear in mind that when he wrote " The Highlanders of Scotland," he knew nothing whatever about the genealogy of the Macleans as it is given in the MS. of 1467. In his " Keltic Scotland " he speaks of that genealogy in the following terms:—" This genealogy is given with so much minuteness up to a certain Sean Dubh-gall Sgoinne, or Old Dugald of Scone, and the ecclesiastical character of the upper links are so obvious, that it is difficult to avoid regarding it as so far trustworthy."

In a work published a few years ago we are told that it is in the highest degree probable that the Macleans and Mackenzies are of Pictish origin. It is possible that such is the case with regard to the Mackenzies; and, if it be the case, and if they feel disposed to glory in the flesh, they have at least as much reason to glory in their Pictish blood as others can have to glory in their Dalriadan blood. So far as the Macleans are concerned, we have no hesitation in affirming that there is not a particle of evidence in existence to indicate in the faintest manner that they are of Pictish descent.

The Macleans are undoubtedly of Keltic origin. It is impossible, however, to determine with anything like certainty, whether their forefathers were Scots, Picts, or Britons. At the same time, it is slightly probable that they were Scots. As Kenneth MacAlpin and his successors on the throne of Alban were Scots, it may be reasonably assumed that, by the year 1100, the majority of the leading men in Scone were of the same stock.

About the year 1125, Constantine, Earl of Fife, Dugald, the son of Mocche, and Maoldomhnach, the son of Machedach, were appointed arbiters by David I. in settling a dispute regarding the boundaries of the lands of Kirkness and Lochore in Fife. Constantine is described as a great judge, or mormaor, in Scotland; Dugald, as an old, just, and venerable man; and Maoldomhnach, as a good and discreet judge. They were all prominent and well-known men. It is probable that Maoldomhnach was mormaor of Lennox, and the father of Muredach, father of Ailin Mór, who was Earl of Lennox in 1193. Mocche probably stands for Mac-che or Mac-he. If it stands for the latter, the letters *he* can only be a part of some such name as Heth or Hedath.

The old, just, and venerable Dugald, who acted as arbiter for King David I., was born probably about the year 1050. Now Old Dugald of Scone, the ancestor of the Macleans, must have been born about that very time, and was undoubtedly, like Dugald the arbiter, a prominent and well-known man. All things considered, it may be regarded as a fact that the two old Dugalds were one and the same person. With this Dugald, then, the authentic history of the Macleans begins; it is impossible to trace them farther back. It may, however, be some comfort for them to know, that so far as authentic pedigrees are concerned, the Campbells, Macdonalds, Mackenzies, Macleods, and Camerons, are no better off than they are themselves.

It may be stated that the Rev. John Beaton, the last seannachie of the Macleans of Duart, agrees with the Skene MS. in deriving the Macleans from Old Dugald of Scone, Erc, and Angus Tuirmeach of Tara. His list of their ancestors has been preserved in the Ardgour MS.

The following were the ancestors of the progenitor of the Macleans :—

I. Dugald of Scone had a son named Raince or Raing.

II. Raing had three sons, Cucatha, Cusithe, and Cuduilig. Cucatha means dog of battle. Cusithe apparently means dog of attack. Duilig seems to be the genitive case of Duileach or Duilleach. If it be, Cuduilig means dog of leaves, or hunting dog. According to the Irish genealogists, Cucatha was the ancestor of the Clan Conchatha in the district of Lennox; Cusithe, of the Clan Consithe in Fife; and Cuduilig, or Cuduilligh, of the Macleans in Mull and its islands.

III. Cuduilligh was lay abbot of Lismore in

Argyleshire. His descendants were all known for some time as Clann Duilligh, or the Clan Dullie.

The Rankins, or Clann Mhic Raing—children of the son of Raing—are descended from Cuduilligh, and were known for a long time as the Clan Dullie. They dropped that name and called themselves Clann Mhic Raing, or Rankins. They were hereditary pipers to the Macleans of Duart, and were highly distinguished for their professional skill.

IV. Neil, son of Cuduilligh or Cudullie, had a son named Maolsuthain.

V. Maolsuthain had a son named Macrath.

VI. Macrath had a son named Gilleoin or Gilleain. Gilleoin was the progenitor of the Macleans.

According to John Maclean of Inverscadle, the name Gilleain is derived from gille leathann, and means the broad-shouldered youth. According to Lachlan Maclean, the Coll scholar and writer, it is derived from gille leoghainn, and means the boy or son of a lion. Both of these derivations are utterly erroneous; they are in direct opposition to phonetic and historic facts. The real meaning of gille leoghainn is servant or attendant of a lion. But Lachlan, who knew the history of the Macleans well, was anxious to make out that they were sons of lions, not only in bravery, but even in name.

The Gaelic word gille means a boy, a youth, a servant. The name John is of Hebrew origin, and signifies one graciously given by Jehovah. There are three different forms of it in Gaelic, Eoin, Seathan, and Iain. Gille Eoin or Gille Sheathain means servant of John, or a person dedicated to serve the Apostle John and enjoy his protection. Gille Eoin is the oldest form of the name Gillean. It was in course of time contracted into Gill' Eoin, or Gilleoin. Gille Sheathain was changed, first, to Gill' Sheathain, and then to Gilleathain. Gilleoin is the most classical form of the name. But this form of it is never used at the present day except in poetic compositions, and even in works of this kind only rarely. As *th* is silent in Gaelic in the middle of words, Gilleathain is frequently written Gilleain, or just as it is pronounced.

Gill-eath-ain or Gill-e-ain is a word of three syllables. As *ath* is silent in *eath*, *eath* really stands for *e*, and is pronounced like the long sound of *e* in met. In its Anglicized form Gill-e-ain is contracted into two syllables, and becomes Gil-lean, the accent being on the last syllable.

The Gaelic word mac means son. The Gaelic word clann means children, and becomes clan in English. Thus, then, Mac Gilleain, or Maclean, means son of Gillean; and Clann Ghilleain, or Clan Gillean, children of Gillean. The expression Clan Maclean should not be used; its real meaning is children of the son of Gillean. But the Macleans are not the children of the son of Gillean; they are the children of Gillean himself. Maclean, Maclaine, and Maclain are all pronounced in the same way.

CHAPTER III.

The First Eight Chiefs.

I. GILLEAIN NA TUAIGHE.

GILLEAIN, or Gilleoin, was the progenitor of the Macleans, and thus their first chief. He was the son of Macrath, son of Maolsuthain, son of Neil, son of Cudullie, son of Raing, son of Old Dugald of Scone. He lived in Argyleshire, and must have been born about the year 1210. He was a prominent man and a distinguished warrior. He was known as Gilleain na Tuaighe, or Gillean of the battle-axe, a weapon which he no doubt wielded with dexterity and power. He had three sons, Bristi, Gillebrìde and Maoliosa.

Tradition relates that while Gilleain was, on a certain occasion, hunting on Beinn Tàlaidh in Mull, he was suddenly enveloped in a fog and lost his way. He wandered about during two or three days, and at last, utterly exhausted by hunger and fatigue, stuck his battle-axe in the ground, near a cranberry bush, and lay down beside it. His companions discovered him in this perilous position, apparently dead, and succeeded in restoring him to consciousness and safety. As to this tradition we strongly suspect that there is no truth in it. The probability is that it is only of recent origin. There is no reference to it in the Ardgour MS., and certainly not in any earlier work.

II. Maoliosa.

Maoliosa, or Malise, had a son named Maolcalum, or Malcolm. It is probable that he had also a son named Maolmoire, or Malmory. Maol and gille, as the first part of a name, mean servant. Thus Maoliosa and Gilliosa, or Gillise, are the same name, and mean servant of Jesus. Maolcalum, or Gillecalum, means servant of Columba. Maolmoire, or Gillemoire, means servant of Mary.

Among the men who rendered homage to Edward I. of England in 1296 was "Gillemoire Mackilyn," apparently Gillemoire Mac Gille-Eoin, or Gilmory Maclean. He belonged to the county of Perth, and was a man of some standing. As the county of Perth included the district of Lorn, it is probable that Gilmory lived in that district. He may, then, have been a son of Malise.

It is necessary to bear in mind that the genealogists do not profess to give the names of the chiefs of a clan. They simply start with the last chief known to them and trace him back through a long line of ancestors. Thus, though Gillemoire Mackilyn should have been chief of the Clan

Gillean, if he died without issue, or if his sons died without issue, he would not appear in the genealogy of the Macleans.

Tradition affirms that **Malise**, or Gillise, fought under Alexander III. at the battle of Largs in 1263. It also asserts that he held some lands in Kintyre.

III. GILLECALUM.

Gillecalum, or Malcolm, son of Malise, married a daughter of the Lord of Carrick, and had three sons by her, Donald, Neil, and John Dubh. In 1296 "Malcolm McCulian en l' isle de Kintyr," or Malcolm MacCulian in the Isle of Kintyre, rendered homage to Edward I. That Malcolm Maclean and Malcolm MacCulian were one and the same person may be regarded as a fact. For this belief there are several good reasons. Malcolm Maclean was known as Malcolm Mac Gille-Eoin; but Mac Gill-e-Eoin would, in the hands of a Frenchified English scribe, become readily transformed into Mac Cul-i-an. Malcolm Maclean must have been born about the year 1270, and Malcolm MacCulian was a prominent man in 1296. According to a tradition related by Hugh Macdonald, of Sleat, the Macleans came to Mull from Carrick. But Carrick, or the southern district of Ayrshire, was opposite Kintyre. Malcolm MacCulian had lands in Kintyre, which in his day was classed as one of the Western Islands. As Malcolm Maclean was married to a daughter of the Lord of Carrick, his wife may have had at least a life interest in some lands in that district. By regarding the two Malcolms as the same person, we find a substantial foundation for Hugh Macdonald's traditional statement. In 1325 Malcolm Maclean's three sons were apparently living in or near Kintyre. In that year Robert Bruce paid a visit to some of the Western Islands. Donald Maclean, Malcolm's eldest son, sent a ship in the King's service around the Mull —evidently the Mull of Kintyre—to West Tarbert. Neil and John, Donald's brothers, sent some of their men to watch the ship, while it remained at Tarbert.

Tradition states that Malcolm Maclean fought under Robert Bruce at the battle of Bannockburn in 1314, and that Bruce granted him some of the lands which had belonged to the Macdougalls of Lorn. It is highly probable that this tradition is true. It is clear that Bruce and Malcolm's sons were on very friendly terms in 1325. Then, at that time or shortly afterwards, the King appointed Neil, Malcolm's second son, constable of the castle of "Scraburgh," which is in all probability a misreading for Karnaburgh or Cairnburgh. In 1329 Neil received ten pounds in part payment for keeping the castle. If the Macleans had not supported Bruce in his hour of need—if they had not fought for him at Bannockburn—it is not likely that one of them would have been placed in charge of a royal garrison, as "Scraburgh," whatever place he meant, must have been.

IV. Iain Dubh.

John, son of Malcolm, was known as Iain Dubh, or Black John. According to the MacFirbis MS. Malcolm had three sons, Donald, Neil, and John. That work tells us, first, that Donald had two sons and, next, that Neil had two sons. Then it makes the following statement: " Eoin diu da mhac maithe leis, *i. e.*, Lochloinn agus Eachdhonn," or John "diu" had two good sons, *i. e.*, Lachlan and Hector. Diu seems to be a misreading for dub or dubh, black.

V. Lachainn Lùbanach.

Lachlan, son of John Dubh, was known as Lachainn Lùbanach, or Lachlan the Crafty. He was a man of ability, determination, and courage.

Hugh Macdonald, of Sleat, wrote a history of the Clan Donald in 1680. His work is full of traditions and very interesting, but by no means trustworthy. He gives the following account of the settlement of the Macleans in the Isle of Mull :—

"John Macdougall of Lorn, commonly called John Bacach, went off to harry Carrick in Galloway, the property of Robert Bruce, afterwards King Robert. Whilst there he met with one Gillean, son of Gillies, son of John, son of Gillies Mór, who went with him to Lorn in quest of better fortune. Macdougall gave him a spot of land, called Bealachuain, in the Isle of Sael. He had three sons : Hector, the eldest, of whom descended the family of Lochbuie; Lachlan, of whom descended the family of Duart; and John, a natural son, of whom descended others of the name Maclean. Whilst Angus Og of the Isles was at Ardtornish in the time of Lent, Macdougall of Lorn sent Hector and Lachlan, the sons of Gillean, as ambassadors to him. After landing they had some conference with him about the Isle of Mull. He refused to grant their request; but desired Mackinnon, who was master of his household, to use them kindly and give them their dinner. Mackinnon caused bread and gruthim to be set before them. The gruthim, which consists of butter and curds mixed together, was so brittle that it was not easy for them to take it up with their long knives. Macdonald came along whilst they were eating, and, seeing their condition, ordered Mackinnon to give them some other sort of food. Mackinnon replied that if they could not eat their food as it was, they should put on the nibs of hens, with which they might gather it up more easily. This reproachful answer touched the sons of Gillean to the quick. On the same day Macdonald left Ardtornish in a small boat to go to Aros in Mull to solemnize the festival of Easter. He gave instructions to Mackinnon to follow him with his large galley, and to take certain men with him. When Mackinnon went to the shore, the sons of Gillean, resolving to be avenged, called him aside, and stabbed him to the heart. They manned the galley with their own followers, pursued Mac-

donald, made him their prisoner, and took him
with them to Dunstaffnage. They remained without the castle. When Macdougall, who was at
dinner when they arrived, heard of what had taken
place, he said that he was very glad to have
Macdonald as his prisoner, but that the sons of
Gillean were very bold, and that he would through
time bridle their forwardness and insolence. One
of Macdougall's sons, a young boy who had been
fostered by Gillean, went to meet the sons of
Gillean, and told them what his father had said
about them. They were now greatly perplexed,
but soon made up their mind. They went to
Macdonald and told him that if he would forgive
their crime in slaying Mackinnon and do them
good, they would deliver him from his present
danger, and inasmuch as he had greater power than
their former master, they would join him and go
along with him. He promised to accede to their
wishes. They took him at his word, brought him
back to his own galley, and went to the Isle of
Mull. Macdougall saw neither him nor them.
Macdonald gave fourscore marklands to Hector,
the oldest brother, and to Lachlan, the youngest,
the chamberlainship of his house. Angus Og had
a daughter who was married to Maclean by her own
inclination of yielding."

The Ardgour MS. gives the traditional history
of Lachlan Lùbanach and Hector Reaganach as
it existed among the Macleans of Mull when that
work was written. It is as follows:—" Lachlan

Lùbanach and Hector Reaganach, the sons of John
Dubh, are said to have gone to the house of Macdougall of Lorn. They were kindly received by
him and obtained much of his favour, but had the
misfortune of awakening the jealousy of his former
favourites, who formed the design of taking away
their lives. The young men, being warned in
time, gave their enemies the slip, and went to the
house of Macdonald of the Isles. Here also
their good behaviour procured them favour, but,
as in the former case, they soon came to be hated
by the previous favourites. The first that vented
his ill-will against them was the laird of Mackinnon, who spoke harshly to them upon their
return from hunting, at which they had been along
with Macdonald. They resolved to take vengeance upon their insulter whenever an opportunity
should offer. In the course of a short time Macdonald left Aros to go to the mainland, and
Mackinnon, who had orders to follow him, was
slain by the offended brothers as he was going on
board of his galley. Having despatched their
enemy, they followed Macdonald, boarded his
galley, and made a prisoner of him. They carried
him to the island of Garbh Eileach, or Garvellach,
and there received from him the most satisfactory
promises. From Garvellach they took him to
Iona, where he solemnly vowed on certain black
stones, which were deemed sacred, to grant them
all their requests and to live in perpetual friendship with them. He gave them charters of lands

in Mull. He gave his daughter to Lachlan in marriage, made him his lieutenant-general, and assigned to the Macleans the privilege of being on the right wing of the army in battle."

According to Seannachie's History of the Macleans, Lachlan Lùbanach demanded of the Lord of the Isles, first of all, full forgiveness for slaying Mackinnon and carrying himself off as a prisoner; secondly, the hand of his daughter in marriage; thirdly, that he would use his influence with Macleod to obtain one of his daughters as a wife for Hector; and fourthly, that he would give, as a dowry to his own daughter, Enisker with its islands. His fifth and last request was that the Lord of the Isles would confer upon him the next post of honor to himself both in peace and war.

All the traditions about Lachlan Lùbanach and Hector Reaganach agree in affirming that they slew Mackinnon, carried off the Lord of the Isles as a prisoner, and compelled him to grant them certain lands in Mull. These assertions may all be regarded as facts. It is evident that the Sleat historian had only a very imperfect acquaintance with the genealogy of the early Macleans. Lachlan and Hector were not the sons of Gillean; they were the sons of John Dubh, great-grandson of Gillean. It was not Angus Og that was taken captive by the two Macleans, but his son, John, first Lord of the Isles. Hugh Macdonald is correct in stating that Macdonald's daughter was married to Maclean, or the chief of the clan; but he is mistaken in calling her husband Hector. It is a historic fact that she was married to Lachlan Lùbanach. The stories about the brittle gruthim and Enisker with its islands are clearly poetic embellishments and nothing more. There is no ground for concluding that Lachlan compelled the Lord of the Isles, when the latter had the honour of sitting on the black stones, to give him his daughter in marriage. It will be noticed that Hugh Macdonald states that Lachlan's wife was married to him " by her own inclination of yielding," or because she really wanted him. Hector Reaganach was not married to a daughter of Macleod of Lewis. It was lands, not wives, that Lachlan and Hector wanted. Probably they took it for granted that a good-looking man, with a charter either of Duart or Lochbuie in his pocket, could get a suitable wife any time without much difficulty. Both of them may, indeed, have been married men when they seized the Lord of the Isles. It is not at all certain that the daughter of the Lord of the Isles was Lachlan Lùbanach's first wife. We know that John Dubh was a grown-up and active man in 1325. It is possible, then, that his sons, Lachlan and Hector, were both born before the year 1330. They may, indeed, have been born before 1325.

Shortly after the death of Robert Bruce in 1329, John Bacach received a charter of the lands of Lorn, Duror, Glencoe, Mull, Jura, Tiree, and Coll;

all of which had been in possession of his father. In 1343 these lands, with the exception of the district of Lorn, were granted to John, Lord of the Isles. In 1354, John Bacach and John of the Isles entered into an agreement by which the former was to surrender to the latter the islands of Mull and Jura, and the castles of Cairnburgh and Ileburgh. John of Lorn was to place Lachlan Mac Alexander, Ivar Mac Lulli, and John Mac Molmari, as hostages in the hands of the Lord of the Isles until the lands and castles referred to should be actually delivered to him; while the Lord of the Isles was never under any circumstances to bestow the constabulary of the castle of Cairnburgh upon any of the Clan Fingon, or the Mackinnons. Thus, the points in dispute between the Macdonalds and the Macdougalls were settled in 1354. We are inclined to think, then, that it was in that year or shortly afterwards that the capture of the Lord of the Isles took place.

It cannot be proved that the Macleans had lands in Mull before the time of Lachlan Lùbanach and Hector Reaganach; at the same time it is tolerably certain that such must have been the case. There is a tradition among all the Macleans that Gilleain na Tuaighe held lands in Mull. As Neil Maclean was constable of Scraburgh, probably Cairnburgh, it is likely that he held some lands near Cairnburgh. Hugh Macdonald tells us that Lachlan Lùbanach and Hector Reaganach had some conference with the Lord of the Isles about the island of Mull. The supposition that they went to Ardtornish as ambassadors for Macdougall of Lorn is out of the question; they went simply on business of their own. What they wanted was evidently a title to some lands in Mull, which they regarded as their own, and which they must have held under Macdougall of Lorn. When they found that talking and pleading were of no use, they resolved to take heroic steps for gaining their ends. They found, in a short time, a fitting opportunity for carrying their purposes into effect. They slew Mackinnon, whom they evidently regarded as their enemy, seized the Lord of the Isles, and carried him off to see the wonders of Iona. In the "Genealogical Account of the Family of Mackinnon" we find the following statements:—"Mackinnon of Strathordill was master of the household to John, Lord of the Isles. Being jealous of the rising influence of Lachlan and Hector Macgillean, he formed the project of assassinating them; but, being made aware of his intention, they anticipated him, and murdered him at his own castle of Kilmorie; the spot is still pointed out." Mackinnon could not dread the rising influence of the Macleans unless they had lands in Mull. He had lands there himself, and what he dreaded was that the Macleans would take some of them from him. The probability is that he had already suffered at their hands. Macdougall of Lorn detested the Mackinnons. He may, then, have allowed the

Macleans to deal with them as they pleased. It
is extremely difficult to believe that the Macleans
would rise at one bound to the influential position
which they occupied in Mull in 1366. The only
rational way of accounting for their influence then
is the supposition that they had been in Mull for
some time, and that they had gradually increased
in strength. Rome did not spring up in a day;
neither did the Macleans.

 Lachlan Lùbanach married, in 1366, Mary,
daughter of the first Lord of the Isles by his wife,
Amy Macrory. As he was related to her within
the prohibited degrees, it was necessary for him
to obtain a dispensation from the Pope, Urban V.
He was chamberlain of the household to the Lord
of the Isles, an office which became hereditary in
his family. He received three different charters
from Donald, second Lord of the Isles. The first
is a charter of the custody and constableship of the
castle of Duart, Torosay, Brolas, and other lands
in Mull; half of the constableship of the castle of
Dunconnel in Scarba; half of the constableship of
the castle of Dunkerd, together with the islands of
Garvellach; certain lands in Luing and Scarba;
the upper half of Jura; lands in Morvern; and
other lands. The second is a charter of the constableship and custody of the castles of Cairnburgh
and Ileburgh, together with the small castles of
Fladda and Lunga; Treshnish, Calgary, and other
lands in Mull; and the office of Fragramanach
and Armanach in the island of Iona. The third

is a charter of the bailiery of all the lands of **Tiree**; certain lands in that island; and the office of steward of the house to the Lord of the Isles. These three charters were granted at Ardtornish on July 12th, 1390. They were confirmed by King James I. They were confirmed again by King James IV., at Glasgow, on July 13th, 1495.

Lachlan Lùbanach died about 1405. He was succeeded in Duart by his son, Hector Roy.

VI. Eachann Ruadh nan Cath.

Hector, sixth chief of the Macleans, was born probably about the year 1367. He was known as Eachann Ruadh nan Cath, or Hector Roy of the battles. He was a distinguished warrior, and was one of the best swordsmen of his day. He was chamberlain of the household to his uncle, Donald, second Lord of the Isles. According to a poem composed by Hector Bacach Maclean in 1651, Hector Roy made an expedition to Ireland, captured a fleet, and entered the town of Dublin as a conqueror. To what extent these statements are true, it is impossible to determine. It is likely, however, that there was some foundation for them. According to a tradition recorded by Seannachie in his history of the Macleans, a celebrated Norwegian came to Mull and challenged the Lord of Duart to a duel with swords. Hector Roy met him at Salen, defeated, and slew him. The Norwegian was buried near the spot on which he fell. A cairn of stones beside the sea-shore is supposed to mark his grave.

The famous battle of Harlaw was fought on the 24th of July, 1411. Donald, second Lord of the Isles, had about 10,000 followers. His army was drawn up in the cuneiform order of battle. The men were on foot and were armed with swords, daggers, battle-axes, bows and arrows, and wooden shields. Donald himself commanded the main body, which consisted of Macdonalds, the Mackinnons, the Macleods of Harris, the Macleods of Lewis, and others. Hector Roy of Duart commanded the right wing, and Malcolm Beag Mackintosh the left. John Mor Tanaistear had charge of the reserve, which was made up of Macdonalds, Mackenzies, and Camerons. The Earl of Mar had only a small army in comparison with Donald's. But the most of his men were trained warriors, and were on horseback. They were armed with long spears, maces, swords, and battle-axes, and were protected by coats of mail. The right wing was led by Sir James Scrymgeour, Constable of Dundee, and the left wing by Sir Alexander Ogilvy, Sheriff of Angus. Mar himself commanded the main body. The men on each side were equally brave, and equally determined to stand and fight. Scrymgeour defeated the left wing of the Highland army, while Hector Roy defeated the left wing of the Lowland army. Mar at the head of his mail-clad knights penetrated Macdonald's centre, but was unable to rout the dense mass before him. The battle raged for a long time, and terminated only when the darkness of night closed around the combatants. During the heat of the fight, Hector Roy of Duart and Sir Alexander Irving of Drum met face to face. They were both skilled swordsmen, and were well matched in every respect. They attacked each other with determination, and fought on until both fell mortally wounded. Of the Highlanders 900 lay dead upon the field of Harlaw. The most prominent of these, besides the brave Hector Roy, were Patrick Obeolan, Lachlan Macmillan, two or three gentlemen of the Clan Monroe, two gentlemen of the Clan Cameron, and a son of Macquarrie of Ulva. Of the followers of the Earl of Mar over 500 were slain; among whom were Sir Alexander Ogilvy, Sir James Scrymgeour, Sir Thomas Murray, Sir Robert Maul, Sir William Abernethy, Sir Alexander Straiton, Sir Robert Davidson, James Lovel, Alexander Stirling, Lesley of Balquhain, and the valiant Sir Alexander Irving. The Earl of Mar was severely wounded. Hector Roy's body was carried home from the field of Harlaw by the Macinneses and Morisons, and buried in Iona. It is said that during several years the Macleans of Duart and the Irvings of Drum were in the habit of exchanging swords on the anniversary of the battle of Harlaw.

VII. LACHAINN BRONNACH.

Lachlan, son and successor of Hector Roy, was known as Lachainn Bronnach, or Big-bellied

Lachlan. He was probably about eighteen years of age at the time of his father's death. He was an intelligent, prudent, and able man. He managed his affairs wisely and extended the influence and power of his family very much. He was with Alexander of the Isles in Lochaber when the latter was attacked and defeated by James I. in 1429. He was taken prisoner and confined along with the Lord of the Isles in Tantallon castle. He was not set at liberty until October, 1431. He was consequently unable to take part in the battle of Inverlochy.

Lachlan Bronnach had a son, named Donald, by a daughter of Maceachern of Kingerloch. He married, first, a daughter of John Borb Macleod of Dunvegan, and had two sons by her, Neil and John Garbh. He married, secondly, Janet, daughter of Alexander Stewart, Earl of Mar, and had one son by her, Lachlan Og, who, in accordance with the terms of the marriage contract between his father and mother, succeeded his father in Duart. As it is generally supposed that Mar's daughter was Lachlan Bronnach's first wife, it is necessary to produce some of the facts which show that such was not the case.

In February, 1443, we find as witnesses to a charter, Lachlan, Lord of Duart, and John, his son, Lord of Coll; in August, 1449, Lachlan, Lord of Duart, and John, his son, Lord of Coll; in April, 1463, Lachlan, Lord of Duart, Lachlan, his son and heir, and Ewen, son of Donald of

Ardgour; in April, 1467, Lachlan, Lord of Duart, and Lachlan Og, Master of Duart; in November, 1467, Lachlan, Lord of Duart, Lachlan Og, chamberlain of the household to the Lord of the Isles, and Ewen, son of Donald of Ardgour; in June, 1469, Lachlan, Lord of Duart, Lachlan Og, Master of Duart, and John of Coll, Lachlan's son; and in 1472, Lachlan Og, Master of Duart, and Ewen of Ardgour. As John Garbh witnessed one charter in 1443 and another in 1449, and as Lachlan Og witnessed a charter for the first time only in 1463, it is clear that John Garbh must have been a good deal older than Lachlan Og.

According to the Exchequer Rolls, the half of Bonnach and Bonnachare was, in 1458, granted for life to Janet Stewart, wife of Lachlan Maclean. As Janet Stewart was the Earl of Mar's daughter, and as she was Lachlan Bronnach's wife in 1458, it is beyond all dispute that she was Lachlan's second wife, and that consequently Lachlan Og, his son by her, was the youngest of his sons.

Lachlan Bronnach acted with wisdom, both for himself and his family, in appointing Lachlan Og heir to Duart and the chiefship of the Clan. By this act he secured the friendship of the Earl of Mar and of the King as well; both of whom in all probability used their influence to obtain for him the lands of Coll, and others. It is probable that Lachlan's marriage with Mar's daughter took place about the end of 1431. He died some time after 1472. He was Lord of Duart over sixty years.

VIII. Lachainn Og.

Lachlan Og was born about the year 1432. He was chamberlain of the household to the Lord of the Isles in 1467. He succeeded his father some time after 1472. He was Lord of Duart at least as early as 1478. He married a daughter of Gillespick Roy Campbell, son and heir of Duncan, first Lord Campbell. He seems to have been a peaceable and good man.

CHAPTER IV.

Hector Odhar and Lachlan Cattanach.

IX. EACHANN ODHAR.

HECTOR ODHAR, or Hector the Swarthy, commanded the Macleans at the long and sanguinary sea-fight of Bloody Bay, in Mull, which was fought about the year 1484. As Maclean of Ardgour was sailing up through the sound of Mull, he noticed Angus Og's fleet, which had just rounded the point of Ardnamurchan. Ardgour at once displayed his colours, and thus showed that he was ready for the contest. Angus Og concluded that the defiant galley in front of him was that of Hector Odhar and steered directly towards it. Hector Odhar, seeing his kinsman in danger, hastened to his relief. He was accompanied by the Macleods of Harris, and the Macneils of Barra. In the course of a few minutes the engagement became general. The result of the fight was that the supporters of the Lord of the Isles were defeated. Hector Odhar and Macleod of

Harris were taken prisoners. The son and heir of Torquil Macleod of Lewis—who commanded the Macleods of that island—was wounded by two arrows, and died a few days after the battle. Macneil of Barra fled towards Coll, and succeeded in making his escape, though pursued by three galleys.

John, the last Lord of the Isles, was deprived of his estates in May, 1494. The Macleans were now, in the eyes of the law, landless; but they did not remain in that position very long. They tendered their submission to James IV., and received charters from him of all the lands which they had formerly held under the Lords of the Isles. They were now an independent clan; but their independence was really of no use to them.

In 1496, Hector Odhar, John Mac Ian of Ardnamurchan, Allan Mac Rory of Moydart, Ewen Mac Allan of Lochiel, and Donald Mac Angus of Keppoch, appeared before the Lords of Council in Edinburgh and bound themselves to the Earl of Argyll, in behalf of the King, under a penalty of five hundred pounds each, to refrain from injuring or molesting one another. The Council had a good object in view; but to what extent they succeeded in attaining it we have no means of learning. It was certainly a difficult matter to keep the men with whom they had to deal in thorough order. Probably, it would require a good tyrant to manage them properly. We know that there was a bitter feud between Hector Odhar and Allan Mac Rory, but we can give no particulars respecting it. It may be taken for granted, however, that the one did as much injury to the tenants of the other as he possibly could.

Hector Odhar had a natural son named Lachlan, who was brought up among the Clan Chattan, and who in consequence of that fact was known as Lachainn Catanach, or Lachlan of the Clan Chattan country. According to tradition Lachlan's mother was a daughter of the chief of the Mackintoshes. On the 8th of October, 1496, Lachlan was legitimated. On the same day his father resigned the whole of his estates to him. Lachlan was now legally Lord of Duart.

X. Lachainn Catanach.

In the summer of 1498, King James renewed his visits to the Western Highlands. On this occasion he held court at his new castle of Kilkerran in South Kintyre. Alexander Macleod of Dunvegan, known as Alasdair Crotach, Torquil Macleod of Lewis, and other land-owners, paid homage to him as their sovereign. He remained a long time at Kilkerran, and resolved, apparently before he left, to abandon his conciliatory policy towards the Islanders. At any rate, shortly after his return to Edinburgh he revoked all the charters which he had granted to those who had been vassals of the Lord of the Isles. Whoever the instigators of this harsh and unwise policy may have been, the men who reaped the greatest benefits from it were Archibald, second Earl of Argyll, Alexander, son and heir of the Earl of Huntly, John Mac Ian of Ardnamurchan, and Duncan Stewart of Appin. James returned to the West Highlands in April, 1499, and held court at Tarbert Castle. He gave Archibald, Earl of Argyll, a commission of lieutenancy over the lordship of the Isles, and appointed him keeper of the castle of Tarbert and bailie of the lands of Knapdale. He also empowered him to let on lease for three years the whole of the lordship of the Isles, except Kintyre and Islay. He gave lands to Alexander, son and heir of the Earl of Huntly, in Lochaber, and lands to Mac Ian of Ardnamurchan in Islay. Upon Duncan Stewart of Appin he bestowed the districts of Duror and Glencoe. These tyrannical proceedings alarmed the Islanders, and led them to rebel against the Government. In 1501 the Macdonalds of Glencoe delivered Donald Dubh, son and heir of Angus Og, from Inchconnell, where he was kept a prisoner by his uncle, Archibald of Argyll. Donald fled to Lewis, and was taken under the protection of Torquil Macleod, who was married to Catherine, daughter of the first Earl of Argyll and sister of Donald's mother. Lachlan Cattanach of Duart, Ewen Mac Allan of Lochiel, John Maclean of Lochbuie, Gilleonan Macneil of Barra, Dunslaff Macquarrie of Ulva, Donald Mac Ranald Bàn of Largie, and others, joined Torquil of Lewis in proclaiming Donald Dubh Lord of the Isles. It seems, however, that the confederates committed no acts of hostility against the Government until 1503. At the end of that year they invaded Badenoch, plundered the country, and laid it waste with fire and sword. They had two reasons for beginning the war in that district; the first was that it belonged to the Earl of Huntly, and the second, that the Clan Chattan of Badenoch were assisting Huntly in his attempt to bring the inhabitants of Lochaber under subjection.

King James put forth the most active efforts to break up the confederacy and crush the rebellion. He commanded Torquil Macleod of Lewis, in 1452, to deliver up Donald Dubh to him. Torquil refused, and was declared a rebel. His lands were at the same time confiscated. In 1503, or early in 1504, Lachlan Cattanach of Duart and Ewen Mac Allan of Lochiel were declared traitors, and deprived of their estates, so far as the law of the land could deprive them of them. Immediately afterwards the Government sent letters to Torquil Macleod of Lewis, Mac Ian of Ardnamurchan, Maclean of Lochbuie, Macleod of Harris, Ranald Mac Allan of Moydart, Macneil of Barra, Mackinnon of Strath, and Macquarrie of Ulva, offering, if they should assist in bringing Lachlan Cattanach and Ewen of Lochiel to justice, to give them half the estates of these chiefs. As the mean and mischievous offer thus made had no effect, the Government resolved to send two armies to the Western Highlands in the spring of 1504. The one was led by the Earl of Huntly, the Earl of Crawford, and Lord Lovat; and the other by the Earl Marshall and the Earl of Argyll. A few months afterwards the Earl of Arran was also sent with a military force against the Islanders. At the same time a fleet, commanded by Sir Andrew Wood and Robert Barton, was despatched to the Isle of Mull, with the result that the strong fortress of Cairnburgh was captured. In the spring of 1505 the Earl of Huntly invaded Ross-shire and made himself master of the castles of Strome and Ellandonan. At the same time King James led an army in person into Argyleshire. He also sent a fleet under the command of John Barton to the islands. The presence of the King, and of the forces at his command, had the desired effect. Lachlan Cattanach wisely gave up the contest and cast himself upon the mercy of his sovereign. As the Macneils of Barra and the Macquarries of Ulva had followed the banner of Maclean of Duart since the forfeiture of the last Lord of the Isles, the submission of Lachlan Cattanach included also that of Macneil and Macquarrie. John Maclean of Lochbuie, Macdonald of Largie, and Ewen Mac Allan of Lochiel followed the example set by the Lord of Duart, and likewise surrendered to the King. Donald Dubh's first rebellion was now over. Torquil of Lewis refused to surrender him to the Government, but handed him over to Lachlan Cattanach, who delivered him to the King. Donald was again placed in confinement.

On May 21st, 1505, Lachlan Cattanach received a full remission for his past misdeeds. On January 23rd, 1506, he was commanded not to intromit with the kirk rents pertaining to the Bishop of the Isles. He was also instructed to help the Bishop in gathering his rents. On January 2nd, 1508, he received permission to sell the lands of Carrequhoul, Auchadalyn, and others, in the lordship of Badenoch, to Alexander, Earl of Huntly. At the same time Ranald Mac Allan of Moydart, John Maclean of Lochbuie, and himself were ordered not to molest Agnes Maclean, prioress of Iona, or the convent in that island. On the 8th of April, 1510, Duncan Stewart, of Appin, obtained a charter of appraising over the lands and castle of Duart for 4,500 marks, due to him by Lachlan Cattanach, the latter having power to redeem his property within seven years. In April, 1510, Lachlan received a letter of safe conduct for himself, his kinsmen, and servants, while visiting the King at Stirling, the letter to be of force during forty days. It is probable that Lachlan Cattanach was forced to part with his lands in Badenoch to pay the Earl of Huntly for the injuries which he had inflicted upon the Earl's tenants in 1502. It is also probable, indeed almost certain, that he plundered some of Duncan Stewart's lands about the same time, and that he was obliged to pay Duncan for his depredations. It is evident that Lachlan had no conscientious scruples about putting some of the Bishop's rents into his own pockets, or seizing the lands which belonged to the monastery of Iona. He was not the only man, however, who was guilty of covetousness in action in these respects.

In 1513, James IV. resolved to invade England. He crossed the border on the 22nd of August at the head of the largest army that any Scottish king had ever yet commanded. He captured Norham Castle and the fortresses of Wark, Etal, and Ford in a short time. Instead, however, of prosecuting the war with vigour, he remained at Ford Castle for quite a long time, either to keep company with Lady Heron, whose husband was a prisoner in his hands, or else to serve the flesh and the Devil. This attractive woman was thoroughly true to her country, and faithfully communicated full information with respect to the purposes and movements of her royal slave to his enemies. In consequence of his delay at Ford Castle, James had only about 30,000 followers when he pitched his camp on Flodden Hill on the 6th of September. He was a thoroughly trained fighter and a brave man ; but his stubbornness, vanity, absurd notions of chivalry, and lack of skill as a general, utterly unfitted him for the position of commander-in-chief of an army. When Lord Patrick Lindsay, a warrior of experience and sense, advised that the King should retire from the army for the safety of his person, James replied in a rage that when he would return to Scotland he would hang Lindsay over his own gate. When the aged Earl of

Angus, Archibald Bell-the-Cat, warned him against making a rash attack upon the English, he scornfully and brutally replied, "Angus, if you are afraid you may go home."

The Earl of Surrey, afterwards first Duke of Norfolk, hastened with an army of 31,000 men to meet King James. On the 9th of September he crossed the river Till and took up a position between the Scots and their country. James could easily have attacked him while crossing the river, but did nothing of the kind. When he saw that the English had crossed it, he could have remained in the strong position which he occupied, at least for a few days. Instead of doing this, however, he descended to the level plain to meet his foe. The right wing of the Scottish army consisted of Campbells, Macleans, Mackenzies, Macdonalds, and other clans, and was commanded by Archibald Campbell, second Earl of Argyll, and Matthew Stewart, second Earl of Lennox. The centre was commanded by the King in person, and the left wing by the Earls of Huntly and Home. The left wing of the English army was led by Sir Edward Stanley; the centre, by Surrey in person; and the right wing, by Sir Edmund Howard and Lord Thomas Howard, Surrey's sons. The Earl of Bothwell had charge of the Scottish reserve, and Lord Dacre of the English reserve. Huntly and Home defeated Edmund Howard; while Thomas Howard, assisted by Lord Dacre and his cavalry, defeated Crawford and Montrose. King James, who had the best armed of the Scottish troops under his command, was driving back the Earl of Surrey, and throwing his squadrons into confusion. At this juncture Thomas Howard and Lord Dacre attacked his flank, but were kept in check by the Earl of Bothwell and the Scottish reserve. Stanley routed the division under Argyll and Lennox with great slaughter. He was now at liberty to make an attack upon the rear of the Scottish army. This attack decided the fate of the day, and also of King James and the brave men who fought around him; the Scots were defeated and driven back to their own country.

King James and about 10,000 of his followers were slain at Flodden; the English lost about 7,000. Among the prominent men who fell with James were the Earls of Crawford, Montrose, Lennox, Argyll, Bothwell, Caithness, Rothes, and Cassilis; Hector Odhar, chief of the Clan Gillean; Sir Duncan Campbell of Glenorchy; Sir William Gordon of Gight; George and William Douglas, sons of the Earl of Angus; Sir John Sommerville of Cambusnethan; and Andrew Stewart, Bishop of Caithness. It is said that two hundred gentlemen of the name of Douglas lay dead upon the field of battle, and that of the followers of the Earl of Caithness only one man ever returned home. It is affirmed by some writers that the Earl of Huntly fled from the field after the first charge, and that Lord Home and his followers began to collect all the plunder they could find. Whether these charges be true or false, Huntly and Home returned to Scotland.

Hector Odhar was a born fighter, an experienced commander, and a highly popular chief. He seems, however, to have been rather too fond of disturbance and war. At all events, he was known as Eachann Odhar nan Imreasan, or Hector Odhar of the strifes. He was about fifty-eight years of age at the time of his death.

A few weeks after the battle of Flodden, Lachlan Cattanach—who was now chief of the Clan Gillean—Malcolm Macleod of Lewis, Alexander Macleod of Harris, Alexander Macdonald of Islay, John Maclean of Lochbuie, Wiland Chisholm of Comar, and Alexander Macdonald of Glengarry proclaimed Sir Donald of Lochalsh Lord of the Isles, and raised the standard of rebellion against the Government. As Lachlan Cattanach was followed, not only by the occupants of his own estates, but also by the Macleans of Ardgour, the Macneils of Barra, the Mackinnons, and the Macquarries, he was by far the most powerful of Sir Donald's supporters. He was also ably assisted by his paternal uncle, Donald, who was a warrior of the same stamp as the brave Hector Odhar. In November, 1513, Sir Donald of Lochalsh, or Dòmhnall Gallda, opened the campaign by invading Glenurchart. He was accompanied by his own immediate followers, the Chisholms of Strathglass, and the Macdonalds of Glengarry.

He seized the castle of Urchart and plundered all the lands near it. About the same time Lachlan Cattanach and Alexander Macleod of Dunvegan besieged and captured the royal garrisons of Cairnburgh and Dunskàich.

On the breaking out of the rebellion, Colin, third Earl of Argyll, was ordered to proceed against Lachlan Cattanach and those who supported him, while Mackenzie of Kintail and Munro of Foulis were instructed to preserve order and peace in Western Ross. At the same time Ewen Mac Allan of Lochiel and William Mackintosh, captain of the Clan Chattan, were guardians of Lochaber. Early in 1515 John Mac Ian of Ardnamurchan was commissioned to treat with the less violent of the rebels, and to promise them forgiveness for their crimes on condition of obeying the Government for the future and making restitution to those whose lands had been plundered by them. The rebellion now speedily collapsed. On the 23rd of August, we find a respite granted to Sir Donald of Lochalsh to enable him to go to Edinburgh and return in safety. While in Edinburgh he was reconciled to John, Duke of Albany, Regent of the kingdom, and pardoned for his rebellious acts. On the 6th of September, 1515, Albany granted a respite to Lachlan Cattanach and Macleod of Dunvegan for all their treasonable deeds, the respite to continue in force until the first day of January. On the 6th of January, 1516, Lachlan and Macleod, together with their kinsmen and friends to the number of one hundred persons, received a respite which was to last until the 15th day of March. They had permission to visit Edinburgh or any other place in the kingdom on lawful business, within that period. On the 30th of March, Sir Donald of Lochalsh came under obligation to the Lords of Council to make redress for all the slaughter and depredations committed by himself or Lachlan Maclean of Duart, and their kinsmen, friends, and assistants, against John Mac Ian of Ardnamurchan and his people. It is thus evident that the Macleans had taken part in plundering expeditions to Ardnamurchan, and that they had been instigated to do so by Sir Donald. They had no quarrel of their own with John Mac Ian.

About the beginning of the year 1517 the Knight of Lochalsh was again in open rebellion against the Government. He succeeded in persuading Lachlan Cattanach, Malcolm Macleod of Lewis, Alexander Macleod of Harris, John of Lochbuie, and Alexander Macdonald of Islay that he had been appointed lieutenant of the Isles by the Duke of Albany. Having procured the support of these restless leaders, he invaded Ardnamurchan at the head of a large body of men and took possession of the castle of Mingarry. The Government sent him a peremptory order to withdraw from that district at once and deliver up the castle to its rightful owner. Instead of complying with this order, he razed the castle to the ground and ravaged the whole country with fire and sword. The Macleans and the Macleods of Harris had by this time found out that Sir Donald had deceived them. They also clearly saw that he was playing the part of a madman, and that he was leading himself and his followers to utter ruin. The result was that they withdrew from all connection with him, and joined the Earl of Argyll in opposing him. Lachlan Cattanach and Macleod of Harris resolved to apprehend him; but as he had discovered their purpose, he succeeded in making his escape. They captured his two brothers, however, and sent them as prisoners to Edinburgh.

The Earl of Argyll, Lachlan of Duart, John of Lochbuie, and Macleod of Harris sent petitions to the Regent and Lords of Council with reference to the rebellion, and making certain requests for themselves. These petitions were considered and acted upon in March, 1517. The Earl of Argyll was appointed lieutenant of the Isles and the adjacent mainland, except the Isles of Bute and Arran and those parts of Lochaber which belonged to Huntly, Mackintosh, or Lochiel. He was at the same time empowered to promise remission for their offences, and the restitution of their lands, to all who should submit to him, except Sir Donald of Lochalsh and the Macdonalds who had supported him. He was also commissioned to pursue the rebels with fire and sword. On the 8th of March Lachlan of Duart received a tack for eleven years of all the lands which had formerly belonged to him in Mull and Morvern. On the 10th, he was empowered to raise and gather all the tenants who had obeyed him in the time of the late King, for the weal of the kingdom and his own just quarrels, but not for the purpose of fighting against the King, the Regent, or the Earl of Argyll, the King's lieutenant. On the 12th, Lachlan, Donald Maclean, his uncle, Gilleonan Macneil of Barra, Neil Mackinnon of Mishnish, Lachlan Mac Ewen of Ardgour, and their kinsmen and servants, received a full remission for all the illegal acts committed by them before that date. On the 14th Lachlan received a gift of the rents of the lands of Tiree, and was appointed collector of the King's dues south of Ardnamurchan, except from the lands which belonged to John Mac Ian of Ardnamurchan. Macleod of Dunvegan and Maclean of Lochbuie were pardoned and allowed to retain possession of their estates.

In his petition to the Lords of Council, Lachlan Cattanach expressed a desire to have the two brothers of Sir Donald of Lochalsh executed for their crimes. It is impossible to believe for a single moment that Lachlan really wished to have these young men punished; he could have no ill-will against them, and he could gain nothing by their death. It may be taken for granted, then, that it was owing to the influence of the Earl of Argyll, or some other person who was anxious to see the power of the Macdonalds utterly destroyed, that the horrible request to have Sir Donald's brothers put to death appeared in Lachlan's petition. When the request was considered by the Lords of Council, Huntly, Lennox, Drummond, Ogilvy, Balwearie, and Ker voted in favour of leaving the fate of Sir Donald's brothers to the decision of the Regent; while Argyll, Cassilis, Erskine, Borthwick, Avondale, Lees, Kincavil, and Otterburn voted in favour of having them dealt with according to their demerits. The desire of the majority was carried into effect, and the young men accordingly put to death. When we consider the way in which the Earl of Argyll, and Cassilis and Erskine, who were married to his sisters, voted, we can scarcely have any doubt respecting the authorship of that part of Lachlan Cattanach's petition which asked for the execution of Lochalsh's brothers.

While Lachlan of Duart was in Edinburgh in March, 1517, he promised under oath in presence of the Lords of Council that he would be true to the King, to the Regent, and the realm; that he would cause the holy kirk to be answered and obeyed within his bounds; that he would assist, supply, and help the Earl of Argyll, lieutenant of the Isles, in governing and maintaining good rule in the islands and districts over which he had charge; and, finally, that as far as it was possible for him to do so, he would keep peace and administer justice among the King's lieges. We have reason to believe that he acted in accordance with these promises.

In 1523 Lachlan Cattanach, having obtained a letter of safe conduct from the Government, paid a visit to Edinburgh. While asleep in his bed at night, Sir John Campbell of Calder and a number of his followers entered his room and assassinated him. He was about forty-eight years of age.

TRADITIONAL HISTORY OF LACHLAN CATTANACH.

The first tradition respecting Lachlan Cattanach has reference to his early life. Seannachie tells us that while he was still quite young, and living among his mother's people, he acted in such a wicked and cruel manner on two different occasions that he narrowly escaped being put to death by persons whom he had grossly injured.—It is certain that Seannachie did not find this story in any old manuscript or any old work of any kind. There is no ground whatever for believing it to be true. We suspect that it is not true—that it is simply a late invention.

The second tradition with regard to Lachlan Cattanach refers to his election to the chiefship of the clan. This tradition also makes its appearance in print for the first time in Seannachie's work. That writer informs us that when Lachlan came to Mull the leading men among the Macleans held a council to consider what to do with him. Some were in favour of excluding him from the succession to the chiefship, on the ground of his depravity and wicked conduct. The majority, however, entertaining strong hopes that time would improve his disposition and render his conduct somewhat tolerable, voted in his favour. Consequently, he was acknowledged as heir and successor to his father.—This tradition is no doubt founded upon facts. Seannachie, however, does not give the facts. But we have no reason to charge him with suppressing them; it is tolerably certain that he did not know them.

That there were men among the Macleans—and probably a large number—who wished to exclude Lachlan from the chiefship of the clan may be regarded as a fact. It was not his wickedness, however, but his being a natural son, that constituted the ground of their opposition to him. In 1496 his father procured an act of legitimation for him, and immediately afterwards gave over the estates to him. His opponents were now under the necessity of accepting the situation in which they were placed and making the best of it. The fact that, in spite of his illegitimacy, the majority of the Macleans were willing to accept him as their chief, clearly shows that Lachlan could not have been such a notoriously wicked wretch as is generally supposed.

The third tradition with regard to Lachlan Cattanach is well known to everyone. It refers to his treatment of his wife, Elizabeth Campbell. The oldest version of it is in a Campbell manuscript written in 1779. According to this manuscript, Lachlan placed his wife on a bare rock in the sea in the full expectation that she would be overwhelmed and drowned by the incoming tide. A person who happened to be passing by in a boat heard her cries, delivered her from her perilous position, and conveyed her to her friends. As soon as the men who had placed her on the rock returned to Duart Castle, they kindled a large fire on the middle of the hall floor, and formed themselves into a circle around it. Then they seized John, second son of Colin, third Earl of Argyll, stripped him naked, and placed him between themselves and the fire. He was only three or four years of age, and had been living with his aunt, Lachlan Cattanach's wife. His cruel tormentors kept rubbing his skin with a hot roasted apple, and compelled him to run around between themselves and the fire. His nurse rushed into the hall, between the legs of Macgillivray of Glencannir, snatched up the boy, and ran to the shore with him, where she accidentally found a boat, in which she was carried to a place of safety. Owing to the treatment which little John Campbell had received at the hands of the ferocious Macleans, there were blue marks on his body ever afterwards. In consequence of this fact he was called Iain Gorm, or Blue John. He was the progenitor of the Campbells of Lochnell. Macgillivray was more humane than the Macleans, and consequently parted his legs for the express purpose of allowing the nurse to have access to the child. When Sir John Calder heard of the barbarous manner in which his sister and nephew had been treated, he resolved to slay Lachlan Cattanach as soon as he should have an opportunity of doing so. Some time afterwards he met Lachlan in Edinburgh and thrust his sword, scabbard and all, through his body.

If the men who placed Duart's wife on the rock acted, on their return, towards a child of three or four years of age in the manner described in the Campbell manuscript of 1779, it is quite clear that they must have been as drunk as any men who could keep on their feet before a fire, or anywhere else, could possibly be. We do not wonder that the nurse found an opening in the circle. The wonder is that there was only one gap in it, and that the little Campbell boy was the only person scorched by the fire. The Macdonalds of Sleat had three chieftains in whose names the word gorm appears, Donald Gorm, Donald Gorm Mor, and Donald Gorm Og. Were these chieftains also men who had been tattooed by apple juice? The general belief is that they were handsome blue-eyed men. Is it not possible, then, that John Gorm of Lochnell was likewise a handsome man, and that he had blue eyes? The Campbells were not Iberians. It is probable that Lachlan Cattanach was as good a swordsman as Campbell of Calder. Is it reasonable, then, to believe that Calder did not think it worth while to unsheathe his sword to attack Lachlan? Among the State Papers of England there is a letter which was written to Henry VIII. by a number of Highland chiefs and chieftains in 1545. In that letter the following sentence occurs :—" The Lord Maclean's father was cruelly murdered under trust in his bed in the town of Edinburgh by Sir John Campbell of Calder, brother to the Earl of Argyll." According to this statement—which is undoubtedly true—Calder was not quite so chivalrous and valiant a hero as the writer of the manuscript of 1779 would have us believe.

According to the Pennycross MS., Lachlan Cattanach's wife tried to persuade her husband to make over the Duart estates to her brother, John of Calder. When she found that he would not take her advice, she attempted to poison him. Lachlan, then, placed her on the rock, which has been ever since known as the Lady's Rock, to suffer for her wickedness and murderous intentions. According to another Maclean version of the story, Argyll's daughter was in love with another man, and was unwilling to marry Lachlan Cattanach. At last, however, urged on by the hope that she could exert an influence over him which would be favourable to the interests of her father's family, she consented to become his wife. She would not, however, part with her lover. She had him disguised as a monk and passed him off as her confessor. When Lachlan found out who his wife's confessor really was, he was greatly enraged, and upbraided his wife for her infidelity. This was the beginning of their quarrel. Another thing which turned him against his wife was the fact that she was constantly plotting against him, and trying to get his estates alienated from the Macleans and made over to her own people. There was also a third source of trouble. While Lachlan's wife would be on some occasions very pleasant, she would be on other occasions exceedingly sulky and refuse to sleep with him. Lachlan's foster-brothers were deeply grieved on account of his domestic infelicity, and resolved to put an end to it. So, on a certain day, Lachlan being away from home, they took his wife out to the Lady's Rock, and left her there to repent of her sins and die.—There is no ground for thinking that Lachlan's wife tried to poison her husband. The story about the lover disguised as a monk is evidently a myth.

Seannachie informs us that Lachlan Cattanach fell desperately in love with a daughter of Maclean of Treshnish, and that in order to be able to marry her he resolved to get rid of his wife, whom he disliked and treated with brutal cruelty. On a certain day he was in excellent humour, and showed every possible attention to his wife. In the evening he asked her to go with him on an excursion on the water near the castle. His galley was manned by a few persons to whom he had communicated his nefarious purpose. He placed his wife on a rock which has been ever since known as the Lady's Rock, and left her there to perish. As soon as he returned, one of those who had been with him reported the state of matters to some of Lachlan's best friends. These men immediately despatched a boat to the Lady's Rock, took the doomed woman on board, and went with her to Lorn. Lachlan, not knowing that his wife had been rescued, pretended that she had died suddenly. He filled an empty coffin with something or other, and went to Inverary to have it buried there. The Campbells met him at Glenara, and professed to be as deeply grieved over the sudden death of his wife as himself. When the funeral party arrived at Inverary, Lachlan was invited by the Earl of Argyll to go in to the castle with him to partake of some refreshment. When he entered the dining-hall he found his wife sitting at the head of the table, and ready to entertain him.

Lachlan Cattanach was by no means a fool; he was a man of both ability and sense. It is pretty certain, then, that if he intended to drown his wife he would not accompany her to the rock. As he would not wish to be blamed for her death he would stay at home and leave others to put her out of the way. The supposition that he went to Inverary with a bodyless coffin is outrageously absurd. What would he have done if the Campbells had desired to see the remains? But even if his wife were dead and her body in a coffin, why should he take the coffin to Inverary? The Macleans buried their dead in Iona. If, then, there was a mock funeral, there was a mock burial, and it must have taken place in Mull. Seannachie's story about the funeral procession to Inverary is beyond all doubt absolutely false. He had no foundation for it except the poetic fancies of Joanna Baillie and Thomas Campbell. There is no reference to it in the Campbell manuscript of 1779.

According to " The House of Argyll and the Collateral Branches of the Clan Campbell "—a work published in 1871—Lachlan Cattanach's wife was delivered from her perilous position by her foster-father, Dugald Campbell of Corranmore, who happened to be on his way to pay her a visit. John F. Campbell of Islay tells us that Lachlan's wife was taken off the rock by her second brother, Archibald of Skipnish. He also states that after the death of Lachlan she was married to Archibald Campbell of Achinbreck, and had a son named John by him.

While the traditions about Lachlan Cattanach and his wife contain several absurd and false statements, they may be true with regard to the main fact. At any rate they all agree in asserting that Lachlan's wife was actually placed on the Lady's Rock.

Colin, first Earl of Argyll, was married about the year 1457, or according to John F. Campbell of Islay, about 1460. He had a large family. Archibald, his son and successor, may not have been his eldest child. It is probable, however, that Archibald was married about 1485. He had four sons and six daughters. Elizabeth, the youngest of his daughters, may have been born in 1497; it is certain that she was not born much earlier. Lachlan Cattanach got into serious difficulties, early in 1517, by joining Sir Donald of Lochalsh, or Dòmhnall Gallda, in his mad projects. He stood in great need of Argyll's assistance, to interfere with the Government in his behalf. But Argyll needed Lachlan's assistance. If he could get the Macleans to support him, or at least to remain neutral, it would be much easier for him to crush the Macdonalds and get possession of their lands. That Argyll and Lachlan Cattanach were on very friendly terms in March, 1517, is certain. If, then, Lachlan happened to be in need of a wife at that time, it would be only natural and proper that Argyll should give him his sister in marriage. She might help to keep her husband on the right track, and might also have a son who would in course of time become Lord of Duart. In view, then, of the friendly terms on which Argyll and Lachlan Cattanach stood towards each other in March, 1517, we are strongly of opinion that the marriage contract between Lachlan and Argyll's sister must have been drawn up about that time. But "The House of Argyll and the Collateral Branches of the Clan Campbell" puts the date of the marriage beyond all doubt; it plainly tells us as a historic fact that it took place in 1517.

The evidence brought forward to prove that Lachlan Cattanach placed his wife on the Lady's Rock to drown her, requires full and careful consideration.

We are told, in the first place, that Lachlan was a monster of iniquity, and that he would therefore murder his wife or any one else to serve his own ends. How do we know that he was a monster of iniquity? It is true that Seannachie in his history of the Macleans states that Lachlan was "a worthless chief," that his violence of temper and neglected education led to acts of "the most savage cruelty," and that "he did not even possess the negative quality of being a brave tyrant." Where did Seannachie get his information? It is certain that he did not find it in old manuscripts or in official documents. All known facts go to show that Lachlan Cattanach was just as good a man as the other chiefs of his day, that he was of a cool temper, that he was kind to his followers, and that he was a warlike and brave man. It is true that he could not sign his name; it does not follow, however, that his education had been neglected. He had certainly the knowledge and training deemed necessary for his position. Seannachie had no ground whatever for his charges against him. That he had heard some bad stories about him, we admit. He had no right, however, to convert these stories into historic facts, and publish them as such. So far as known, Lachlan Cattanach never murdered any one. It is utterly unreasonable, then, to believe, without clear proof, that he had murderous intentions towards his wife.

We are told, in the second place, that Lachlan Cattanach had very strong motives for purposing to murder his wife. It is said that he disliked her and wanted to get rid of her; that he had no children, and that, like Napoleon, he was anxious to have an heir; and that he was passionately in love with Treshnish's daughter and desired to marry her.

It is quite possible that Lachlan Cattanach disliked his wife, that he could not honestly pray for long life and prosperity to her, and that he could wish to see her in the grave. It does not follow, however, that feelings of this kind would lead him to place her on the Lady's Rock to be drowned. The body might float ashore and his crime be discovered. If it should be found out that he had murdered his wife, the best men among his own followers would turn against him, while the Earl of Argyll would become his bitterest enemy. It may be safely affirmed that mere dislike to his wife could never tempt Lachlan to murder her. The supposition that Lachlan Cattanach was extremely anxious to have an heir, is preposterous in the extreme. When he married Elizabeth Campbell in 1517, he had two sons who were nearly grown-up men, Hector Mor and Ailein nan Sop. The story about his falling violently in love with Treshnish's daughter, after his marriage with Elizabeth Campbell, is entirely false. It is admitted both by the Macleans and the Campbells—even by Seannachie himself—that Treshnish's daughter was the mother of Hector Mor and Ailein nan Sop. She was thus Lachlan's first wife.

We are told, in the third place, that there is a tradition in Argyleshire to the effect that Lachlan

Cattanach placed his wife on the Lady's Rock in the full expectation that she would be drowned, that the tradition is old, and that consequently it must be true.—It is by no means certain that the tradition which represents Lachlan Cattanach as trying to drown his wife, is old. Probably the earliest work in which it is recorded is the Campbell manuscript of 1779. The writer of that work gives no authority for his narrative except "common report." If the common report in 1779 were that Lachlan Cattanach had actually drowned his wife at the Lady's Rock about 1519, it would probably be true. But that was not the report. It was admitted that Lachlan's wife was not drowned; what was affirmed was that Lachlan wanted to drown her. Thus, the report in circulation had reference, not to an actual occurrence, but to the purposes of a man's heart. We cannot always trust common report with regard to actual events; how, then, can we trust it with regard to thoughts and intentions?

It is possible that the Macleans placed Elizabeth Campbell on the Lady's Rock. But they may have placed her there simply to drive her out of Mull. They could have no motives for drowning her; but they might have motives—and very strong motives from their point of view—for sending her back to Inverary. It is quite likely that there was a good deal of dissatisfaction with their chief among them. They would blame him for his acts of rebellion and for bringing himself into a position in which it was necessary for him to support the Campbells against the Macdonalds. They would very probably look upon him as a tool in the hands of Argyll. They would also be dissatisfied with his wife, and might look upon her as a source of danger to their clan. It is strongly probable that when Lachlan married her he came under obligation, if he should have a son by her, to make her son his heir, and thus disinherit Hector Mor. The Macleans would naturally wish that she would never have a son. All things considered, they may have sent her to the Lady's Rock, and thence to Lorn, just to get rid of her. If they had really intended to drown her, they would no doubt have carried their purpose into effect.

While it is possible that the Macleans sent Lachlan Cattanach's wife out of Mull, the probability is that she left of her own accord. Love had nothing to do with uniting Lachlan and Elizabeth Campbell in marriage. It was the political craft of the Earl of Argyll that brought them together as man and wife. Consequently, it is not necessary to assume that Lachlan was a brute, or that his wife was a dabbler in poison, to account for their separation. It is probable that they were not happy together and that they could not be very anxious to remain together. Lachlan's wife, then, may have desired to be rid of Lachlan just as much as Lachlan desired to be rid of her. It is certain that she must have felt exceedingly uncomfortable in Duart. She may even have heard whispers of ugly threats against her life. She was in no danger from Lachlan Cattanach, but she may have been in danger from others. According to "The House of Argyll and the Collateral Branches of the Clan Campbell," she was taken away from the Lady's Rock by her foster-father, Dugald Campbell. According to Campbell of Islay, she was taken off the rock by her brother, Archibald of Skipnish. According to the Campbell manuscript of 1779, the nurse of John Gorm Campbell fled from Duart with her charge on the same night on which her mistress was placed on the Lady's Rock. If, then, Lachlan Cattanach's wife was carried away from the Lady's Rock, either by her foster-father or her brother, is it not probable that her deliverer had come to the rock for the very purpose of taking her away? Again, if John Gorm's nurse found a boat at the shore, at the very moment in which she needed a boat, is it not likely that the boat was actually waiting for her where she found it? The story which states that she broke through a circle of ferocious Macleans, snatched up John Gorm, ran off to the shore with him, and immediately found a boat by accident, is absurd. The traditions with regard to Lachlan and his wife clearly teach two things; first, that his wife had some friends in Mull who conveyed her to the Lady's Rock; and, secondly, that she was met there by her foster-father and her brother and taken to Lorn. In 1523 Sir John Campbell of Calder slew Lachlan Cattanach, and thus set his sister at liberty to get a second husband.

Dean Munro, who travelled through the Western Islands in 1549, gives a very minute account of the islands and rocks of that region; but makes no reference to Sgeir na Baintighearna, or the Lady's Rock. If he had heard that the chief of the Macleans had tried to drown his wife on it, it is exceedingly probable that he would have stated that there was such a rock, and that he would, also, have mentioned the circumstance from which it derived its name.

We have now examined all the facts and traditions which have any bearing upon the charge of murderous intentions made against Lachlan Cattanach. Judging by the evidence before us, the only conclusion at which it is possible for us to arrive with respect to him is, NOT GUILTY.

CHAPTER V.

Hector Mor and Hector Og.

XI. EACHANN MOR.

HECTOR MOR was born about the year 1497. He was on terms of close friendship with Alexander Macdonald of Islay and the Glens, Alasdair Mac Iain Chathanaich, and married his eldest daughter, probably about 1520. He became Lord of Duart in 1523. He hated the Campbells for murdering his father, and for other wrong acts of their aggressive policy; and was ready to attack them whenever a favourable opportunity should offer. He could always count upon the assistance of the Macdonalds of Islay, and indeed upon that of all the Macdonalds of the South Isles. He would have invaded the lands of the Campbells immediately after his father's death, but was prevented from doing so by the interference of the Government.

In May, 1520, Alexander of Islay obtained from John Campbell of Calder a grant for a term of five years of forty-five marklands in Islay, and the whole of Jura and Colonsay. On the 25th of December, 1524, we find a remission granted to Calder for having laid waste the lands of Colonsay. The acts for which the remission was granted were no doubt committed either in the autumn of 1523 or the spring of 1524. Thus, the Campbells began to attack the Macleans and the Macdonalds of Islay about the same time. They first slew Lachlan Cattanach, and then plundered Colonsay. The friendship which existed between the Macleans and the Macdonalds was evidently a source of annoyance to them. They may also have been anxious to provoke a fresh rebellion. In June, 1527, the Government granted a letter to "Hector Maclean of Duart, son and heir of the late Lachlan Maclean of Duart, charging the Sheriff of Inverness to command Colin, Earl of Argyll, Sir John Campbell of Calder, and their accomplices, to make no hosting convocation of the lieges, or invasion upon the said Hector Maclean of Duart, his kin, and friends." This letter clearly proves that, at the time in which it was issued, the Campbells were threatening to attack the Macleans. It is, indeed, probable that they had already committed some acts of hostility against them.

When James IV. fell at Flodden in 1513, his son James was only two years of age. Archibald Douglas, sixth Earl of Angus, was practically Regent of the kingdom from November, 1524, to July, 1528, at which date James V. took the reins of government into his own hands. When

Angus held the supreme power he made grants of crown lands to several persons in the lordship of the Isles, his object evidently being to attach these persons to his own cause, and thus increase the number of his adherents. In November, 1528, the King and Lords of Council declared the grants made by Angus to be null and void, and decreed that for the future no grants of lands should be made in the Isles and adjacent mainland except by the advice of the Lords of Council and Colin, Earl of Argyll, the King's lieutenant. The cancellation of the grants made by Angus, and the power placed in the hands of Argyll with regard to future grants, caused great dissatisfaction among the Macleans, Macdonalds, and other clans. Some of them were deprived of lands to which they had a just claim, while they were all more than ever at the mercy of Argyll.

In the spring of 1527, Alexander Macdonald of Islay, Hector Mor of Duart, and Macdonald of Largie ravaged Roseneath, Craignish, and other lands belonging to the Campbells, and slew several of the inhabitants. The Campbells, under the command of Archibald, son and heir of the Earl of Argyll, retaliated upon the Macleans at once, and laid waste a part of Mull, the Maclean lands in Morvern, and the island of Tiree. They also put a number of persons to the sword. In the month of August, Argyll sent an urgent appeal to the Government, through his brother Calder, asking for a strong force to enable him to subdue the Macleans, Macdonalds, and other rebellious clans. Instead of the army which he wanted, the Government sent him two cannons and three barrels of gunpowder. At the same time they sent a herald, named Robert Hart, to Alexander of Islay, with directions to summon him to lay down his arms, and ask him to bring his grievances before the King in person. Alexander refused to comply with these requests, and thus unwisely put himself and his associates in the position of being rebels, not only against Argyll, but against the King as well. At the very time in which the Macleans and Macdonalds of Islay were in rebellion in the South Isles, the Macleods of Harris and the Macdonalds of Sleat were causing trouble in the North. Thus, the whole of the Isles were in a state of commotion. In the spring of 1530 King James began to make extensive preparations for an expedition against the Islanders. Alarmed by these preparations, nine of their principal leaders sent to the King in the month of May, by the hands of Hector of Duart, an offer of full submission to his authority. The King at once granted to them letters of protection against Argyll and all other opponents, so that they might have an opportunity of appearing before him and returning to their homes in safety. The men who had offered to tender their submission to the King were, Hector Maclean of Duart ; John Maclean of Lochbuie ; John Muidartach, captain of the Clanranald ; Alexander Mac Ian of Ardnamurchan ;

Alexander Macleod of Harris; John Abrach Maclean of Coll; John Macleod of Lewis; and Donald Gruamach of Sleat. In the spring of 1531, Alexander of Islay also sent an offer of submission to the King. In the month of June, Hector Mor and himself appeared before the King in Stirling, and "in the most humble manner offered their service" to him. Alexander was pardoned on the 7th of June, and ordered to set at liberty all the men belonging to the Earl of Argyll that he held as prisoners. On the following day—the 8th of June, 1531—Hector Mor and his associates received a remission for treasonably burning the houses of Roseneath, Lennox, Craignish, and others. The other land proprietors who had violated the laws of the land followed the example of Alexander of Islay and Hector Mor, and were dealt with in the same lenient manner. The Western Islands were now once more in a state of peace. Colin, third Earl of Argyll, died in 1530, and was succeeded by his son Archibald. We find that on the 17th of March, 1532, the Government granted to Archibald, Earl of Argyll, and eighty-two others, remission for the depredations committed by them in Mull, Morvern, and Tiree, on condition that the Earl should give satisfaction to "Donald Ballo Mac Auchin, Donald Crum Mac Cownane, and Farquhar Mac Sevir."

About 1533 Hector Mor captured an English ship, and for his services received from King James a remission of the rents and duties of the island of

Tiree. Shortly afterwards the Clanranald complained to the Lords of Council of the aggressive acts of Hector Mor and his two brothers, Ailein nan Sop and Patrick. Hector was compelled to give securities for proper behaviour on his own part towards the Clanranald, and to become security himself for his brothers. On the 9th of January, 1540, Hector Mor appeared before the King at Linlithgow and resigned all his lands in favour of his son and heir, Hector Og, reserving of course a life interest for himself. The lands thus placed in the King's hands were erected into the barony of Duart, and, according to the terms of resignation, conveyed by charter to Hector Og. On the 11th of February, Hector Mor received a respite for all past crimes, the respite to continue in force for nineteen years. In November, 1542, he received a charter of the lands of Kilmichael and Kilmore in Islay. The lands were granted in life rent to himself and in fee and heritage to his heir, Hector Og.

In May, 1540, James V. sailed with a fleet of twelve large ships from Leith to the Orkney Islands, and thence along the western coast of Scotland to the Clyde. He landed in several places in the islands and on the adjacent mainland. He apprehended Donald Mackay of Strathnaver and carried him along with him. He received voluntary visits from Rory Macleod of Lewis, Alexander Macleod of Harris, John Muidartach, Alexander Macdonald of Glengarry, John Mackenzie of Kintail, Hector Mor of Duart, and James Macdonald of Islay. These imperious rulers were also under the necessity of accepting a free passage from him and accompanying him on his voyage. He set some of them at liberty without much delay, but brought others to Edinburgh and kept them there as long as he lived. King James died in 1542, and was succeeded by his infant daughter, Mary Queen of Scots. Early in 1543 Donald Dubh was allowed to escape from Edinburgh Castle, where he had been confined during the last thirty-seven years, and was once more at liberty to assert his claim to the lordship of the Isles and the earldom of Ross. Shortly after Donald Dubh's escape from Edinburgh, the Earl of Arran, Regent of the kingdom, liberated the turbulent chiefs and chieftains who had been placed in confinement by James V. in 1540. Donald Dubh was now ready for action. He styled himself Lord of the Isles and Earl of Ross, and resolved to expel Argyll and Huntly from the lands which had belonged to his grandfather, John, fourth Lord of the Isles. He was joined by the Macleans, Macneils, Mackinnons, and Macquarries, by the Macleods of Harris and Lewis, and by all the Macdonalds except James of Islay. At the head of 1800 warriors he invaded Argyll's territories, slew quite a number of persons, and carried off an immense quantity of plunder.

When Donald Dubh raised the standard of rebellion the whole of Scotland was in a state of turmoil. The Protestants and Roman Catholics were quarrelling over religious matters, while Henry VIII. of England was threatening to invade the country with an army and reduce it to subjection. The Earl of Lennox, disappointed in his expectations of obtaining the regency, went to England, and sold himself to King Henry. According to the terms of agreement between them he was to assist Henry in conquering Scotland, while Henry was to appoint him Regent under himself. In May, 1544, an English army of 10,000 men, under the Earl of Hertford, landed at Leith and burnt the city of Edinburgh. At the same time Lord Evers entered Scotland at Berwick with 4,000 horse, and advanced to join Hertford, plundering the country as he marched along, and reducing castles, abbeys, villages, and farmhouses to utter ruin. In the following August the Earl of Lennox led an expedition from Bristol to the Clyde. He plundered the island of Arran, and reduced the village of Dunoon to ashes. He also made devastating excursions to Kintyre, Kyle, Carrick, Cunningham, and Galloway. His wrath was especially directed against the Earls of Arran, Argyll, and Glencairn. While engaged in this expedition, he entered into communication with Donald Dubh, the new Lord of the Isles.

On the 23rd of July, 1545, Donald Dubh and his leading supporters held a meeting on the island of Ellancarne, or Eigg. They agreed unanimously to recognize the Earl of Lennox as Regent of Scotland, and to send two commissioners to England to enter into a treaty, through the Earl of Lennox, with King Henry VIII. The persons selected to go to England were Rory Mac Alister, dean of Morvern, and "Mr. Patrick Maclean, brother-german of Lord Maclean and justice-clerk of the South Isles." The men who elected them and signed their commission were, "Donald, Lord of the Isles and Earl of Ross; Hector Maclean, Lord of Duart; John Mac Alister, captain of Clanranald; Rory Macleod of Lewis; Alexander Macleod of Dunvegan; Murdoch Maclean of Lochbuie; Angus Macdonald, brother-german to James Macdonald; Allan Maclean of Torloisk, brother-german to Lord Maclean; Archibald Macdonald, captain of Clan Uisdein; Alexander Mac Ian of Ardnamurchan; John Maclean of Coll; Gilliganan Macneil of Barra; Ewen Mackinnon of Strathordill; John Macquarrie of Ulva; John Maclean of Ardgour; Alexander Mac Ranald of Glengarry; Angus Mac Ranald of Knoydart; and Donald Maclean of Kingerloch." Among all those influential men there was not one who could sign his name. Patrick Colquhoun, brother of Colquhoun of Luss, Walter Macfarlane of Ardlish, Archibald Macgillivray, vicar of Killane, and Mr. John Carswell, afterwards Bishop of the Isles, were present as witnesses. Colquhoun and Macfarlane were agents of the Earl of Lennox. Rory Mac Alister was a brother of John Muideartach. Allan Maclean of Torloisk was the well-known Ailein nan Sop. Angus Macdonald was a brother of James Macdonald of Islay.

Donald Dubh and his supporters had 8,000 armed men at their command. They left 4,000 at home to protect their lands against Argyll and Huntly, and crossed over to Ireland with a fleet of 180 galleys and 4,000 men. They held a meeting in the chapter house of the monastery of Greyfriars at Knockfergus on the 5th of August, and drew up articles, addressed to the King of England, stating their grievances, desires, and purposes. The commissioners from the Islanders, Rory Mac Alister and Patrick Maclean, appeared before Henry VIII. in the manor of Oatlands on the 4th of September, and were received with great cordiality. The agreement arrived at was substantially as follows:—The Lord of the Isles and his adherents were to serve the King of England truly and faithfully. They were not to come to any agreement with Huntly or Argyll, which should be prejudicial to the interests of the King of England. They were to place 8,000 men at the disposal of the Earl of Lennox, while he should remain in the country of the Earl of Argyll, and 6,000 when he should be in any other part of Scotland. Henry was to give the Lord of the Isles an annual pension of 2,000 crowns, and to include himself and his adherents in any treaty that he should make with the Earl of Arran, Regent of Scotland. He was also to send the Earl of Lennox and the Earl of Ormond and Ossary with a number of men to invade the Campbell districts of Argyleshire, and to march then to Stirling, burning, harrying, and spoiling. Lastly, he was to pay 3,000 of the Islesmen for the period of two months the same sum per day which he was accustomed to give to his own men. Immediately after the conclusion of the treaty the commissioners returned to Knockfergus. In the despatches from the Irish Privy Council to Henry VIII. we find the troops that accompanied Donald Dubh to Knockfergus described in the following terms:—"Three thousand of them are very tall men; clothed, for the most part, in habergeons of mail, and armed with long swords and long bows, but with few guns. The other thousand are tall mariners that rowed in the galleys."

Some time after the arrival of the commissioners, Donald Dubh and his adherents returned to Scotland, where his army became dispersed. This result was brought about by two things. In the first place, the Earl of Lennox remained in England too long. He should have made the greatest possible haste to join the Islesmen. In the second place, the manner in which a sum of money, sent by the King of England, was distributed among Donald Dubh's adherents, caused a good deal of grumbling. The money was entrusted to Hector Mor of Duart. While some were satisfied with the amount given to them, others complained that they did not receive enough.

Lennox and Ormond sailed from Dublin on the 17th of November with a large fleet and an army of 2,000 men, but did not attempt to invade the lands of the Campbells. They returned to Ireland without accomplishing anything. Shortly afterwards Donald Dubh died of fever at Drogheda. He was a brave but unfortunate man.

When Donald Dubh was dying he commended his only child, a natural son, to the protection of the King of England. He also nominated James Macdonald of Islay as his successor in the lordship of the Isles.

In a letter written by James of Islay on the 10th of February, 1546, we find him ready to accept the position of Lord of the Isles. The Macdonalds, Camerons, and Ailein nan Sop were willing to support him; but Hector Mor of Duart, Maclean of Lochbuie, Maclean of Coll, Maclean of Ardgour, Maclean of Kingerloch, Macneil of Barra, Mackinnon, Macquarrie, Macleod of Harris, and Macleod of Lewis refused to proceed any further in the vain attempt to re-establish the lordship of the Isles. The followers of Donald Dubh were never punished for their treasonable conduct. They were all apparently on good terms with the Earl of Arran, Regent of the kingdom, by the end of the year 1546.

Hector Mor made extensive additions to the castle of Duart, and at the same time made it much stronger than it had been. The work was completed probably about the year 1547.

According to the Pennycross MS., when Hector Mor was repairing his castle, the Earl of Argyll threatened to invade Mull, and ordered all his vassals to meet him on a certain day at Clachan Saol. Campbell of Duntroon told him that he had no galley, but Argyll would take no excuse. The day before the invaders were to leave, Duntroon went to Duart and asked Hector Mor to loan him one of his galleys for a few days. Hector asked him where he was going with it. He replied that he was going to assist Argyll to invade Mull the next day. Hector at once gave him one of his best galleys, and requested him to tell Argyll that if he should come to Duart in peace he would be glad to see him, but that if he should come for war he would be prepared to give him an opportunity of fighting. On the next morning Duntroon went to Clachan Saol, where Argyll and his vassals were assembled. Argyll asked him where he had been. He told him that as a matter of necessity he had to go to Mull to borrow a galley from Hector Mor, and that when he was asked what he was going to do with it he told the whole truth. He also delivered Hector Mor's message. Then he advised Argyll to go to Mull in peace, to ask Hector Mor to give him his daughter in marriage, and to try to have a match made between Hector Mor's son and his own daughter. Argyll was highly delighted with Duntroon's advice, and acted at once in accordance with it.

Whether Duntroon had anything to do with bringing about a marriage between the Earl of Argyll and Hector Mor's daughter or not, it is a fact that they were married. It is also a fact that Hector Og and Argyll's daughter were married. But the two marriages did not take place at the same time. According to "The House of Argyll and the Collateral Branches of the Clan Campbell," the Earl of Argyll granted a charter of the estate of Craignish, in life rent, in favour of Catherine Maclean, on the 23rd of January, 1546. This charter determines the date of the marriage of Argyll with Hector Mor's daughter. Argyll died in 1553. On the 26th of January, 1557, Hector Og, with his father's consent, bestowed upon Janet Campbell, daughter of Archibald, Earl of Argyll, "Dunnowlycht, Rannochquhen," and other lands in Knapdale and Lochaber. Thus, Hector Og's marriage took place in 1557.

In February, 1549, Hector Mor received a charter of the lands of Ardgour. Shortly afterwards he received a gift of the patronage of the kirks of Kilcomar and Kilmarrow in Islay, in the diocese of the Isles, and also of the kirks of Kilcolmkill, and "Kilsynnye," in the diocese of Argyll. In June, 1553, he received a charter of the lands of Ulva, Laganvalsagary, and others in the shire of Tarbert. The charter of 1549 made Hector feudal lord of Maclean of Ardgour; while the charter of 1553 put him in the same position towards Macquarrie of Ulva.

Hector Mor tried to persuade Hector Maclean of Coll to acknowledge him as his feudal superior, and to follow him in all his wars and expeditions.

Finding that persuasion had no effect on the laird of Coll, he sent, in August, 1561, an armed force under the command of his two sons, Hector Og and John Dubh, to plunder the lands of Achalennan and Drimnin. The laird of Coll was in Edinburgh at the time. Hector Mor's sons carried off all the horses, cattle, sheep, goats, and provision they could find—the whole amounting in value to 4,000 marks. They also took possession of the lands they plundered, and kept possession of them for nearly three years and a half. In January, 1565, Hector Roy, younger of Coll, appeared before the Privy Council for his father, and Hector Mor for himself. Hector Mor was compelled to restore the lands of Achalennan and Drimnin to their lawful owner. He was also commanded not to oppress or molest Hector of Coll in any way. The amount to be paid by him for the depredations which he had committed was left to the decision and judgment of Archibald, Earl of Argyll.

In July, 1539, Ailein nan Sop received from the Government a gift of the non-entry mails of Gigha and certain lands in Kintyre and Islay. In 1552, Hector, his son and successor, received a gift of the same lands. In 1554, Neil Macneill, who had unquestionably a better right to Gigha than Hector Mac Allan, sold his claim to James Macdonald of Islay. Hector Mac Allan, who was in possession of Gigha, refused to part with it. His uncle, Hector Mor, took his part. The result was that Hector Mor and James of Islay became enemies. Shortly afterwards they quarrelled about the Rhinns of Islay. The Macleans were in actual possession of the lands, but James of Islay had received a claim to them from the Crown. From hard feelings and angry words Hector Mor and James came to acts of hostility and war. In 1562 the Macdonalds of Islay, assisted by the Macdonalds of Sleat, invaded Mull, Tiree, and Coll, plundering and slaying; and we may feel quite sure that the Macleans paid them back in a similar manner. On December 14th, 1563, we find a letter from Hector Mor read before the Privy Council, in which he claimed the Rhinns of Islay as his by right, but stated that he was "unable to travel to Edinburgh by reason of infirmity to prove his right." James of Islay appeared with witnesses to prove his claim to the Rhinns. It is just possible that Hector Mor was not quite so unwell as he pretended to be. At any rate some members of the Council were of the opinion that his infirmity was only feigned. In 1564, the Privy Council determined the points in dispute in favour of James of Islay, but Hector Mor refused to accept its decision. The consequence was that James and himself continued their plundering raids into each other's lands. About the beginning of 1565 they were both summoned before the Privy Council and bound down, under a penalty of £10,000 each, to abstain from their barbarous warfare. James died a few months afterwards. In 1566 Hector Mor ravaged the island of Gigha with fire and sword. In April, 1567,

Queen Mary commissioned the Earl of Argyll to proceed against him, and compel him to obey the laws of the country. It may be taken for granted that he made some compensation for his ravages in Gigha, and thus settled matters amicably with the Queen's lieutenant.

Hector Mor died in 1568. He was a prominent man, and well fitted for taking his own part in the time in which he lived. He had strong intellectual powers, but he was arbitrary and stubborn, and could do exceedingly harsh things. His treatment of the family of Coll was utterly inexcusable. He was a shrewd manager, and amassed a good deal of wealth. He lived in princely style, and was, like all the Highland chiefs, given to hospitality.

XII. Eachann Og.

Hector Og married, in 1557, Janet, only daughter of Archibald, fourth Earl of Argyll, by his wife, Mary, daughter of William Graham, sixteenth Earl of Menteith. He took an active part along with John Dubh, his brother, in the plunderings, quarrels, and wars of his father. He was not, however, of a warlike disposition. After his father's death in 1568 he led a life of ease and pleasure, and in a short time squandered all the money that had been left him. According to a song composed by Malcolm Macleod, third of Raarsay, the most bountiful hand seen by the Gaidels of Scotland in his day was that of Hector Og. By his folly and extravagance Hector Og actually plunged his estate into debt. He died some time after May 14th, 1573. He was succeeded by his famous son, Lachlan Mor.

CHAPTER VI.

XIII. LACHAINN MOR DHUBHAIRT.

Lachlan Mor of Duart, only son of Hector Og and Janet Campbell, was born about the end of the year 1557. He spent a few years in the Lowlands, and received a good education. He was brought up a Presbyterian, both by his mother and those who had charge of him when going to school. He was knighted by King James.

John Dubh of Morvern was the next heir to Lachlan Mor, and was entitled to the position of leader of the Macleans during the minority of the latter. Hector of Torloisk, or Hector the son of Ailein nan Sop, was the next heir to John Dubh. Hector was like his father an able and active man. He was also an ambitious man, and anxious to get the management of the Duart estate into his own hands. John Dubh, however, stood in his way. In May, 1573, John Dubh was seized without any legal authority by Archibald, fifth Earl of Argyll, and imprisoned in Inchconnell

Castle in Lochow. Argyll was instigated to take this step by Hector Mac Allan, or Hector of Torloisk. It is certain, however, that Argyll was just as anxious as Hector himself to prevent John Dubh from being leader of the Clan Gillean. In 1574, or thereabouts, Hector married Janet Campbell, Hector Og's widow, and succeeded in obtaining the leadership of the clan. Archibald of Argyll died in September, 1575, and was succeeded by his brother Colin, a rapacious and quarrelsome man, and a bitter enemy to the Macleans.

About the beginning of 1576, Lachlan Mor returned from the Lowlands to take charge of his estates. Some time afterwards, probably about the end of the year, John Dubh was, by order of the Privy Council, released from his confinement. In March, 1577, Colin, sixth Earl of Argyll, tried to persuade John Dubh, by promising him great rewards, to murder Lachlan Mor, his own sister's son. John Dubh made known to Lachlan that the Earl of Argyll was plotting against his life. Lachlan also became acquainted with facts which led him to believe that Hector Mac Allan was associated with Argyll in planning his destruction. On May 23rd, 1577, he seized Hector and his son, Allan Og, and carried them off to Duart Castle, where he imprisoned them and put them in irons. In the summer of 1577, Argyll induced Angus Macdonald of Islay to besiege the castle of Lochgorm in Islay, which belonged to Lachlan Mor, and ravage the lands around it. Angus led 1200 men to attack the castle, and was assisted by Argyll with a force of 250 men. Lachlan Mor, however, remained in possession of Lochgorm.

While the Macleans were engaged in defending Lochgorm Castle, Argyll sent two hundred of his followers, under the command of Dugald Campbell of Inveraw, to plunder the Macleans of Luing. Inveraw carried out his instructions with fidelity and energy. He took away all the cows, horses, and sheep that he could find, and despoiled the women and children of their clothing. About the same time Campbell of Lochgoilhead, at the special command of the Earl of Argyll, seized Lachlan Mor's servant, while on his way to the Lowlands, and imprisoned him. The Earl in fact made it impossible for Lachlan Mor's followers to travel through Argyll, to trade with the Lowlands. He was in the habit of arresting them and keeping them in prison until ransomed by their friends. He was evidently an admirer of the ways and doings of the pirates of Algiers. In November, 1577, Lachlan Mor, John Smollet, Ewen of Ardgour, and "John Dubh Mac Charles Mac Eachann" seized Adam Mackay, with the intention of sending him a prisoner to Dumbarton. He was taken from them by John Og Maclean and his accomplices, servants to Colin, Earl of Argyll. Shortly afterwards, George Smollet, captain of the Isle of Luing, was seized and imprisoned by Argyll.

Alexander Cunningham, fifth Earl of Glencairn,

was among the first of the Scottish noblemen who favoured the Reformation. He became a member of Queen Mary's Privy Council in 1560, and was a very influential man in his time. He died in 1574. His daughter, Jane, was married to Archibald, fifth Earl of Argyll. William, his son and successor, had two sons and six daughters. Lachlan Mor entered into a contract of marriage with Margaret, the second of Glencairn's daughters, on the 30th of December, 1577. They were married shortly afterwards.

About the beginning of the year 1578, Lachlan Mor lodged a complaint with the Privy Council against the doings of Argyll in Luing and other places. In the following December the Council ordered Argyll to return answers to the complaints made against him. Shortly afterwards Lachlan Mor made preparations to enter the country of the Campbells and exact satisfaction by fire and sword for the injuries done to his followers. Argyll, dreading the consequences of an invasion, hastened to come to terms. Two arbitrators were appointed to determine the value of the property carried away from Luing. Argyll paid the sum agreed upon, and thus saved his warlike opponent the trouble of collecting it among the Campbells.

In January, 1578, John Dubh of Morvern invaded the Island of Gigha with a strong force, plundered it, burnt and destroyed the houses, and slew nine men and two women. He carried off with him 500 cows, 300 horses, 2,000 sheep and goats, and all the valuable articles to be found. Of course John Dubh was acting nominally under Lachlan Mor's orders. Still it is probable that for all the acts done by Lachlan Mor during the first few years of his chiefship, John Dubh's share of the responsibility was greater than Lachlan's. He was practically the leader of the clan. In February, 1578, we find the Government charging Lachlan Mor of Duart, Lachlan Dubh Mackinnon of Strathordill, and others, not to attack or pursue Donald Mac Angus of Glengarry.

In April, 1578, Lachlan Mor seized Donald Maclean, son of John Diurach, son of Hector Mac Allan, and imprisoned him in the castle of Cairnburgh. On the 20th of April he invaded Coll, seized the castle of Breacachadh, and garrisoned it with his own followers. He kept possession of the estates of Coll for some time. Rory Beg Maclean acted as his deputy and collected the rents for him. Shortly after he had made himself master of Coll, he sent Hector Mac Allan and Allan Og, Hector's son, to that island. Hector was beheaded there by his order, and Allan Og placed in confinement.

The feud between the Macleans and the Macdonalds, with regard to the Rhinns of Islay, was renewed by the attack of the latter on the castle of Lochgorm in 1577. The one clan was in the habit of making plundering expeditions into the lands of the other. Consequently the losses and sufferings endured by the tenants of both clans were very great. In January, 1579, the Government resolved to put a stop to the mischievous work that was going on. They enjoined Lachlan Mor and James of Islay to sign an agreement, within a certain number of days, forgiving one another for the past, and promising obedience to the laws of the land for the future. They also made known to them in the plainest terms that if they would not comply with the orders given them, they would be proceeded against for treason. The result of the firm action of the Government was to bring the barbarous guerilla warfare of the Macleans and the Macdonalds to an end. Shortly afterwards Angus of Islay married Lachlan Mor's sister. There was now some ground for hoping that the Macleans and the Macdonalds would for the future act with wisdom and fight side by side against their common enemies as in the days of yore.

On April 30th, 1579, the Privy Council issued letters of denunciation and warning against Lachlan Mor for his unjust treatment of the Macleans of Coll, for keeping Allan Og and Donald, son of John Diurach, in confinement, and for the depredations committed by John Dubh in the Isle of Gigha. Shortly afterwards he restored the estates of Coll to their lawful owner, released his prisoners, and probably made some compensation to Agnes Campbell, who had through her husband, James Macdonald of Islay, a life interest in Gigha. In 1578 some of Lachlan Mor's followers plundered the lands of "Shane O' Dochtrie of Glach."

On the 10th of August, 1579, Colin, sixth Earl of Argyll, was appointed Lord High Chancellor of Scotland. On the 27th day of the same month he compelled Lachlan to give pledges for standing his trial at a future date for the losses sustained by O' Dochtrie. In May, 1580, Lachlan was under the necessity of surrendering to the High Chancellor lands of the yearly value of 200 marks, to compensate for the injuries done to O' Dochtrie. We do not know what became of these lands. It is possible that Lachlan paid the amount due to O' Dochtrie and got his lands back. The probability, however, is that the Earl of Argyll retained possession of them. Lachlan Mor seems to have spent a few weeks in Ulster in 1584.

In the summer of 1585 Donald Gorm Mor of Sleat, left the Isle of Skye, accompanied by a large retinue, with the intention of paying a visit to Angus Macdonald of Islay. Owing to a severe storm which had sprung up, he was forced to seek shelter in the northern part of Jura, which part of the island belonged to Maclean of Duart. Hugh, son of Archibald the Clerk, and another Macdonald, a descendant of Donald Herrach, were driven by the same storm to Jura. During the night these two men collected a large number of the cattle which belonged to the Macleans who lived near the place in which Donald Gorm Mor had cast anchor, and carried them off in their galleys. Their sole object in taking away the cattle was to get Donald Gorm Mor into trouble.

They knew that the Macleans would believe that the theft was committed by Donald Gorm Mor, and they hoped that they would attack him and put him to death. The men whose cattle had been stolen went at once to Lachlan Mor to lay their complaint before him. As no one in Jura had seen the men who had taken away the cattle, Lachlan Mor believed the story told him, and immediately prepared to take vengeance upon the supposed plunderers. He sailed to Jura with a number of men and made a sudden attack upon Donald Gorm Mor, who was utterly ignorant of what had taken place. He slew sixty of the Macdonalds, but the rest of them, Donald Gorm Mor included, succeeded in making their escape. Lachlan Mor's conduct was utterly inexcusable. Even if Donald Gorm Mor and his men had carried off the cattle, the punishment inflicted upon them was monstrous. Of course it may be said that Lachlan Mor acted in accordance with the custom of the age in which he lived. That may be true enough ; but the fact that it is customary to do wrong does not justify a man in disregarding the moral law. The place at which the Macdonalds were slain was known as Innis a Chnoic Bhric, Innis Knock Breck, or the grazing field of the speckled hill.

Donald Gorm Mor hastened back to Skye, burning with anger, and fully resolved to take vengeance upon the Macleans. He despatched messengers to the chieftains of the various branches of the Clan Donald, calling upon them to assist him in attacking his assailants. The conduct of Lachlan Mor in slaying a number of innocent men created feelings of indignation and vengeance among all the Macdonalds. The league formed against him was so powerful that he found himself in great difficulties. The Macdonalds were committing acts of depredation on his lands in various quarters, and threatening to invade Mull with all their forces. They had found out that the cattle had been actually stolen, and stolen by two Macdonalds, still they felt so indignant over the slaughter of their clansmen at Knock Breck that they were unwilling to come to terms with their antagonist. In the month of September King James wrote Macleod of Dunvegan, requesting him to assist the Macleans against the Macdonalds. We may be sure that he urged the Macdonalds at the same time to desist from their hostilities. Owing to the action of the King, the Macdonalds felt disposed to settle their disputes with the Macleans in a proper manner. Even if they should be able to defeat both the Macleans and the Macleods of Harris, they could not possibly defeat the forces at the King's command.

In the spring of 1586 Angus Macdonald of Islay went to Skye to consult Donald Gorm Mor with regard to a settlement with Lachlan Mor. On his way back he called at Duart Castle to try to persuade Lachlan to come to an amicable settlement with his opponent. On the day after his arrival, the Lord of Duart seized both Angus and his attendants, and threw them into prison, where he kept them until Angus consented to renounce his claim to the Rhinns of Islay. Angus was also under the necessity of giving James, his son, and Ranald, his brother, as hostages to Lachlan until the latter should be put in possession of the lands promised to him. The harsh treatment received by Angus at the hands of Lachlan Mor put an end to his peaceful intentions. He went back to Islay a bitter enemy to the Lord of Duart.

In July, 1586, Lachlan Mor went to Islay to receive possession of the disputed lands of the Rhinns, and took up his quarters at the fort of Lochgorm, where he remained three days. He received repeated invitations from Angus of Islay to pay him a visit at Mullintrea. He yielded at last, and went to spend a night with him. He was accompanied, according to one account, by seventy of his followers, but according to another account by eighty-six. He was received in the most friendly manner, and entertained in grand style. During the evening Angus's wife saw reasons for thinking that her brother was likely to be attacked, but could find no opportunity of making her suspicions known to him. She ventured, however, to make the simple remark, "Tha 'n oidhche stoirmeil 's bu chòir do gach buachaille sùil a bhith aige air a threud," the night is stormy, and every shepherd should have an eye on his flock. Lachlan understood the hint. He refused to comply with Angus's request to remain in the castle all night, and went to sleep in one of the buildings in which his followers were lodged. He took his nephew with him, James, the son and heir of Angus, who was still a hostage in his hands. At midnight Angus of Islay, at the head of nearly 400 armed followers, went to the door of the building in which Lachlan was sleeping, and asked him to get up and have a drink with him. Lachlan was on his feet in an instant, and, with little James in his left hand as a shield and his sword in his right hand, went to the door. While Lachlan saw that it was impossible for him to escape, Angus saw that if a fight took place his son would be certainly slain. Angus now solemnly promised that if the Macleans would give up his son to him, and surrender as prisoners, their lives would be spared. Lachlan Mor accepted the terms offered and delivered up his sword. All those who were with him, except two, followed his example. One of these was John Dubh of Morvern, the commander of the expedition to Gigha; the other was Macdonald Herrach, the man who, along with Hugh, son of Gillespick the Clerk, had occasioned the slaughter of the Macdonalds at Knock Breck. As these men knew that they would receive no mercy they refused to give up their arms. They stood in the door of the building in which they lodged and defied their opponents to capture them. The Macdonalds, knowing their prowess and determination, and unable to subdue them by the sword, set fire to the building which they occupied. Both of them perished in the flames. The prisoners were tied together two by two and placed in confinement.

The day after the black night of Mullintrea a report was circulated in Islay to the effect that Ranald Mac James, who was a hostage in Duart, had been executed. On hearing this absurd story Angus ordered his brother Coll to lead out the prisoners in couples and put them to death. The work of butchery was carried on for several days, perhaps for several weeks. At last there was none left except Lachlan Mor. It is said that on the day on which the ferocious Angus intended to decapitate the Lord of Duart, he fell from his horse and received an injury which rendered him unable to go out to the place of execution. Owing to this accident, he spared the life of his enemy until he should be able to mount his horse and ride out to see him put to death. This story may or may not be true. It is likely, however, that it is not true. We suspect that Angus spared Lachlan Mor's life simply to exchange him for his own brother, Ranald.

A work recently published conveys the idea that all the prisoners put to death by Angus of Islay were slain on the same day. This statement is wholly unwarranted. The history of "The Feuds and Conflicts of the Clans" was written in the time of James VI., and published in 1764. In that work we are told that "as soon as the report came to Angus's ears that his brother Ranald had been slain, he revenged himself fully upon the prisoners;

for Maclean's followers were by couples beheaded the days following, by Coll, the brother of Angus." The Ardgour MS. tells us that Angus "hated two of the prisoners more than any of the rest and caused the barn to be set on fire over them, and that next morning, contrary to the terms of capitulation, he caused two more of them to be put to death and continued doing so daily until only Lachlan Mor and his uncle, John Dubh, remained alive." It is certainly difficult to believe that Angus of Islay spent several days in butchering his prisoners; but the foregoing evidence—especially that of the history written in the time of James VI.—clearly proves that such was the case.

Lachlan Mor's conduct towards Angus of Islay was ungenerous and unjust, but Angus's conduct towards Lachlan Mor was utterly atrocious. Angus went of his own accord to Duart, but Lachlan was invited and coaxed to visit Mullintrea. Lachlan acted in a cruel manner towards Angus, but Angus added treachery to cruelty in dealing with Lachlan. Lachlan did not injure any of Angus's followers, but Angus put to death all the men who accompanied Lachlan. Even if his brother had been murdered in Duart, the murder of one man could be no excuse for murdering seventy, or eighty-six, men whose lives he had promised to spare. But it is not at all likely that he believed the story regarding the execution of his brother. If he believed it, he must have also believed that the execution took place by

Lachlan Mor's orders. Why then should he have spared Lachlan, and slain his followers? The probability is that the main reason which influenced Angus to murder his prisoners was the desire to weaken his opponents by cutting off their leading men.

The author of the report respecting the execution of Ranald Mac James was Allan Og Maclean, son of Hector Mac Allan. Allan Og hated Lachlan Mor, and was ready to invent and circulate any story that would give Angus of Islay a plausible excuse for putting him to death. But he was under the influence of other motives besides hatred. If he could get Lachlan out of the way, he himself might become leader of the clan during the minority of Lachlan's son and heir.

Shortly after the imprisonment of Lachlan Mor, the Macleans succeeded in capturing Ranald, son of Coll, third son of Alexander of Islay. They had now Angus Macdonald's brother and his first cousin in their hands. As soon as King James had heard of Lachlan Mor's danger, he took active steps to procure his release. Colin, sixth Earl of Argyll, died in 1584. As Archibald, his son and successor, was under age, the government of the earldom was in the hands of guardians. These guardians were instructed by King James, to act as peacemakers between the Macleans and the Macdonalds, and to procure his freedom for Lachlan Mor. The Campbells performed the duties entrusted to them with fidelity and success. According to the settlement arrived at, Lachlan Mor renounced his claim to the Rhinns of Islay in favour of Angus Macdonald, and promised to leave him in undisturbed possession of these lands. He also agreed to release Ranald Mac James and Ranald Mac Coll as soon as he should arrive in Duart. The Campbell peacemakers, who represented the King, promised Angus a full pardon for all the crimes committed by him. They also placed in his hands eight hostages, of whom he was to retain possession until the remission promised should be actually granted to him. These hostages were, Hector Maclean, Lachlan Mor's eldest son; Alexander, brother of William Macleod of Dunvegan; Lachlan and Neil, sons of Lachlan Mackinnon of Strathordill; John and Murdoch, sons of Rory Macneil of Barra; Allan, son of Ewen Maclean of Ardgour; and Donald, son of Hector Maclean, constable of Cairnburgh. Lachlan Mor was now liberated. As soon as he arrived in Mull, he gave their freedom to Ranald Mac James and Ranald Mac Coll.

The Ardgour MS. tells us that Angus of Islay murdered all his prisoners except Lachlan Mor and John Dubh. When the former was set at liberty, the latter was kept in prison as a hostage until Ranald Mac James and Ranald Mac Coll should arrive in Islay. A few days after Lachlan had been released, Macdonald of Ardnamurchan came to Islay and assured Angus that his brother Ranald had been put to death. Angus then caused John Dubh to be executed.—There is no truth in this story. The eight hostages placed by the representatives of the King in Angus's hands would be a sufficient guarantee to him that the prisoners in Duart Castle would be liberated. According to "The Feuds and Conflicts of the Clans," the man who was burnt to death with Macdonald Herrach "was a very near kinsman to Maclean, and the eldest of his surname, renowned both for counsel and manhood." According to Seannachie's history, he was a Maclean from Morvern. As John Dubh was Lachlan Mor's uncle, as he was well advanced in years, as he was the most influential counsellor among the Macleans, as he was an experienced warrior, and as he was bailie of Morvern, it is beyond all doubt that he was the man who perished with Macdonald Herrach. It is clear, then, that Macdonald of Ardnamurchan was not responsible for his death.

Lachlan Mor paid a visit to King James in Edinburgh in the spring of 1587. His object was undoubtedly to urge the King to secure the release and safety of the hostages who were in the hands of Angus of Islay. It is evident that he received a very favourable reception. At a meeting of the Privy Council held at Holyrood House on the 16th of April, we find the King stating that he had remitted the great crimes of Angus Macdonald of Islay, that he had delivered eight hostages into his hands to procure the liberation of Lachlan Maclean of Duart, that it was unreasonable that the hostages should always remain in their state of bondage, and that he himself intended to take immediate steps to settle in an equitable manner the controversies between Angus of Islay and Lachlan of Duart. He then orders that Angus Macdonald, Ranald Macdonald of Smerby, John Mac Ian of Ardnamurchan, Archibald Macdonald, son of Angus Ileach, Neil Mackay, officer of the Rhinns of Islay, Hector Mac Alister of Largie, Mac Alister, tutor of Largie, John Dubh Mac Ranald, and John Mor Mac Ian be commanded to deliver the eight hostages in their hands to Archibald, Earl of Argyll, or to any of his tutors, in order to be conveyed to His Majesty and kept by him until all the matters in dispute shall be settled. On the 20th of the same month, King James wrote a letter to the Earl of Huntly, requesting him to use all diligence to keep Donald Gorm Mor, Macleod of Lewis, Macleod of Harris, the captain of the Clanranald, and all others within the bounds of his lieutenancy, from taking part in the disputes between Lachlan Mor and Angus of Islay, as he himself intended to take special pains to settle these disputes as soon as possible.

On the 30th of May, 1587, we find Donald Gorm Mor of Sleat and Angus of Islay entering into an alliance, offensive and defensive, with Lachlan Mackintosh, captain of the Clan Chattan, against all persons, except the King and the Earl of Argyll. The Macdonalds were evidently preparing for a renewal of the war with Lachlan Mor, while

Mackintosh was seeking to strengthen himself against the Earl of Huntly. Angus of Islay refused to give up the hostages in his hands, and thus placed himself in direct opposition to the King, the result being that he was outlawed. His associates were outlawed at the same time.

In the summer of 1587, **Lachlan Mor** renewed the war against the Macdonalds. He invaded Islay, laid the greater part of it waste, and put to death a large number of persons; he slew every Macdonald, capable of bearing arms, that fell into his hands. At the time of this invasion Angus Macdonald was in Ireland attending to his affairs in that country. He returned as speedily as possible, vowing vengeance upon his fierce opponent. Donald Gorm Mor and himself collected their vassals and friends, and at the head of a large force invaded the island of Tiree. As Lachlan Mor was utterly unprepared to attack them, he ordered his tenants in Mull to leave the sea-coast and valleys and to seek shelter, with their cattle and horses, in the mountains. The invaders sailed from Tiree to Loch-nan-Gall in Mull, and landed at Derryguaig, near Knock, at the foot of Ben Mor. The Macleans occupied a strong position at Lecklee, back of Gernadu. The Macdonalds pushed forward their outposts as far as Sròn-na-Cranalaich, which was about three miles from Lecklee. They could advance no further without going through a narrow pass, which was guarded by a body of Macleans in command of John

Maclean of Inverscadle, one of the ablest warriors of his day. Contrary to his instructions, the fiery Inverscadle left his post and attacked the Macdonalds who were at Sròn-na-Cranalaich. He was of course defeated. He himself returned, but the most of his followers were slain. On the morning of the next day the Macdonalds came to the conclusion that it would be sheer madness to attempt to march through the mountain passes to attack their foes. Consequently, they resolved to go away and plunder some unprotected districts. As they were making their way back to their galleys the Macleans suddenly attacked them and inflicted some loss on them.

During their expedition the Macdonalds laid waste the whole of Tiree, the Isle of Iona, and parts of Mull. They put to death all the Macleans whom they could find, and killed all the cattle, sheep, and goats which they could not carry away with them. Their whole aim was to exterminate the Macleans. But the latter were not idle. They invaded Kintyre and ravaged a large portion of that district with fire and sword. Angus Macdonald was now compelled to hasten back to protect his tenants.

In the sanguinary and destructive war which raged between Lachlan Mor and Angus of Islay, Lachlan was supported by the whole of the Macleans, the Macquarries, the Macneils of Barra, and the Mackinnons, and also by the Macleods of Harris; while Angus was supported by the whole

of the Macdonalds, the Mac Alisters of Loup,
the Macphies of Colonsay, and the Macneills of
Gigha, and likewise by the Macleods of Lewis.
So far as the Macleods were concerned, it is not
likely that they took an active part in the war.
The one branch would require to watch the other.

John Mac Ian of Ardnamurchan became a suitor
for the hand of Lachlan Mor's mother in marriage,
some time after the death of her second husband,
Hector Mac Allan of Torloisk. Lachlan was
originally strongly opposed to the match. Early
in 1588 he gave Mac Ian to understand that he was
anxious to enjoy his friendship for the future, and
was willing to give him his mother in marriage.
His aim, evidently, was to detach Mac Ian from
the party headed by Angus of Islay and Donald
Gorm Mor. The marriage took place at the
bride's residence, Torloisk House, on the 12th of
April. The evening was spent pleasantly in feasting and drinking. After the newly married couple
had been put to bed the most of the Macdonalds
retired to a barn to sleep. A few of them, however—probably the more prominent of them—
remained in the house and continued drinking
with Lachlan Mor and some of his principal men.
During the conversation which took place, one of
the Macdonalds boasted that Mac Ian had married
Lachlan's mother for her wealth, and not from
any love he had for her. He was also indiscreet
enough to state that Mac Ian would still continue
to support Angus of Islay and Donald Gorm Mor.

A Maclean who was sitting beside him called out, "Drunken men always tell the truth," and stabbed him to the heart with his dagger. The Macleans immediately rushed upon the Macdonalds. They slew, first, the men who were drinking with them, and, next, those who were sleeping in the barn— in all over eighteen persons. Their next object of attack was Mac Ian himself. They broke into his room, and would have despatched him on the spot, if the cries and tears of his wife had not softened their hearts. They did not allow him, however, to remain in his room. He was dragged away and thrown into the dungeon. Two of his followers, who had escaped the general massacre, were imprisoned along with him. These were, Allister Mac Ian and Angus Mac Ian. The latter was Mac Ian's page. Some of the foregoing details may not be strictly accurate. There are two things, however, which can be depended upon as facts; first, that when the marriage took place, the Macleans had no intention of murdering the Macdonalds; secondly, that the real cause of the massacre was the discovery by the Macleans on the night of the marriage that Mac Ian would not support them against Angus of Islay and Donald Gorm Mor. The Lord of Duart was a politician. When he found that he could not get the Mac Ians to fight for him, he concluded in a moment of anger that the best thing he could do was to disqualify them from fighting against him. David Mac Gill of Nesbit, King's Advocate, wrote to the Privy

Council complaining of Lachlan Mor's conduct and asking that steps be taken to secure the release of Mac Ian and his two companions. Lachlan was summoned to appear before the Council, but refused to obey. The consequence was that on the 18th of June he was denounced a rebel.

In the autumn of 1588, the Florida, one of the largest ships that belonged to the Spanish Armada, was compelled by a storm to seek shelter in the harbour of Tobermory. Lachlan Mor supplied the captain with provisions, and received in return the use of 100 Spanish soldiers for a few weeks. With this force and some of his own followers he left Mull in the month of October on an expedition against the Macdonalds of Ardnamurchan and Moydart. He plundered the islands of Canna, Rum, Eigg, and Muck, and destroyed the houses by fire. According to David Mac Gill of Nesbit, the King's Advocate, he slaughtered in the "most barbarous, shameful, and cruel manner, all the men, women, and children." He laid siege to the castle of Mingarry in Ardnamurchan during three days, but was unable to take it. He laid waste with fire and sword all the lands in the vicinity of it, and then returned to Mull. When Lachlan was away on this expedition, or soon afterwards, Angus of Islay, having procured the assistance of 100 English soldiers, ravaged with fire and sword some lands which belonged to the Macleans.

Shortly after the return of the Macleans and the

Spaniards from their ferocious work, the Florida exploded in Tobermory Bay, the result being that all the men who were on board perished, except three or four. According to the records of the Privy Council the ship was blown up at the instigation of Lachlan Mor. Martin in his "Description of the Western Islands," a work written about 1695, states that it was destroyed by one Smollet, a native of Dumbarton. The Ardgour MS. assures us that the destruction of the Florida was purely a matter of accident. Seannachie gives a minute account of it. He tells us that Don Fareija, the captain of the ship, intended to go away without paying the people of Mull for the supplies which he had received from them; that Lachlan Mor sent Donald Glas, son of John Dubh of Morvern, to demand a settlement; that the captain kept Donald on board and intended to carry him off to Spain; and that Donald, exasperated by the dishonesty and treachery of the Spaniards, took vengeance upon them by setting fire to the powder magazine. According to a well-known legend the author of the destruction of the big Spanish ship, an long mhór Spainteach, was the Doideag Mhuileach, a celebrated Mull witch who invariably exerted her influence in behalf of the Macleans of Duart. Upon the whole we are inclined to think that Martin's statement is correct, and that the Smollet to whom he refers was either George Smollet, captain of the island of Luing, or else John Smollet, who was evidently George's brother. It is certainly possible that Lachlan Mor was not in a state of total ignorance regarding Smollet's intentions. It is also possible that Donald Glas was one of Smollet's assistants.

The treaty of peace effected by the King and the guardians of the young Earl of Argyll between the Macleans and the Macdonalds was concluded in the autumn of 1586. The Government, as we have seen, placed at that time eight hostages in the hands of the Macdonalds as a guarantee of remission for their crimes, and also as a pledge of abstinence from hostilities on the part of the Macleans. On the 30th of May, 1587, Angus of Islay and his associates were denounced rebels for refusing to deliver up the hostages in their hands to the Earl of Argyll, and, through him, to the King. Shortly afterwards Lachlan Mor renewed the war and swooped down upon Islay with fire and sword. On the 18th of June, 1588, he was declared a rebel for his treatment of John Mac Ian of Ardnamurchan. On the 3rd of January, 1589, he was again declared a rebel for his cruel expedition to Canna, Rum, Eigg, Muck, and Ardnamurchan. The war between himself and the Macdonalds had now raged during the long period of two years and three months. The King and his Council, however, had done nothing to crush it. Indeed, it looks as if they did not care very much whether the belligerent clans should extirpate each other or not. They knew that the more they would fight the weaker they would become. They knew also that as a result of their weakness their lands could by-and-by be easily gobbled up. To some of the rulers of the country the destructive feud between the foolish and sanguinary belligerents must have been an exceedingly enjoyable sight.

About the beginning of the year 1589, the Macleans and the Macdonalds began to come to their senses, and to see that their raids, battles and butcheries, while injurious to both, were of no advantage to either. In their glimmerings of sanity they resolved to sheathe the sword and live at peace. The eight hostages who had been in the hands of the Macdonalds since the autumn of 1586, were now set at liberty. John Mac Ian and the other prisoners in the hands of the Macleans were also allowed to return to their homes.

In March, 1589, remissions were granted by the Government to Lachlan Mor, James of Islay, and Donald Gorm Mor, for all the crimes committed by them during their late feud. A few months afterwards they were induced to pay a visit to Edinburgh, ostensibly to communicate their views to the King and Council with regard to the best means of preserving order and peace in the Highlands, but really to be dealt with as criminals. Contrary to all ideas of justice and fair dealing, they were at once arrested and thrown into prison. About the beginning of 1591 they were brought to trial for the crimes already pardoned by the Privy Council. They made no attempt to defend their actions; they simply cast themselves on the

King's mercy. They were fined to the amount of £20,000 Scots each. Donald Gorm Mor was fined at the same time, the sum to be paid by him being £4,000 Scots.

On the 24th of December, 1589, we find Lachlan Mor giving to Neil Campbell, Bishop of Argyll, and the heirs male of his body, a charter of the lands of Tarbert in the Isle of Jura. On March 23rd, 1591, we find him entering into a bond of friendship with Duncan Campbell of Glenorchy and Sir James Campbell of Ardkinglass, who were acting in behalf of the young Earl of Argyll. As James, Earl of Glencairn, and Neil Campbell, Bishop of Argyll, were witnesses to this bond, it is very likely that they had something to do with getting it made. It is evident that Lachlan Mor's object in giving a piece of land to the Bishop of Argyll, and in entering into a bond of friendship with Glenorchy and Ardkinglass, was to procure, or rather to purchase, the favour and support of the Campbells. He was in a difficulty and needed their help. In the summer of 1591 John Campbell of Ardkinglass, son and successor of Sir James, became security for Lachlan Mor for the fine imposed on him; while Sir John Campbell, third of Calder, became security for Angus of Islay and Donald Gorm Mor. Lachlan Mor promised to give, within a certain date after his release, three hostages to the King. The hostages to be given by him were, Hector Og, his son and heir; John, eldest son of the captain of Cairnburgh, and Malcolm, eldest son of the captain of Aros. Angus of Islay and Donald Gorm Mor were under the necessity of giving hostages before being set at liberty. The island rulers were now allowed to return to their homes.

Shortly before his release from confinement Lachlan Mor offered, through Bowes, the English ambassador, his services to Queen Elizabeth. He expressed his readiness to cross over to Ireland and assist in putting down all rebellions against her authority in that country. Elizabeth was glad to have his goodwill, but probably unwilling to expend the money which would be required.

Lachlan Mor, Angus of Islay, and Donald Gorm Mor failed in carrying out their promises, especially in paying the King's rents. At the meeting of Parliament in June, 1592, it was resolved to "punish and repress all the treasonable and barbarous rebels of the Highlands and islands." Lachlan Mor, Angus of Islay, and Donald Gorm Mor were commanded to appear before the Privy Council on the 14th day of July to fulfil the conditions which had been imposed upon them, and to give sufficient security for the payment of the Crown rents. In the event of non-compliance, the King could declare their lives, lands, and goods forfeited. On March 16th, 1593, the following persons were relaxed from the horn and received to the King's peace: Lachlan Mor of Duart; Maclean of Lochbuie; Maclean of Coll; Macleod, tutor of Harris; Lachlan Mackinnon of

Strathordill; Hector Macquarrie of Ulva; Charles Maclean, tutor of Ardgour; John Og Mac Ian of Ardnamurchan; Allan Maclean, bailie of Morvern; John Maclean, bailie of Ross; Neil Mac Gillecalum, captain of Aros; Hector Maclean, captain of Cairnburgh; and Macneil of Barra.

In June, 1594, the Earls of Huntly, Errol, and Angus were forfeited for conspiring with Philip of Spain to re-establish Roman Catholicism in Scotland. Lachlan Mor and Angus of Islay were forfeited at the same time for not carrying out the promises made by them in 1591. Shortly afterwards, Archibald, seventh Earl of Argyll, who was only in the nineteenth year of his age, was commissioned to reduce the three Roman Catholic earls to submission. He raised an army of 4,000 or 5,000 men, and marched into Badenoch, where he arrived on the 27th of September, and was joined by the Mackintoshes and Grants. He tried to capture Ruthven Castle, which was defended by the Macphersons, but failed. He led his army from Badenoch to Glenlivet, and was attacked there by the Earls of Huntly and Errol on Thursday, the 3rd day of October.

At the battle of Glenlivet the Earl of Argyll had about 7,000 men. The Macleans were at the extreme right and the Mackintoshes next to them. The centre was commanded by Duncan Campbell of Auchinbreck. The left wing consisted of the Grants, Macgregors, and others. The rear was commanded by Argyll himself. The Earls of

Huntly and Errol had only about 1500 men, but most of these were horsemen. They had three field pieces, which were under the direction of Captain Andrew Gray. Grant of Gartanbeg, in accordance with a promise given to the Earl of Huntly, fled at the very commencement of the fight. The Campbells of Lochnell, who were enemies to the Earl of Argyll, seem to have followed his example. The artillery struck terror into the ranks of those of the Campbells who remained with their chief. The Camerons, under Allan Mac Ian Duibh, attacked their old foes, the Mackintoshes, and routed them. The Earl of Argyll fought bravely; but being deserted by his followers he was compelled to flee with them. Lachlan Mor displayed the highest skill as a commander. He held his ground and inflicted upon Huntly and Errol nearly all the losses which they suffered. He was the last man to quit the field. He led his followers away in good order. He lost only a few men in the battle, and none in the retreat.

About the beginning of July, 1595, Donald Gorm Mor and other Macdonald leaders crossed over to Ireland to assist Hugh Roy O' Neil, Earl of Tyrone, and Hugh Roy O' Donnell, who were at that time in rebellion against Queen Elizabeth. About the middle of July another party of Macdonalds, numbering 900 men, left the Highlands for the same purpose. On the evening of the day on which they left, they landed on the small island of Calve in Tobermory Bay. Through the night

Lachlan Mor, at the head of 300 men, seized their galleys and boats and then captured themselves. Among the prisoners taken by him were, the captain of Clanranald and three of his uncles, the laird of Knoydart, Mac Ian of Ardnamurchan, a brother of Donald Gorm Mor, and a number of other prominent men. All the leading men taken were placed in confinement. The common soldiers were conveyed to Ardnamurchan, and set at liberty. Queen Elizabeth was so well pleased with the Lord of Duart for capturing the Macdonalds that she sent him a present of 1,000 crowns, and also promised him a pension.

Young Mac Ian of Ardnamurchan was murdered at Kintra, about the year 1596, by his uncle, Angus Mor Macdonald. The murderer was the next heir and expected to obtain the estate for himself. He was a man of great size and strength, and also of great ferocity. He lived at Ath-na-h-Eilde, near Strontian. Allan Cameron of Lochiel, to whose daughter young Mac Ian was engaged to be married, invaded Ardnamurchan to punish the assassin. Angus Mor, aware of his danger, placed himself under the protection of Lachlan of Duart. A conflict took place between the invaders and the Clan Ian at Leachd-nan-Saighead, or the ledge of the arrows, in Morvern. Angus Mor raised his helmet to cool his brow. A Cameron who had been watching for a chance, immediately sent an arrow into his skull. When the Clan Ian saw that their leader was slain they became discouraged and fled. Immediately afterwards Lachlan Mor arrived in Morvern to support and protect them. The victorious Camerons were now under the necessity of desisting from pursuing the Mac Ians, and of returning to Lochaber. The chieftain of the Mac Ians was buried in the churchyard of Keill in Morvern. According to tradition, the archer who slew Angus Mor was known as Iain Dubh Beag Innse-righ.

Hector Maclean of Coll died about the end of the year 1593. Lachlan, his son and successor, was at that time only about eighteen years of age. Shortly after Hector's death, Lachlan of Duart seized the castle of Breacachadh and took possession of all the Coll estates. He appointed Rory Beg Maclean as his deputy to collect the rents in Coll. When Lachlan of Coll reached his majority he complained to the Privy Council against the oppressive conduct of Lachlan Mor and petitioned for redress. The Council considered his complaint and petition on November 11th, 1596. Lachlan Mor and himself were both present. The Council ordered Lachlan Mor to deliver up the castle of Breacachadh to Sir William Stewart of Houston, the King's lieutenant of the Isles and Highlands, to surrender the Coll estates to their lawful owner, and to allow the owner and his tenants to possess and use these estates without molestation from him. The Council also decreed that in case Lachlan Mor should fail to carry out their orders he should pay as a penalty the sum of 10,000 marks.

Lachlan of Coll obtained possession of his estates, and was allowed to hold them in peace. We presume that Lachlan Mor's object in seizing the estates of Coll was not to keep them for himself, but to compel Lachlan of Coll to hold them of him, and thus acknowledge him as his feudal superior.

In May, 1596, King James issued a proclamation declaring his intention of leading an expedition in person against the Islanders. Lachlan Mor and Donald Gorm Mor immediately repaired to Edinburgh, gave in their submission to the King, settled with the Exchequer, and agreed to augment their rents. They were at once received into favour and had their estates restored to them. The Earl of Argyll and Kenneth Mackenzie of Kintail became securities for Lachlan Mor's obedience, in the sum of 30,000 marks. Rory Macleod of Harris and Donald Mac Angus of Glengarry obtained remissions shortly afterwards. The Macleods of Lewis also tendered their submission. Angus Macdonald of Islay still refused to yield to the King. The King showed his displeasure with him by granting Lachlan Mor a lease of the Rhinns of Islay. At last, in the month of October, Angus sent in his submission by James, his son and heir. In January, 1597, he went to Edinburgh to see the King. He was asked to find security for the arrears of his crown rents, to remove all his followers from Kintyre, and the Rhinns of Islay, and to deliver the castle of Dunnyveg to the Government. It was agreed that if he should carry out these conditions, all the lands which he had held in Islay should be restored to him, except the Rhinns. He returned to Islay, but took no steps to comply with the obligations imposed upon him.

Towards the end of the year 1597 Lachlan Mor and Angus of Islay came to some sort of settlement and agreed to proceed together to Ireland to fight in behalf of Queen Elizabeth against the Earl of Tyrone. They were to take with them between 2,000 and 3,000 men. They did not, however, carry out their purpose. It is evident, then, that Elizabeth did not give them the encouragement expected by them. The conditions on which Lachlan Mor and Angus of Islay became reconciled, we do not know. It may be taken for granted, however, that one of the terms was that Lachlan should be left in undisturbed possession of the Rhinns.

In October, 1596, Angus of Islay made over his estates to his son James, reserving for himself only a life interest. But Angus had no legal claim to the estates at that time; they belonged to the King; consequently the deed given to James was absolutely worthless. In 1597 James received the honour of knighthood from the King. Shortly afterwards he resolved to deprive his father of all influence and to take the management of the estates entirely into his own hands. An opportunity for carrying out his purpose with respect to his father soon presented itself. Gorrie Macalister, the young laird of Loup, slew his tutor, and also intended to slay his two sons. The young men fled to Askamull, the residence of Angus of Islay, and enjoyed the protection of the latter. In January, 1598, James Mac Angus, accompanied by the laird of Loup, his own brother Angus Og, and two or three armed followers, went to Askamull in the dead of night to arrest the Macalisters. When the men whose lives he sought refused to come out of the house to be executed, he placed a number of trees around it and set fire to it. He evidently expected that his father and mother would be burnt to death. They managed, however, to get out of the burning building in time to save their lives. He immediately arrested his father, and sent him to Smerby in Kintyre, where he kept him in irons for several months. He had now full charge of the estates. He acted, however, in such a violent manner that it became necessary in the month of June to issue a proclamation for a royal expedition to Kintyre.

In the spring of 1598, Sir James Macdonald determined to deprive Lachlan Mor of the Rhinns of Islay, and thus to make himself master of all the lands which had belonged to his father. As Lachlan Mor had received the Rhinns from the King he refused to part with them. Both parties prepared for war. The end of their disagreement was that Lachlan Mor was slain at Gruinnart in Islay on the 5th of August, 1598.

Tytler in his history of Scotland gives the following account of Lachlan Mor's death:—"Lachlan Maclean of Duart was treacherously slain in Islay by his nephew, Sir James Macdonald, who persuaded him to visit the island; alleging, as a pretext, his desire to make an amicable settlement of their differences. So little did the brave Lord of Duart suspect any foul play, that he came to the meeting without armour, in a silk dress, and with only a rapier at his side. Along with him were his second son, and the best of his kin, in their holiday garb, and with little other arms than their hunting-knives and boar spears; but, although set upon by an ambush of nearly 700 men, they made a desperate defence. Maclean, a man of herculean strength, slew three of the Macdonalds at the first onset. When he saw that there was no hope, he commanded his son, who fought beside him, to fly, and live to avenge him; but the chief himself, and a little knot of his clansmen, stood shoulder to shoulder, and were not cut down till after fifty of their assailants had fallen. The death of this great chief was little resented by the King, for James had long been jealous of his dealings with Elizabeth."— Tytler founds his statements on the contents of a letter written to Sir Robert Cecil, on the 10th of August, 1598, by Nicholson, the English envoy at the Scottish court. They are thus in all probability substantially correct.

According to the Ardgour MS., Lachlan Mor

and Sir James Macdonald agreed to meet at Gruinnart on the 5th of August, 1598, to adjust in a friendly manner all the matters in dispute between them. Accordingly Lachlan Mor went to Islay on the day appointed, with Hector Og his eldest son, and his whole clan. He landed on Nave Island, where he left Hector Og and the most of his followers. He took sixty men with him to Gruinnart. He sent his proposals to Sir James, who sent a few gentlemen of his clan back with answers. Sir James learned from his scouts that Lachlan Mor had only a few men with him, and that the men whom he had left on Nave Island could not, owing to the ebb of the tide, leave the place in which they were. Sir James immediately attacked his uncle with the Islay men, the Kintyre men not having yet arrived. Lachlan Mor made a desperate resistance, and forced the Macdonalds to retire several times. At last the Kintyre men came up. Sir James now attacked the Macleans with his whole force and overpowered them. Lachlan Mor was shot in the belly through his target. His followers were all cut down, except a few who succeeded in making their escape by flight.—The Ardgour MS. undoubtedly gives the story current in Mull in 1762. Lachlan Mor's "whole clan," or followers, would number about 600 men.

According to Seannachie's history of the Macleans, Lachlan Mor sailed to Islay at the head of 600 men. He left 340 men on Nave Island and took 250 with him to Gruinnart. He was accompanied by Lachlan Og, his second son. Sir James Macdonald had 1500 men with him, nearly all of whom were hidden behind the hills. When Lachlan Mor saw that he was in danger he took up a strong position on a hill, from which he drove away some Macdonalds who had occupied it. Sir James attacked him with 800 men, but was driven back. Shortly after the fight had begun Lachlan Og was wounded. His father immediately sent him off in charge of ten or twelve men to Nave Island. In his second attack upon his uncle, Sir James had 900 men under him. Lachlan Mor moved down the hill to meet his nephew. When he was almost within striking distance of him he called out to him, A Sheumais, a Sheumais a mhic mo pheathar, fàg mo rathad, James, James, son of my sister, get out of my way. These words had scarcely been uttered when a shot from one of Sir James's followers brought the hero of Glenlivet to the ground. The Macleans, enraged by the fall of their chief, fought on with uncontrollable fury. Sir James was at last under the necessity of calling up his reserve. The Macleans were now overpowered and all slain except seven or eight.— This account of the fight at Gruinnart cannot be depended upon. It is not in accordance with the traditions of the Macleans. Neither is it in accordance with any of the old histories which refer to Lachlan Mor's death. It is probably correct in stating that Lachlan left Mull with 600 men. It is certain, however, that James

Macdonald had not 1500 men with him. Nicholson's letter, which fixes the number of the Macdonalds at 700, evidently contains the truth. It is absurd to suppose that an experienced warrior like Lachlan Mor would leave an advantageous position to attack 900 men with 250 men. It is equally absurd to think that Sir James Macdonald would have found it necessary to call up his reserve to crush a handful of leaderless Macleans.

According to "The History of the Feuds and Conflicts of the Clans"—a work written in the time of James VI.—Sir Lachlan Maclean claimed the whole of Islay. He assembled all his forces, and invaded that island to take possession of it. Sir James Macdonald likewise assembled his forces and went to Islay to prevent his uncle from carrying out his intentions. Certain persons who were interested in both of them tried to effect a reconciliation between them. Sir James agreed to let his uncle have the half of the island during his lifetime, providing he would consent to hold the land of him as his feudal superior. Moreover, he offered to submit the controversy to the arbitration of the King. Sir Lachlan refused to come to any settlement with his nephew unless the latter "would resign to him the title and possession of the whole island." The consequence was that both prepared for battle. Sir James Macdonald was far inferior, in the number of men, to his uncle, but some of those who were with him had been trained in the wars in Ireland and were better

disciplined than the Macleans. At the beginning
of the battle Sir James caused his vanguard to
pretend to retreat, in order to get possession of the
top of a hill which was near them, and also to get
the sun to their back. In the end he defeated the
Macleans. Sir Lachlan and eighty of his leading
men, together with 200 common soldiers, were
slain. Lachlan Og and those who survived with
him were chased to their boats. Sir James was
dangerously wounded by an arrow, and was left
during the greater part of the night on the field
along with the slain. Thirty of the Macdonalds
were killed and sixty wounded.

It is quite clear that the foregoing account of
the origin of the fight at Gruinnart and the fight
itself is entirely erroneous. Lachlan Mor obtained
a right to the Rhinns of Islay in 1596. It is
likely, then, that he had possession of that district
before August, 1598. It is unreasonable to suppose that he claimed the whole of Islay. On
what ground could he claim that part of it which
was still in the hands of the King? As James
Macdonald had no legal claim either to the whole
or a part of Islay, it was impossible for him to
resign to Lachlan Mor " the title and possession
of the whole island." How could he give to another that which did not belong to himself? The
assertion that Sir James was willing to leave the
matters in dispute to the King's decision is entirely
groundless; it cannot be true. What was the King
to decide? Was it whether Sir James had a right

to the whole of Islay or not? The decree of forfeiture pronounced against Angus Macdonald in June, 1594, had already settled that point. Was the King to decide whether Lachlan Mor should hold the Rhinns of Islay of James Macdonald as his feudal superior or not? Surely the fact that the King, who was the actual owner of those lands, had leased them to Lachlan Mor was as clear and full a decision with regard to this matter as could be given. How could Lachlan Mor be the vassal of a man who had no lands for himself? It is likely that so far as courage and strength were concerned the Macleans were equal, man for man, to the Macdonalds; it is also likely that the warriors of Glenlivet were just as well disciplined as the men who had been fighting in Ireland, and it is certain that Lachlan Mor was an abler strategist than James Macdonald. It is extremely difficult, then, to believe that the victorious Macdonalds were far inferior in numbers to the defeated Macleans. The assertion that James Macdonald was severely wounded is unquestionably incorrect. The truth is that "The History of the Feuds and Conflicts of the Clans" mixes together two different events. It deals with the fight at Gruinnart and the battle of Benvigory as if they were one and the same conflict. It makes no reference at all to the latter; it is a well-known fact, however, that there was such a battle.

Our own conclusion respecting the things which took place at Gruinnart, is that Lachlan Mor and

James Macdonald met there to settle their disputes in a friendly manner, that when Sir James found out that the men on Nave Island could not get off, he resolved to attack Lachlan Mor at once, that Lachlan Og was sent away to Nave Island either for safety or for assistance, and that Sir James Macdonald fell upon the Macleans with a strong force and slaughtered them. There are strong reasons for this view. In the first place, it is impossible to accept the statements of Seannachie's history or of "The History of the Feuds and Conflicts of the Clans" as facts. In the second place, Nicholson's letter and the Ardgour MS. support our view. In the third place, the Register of the Privy Council informs us that one of the crimes for which Sir James Macdonald was committed to prison in 1604 was "the treasonable murder of Sir Lachlan Maclean of Duart, his uncle, committed under trust and credit." In the fourth place, one of the crimes for which Sir James received a remission in 1620 was "the slaughter of Maclean."

Lachlan Mor was a man of uncommon strength and activity, and an excellent swordsman. He possessed a strong and vigorous intellect, and thoroughly understood the art of governing those over whom he ruled. His military genius was of a high order. As a commander he had no equal in the Highlands in his day. He was of an imperious disposition and determined, at all hazards, to have his own way. His weak point was his readiness to believe his enemies. He acted foolishly when he went to Mullintrea, and he acted still more foolishly when he went to Gruinnart with only sixty men. He was forty-one years of age at the time of his death. He was buried at Kilchoman in Islay. His grave is on the outside of the church, and near the south wall. He was slain on August 5th, 1598.

TRADITIONS ABOUT LACHLAN MOR.

Seannachie relates the following story concerning Lachlan Mor's courtship and marriage :—In the beginning of December, 1577, Lachlan Mor paid a visit to the Scottish court. King James was exceedingly anxious that he should marry Dorothea Stewart, eldest daughter of John, fifth Earl of Atholl. All the parties concerned fell in with the King's plan. The consequence was that a contract of marriage between Lachlan and Dorothea Stewart was drawn up and signed. The marriage was to take place in the course of a few weeks. While Lachlan was on his way back to make ready for the coming event he called to see the Earl of Cunningham and staid a few days. He fell in love with Margaret, one of the Earl's daughters, proposed to her, and was accepted. When King James heard of his marriage he was much displeased with him for his fickleness and dishonourable conduct.

There can be no truth in this story. It is probable that when Lachlan Mor was a boy he spent a good part of his time with his maternal uncle, the Earl of Argyll. But Argyll's wife was Margaret Cunningham's aunt. It may be taken for granted, then, that Lachlan was acquainted with the fascinating Margaret long before December, 1577. James VI. was only eleven years old in 1577 and could scarcely at that early age have been an accomplished match-maker. John Stewart, fifth Earl of Atholl, was not born before the year 1550. Consequently, it is exceedingly improbable that he had a daughter who was old enough in 1577 to be married to Lachlan Mor or any one else, except a heathen Chinee.

According to a tradition recorded in the Ardgour MS., the Macdonalds held a council of war on the morning of the day on which they intended to attack the Macleans at Lecklee. They noticed that Maclean of Boreray, a vassal of Macdonald of Sleat, looked extremely sad. "It cannot be a pleasant business for you," said Donald Gorm Mor to him, "to go with us to-day to slay your chief and his followers; you may therefore remain in the rear." "I am much obliged to you for your offer," replied Boreray, "but I cannot accept it; it is not unwillingness to fight against my own clan that makes me so sad; it is something else." "What is the cause of your trouble, then?" asked Macdonald. After a good deal of urging, Boreray told him that about the middle of the night, just as he had fallen asleep, he heard a man uttering in a melancholy voice the following words:—

> A Lic-lì sin, O Lic-lì,
> 'S ann ort-s' a bheirear an dìth.
> Clann-Ghilleain bheir iad buaidh
> Air an t-sluagh a thig air tìr.
> 'Ghearna dhubh, 's i Ghearna dhubh!
> 'S ann uimp' a dhoirtear an fhuil,
> Marbhar an Ridire Ruadh
> Mu'n déid lann an truaill an diugh.

These lines may be rendered into English as follows:—

> O Lecklee, thou dread Lecklee,
> Great the carnage thou shalt see.
> The Macleans shall win the day;
> The invaders slain shall be.
> Gerna Dubh, thou hill of woe,
> Tides of blood shall round thee flow,
> Ere the gleaming swords shall rest
> The Red Knight shall be laid low.

Donald Gorm Mor believed that Boreray had actually heard the prophetic words which he rehearsed, and became alarmed for his own safety and that of the men who were with him. The consequence was that the invaders hastened back to their boats as fast as they could.

Donald Gorm Mor, who is undoubtedly the person meant by the Red Knight, was neither a baronet nor a knight. Donald Gorm Og, who succeeded him, was created a baronet in 1625. It is certain, then, that the poetic version of Boreray's dream was not composed prior to that date. It is possible that Boreray was at Lecklee, and that he was something of a poet. It is utterly improbable, however, that he would have tried to fool a sensible man like Donald Gorm Mor by telling him that he had been taught two verses of poetry in a dream. The Macdonalds left Lecklee simply because they knew that it would be certain death for them to attack the Macleans in the strong position occupied by them. At all events, it was not Boreray's dream that caused them to go away.

According to the Ardgour MS. the Macdonalds prepared to invade Mull a second time. They appointed the small island of Bakka, am Bac, at the south end of Kerrera, as their place of rendezvous, their object being to attack Lachlan Mor in Duart Castle. Lachlan, aware of their intentions, collected a large force of Macleans, Macneils, Macquarries, and Mackinnons. He had also Maclean of Boreray with him. He left Duart at the head of his followers and sailed towards Bakka. The Macdonalds were drawn up on the shore prepared to receive their opponents. The Macleans sent several volleys of arrows among them and compelled them to retreat from the shore. Lachlan Mor immediately landed his forces, and advanced to the attack. He defeated the Macdonalds and forced them to seek safety in their galleys, which lay on the other side of the island. Macneil of Barra and Maclean of Boreray had command of the archers, and displayed signal valour in the battle. After their defeat at Bakka the Macdonalds made no further attempt to invade Mull and beard the lion in his den.

We are inclined to think that there was no such contest as the battle of Bakka, and that the affair really referred to is the capture of the Macdonalds on Calve Island in July, 1595. It is not at all likely that Maclean of Boreray fought against Macdonald of Sleat. The probability is that in the war between the Macdonalds and the Macleans he was allowed to remain neutral.

In 1873, J. F. Campbell of Islay published the following story, as a short sample of popular local history:—There was a quarrel between Maclean of Duart and his brother. The latter was under the necessity of seeking refuge in Ireland, where he remained three years. Duart sent word to his brother, asking him to return and promising to forgive his past offences. The exile returned, but was immediately seized and condemned to death. Duart ordered Neil Mor Maclean to cut off the doomed man's head. He was told that unless he would do so his own head would be cut off. Through fear Neil Mor beheaded Maclean's brother. The sword became fast in the block. In order to draw it back Neil put his foot against the head. Maclean became enraged and said to him, Although I ordered the blow I will not suffer the insult. He commanded that Neil should be put to death. Neil fled and escaped. He succeeded in keeping out of the hands of Maclean and his followers for three years. Maclean sent for a powerful man named Allan Macdonald and persuaded him to go in search of Neil to arrest or slay him. Allan took fifteen men with him and went to Drimnacross, where Neil resided. When they entered Neil's house they asked his wife if her husband was at home. She went to the other end of the house, where she had Neil concealed, and took out a large bar of iron. She broke a piece of the bar off with her hands and gave it to the ploughman, saying, When your master went to the forge he told me to send you after him with a piece of iron; take this with you and tell him that there are men in the house who want to see him. Don't tell him that, said Allan Macdonald; we have no business of any importance with him. Allan and his men immediately left the house. When they were out of hearing, Allan said to those with him, We should be thankful to the Almighty that Neil's wife did not know the business we were on; had she known it, she would have killed us all with that iron bar. Some time afterwards Maclean sent word to Neil Mor that he wanted him to come to see him so that they would make peace. Neil went to see Maclean. They settled their disputes and parted on good terms. On returning Neil said to his wife, Thank God I can sleep in my own bed to-night, a thing that I have not done for three years. His wife advised him to sleep in his hiding-place that night also, but he did not heed her. Through the night a body of men, sent by Maclean, came to the house. They broke in the door; but Neil escaped and fled towards Bealach Ruadh. At Clachan Dubh he was met by a band of Maclean's men. A fight took place and Neil was left half dead on the ground. When his assailants were some distance on the way home, one of them, Dugald Roy Mac Alpin, said, I should not wonder if Neil Mor would come alive yet. The whole band immediately returned. They found Neil on his knees and the palms of his hands. They attacked him again and tore him apart into such small bits that it was in a bed-rug he was taken home.

Ridiculous as the foregoing story is, we have reason to think that there are some persons who regard it as genuine history. They heard it from their fathers, and they believe that their fathers had it word for word as it existed originally. They make no allowance for the changes which a story undergoes in being handed down from one generation to another.

The Maclean referred to is Lachlan Mor. He had no brother, but he had a step-father, Hector Mac Allan, and a step-father who was plotting against his life and deserved to be put to death. Hector Mac Allan was not in Ireland at all, but Lachlan Mor was in the Lowlands about three years. Thus Hector Mac Allan and himself were parted during the period stated. Hector Mac Allan was beheaded in Coll in 1578; but Lachlan Mor was not present at the execution; neither was

Neil Mor. Lachlan Mor took possession of Coll in 1593, and compelled his opponent, Neil Mor, to flee for his life. He gave up Coll to its owner in November, 1596. Thus Neil Mor was in danger from Lachlan for three years. He was slain evidently about the end of 1596 or the beginning of 1597. The part of the story which states that Lachlan Mor had patched up a false peace with Neil Mor is a pure fiction. It can easily be shown that Lachlan committed some high-handed and wrong acts; it cannot be shown, however, that treachery had a resting-place in his nature; it had not.

We are told in "The Feuds and Conflicts of the Clans" that Lachlan Mor consulted a witch before leaving for Gruinnart. She gave him two advices. The first was, not to land on Islay on a Thursday; and the second, not to drink of the water of a certain spring near Gruinnart. He was driven to Islay by a tempest on Thursday, and drank of the water of the forbidden spring before he knew that he was in the wrong place. According to Dr. Norman Macleod's Cuairtear nan Gleann, the Macleans, before starting on an expedition, were in the habit of walking sunwise three times around a small island in Loch Speilbh. Lachlan Mor ridiculed this practice and walked three times around the island in the opposite direction. The superstitious men among his followers were greatly discouraged by this act.

It may be regarded as pretty certain that such

an intelligent man and skilful strategist as Lachlan
Mor never consulted a witch with regard to the
steps to be taken for winning a battle. Then, it
is probably equally certain that he did not go to
the trouble of walking around the island in any
direction whatever. We may be sure that he
would do nothing to dampen the ardour of his
followers.

Tradition tells us that the man who slew Lachlan Mor was known as Dubhsìth and that he was a native of Jura. He was short in stature, but a good marksman. William Livingstone, the distinguished Islay poet, describes him as a dwarf hatched by the devil in the hollow in Jura,—
"troich a ghuir an diabhal 'san lag an Diura."
Dubhsìth offered his services to Lachlan Mor on the morning of the fight at Gruinnart. Lachlan gruffly told him that he would not disgrace his followers by having such a contemptible-looking creature as he was among them. Dubhsìth went immediately to James Macdonald and asked permission to fight under him. James spoke kindly to him, and told him that he should be very glad to have him with him. According to one account Dubhsìth had a gun and was on the look-out all day for an opportunity to kill Lachlan Mor. As Lachlan was climbing a hill he bent, and thus caused an opening in the joints of his defensive armour. Dubhsìth took immediate aim and fired at him. According to another account, it was a bow and arrow that Dubhsìth had. As Lachlan

Mor raised his arm he exposed a part of his side. Dubhsìth instantly launched an arrow into his side just below the arm.

There is not the slightest ground for believing that Dubhsìth had proffered his services to Lachlan Mor on the morning of the fight. He was undoubtedly with James Macdonald when the Macleans arrived at Gruinnart. William Livingstone agrees with the Ardgour MS. in affirming that Lachlan Mor was shot in the belly.

CHAPTER VII.

Hector Og and Hector Mor.

XIV. EACHANN OG.

Hector Og was brought up and educated with Colin Cam Mackenzie of Kintail. He received a royal charter, in March, 1588, of the island of Iona and certain lands in Mull, Tiree, and Islay; all of which had formerly belonged to the abbot of Iona. He was about twenty years of age when he became Lord of Duart. He felt it to be his first duty to punish the Macdonalds of Islay for the murder of his father. He was assisted in carrying out his purpose by Rory Mor Macleod of Harris, and especially by Allan Cameron of Lochiel. Maclean of Lochbuie supported Sir James Macdonald. Hector Og and his assistants invaded Islay with a large force. They encountered the Macdonalds and their associates at Benvigory, and inflicted a severe defeat upon them. Sir James was dangerously wounded by an arrow, and

Lochbuie taken prisoner by Allan of Lochiel. Immediately after their victory the confederates ravaged the greater part of Islay with fire and sword. The wars between the Macleans of Duart and the Macdonalds of Islay were now over. Benvigory was their last battle. In 1602 Hector Og was summoned to appear before the Privy Council to render obedience to the King, to give security to pay the King's mails and duties, and to answer "touching the slaughters, herships, and depredations committed by him upon the King's own tenants in the Isles of Oronsay and Colonsay." As he refused to appear he was declared a rebel and put to the horn. The people of Oronsay and Colonsay were active supporters of Sir James Macdonald. That, no doubt, was Hector Og's reason for attacking them.

In the autumn of 1602, Kenneth, first Lord Mackenzie of Kintail, obtained a commission of fire and sword against the Macdonalds of Glengarry. As the latter were assisted by the Macdonalds of Moydart and Ardnamurchan, he paid a visit to Mull for the purpose of procuring the help of Hector Og, who had married his sister. Hector Og, at his request, invaded Ardnamurchan and ravaged that district. These acts brought Hector into trouble with the Earl of Argyll, who was the legal owner of Ardnamurchan. As, however, Lord Kintail, who had a right to punish both the Macdonalds of Glengarry and their supporters, offered to hold himself responsible for Hector Og's doings, Argyll did not press his complaint against the latter.

On the 20th of September, 1603, Argyll obtained letters from the King charging Angus Macdonald of Islay and Hector Og of Duart to give up the castles of Dunnyveg and Duart to him. In case they should refuse to comply with this request, they were to be held as traitors and to be deprived of their estates. The authority thus given to Argyll proved of no use to him. But the fact that he went to the trouble of procuring it shows the hostile feelings which he entertained towards both the Macdonalds and the Macleans.

On September 4th, 1604, James Cunningham, Earl of Glencairn, came under obligation to David Murray, Lord Scone, Comptroller of Scotland, to deliver Duart Castle to the King whenever required to do so, and to see the following payments made to the Comptroller, as part of the crown rents due by Hector Og: at Martinmas, 1604, 2,500 marks; in August, 1605, 5,000 marks; and at Martinmas, 1605, £5,000. Hector Og was now relaxed from the horn.

In 1603, Angus Macdonald of Islay received information that his son and heir was meditating another plot against him. He arrested Sir James at once, and delivered him to Campbell of Auchinbreck, who handed him over to the Earl of Argyll. In 1604 the Privy Council confined him as a prisoner in the royal castle of Blackness. He tried twice to escape, but did not succeed. In 1607

Argyll obtained from King James a charter of all those lands in Kintyre and Jura, which had been forfeited by Angus Macdonald of Islay. One of the conditions on which the lands were given him was that he would not let any of them to persons of the name of Macdonald or Maclean without the King's consent. These lands are still in possession of the Campbells.

In 1608, Andrew Stewart, Lord Ochiltree, was appointed by the King and Privy Council lieutenant over the Isles. Andrew Knox, Bishop of the Isles, Sir James Hay of Kingask, and others were appointed a council to assist him. He made an expedition to the Western Isles in the month of August. He had a small fleet and army under his command. The first place he visited was Islay. Angus Macdonald handed over to him the castle of Dunnyveg and the fort of Lochgorm. He placed a garrison of twenty-four men in the former, and razed the latter to the ground. He left Islay on the 14th of August and, after a very stormy passage, landed at Duart on the 15th. Hector Og surrendered Duart Castle to him without hesitation. He took possession of it on the 17th, but gave it back to its owner in the course of a few days. From Duart he went to Aros, where he held a court. Among the Islesmen who attended were the following :—Angus Macdonald of Islay ; Donald Gorm Mor Macdonald of Sleat ; Donald Mac Allan, captain of the Clanranald ; Rory Mor Macleod of Dunvegan ; Hector Og of Duart ;

Lachlan Maclean of Ardnacross, Hector Og's brother; Allan, son of Charles Maclean, tutor of Ardgour; and Neil Mac Ilduy and Neil Mac Rory, two of Hector Og's principal vassals, both undoubtedly Macleans. Angus Macdonald of Islay readily agreed to all the conditions imposed on him, and was allowed to return home. As the other landlords were not quite so pliable, Lord Ochiltree, by the advice of the tricky Bishop Knox, resolved to kidnap them. He invited them to go with him on board the King's ship, called the Moon, to hear a sermon from the Bishop. All of them accepted the invitation except Rory Mor of Dunvegan. When the sermon was over, Lord Ochiltree prevailed upon the Islesmen to dine with him. As soon as the dinner was finished he told them that they would have to accompany him to Edinburgh, and immediately weighed anchor and sailed off with them. He arrived in Edinburgh about the beginning of October. Some of the captives were confined in Dumbarton, some in Blackness, and some in Stirling. King James was greatly delighted with the success of the expedition. He could now compel the Macleans and Macdonalds to obey his laws and pay him the rents which he demanded of them. Besides, he had a bishop after his own heart. Hector Og, Lachlan, his brother, Allan, son of the tutor of Ardgour, Neil Mac Ilduy, and Neil Mac Rory seem to have been all imprisoned in Dumbarton. On February 24th, 1609, Hector Og appeared in Edinburgh before the commissioners of the Isles and offered to be answerable for all the inhabitants of Tiree and Morvern, the inhabitants of his part of Mull, and the inhabitants of the lands which belonged to him in Islay, Coll, Jura, Kintyre, Scalpa, and Lochaber. He offered at the same time to give as pledges of his obedience such of his sons or brothers as the commissioners should name. As these offers were rejected, Hector was sent back to Dumbarton Castle. His brother, Lachlan Og, was sent back along with him. Allan Maclean, Neil Mac Ilduy, and Neil Mac Rory were confined in the Tolbooth in Edinburgh. On May 12th, 1609, Angus Macdonald of Islay was imprisoned in the castle of Blackness.

In the summer of 1609 Bishop Knox was sent by King James as commissioner to the Western Islands to make such arrangements with the chiefs and chieftains as would tend to support the cause of law and order, and advance the civilization and welfare of the people. The Bishop, accompanied by Angus of Islay and Hector Og of Duart, arrived in Iona about the middle of July. At the meeting held by him the following prominent persons were present:—Angus of Islay; Hector Og of Duart; Donald Gorm Mor of Sleat; Rory Mor Macleod of Dunvegan; Donald Mac Allan of Moydart; Lachlan Maclean of Coll; Lachlan Mackinnon of Strathordill; Hector Maclean of Lochbuie; Lachlan Og Maclean; Allan Maclean, brother of Hector Og and Lachlan Og; Gillespick Macquarrie of Ulva; and Donald Macphie from

Colonsay. All these men professed their adherence to the Episcopalian Church and acknowledged King James as "supreme judge under the eternal God in all causes, and above all persons, both spiritual and temporal." They also bound themselves in the most solemn manner to act in accordance with the following regulations or statutes :—1. That the ministers planted or to be planted in the parishes of the Isles should be reverently obeyed, that their stipends should be dutifully paid, that ruinous churches should be repaired with reasonable diligence, that the Sabbaths should be solemnly kept, and that the marriages contracted for certain years should be considered illegal and those entering into such marriages punished as fornicators. 2. That inns should be established at convenient places for the convenience of travellers and the benefit of the people, who were put to inconvenience and trouble in entertaining travellers. 3. That no idle persons or masterless vagabonds should be allowed to reside within the Isles. 4. That all persons, who were not natives of the Isles, and who should be found sorning, or living upon the inhabitants, should be punished as thieves and oppressors. 5. That while men of wealth might import wines and other liquors for their own use, and while any person could brew as much whiskey as he required in his own family, no merchant should be allowed to keep wines or any other liquors for sale. Liquor found with a merchant could be seized and destroyed; while a person buying liquor from a merchant could be fined forty pounds for the first offence, one hundred pounds for the second, and be deprived of all he possessed for the third. 6. That every gentleman or yeoman within the Isles, worth in goods sixty cows, should send his eldest son to school in the Lowlands and keep him there until he should learn to speak, read, and write English. If he had only female children, he was to send his eldest daughter. 7. That no firearms should be used. 8. That wandering bards should be punished.

These regulations were upon the whole well observed and had a beneficial effect. Bishop Knox took Angus of Islay and Hector Og back with him to Edinburgh. They were both released shortly afterwards. James, Earl of Glencairn, and Kenneth Mackenzie of Kintail became securities for Hector Og. They were bound under a penalty of £30,000 for his appearance before the Council whenever required.

On the 28th of June, 1610, Hector Og of Duart, Angus Macdonald of Islay, Donald Gorm Mor of Sleat, Rory Mor Macleod of Dunvegan, Donald Mac Allan of Moydart, Lachlan Mackinnon of Strathordill, and Allan Cameron of Lochiel appeared before the Privy Council in Edinburgh. They bound themselves by a solemn promise to assist the King's lieutenant, justices, and commissioners in securing obedience to the laws of the land; to live at peace with one another; and to bring such disputes as might spring up among them before the courts of law and justice. This agreement, if carried out, would put an end to their ferocious feuds. About a month afterwards the Bishop of the Isles was appointed for life steward and justice of all the West and North Isles of Scotland, except the Orkney and Shetland Islands. He was at the same time appointed constable of the castle of Dunnyveg in Islay. In 1613 we find Hector Og of Duart, Donald Gorm Mor of Sleat, Rory Mor of Dunvegan, and Donald Mac Allan of Moydart referred to as persons who had settled with the Exchequer. In the same year, Sir James Campbell of Lawers tried to obtain from King James a charter of the Maclean lands in Morvern. The King was willing to grant these lands to him. He was to receive them, however, on condition that in case the Macleans should rise up in rebellion, the Earl of Argyll and himself were to reduce them to subjection at their own charge, or else give the lands back to the King. For some reason or other Sir James did not receive the lands which he was so anxious to obtain. Probably the Earl of Argyll was not disposed to give him the assistance which he would in all likelihood require to gain possession of them.

In December, 1613, Allan Cameron of Lochiel was proclaimed a rebel. The Government gave a commission of fire and sword against him to the Marquis of Huntly and his eldest son, the Earl of Enzie, both of whom were acting very unjustly towards the Camerons. The Gordons tried to capture Lochiel, but did not succeed. In the spring of 1614, the Privy Council summoned Hector Og of Duart, Sir Rory Mor Macleod of Dunvegan, Mackinnon, Maclean of Coll, and Maclean of Lochbuie "for the reset of Allan Cameron of Lochiel and for remaining from the army of the Earl of Enzie." On the 8th of July we find the summons continued in force until the 10th of next July. As the word "reset" means harbouring an outlaw, it is evident that Lochiel had to flee from Lochaber. The Government called upon the Macleans, Macleods, and Mackinnons to support the Gordons against the Camerons. Of course they did not comply with this cruel order; and it is very much to their credit that they did not.

Angus Macdonald of Islay died about the year 1612. Shortly after his death, Sir Ranald Macdonald, afterwards Earl of Antrim, obtained a lease of the lands of Islay and held them about two years. In the spring of 1614, Ranald Og, an illegitimate son of Angus of Islay, seized the castle of Dunnyveg, which was in charge of the Bishop of the Isles. Angus Og, a legitimate son of Angus, besieged the castle, captured it, and compelled his brother Ranald Og to flee for safety. He placed Coll Macdonald, Colla Ciotach, in charge of it, and professed his readiness to restore it to the Bishop. Through the influence of the Earl of Argyll, Angus Og was led to keep possession of the castle, and thus to put himself and his clan in the position of being in rebellion against the Government. Sir John Campbell, fourth of Calder, offered a very high feu-duty, or perpetual rent, for Islay, and agreed to accept a commission against Angus Og and his followers. On the 21st of November the King granted him a charter of the whole island. He landed in Islay with a strong force on the 6th of January, 1615, and captured Dunnyveg on the 3rd of February. The Campbells had now possession of all the lands which had at one time belonged to Angus Macdonald of Islay.

In May, 1615, Sir James Macdonald escaped from prison. He went directly to Lochaber, and thence through Moròr and Knoydart to the Isle of Skye. He sailed from Eigg at the head of about 350 men, and landed in Colonsay about the 18th of June. He went from Colonsay to Islay, and made himself master of the castle of Dunnyveg about the 24th of the month. The Earl of Argyll was sent against him by the Government with a strong force in September. As he was unable to resist Argyll, he fled to Ireland, whence he made his escape to Spain. In 1626, King James recalled him from Spain, pardoned him for all his past offences, and gave him a pension of 1000 marks sterling a year. He died shortly afterwards.

The Ardgour MS. informs us that a few hours after the battle of Glenlivet in 1594, Lachlan Mor of Duart offered the Earl of Argyll, if he would give him 500 men, to attack the Earl of Huntly with his own followers and these men, and to bring that nobleman, dead or alive, to him. The offer was rejected, but Huntly heard that it had been made, and was greatly annoyed. He had no opportunity to take vengeance upon the author of it. Hector Og, however, was not allowed to escape. At a convention of estates which was to be held at Stirling all the Highland landlords were to appear. Hector Og arrived on the morning of the day appointed for the meeting. He met Huntly on the street, and told him that he should like to change his clothes before going to the convention if he would have time. The latter gave him to understand that there was no special reason for hastening to the convention. As soon as Huntly had parted with Hector Og he went to the convention and caused Hector's name to be immediately called in connection with the estate of Garbhdhabhach in Lochaber. As Hector was not present to answer his name he was instantly deprived of that estate. Shortly afterwards the King granted it to Huntly's son George, Lord Gordon.

There may be some truth in the foregoing story. It is probable, however, that the real cause of the animosity of the Gordons against Hector Og was the sympathy of the Macleans with the Camerons in 1614. We know that the Macleans possessed Inverlochy and other lands in Lochaber, and that they were deprived of them by the Gordons about the year 1615. That the Lochaber lands were taken from them by some very unfair means, is pretty certain. In June, 1616, Hector Og, Allan of Ardtornish, Allan's sons, and others attacked the castle of Inverlochy, cut down its gates with axes, took possession of it, and drove away its defenders. On the 11th of the following July the Privy Council ordered the Macleans to deliver up the castle of Inverlochy to George, Lord Gordon, its legal owner. The Macleans, of course, were under the necessity of complying. Lord Gordon became Marquis of Huntly in 1636. He was a Jacobite, but through spite and jealousy refused to co-operate with the great Montrose. He was beheaded in Edinburgh in March, 1649.

On July 12th, 1616, Hector Og appeared before the Privy Council and consented that a tack of his lands should be given for five years to James, Earl of Glencairn. On the 26th of July he named upon oath the following persons as his chief vassals: Lachlan Og, Allan, Gillean, and Charles, his brothers; Allan Mac Iain Duibh; Hector, son of Lachlan Og; John Garbh Maclean; Lachlan Mac Donald Mac Neil; Hector, son of Allan Mac Iain Duibh; Neil Mac Ilduy; and Donald Mac Rory, captain of Duart. In the same month Hector Og, Sir Rory Mor Macleod, Donald Mac Allan of Moydart, Hector Maclean of Lochbuie, Lachlan Maclean of Coll, Sir Lachlan Mackinnon of Strathordill, and Lachlan Og Maclean appeared before the Privy Council, and bound themselves to act in accordance with the following obligations :—1. That they should keep good order among their vassals and appear before the Privy Council annually on the 10th of July. 2. That they should bring with them to the Council annually a certain number of their principal kinsmen. Duart was to bring four, Macleod three, Clanranald two, and Lochbuie, Coll, Mackinnon, and Lachlan Og one each. 3. That they were to maintain in their households only a certain number of gentlemen. Duart was allowed to maintain eight, Macleod and Clanranald six, and the others three each. 4. That they were to expel from their lands all sorners and idlers. 5. That they were not to carry pistols, except when employed in the King's service, and that none but themselves and their household gentlemen were to wear swords or daggers. 6. That they were to reside in certain places allotted to them. Hector Og was to reside at Duart, Sir Rory Mor Macleod at Dunvegan, Clanranald at Ellantirim, Lochbuie at Moy, Coll at Breacachadh, Mackinnon at Kilmorie, and Lachlan Og Maclean at Ardnacross. 7. That they were to let lands to tenants at a certain fixed rent, in lieu of all exactions. 8. That none of them should keep more than one birlinn or galley. 9. That they should send those of their children who were over nine years of age to school in the Lowlands to be instructed in speaking, reading, and writing the English language. 10. That they were to use in their houses annually only a certain quantity of wine. Hector

Og and Rory Mor were limited to four tuns each, Clanranald to three tuns, and the others to one tun, or about 252 gallons, each.

Donald Gorm Mor was prevented by sickness from appearing before the Council, but came under the same obligations as the other Islanders in September. He was to exhibit three of his kinsmen to the Council annually, to have six household gentlemen, and to reside in Duntulm. He was allowed to use three tuns of wine yearly.

On July 28th, 1616, Hector Og and his brother Lachlan were committed to ward in the castle of Edinburgh for not giving the securities required of them by the Privy Council. On the 2nd of September, Hector Og was permitted to leave the castle and reside with his father-in-law, Archibald Acheson of Gosford, who lived in Edinburgh. Acheson came under obligation to present Hector before the Privy Council whenever he should be required to do so. Lachlan, Hector Og's brother, was not liberated until the following year.

On April 3rd, 1617, the Privy Council gave to Sir Rory Mackenzie of Coigeach a commission of justiciary and general rule over the lands which belonged to Hector Maclean of Duart and enfeoffed him in these lands instead of Hector Og. On the 30th of April the Privy Council empowered William Cunningham to apprehend Hector Og for a debt of £1020 and to seize his house. The debt was originally only 850 marks, which Hector Og had borrowed from Alexander Cunningham of

Craigends. Through interest at "ten per cent." this small sum gradually swelled up to the amount mentioned. Shortly after William Cunningham had been empowered to arrest Hector Og, William Stewart, son of William Stewart, constable of Dumbarton Castle, sued Sir Rory Mackenzie of Coigeach, possessor of the lands of Hector Maclean of Duart, for the repayment of 1,000 marks, with expenses, for money advanced by his father to Hector during the imprisonment of the latter in Dumbarton Castle.

On June 11th, 1618, Sir Rory Mackenzie of Coigeach made the following complaint to the Privy Council:—Out of his tender respect and regard for Hector Maclean of Duart and the standing of his house, he took upon him the burden of a great number of his debts, for which he was sorely distressed within the burgh of Edinburgh, and through which he was likely to lose his whole estate. He was put in possession of Hector's estates, and finds that he is answerable in law for the whole of Hector's men, tenants, and servants. It is necessary that in the matter of preserving order and peace he should be properly supported by Allan Maclean of Carnnacallych, Gillean Maclean of Coull, Hector Maclean, son of Lachlan Maclean of Ardnacross, Donald Macgillivray of Pennyghael, John Garbh Maclean of Bunessan, Allan Mac Ewen in Ormasay, and Neil Mac Donald Vic Iain Uidhir in Ballinahard. These men had refused either to support him or to find caution for their own good behaviour, and he asks that the Council compel them to do both. The Council denounced the persons named as rebels. Of course as Sir Rory Mackenzie had possession of the Duart estates, the rents were uplifted by him. On the 27th of July, 1620, Hector Macneill of Taynish complained to the Privy Council that he had been employed by the friends of the House of Argyll, who were acting for the young Lord Lorn, to plant the Isle of Jura with good tenants and to see them suitably settled; that he was interrupted in that work by Charles Maclean, brother of Hector Maclean of Duart, who came to the island with a number of mastiff dogs, chased away the cattle, and assaulted and terrified the new tenants; and that the said Charles Maclean had threatened to return with a large force. Hector Og and Charles, his brother, were both proclaimed rebels. It is evident that Macneill of Taynish was expelling the Macleans from Jura and introducing Campbells in their place. On February 22nd, 1621, Lachlan Maclean of Ardnacross petitioned the Privy Council, asking that his yearly appearance before the Privy Council in Edinburgh be dispensed with, inasmuch as he was only a poor tenant. He states that he was a minor at the time of his father's death, that his father made no provision for him, and that his brother, Hector Og, had so carelessly and slothfully governed and husbanded his estate that he could never provide for him or even for himself. About 1620,

Sir John Macdougall began to impose a toll upon the cattle landed by the people of Mull in Lorn. On March 28th, 1622, Sir Rory Mackenzie of Coigeach complained to the Privy Council of Sir John's conduct. In his complaint he states that he had become responsible for the whole of Hector Og's debts and also for the payment of the crown rents due by Hector, which rents amounted to the sum of 2,500 marks yearly. Sir John's unjust interference with his tenants was making it difficult for him to pay the crown rents. Sir John and his officers were proclaimed rebels.

The history of the Macleans in the time of Hector Og is very unpleasant reading. It is the history of a declining power. It is probable that owing to the sanguinary wars in which Lachlan Mor was engaged he left some debt on the estate. It is also probable that in procuring assistance and fitting out an expedition to take vengeance on the slayers of his father, Hector Og was under a good deal of expense. Then, it is well known that the crown rents imposed by King James upon the Lord of Duart and other Islesmen were unreasonably heavy, so heavy indeed that it was scarcely possible to pay them. The truth is that James was always in need of money, and frequently committed very unjust acts to increase his income. He was not naturally cruel, but he hated the Islanders, and was ready to deprive them both of their lands and their lives. They had too much of the spirit of independence in them to suit his tyrannical notions of the rights of kings ; especially of the rights of such a wise king as he deemed himself to be. In 1607 he was ready to grant a commission to the Marquis of Huntly to extirpate them ; and the Marquis was equally ready to take the work in hand for a proper reward. But while Hector Og laboured under some disadvantages from the beginning of his chiefship, it is plainly evident that he was utterly unfit for the position which he occupied. He was, like David Bruce and Richard Cromwell, the weak son of a great father. He lacked sagacity and energy, and could neither manage his own affairs nor those of his clan. He was exceedingly careless, and probably extravagant; at any rate he was continually getting into debt. He died about the beginning of 1623.

XV. Eachann Mor.

We find Hector Mor described as "Hector Maclean now of Duart" on September 12th, 1623. He was a quiet and good-natured man. He possessed none of the fiery qualities of his grandfather, Sir Lachlan Mor. His brother Lachlan and himself took possession of the island of Iona some time after 1626. It is pretty certain, however, that Lachlan was far more responsible for this act than he was. The Ardgour MS. tells us that he was "a good man, but somewhat inactive." He died apparently about the year 1630. He was succeeded by his brother Lachlan.

CHAPTER VIII.

Sir Lachlan and His Sons.

XVI. SIR LACHAINN.

We find Lachlan, second son of Hector Og, described on September 12th, 1623, as "Lachlan Maclean now of Morvern." On that day Hector, his brother, and himself became sureties for the annual appearance of Sir Rory Mor Macleod of Dunvegan before the Privy Council during the next three years. He received a charter of the barony of Duart on July 24th, 1631. He was created a baronet by Charles I. on the 3rd of the following September. In both the charter and the patent of baronetcy he is described as Lachlan Maclean of Morvern. The title conferred upon him was not limited to heirs male of his body; it was to descend " to his heirs male whatsoever."

There must have been a good deal of debt on the Duart estates when Sir Lachlan obtained possession of them. At any rate he was under the necessity of borrowing money in 1634. For the payment of the amount borrowed by him, Lord Lorn, afterwards Marquis of Argyll, became security for him. At the same time Sir Lachlan accepted Lord Lorn as his feudal superior in the lands of Brolas.

During a vacancy in the see of the Isles, Hector Mor of Duart took possession of the island of Icolmkill, or Iona. Bishop Neil Campbell demanded the island of him, but met with a refusal. The Bishop then sent a complaint against Sir Lachlan to the King. On March 10th, 1636, Charles I. instructed the Lords of the Exchequer to assign to the Bishop for the purpose of repairing the cathedral of Iona the sum of £400 sterling out of the feu-duties payable to the crown by Sir Lachlan. On the 14th of the same month Charles wrote to Sir Lachlan, ordering him to restore to the Bishop " the absolute possession of the island of Icolmkill without further hearing or delay." Sir Lachlan had no right to the island of Iona ; at the same time it is well known that he was not the only prominent man who was guilty of seizing church lands. It is said that John Campbell, Bishop of the Isles from 1572 to 1605 "dilapidated the benefice in favour of his relations." Surely a Maclean laird might follow the example of a Campbell bishop.

In 1641 the Marquis of Argyll used his influence to persuade Sir Lachlan of Duart to join the political party to which he belonged himself. Sir Lachlan received a letter from the King in that year. Argyll was exceedingly anxious to know the contents of the letter, but received no satisfaction from the Lord of Duart. When he found that he could not persuade Sir Lachlan by arguments to join him in his plans, he resolved to compel him to join him, or else to ruin him. He immediately purchased a right to some old crown rents due by Sir Lachlan, and also a right to some feu-duties claimed by the Bishop of the Isles for the island of Icolmkill. He obtained each of these claims for a comparatively small sum. By means of the crown rents, the Bishop's feu-duties, the amount for which he was security, and several smaller items, he succeeded in patching up an account against Sir Lachlan for £30,000. For the whole of this claim—the sum for which he was security included—he paid in all only about £10,000. He was thus making a clear gain of £20,000 by the disreputable business in which he was engaged. Sir Lachlan went to Inverary to try to come to a settlement with Argyll. The latter immediately arrested him and imprisoned him in the castle of Carrick, where he kept him for over a year. At last, in order to procure his liberty, Sir Lachlan gave him his bond for £16,000, and signed an account for £14,000. Sir Lachlan thus came under obligation to pay to Argyll the £30,000 which the latter claimed. Argyll had now both Sir Lachlan and his estates to a large extent at his mercy. The imprisonment of Sir Lachlan in Carrick Castle is the subject of one of John Lom's poems. The honest bard praises the chief of the Clan Gillean, hurls his fiercest anathemas against the race of Diarmid, and calls upon the Macleods of Harris, the Macdonalds of Sleat, the Macdonalds of Glengarry, and the Camerons of Lochiel to invade Argyll's lands, to plunder and lay them waste, and to plunge their red daggers into the bodies of the Campbells. On March 2nd, 1643, Sir Lachlan resigned his lands in favour of his son, Hector, reserving to himself a life interest.

On the 1st of February, 1644, James Graham, Earl of Montrose, received a commission from Charles I. as Lieutenant-General of His Majesty's forces in the kingdom of Scotland. On the 6th of the following May he was raised to the rank of Marquis. He left Carlisle on the 18th of August to make his way to the Highlands, and after four days of hard riding reached Tilliebelton House in Perthshire, the residence of his cousin, Patrick Dubh Graham of Inchbrakie. He was accompanied only by two persons, Sir William Rollock and Colonel Sibbald. He remained at Tilliebelton for some time, waiting for the arrival of a body of men that the Marquis of Antrim had promised to send to Scotland, to support King Charles in his war with the English Parliament and Scottish Covenanters.

Alexander Macdonald, Alasdair Mac Cholla, sailed from Ireland for Scotland on the 27th of June, 1644. He had 1,500 men under him. He landed in Morvern on the 5th of July. He captured and garrisoned the castle of Kinlochaline. Shortly afterwards he laid siege to Mingarry Castle and made himself master of it in the course of a few days. Having garrisoned it, he marched to Kyle-rhea, as he was anxious to see Sir James Macdonald. From Kyle-rhea he led his forces over the mountains of Cuaich and thence to Glengarry, where he was joined only by a very few persons. From Glengarry he marched to Badenoch, where Ewen Og Macpherson, the son of Andrew, the son of Ewen, joined him with 300 men. He went from Badenoch to Blair Atholl, and was joined on the way by the Farquharsons of Braemar, under Donald Og, son of Donald, the son of Finlay.

Montrose came to Blair Atholl a day or two after the arrival of Alexander Macdonald. He was dressed in the Highland garb, and on foot. He had neither troops nor money; he had nothing whatever but the King's commission and his own military genius. He took immediate charge of the small army which he found awaiting him, and displayed the royal standard, which he placed on Blair Castle. On the next day he was joined by 800 Atholl men, consisting chiefly of Stewarts and the Clan Duncan, or Robertsons of Struan. He had now about 2,500 men under him. He left Blair Atholl as soon as possible and marched towards Perth. He attacked the Menzies, who had assailed his rear guard, destroyed their ripe cornfields, and set fire to a number of houses. He crossed the river Tay on the 31st of August. He defeated Lord Elcho at Tippermuir on Sunday, the 1st of September. On the day following, the city of Perth surrendered to him. He defeated Lord Burleigh at Aberdeen on the 12th of September. The Earl of Argyll attacked him with a large force at Fyvie on the 29th of October, but was compelled to retire. Montrose left Fyvie on the 31st of October and marched through Strathbogie into Badenoch, where he was joined by John Muideartach and others. He led his army across the mountains to Atholl, and was joined there by the Atholl men, some of the Macdonalds of Knoydart and Glengarry, some of the Camerons, the Stewarts of Appin, the Macdonalds of Keppoch, and the Macdonalds of Glencoe. He left Blair Atholl about the middle of December, to invade the Campbell territories. He marched through Breadalbane to the head of Loch Tay, burning the houses, slaughtering the cattle, and killing the able-bodied men who fell into his hands. He was now joined by the Macgregors and Macnabs. At the head of Loch Tay he placed a division of his army in charge of John Muideartach with instructions to lay waste the northern part of Glenorchy and the northern and western parts of Lorn. He gave him, in addition to his own followers, the Macdonalds of Glengarry and Knoydart, and the Macdonalds of Keppoch. Montrose marched through Glen Dochart and the valley of the river Lochy to Loch Awe, and thence through Glen Aray. Argyll knew nothing about his movements until he was within three miles of Inverary. As soon, however, as he had heard that Montrose was so near him, he fled from his castle, entered a fishing boat, and sailed off to the Lowlands, both for safety and assistance. Montrose proceeded to Kilmartin near Loch Crinan. There he met John Muideartach with a drove of 1,000 of the fattest cows that he was able to pick up in the districts traversed by him. He now divided his army into brigades. He sent Alister Mac Coll and his followers in one direction, and John Muideartach and those who had been with him, in another direction. He kept the Atholl men and others with himself. We are told that Glenorchy, Inveraw, Auchinbreck and other places in Kintyre were plundered, and that 895 of Argyll's followers were slain. The fact is that the invaders went everywhere among the Campbells plundering, burning, and slaughtering. About the 26th of January, Montrose called in his predatory bands, and marched by way of Connel Ferry to Inverlochy, and thence to Kill-Cummin, now Fort Augustus, where he halted on the 29th. At Inverlochy he was joined by Sir Lachlan Maclean of Duart, who had come with about twenty men to meet him. At Glengarry he was joined by Angus Macdonald, son and heir of Donald Macdonald of Glengarry. On the 31st a messenger came to him from Allan Cameron of Lochiel stating that Argyll had entered Lochaber plundering, burning, and laying waste the country. It is probable that John Lom, the poet, arrived from Keppoch about the same time, and that there were thus two messengers. Montrose resolved to attack Argyll at once. He led his army along the river Tarf, over Laire Thuirard, through Glenroy, and over the mountains into Glennevis, where he arrived on the evening of Saturday, the 1st day of February. Argyll left his army as soon as Montrose arrived, and sought safety on his galley. He appointed Sir Duncan Campbell of Auchinbreck to the chief command. At dawn on Sunday morning both parties began to prepare for battle. Sir Duncan Campbell placed a regiment of Lowland infantry with two field-pieces on the right; the Campbells in the centre; and a Lowland regiment with two field-pieces on the left. He planted about forty or fifty musketeers in Inverlochy Castle. His reserve occupied a rising ground, and had a field-piece. Montrose also drew up his men in four divisions. The left wing consisted of a regiment of Antrim men under Colonel Magnus O' Cahan or O' Kean; the centre was composed of the Macdonalds of Glengarry, the Macleans, the Clanranald, the Macdonalds of Glencoe, the Macdonalds of Keppoch, the Camerons, the Stewarts of Appin, and the Robertsons, Stewarts and other Atholl men; the right wing consisted of an Antrim regiment under Alister Mac Coll. An Antrim regiment under Colonel Sir James Macdonald formed the reserve. The Antrim men were all musketeers. The battle was begun shortly after sunrise. George Stewart, son of Alexander Stewart, laird of Urrard, charged from Montrose's line without orders, and was the means of hastening a general engagement. Colonel O'Cahan attacked the Lowlanders on Auchinbreck's right wing and defeated them. Montrose's centre and right wing now pressed forward and routed those opposed to them. The battle was over in a few minutes. The Lowland regiments fired only once; they were assailed by the claymores before they had time to reload. The pursuit continued for a long distance. Argyll lost fourteen barons of his own clan and 1,500 common soldiers. Montrose lost only eight men, Lord Ogilvie, Captain Brain, and six privates. Sir Duncan Campbell of Auchinbreck, who was a very brave man, was slain after the battle by Alister Mac Coll.

Montrose defeated General Urry at Auldearn on May 9th, 1645. He defeated General Baillie at Alford on July 2nd. A few weeks afterwards he was joined by 700 Macleans, under the command of Donald of Brolas.

Shortly after the Macleans had left Mull to join Montrose, the Campbells invaded their possessions and pillaged and destroyed as they marched along. As there were only women and children and a few old men to meet them, they were free from fear and took time, like Joel's locusts, to make everything "clean bare." The land was as the Garden of Eden before them, and behind them a desolate wilderness.

As Montrose was leading his army down the vale of the Devon to the wood of Tullibody, the Macleans laid waste the lands of Muckart and Dollar, which belonged to the Marquis of Argyll. They also reduced Castle Campbell to ashes. They committed these acts to pay back Argyll for wrongs which they had suffered at his hands. A few days afterwards Argyll burnt the house of Menstrie, which belonged to the Earl of Stirling, and the house of Aithrie, which belonged to Montrose's uncle, Sir John Graham of Braco.

The battle of Kilsyth was fought on August 15th, 1645. Montrose had 5,000 infantry and 500 horse; General Baillie had 7,000 infantry and 800 horse. Montrose planted his troops at Auchincleugh, about two miles east of Kilsyth. There were a few cottages and gardens in front of him. Within the cottages and behind the walls he placed 100 of his best marksmen. A regiment of cavalry, acting of its own accord, attacked these marksmen, but was driven back with considerable loss. The Macleans, the Clanranald, and the Macgregors occupied the nearest position to the marksmen who were in the houses and enclosures. Without waiting for orders they rushed forward to attack Baillie's army. They were met by 2,000 foot, divided into three regiments, and flanked by three troops of horse and one of lancers, and were in danger of being surrounded and cut off. Lord Aboyne with a few horse made a sudden charge upon one of the infantry regiments and broke right through it. James Ogilvie, Earl of Airlie, then in the seventieth year of his age, charged the horse with a strong body of cavalry and threw them into confusion. Montrose now made a general attack. In a very short time the Covenanters were routed and dispersed in every direction. Of Baillie's foot-soldiers, only about 300 escaped. Montrose lost only a few men. The Marquis of Argyll and other noblemen accompanied Baillie to the battlefield. Argyll saved himself by the fleetness of his horse. He fled to South Queensferry, where he found a vessel which carried him off to Berwick.

On the 3rd of September, Montrose was appointed Lieutenant-General, and Captain-General of Scotland. On the same day he conferred the honour of knighthood on Alister Mac Coll, who immediately afterwards departed with most of his followers to Kintyre. The Macleans, Macdonalds, and other clans left Montrose at the same time.

As Sir Alister Mac Coll and Sir Lachlan Maclean were passing through Lorn with their men, they defeated 700 of Argyll's followers at Mamore. They had only about 200 men with them, as the main body of their followers had been delayed by the way.

Montrose was surprised and defeated by David Leslie at Philiphaugh on September 13th, 1645. King Charles was defeated at Chester on the 24th of September. The King gave himself up to the Scottish army on May 5th, 1646. On the 19th of

May he sent a letter to Montrose, ordering him to disband his forces and retire to France. The Scots surrendered King Charles to the English Parliament on January 28th, 1647. On January 30th, 1649, he was executed in front of Whitehall. He was an arbitrary and untrustworthy man.

General David Leslie arrived at Inverary on May 21st, 1647, with a strong force, to expel Sir Alister Mac Coll, who had been in possession of Kintyre since the end of September, 1645. He attacked the latter on the 25th, and easily defeated his small army. He then besieged Dunaverty, which was defended by 300 men, partly Irishmen, and partly Macdougalls and other Highlanders. After losing about forty men, the besieged surrendered. With the exception of one or two, they were all put to death. Leslie went from Kintyre to Islay, and laid siege to Dunnyveg, which was defended by Colla Ciotach Macdonald with 200 men. Coll, who was in his seventy-seventh year, went out of the garrison to have a talk with Campbell of Dunstaffnage, and was treacherously captured. The garrison surrendered on condition of having their lives spared. Colla Ciotach was hanged by the Campbells at Dunstaffnage. Sir Alister, his son, made his escape to Ireland. From Islay, Leslie went to Jura and thence to Mull. Sir Lachlan Maclean surrendered the castles of Duart and Aros to him, and along with the castles fourteen Irishmen who were with him. He also gave Leslie his son, Hector Roy, as a pledge of his fidelity. The Irishmen were all, except perhaps one, put to death by Leslie.

Sir James Turner, a major-general who served under Leslie, blames Sir Lachlan Maclean for delivering the Irishmen to Leslie. He tells us that "Maclean saved his lands with the loss of his reputation." The simple truth is that Sir Lachlan was utterly unable to protect either himself or the Irishmen. Sir Donald Campbell of Ardnamurchan and other Campbells were exceedingly anxious to have an opportunity of slaying the inhabitants of Mull. Turner tells us "that with all imaginable violence Sir Donald pressed that the whole Clan Maclean should be put to the edge of the sword." Leslie had 5,000 men in Mull. He could easily capture Duart and Aros in a few days. If he had been compelled to take these castles by storm, he would have put all the defenders to the sword. Besides, the Campbells would have laid Mull waste and butchered the defenceless inhabitants while the siege was going on.

We are told by the Maclean historians that Argyll seized Sir Lachlan's heir at Dumbarton, where he was going to school; that he took him with him to Mull; and that he threatened to put him to death, unless Sir Lachlan would surrender his castle to Leslie. There is evidently no truth in this story. Hector Roy was probably about twenty years of age in 1647. Argyll was greedy and crafty, but he was not a murderer. Then, the likelihood is that he really desired that Sir Lachlan would refuse to surrender to Leslie. The more the latter should oppose the Government, the greater the probability that he would lose his lands. We suspect that the seizure of Hector Roy took place at the time of Sir Lachlan's imprisonment in Carrick Castle.

It is said that Marion, Sir Lachlan's youngest daughter, placed a horse at the disposal of an Irish officer and thus enabled the latter to escape to a boat, by which, like the Marquis of Argyll on three different occasions, he was carried to a place of safety. It is probable that this story is true.

Through the influence of Argyll, the Government planted a garrison in the castle of Duart and kept possession of it. In 1648 Sir Lachlan besieged the castle of Cairnburgh, but did not succeed in getting possession of it. He died shortly afterwards. He was buried in Icolmkill. He left two sons, Hector Roy and Allan. He was an honourable man and an excellent chief.

XVII. EACHANN RUADH INBHIRCHÉITEINN.

Sir Hector Roy, popularly known as Hector Roy of Inverkeithing, was a man of good ability and great energy, and possessed to a large extent the warlike qualities of his great-grandfather, Lachlan Mor. About the year 1648 he complained to the Marquis of Argyll of the depredations committed by his followers in Ardnamurchan and Lorn upon the Macleans of Morvern and Mull. As Argyll paid no attention to his complaints, he entered Ardnamurchan, seized two of the principal offenders, and hanged them. He compelled the other plunderers to make full restitution for all the cattle which they had carried off. He then entered Lorn and dealt in a similar manner with some of the cattle-lifters of that district. When Argyll remonstrated with him, he told him that unless he would control his thieves himself he would control them for him. About the same time some of the Camerons who lived in Morvern made a plundering expedition into Kingerloch, slew the laird of that district, and wounded his son. Sir Hector tried to bring them to justice, but as they fled he was not able to arrest them. The only punishment he could inflict upon them was to kill three or four hundred of their cattle.

During the period of the civil war, or from 1642 to 1649, the estate of Duart paid none of the public dues. As the Macleans were fighting for their king and country, they assumed that they had a perfect right to these dues to meet the heavy expenses incurred by them. Indeed, after the invasion of their lands by Argyll and General Leslie in 1647, they were utterly unable to pay anything. Argyll, taking advantage of their difficulties, bought up all the public debts on their estate. He purchased also the private debts for which Sir Hector was responsible. By means of these purchases, and the £30,000 promised him in 1642, together with all the interest that he could possibly charge, he made up an account against

Sir Hector, in 1650, for £70,000. In that year Sir Hector paid him £10,000, and gave him his bond for the remaining £60,000.

On the execution of his father on February 8th, 1649, Charles II. assumed the title of King. He left France for Scotland in June, 1650, and landed at the mouth of the Spey on the 23d of the month. He professed to be a Presbyterian and signed the Covenant. He was crowned at Scone on January 1st, 1651. Cromwell had no idea of permitting Charles to rule in Scotland. He marched against him, and defeated the Scots under David Leslie at Dunbarton September 3d, 1650. In June, 1651, Cromwell led his army against the Scots, who occupied a strong position in front of Stirling. Shortly after the middle of July he sent a division of his army, under General Lambert, across the Forth at Queensferry, to intercept the supplies of the Scottish army. Holburn of Menstrie was sent by the Scots to oppose Lambert. The two forces met at Inverkeithing on Sunday, July 20th. Lambert had about 4,000 men under him, 2,000 of whom were probably cavalry. Holburn had about 3,500 men under him. His force consisted of 1,000 horse under his own immediate command, 200 horse and 800 Lowland infantry under Sir John Brown of Fordel, 800 infantry under Sir Hector Roy Maclean of Duart, and 700 infantry under Sir George Buchanan, chief of his clan. Holburn, who was both a traitor and a coward, fled with his cavalry ere the battle had scarcely begun. The left wing, which was commanded by Sir John Brown, was, after a brave resistance, overwhelmed by numbers and forced to retreat, leaving their commander a prisoner, and mortally wounded. The Macleans and the Buchanans were suffering dreadfully from Lambert's artillery. They moved up the hill against their enemies as rapidly as they could. They were in a short time encircled by the English, the result being that they were nearly all cut to pieces.

During the battle, one of the Macleans, seeing his young chief in danger, sprang in between him and his foes, but was soon cut down. Immediately another Maclean, calling out, Fear eile airson Eachainn, Another for Hector, assumed the same post of danger, and was likewise slain. Another and another followed, with the same self-sacrificing cry and the same result, until eight brave clansmen had unselfishly and gloriously yielded up their lives, trying to shield their heroic chief.

In spite of the treachery of Holburn, the battle of Inverkeithing lasted during four long hours. Hector Roy fell, towards the close of the fight, from a musket-ball which pierced his breast. He was covered with wounds. Of the famous 800 whom he led to the field, 700 at least were Macleans. The remainder consisted of the Macquarries and scattered members of other clans. Of the 800 only about thirty-five returned to their homes. Sir John Brown was taken prisoner, but died a few days after the battle. Sir George Buchanan was also taken prisoner. He died towards the end of the year. There were about 2,000 Scotsmen killed at Inverkeithing.

Among the killed of the Maclean regiment at the battle of Inverkeithing were the following :—Sir Hector Roy Maclean of Duart, Colonel; Ewen and Lachlan Cattanach, sons of Lachlan Og Maclean of Torloisk; Donald and John Og, sons of Allan Maclean of Ardgour; Archibald, son of Maclean of Boreray; Ewen Maclean of Treshnish; Charles, son of Maclean of Inverscadale; Murdoch, Allan, Lachlan, Ewen, and John, sons of Lachlan Odhar Maclean of Ardchraoishnish; Ewen, son of John Garbh Maclean of Coll; Ewen, son of the first Maclean of Muck; and Allan, son of Macquarrie of Ulva. Among the men wounded were :—Donald Maclean of Brolas, Lieutenant-Colonel; John Maclean of Kinlochaline; John Diurach Maclean of the Morvern family; John Maclean of Totaranald; and Neil Maclean of Drimnacross.

The foregoing list is very defective; but it is the fullest that we can give. Sir Hector Roy was an accomplished chief, a born fighter, and a valiant man. His fiery nature, however, unfitted him for being a successful commander. His conduct in continuing the unequal fight at Inverkeithing so long, when he might have retreated or surrendered, was utterly unreasonable. It was useless to his king, and injurious to his clan. His own life and the lives of his loyal followers were too valuable to have them thrown away in trying to accomplish an impossibility. While, then, we admire Sir Hector's bravery and determination, we deplore his recklessness and folly. He was probably about twenty-five years of age at the time of his death. He was succeeded by his brother, Allan.

XVIII. Sir Ailein.

Sir Allan Maclean of Duart was born about the year 1641. He was thus only ten years of age when he succeeded his brother, Hector Roy. His uncle, Donald Maclean of Brolas, was appointed tutor to him.

Shortly after the battle of Inverkeithing, Charles I. led his army to England. Cromwell followed after him, and defeated him at Worcester on September 3d, 1651. Of the Scots, 3,000 men were slain, and 10,000 taken prisoners. Those of the prisoners who recovered from their wounds were shipped off to the plantations, or colonies, in America, and sold into slavery. The Macleods of Harris, who had always been friendly to the Macleans, suffered severely at Worcester. Of the 700 men who formed their regiment only a few lived to return to their native Isles.

When Cromwell went in pursuit of Charles, he left General Monk behind him with a force of 5,000 horse and foot to complete the subjugation of Scotland. Monk accomplished the work entrusted to him without any difficulty. In July, 1653, some of the followers of King Charles met at Lochaber and organized a rebellion against the authority of Oliver Cromwell. Among those who joined this foolish project were:—William Cunningham, ninth Earl of Glencairn, the Marquis of Montrose, the Earl of Seaforth, the Earl of Selkirk, Lord Lorn, Lord Balcarres, Lord Forrester, Lord Kenmore, Glengarry, Lochiel, Donald Maclean of Brolas, Robertson of Struan, the tutor of Macgregor, Farquharson of Inverey, the chief of the Macnaughtons, Sir Arthur Forbes, and Graham of Duchray. The Earl of Glencairn was appointed to the chief command. The rebels lay in a wood about three miles from Ruthven Castle during the 12th, 13th, and 14th of August. On the night of the last of these days they received information with regard to the victories of Cromwell's fleet over the Dutch. This information led them to disperse immediately. Glencairn went to Lochaber. Lord Lorn and Donald of Brolas started together with their followers and travelled homewards over the hills. Lord Lorn joined Glencairn towards the end of the year with 1,000 men, but deserted him on January 1st, 1654. In the month of March, Glencairn was superseded by Major-General Middleton. The defeat of the latter at Lochgarry by Colonel Morgan, on July 26th, 1654, brought the insurrection to an end.

The Marquis of Argyll pretended to be very much opposed to the conduct of his son and heir, Lord Lorn, in joining Glencairn. It is pretty certain, however, that Lorn was not really acting against his father's will. When the insurrection began the Marquis could not foresee what turn political events might take. He deemed it, therefore, good policy to have his heir fighting for Charles while he himself was supporting Cromwell. If Glencairn should be defeated, the Marquis would not be disturbed in his estates. If Glencairn won, the estates would be safe with Lord Lorn.

On September 3d, 1653, Colonel Cobbet entered Mull and took possession of Duart Castle for Cromwell. The Marquis of Argyll arrived a few days afterwards, and by his advice and assistance the heritors of the Duart estate were compelled to promise that they would live peaceably, obey the authority of Parliament, and pay sess like the rest of the shire of Argyll. They were also forced to promise that they would not pay any rent to the tutor of Duart, who was in rebellion against Cromwell. At the request of the Marquis, Cobbet planted an English garrison in Duart. The steps thus taken prevented Donald of Brolas, the leader of the Macleans at the time, from giving any assistance to Glencairn.

After the retirement of Richard Cromwell in May, 1659, the Marquis of Argyll felt at liberty to renew his attacks on the Macleans. Of the £60,000 for which Sir Hector gave his bond in 1651, the guardians of Sir Allan paid £22,000 between 1652 and 1659. In 1659 Argyll obtained a decreet of adjudication in the sum of £85,000 against the Duart estate. After the restoration of

Charles II. in May, 1660, Donald Maclean of Brolas, tutor of Sir Allan, sent a complaint to the Scottish Parliament against the doings of Argyll, and clearly proved that no credit had been given by him for a large portion of the sums which had been paid him. The King's Advocate, by the authority of the Parliament, stopped the execution of the decreet against the Macleans. The forfeiture and execution of Argyll in May, 1661, allowed them to live in peace for a few years.

Sir Allan attained his majority in 1661, and was legally recognized as Lord of Duart in January, 1662.

In the year 1662 some Maclean women who lived in Strathglass were accused of the crime of witchcraft. An application was made to the Privy Council for a commission to try them and put them to death. The application was granted at Edinburgh on June 26th, 1662, and the following persons appointed commissioners:—Alexander Chisholm of Comar; Colin Chisholm, his brother; and John, Valentine, and Thomas Chisholm, his cousins. John Mac Rory Maclean went to Mull to see Sir Allan, the chief of the Clan Gillean, and to ask his protection against the Chisholms and their commission. Sir Allan immediately petitioned the Privy Council in behalf of the women whose lives were in danger. In his petition he states that the Macleans had been kindly tenants in Strathglass for two or three hundred years, and that Alexander Chisholm of Comar, laird of

Strathglass, had conceived an inveterate hatred against them and was anxious to remove them from their lands and possessions. Sir Allan's petition was considered on July 3d, 1662. The result was that the commission to the Chisholms was cancelled, and that the Strathglass witches were neither put to death nor banished.

On August 26th, 1662, Archibald, ninth Earl of Argyll, the Lord Lorn of Glencairn's rebellion, was with gross injustice condemned by the Scottish Parliament to be put to death and to forfeit all his estates. The crime for which he was tried was that of leasing-making, or creating dissension between the King and his subjects. As the time for carrying out the sentence against him was left to the judgment of the King, Charles II., he was allowed to lie in prison in Edinburgh. He was released on June 4th, 1663, restored to the honours and estates of his grandfather, and appointed a Privy Councillor and one of the Commissioners of the Treasury. He went immediately to work with hereditary zeal and diligence and bought up all the debts which he could find against the Duart estate. He was now in a position to press his claim against Sir Allan. In 1669 this claim was £85,000. Argyll had at the same time a debt of £20,000 Scots against Clanranald.

On June 25th, 1664, the Earl of Argyll wrote a letter to Lauderdale, from which it appears that 100,000 marks Scots would, at that time, have nearly satisfied all his claims on his neighbours.

As there are only thirteen shillings and sixpence of Scottish money in a mark Scots, 100,000 marks are equal only to £66,000 Scots. On November 11th, 1665, Argyll claimed from Maclean of Duart alone £121,000 Scots, or nearly double the amount which he claimed from all his neighbours in June, 1664. It is thus evident that the Lords of Argyll thoroughly understood the art of investing money to the best advantage. Whether they were honest or not, is another question.

In 1672, or thereabouts, Sir Allan Maclean crossed over to Ireland and went thence to London, to complain to the King with regard to the manner in which Argyll was acting towards him. The King ordered Lauderdale, the Secretary of State for Scotland, who happened to be in London at the time, to see justice done to him. Lauderdale, who was a tyrannical and unscrupulous man, and a friend of Argyll, made no attempt to render justice to Sir Allan. Instead of trying to see justice done to him, he used all his powerful influence against him. The consequence was that Argyll obtained full control of Duart, Morvern, Tiree, and the other lands which belonged to Sir Allan's estate. He had power to uplift the rents and to keep them all, except a small allowance which was to be given to Sir Allan for maintenance. To this settlement the Lord of Duart was a consenting party.

Sir Allan Maclean of Duart died early in 1674. He was in the thirty-fourth year of his age. He was succeeded by his only son, John.

CHAPTER IX.

Sir John and Sir Hector.

XIX. SIR IAIN.

Sir John Maclean was only four years of age at the time of his father's death. Lachlan Maclean of Brolas and Lachlan Maclean of Torloisk were appointed tutors to him.

Immediately after the death of Sir Allan, in 1674, Archibald, ninth Earl of Argyll, procured letters of ejection against the Macleans of Duart, on the ground that they had refused to give him possession of the castle of Duart. He then charged them with treasonable gatherings, keeping garrisoned houses, and making unlawful leagues among themselves; and cited them to appear before him, as justiciary of the Isles, at his court in Inverary. As they were wise enough to keep away from Inverary, Argyll complained of them as rebels to the Privy Council, and obtained a commission of fire and sword against them. He got 500 men from the Government, and with these men and 1800 of his own followers he invaded Mull in the month of September. As the Macleans were not in a position to fight against both Argyll and the King, they removed to the mountains, taking the most of their cattle with them. The invaders landed in three different places, and committed numerous acts of cruelty. Lord Neil Campbell of Ardmaddy, Argyll's uncle, took great delight in going about from place to place and houghing all the cattle that he could find. Some of the Campbells entered the house of Maclean of Ardnacross, stripped Sir John naked, and took all his clothes away. According to the Ardgour MS. they attempted to murder him. On the 8th of September, 1674, the Macleans, acting under compulsion, promised to pay the rents of Duart, Morvern, and Tiree to Argyll's agents until the sum claimed by the latter should be paid in full. At the same time Argyll, by the authority of the Privy Council, granted them a remission for all their past offences. The oppressive coveter of his neighbours' lands now returned to Inverary a happy man. Of course he left a garrison in Duart Castle.

In 1634, Sir Lachlan of Duart became a vassal of Lord Lorn for the lands of Brolas. Immediately after obtaining possession of Duart, in September, 1674, the Earl of Argyll tried to compel Lachlan of Brolas, tutor of Sir John, to accept a new charter of these lands. As the charter was binding the grantee to renounce allegiance to his own chief and to follow Argyll in all things, Brolas refused to have anything to do with it. Argyll now trumped up some charges against him, and took steps to prosecute him and obtain a commission of fire and sword against him. The Macleans, seeing that concessions were of no avail, and that their existence as an independent clan was in danger, resolved to withhold the rents from Argyll, and to resist his fresh attacks with the sword. The Macleans of Kinlochaline and the Macleans of Ardgour joined Brolas at once. The Macleans of Torloisk, Lochbuie, and Kingerloch promised to support him. The Macdonells of Glengarry, the Macdonalds of Keppoch, and the Camerons, also assured him of their assistance. In April, 1675, the Macleans sent fiery crosses through Mull, Morvern, and other places, and assembled, to the number of 400 men, in arms. It is evident that they expected to be attacked by the Campbells. On the 20th of the same month they appeared in a warlike posture on the lands of Knockmartin. Shortly afterwards, 100 of them gathered together at Gaderly and Glenforsay.

In a letter, dated at Coll, May 2d, 1675, Lachlan Maclean writes the Earl of Argyll that all the Macleans aimed at his life and had sent to Tiree to apprehend him. By information from the laird of Coll, he escaped and found refuge in Coll's castle. He had lost most of his means. In a second letter to Argyll, dated at Coll, April 20th,

1676, he states that he had been bailie of Tiree
until 1675, that John Maclean of Kinlochaline
forced him to leave that island, that he had a wife
and children, and that his losses amounted to
£3,090 Scots. He asks Argyll to send him relief,
or compensation for his losses. We do not know
who Lachlan was. It is evident, however, that
the Macleans regarded him as a traitor to his clan.
John of Kinlochaline was probably the most experienced warrior among the Macleans in 1675.
He was one of the heroes of Inverkeithing. It
seems that when he scared Lachlan Maclean out
of Tiree, he seized a number of horses and swine,
and also some corn. Probably the swine and corn
would be of more use to him than Argyll's bailie.

In May, 1675, Argyll cited a number of the Macleans to appear at court in Inverary before John
Campbell, Sheriff depute, to answer for crimes and
treasonable acts of various kinds. Some of the
charges referred to matters which took place prior
to September 8th, 1674. The others referred to
the doings of the Macleans in April. The principal persons cited to appear at Inverary were:—
Lachlan Maclean of Brolas; Hector, his brother;
John Maclean of Ardgour; Ewen Maclean, fiar of
Ardgour; Allan Maclean of Inverscadale; John
Maclean of Kinlochaline; and Hector, son of Kinlochaline. Of course the Macleans were not foolish
enough to go to Inverary. Consequently they were
dealt with as fugitives from justice, and rebels.
But they were not rebels against the King; they

were rebels simply against the petty kinglet of Inverary. About the first of September, 1675, Argyll received from the Privy Council a commission of fire and sword against the Macleans of Duart, Kinlochaline, and Ardgour. He also obtained a body of soldiers to assist him. About the 12th of September, the Macleans, the Macdonells of Glengarry, the Macdonalds of Keppoch, and the Camerons, in fourteen boats and to the number of 300 men, attacked a frigate belonging to Argyll, near the castle of Ardnamurchan; but were beaten off. The frigate was coming from Leith and was laden with provision for Argyll's army. Shortly after this event Argyll sailed for Mull with a force of 2,200 men. But this formidable force never reached its place of destination. A dreadful storm, which raged for two days, drove back the ships and disabled some of them. The superstition of the times ascribed the storm to the influence of the witch known as an Doideag Mhuileach, or the Mull Doideag. It seems that this famous witch had promised the Macleans that so long as she lived Argyll should not enter Mull. It is just possible that when Argyll found that the Macdonalds and Camerons were assembling to help the Macleans he had no particular desire to go to Mull. He may perhaps have begun to think about the fate of the Campbells at Inverlochy.

When the Campbells were preparing to invade Mull in September, 1675, the Macleans sent Sir John, who was only six years of age, to Cairnburgh for safety. In the course of a few months he was taken back to Ardnacross, where we find him in 1676. It was felt, however, that his life was not safe there from his deadly foes. Consequently he was sent in 1677 to Brahan Castle. Lachlan, eldest son of Allan Maclean of Grulin, accompanied him to his new home. Both of them remained with the Earl of Seaforth until they were old enough to go to college.

On October 18th, 1675, Hector Maclean of Lochbuie, and the brothers of Kingerloch, with sixty men in three birlinns, invaded the islands of Garvellach and plundered them. Shortly afterwards, Lachlan of Brolas, Hector of Lochbuie, Major David Ramsay, and others, raided the island of Kerrera, which was occupied by William Campbell, and carried off everything of value they could find. John Mac Charles Maclean, with sixty men, broke into the house of John Maclachlan of Kilbride and plundered it. They also carried away fifty-two cows, sixteen stirks, four horses, and twelve sheep. But the Campbells were not idle ; they were plundering the Macleans.

Argyll went to Edinburgh and tried to obtain additional assistance from the Privy Council. As he did not meet with the encouragement which he expected, he started for London about the end of the year 1675, to lay his complaints before the King. He felt confident that through Lauderdale's influence he would be successful in obtaining everything that he wanted. Lachlan of Brolas and Lachlan of Torloisk, accompanied by Lord Macdonell, and probably by Sir Ewen of Lochiel, followed him to London. In February, 1676, the King remitted the matter in dispute to three lords of the Privy Council of Scotland for adjudication. Argyll lodged his complaints against the Macleans with the Council. Lachlan of Brolas and Lachlan of Torloisk gave in their answers to these complaints. The Macleans had now strong hopes that the disputed points would be finally settled. But Argyll, who did not desire a settlement, continued to have the decision put off for several years. We have seen that in 1665 Argyll's claim against the Duart estate was £121,000. In 1676 he claimed £200,000. Perhaps he was an unscrupulous usurer; perhaps he was a manufacturer of bogus accounts; he was certainly either the one or the other.

On February 24th, 1677, some of the Campbells who were garrisoning Duart Castle captured a boat loaded with Irish victuals, six miles from Duart, and brought it with them to the castle; but before they could unload it, the Macleans, under Archibald Maclean, uncle of Ardgour, and the laird of Kingerloch's brother, seized it, carried it away, and kept possession of it. On May 23d, 1677, we find Campbell of Inverawe writing Argyll that frequent meetings had lately taken place between the Macleans and the Macdonalds, that the former expected a vessel with guns from Lord Macdonell, that a trench had been constructed near Tobermory to hinder vessels from entering the Sound of Mull, and that Brolas and Lochiel were to meet in Morvern on the following day. Shortly afterwards, Brolas and Lochiel raided Migharie, Carwallan, and other lands belonging to Alexander Campbell of Lochnell, and carried off 650 lambs, 650 sheep, 161 horses, 500 goats, 230 bolls of corn, and twenty-four bolls of barley. About the same time the Macleans and Camerons took away from Ardnamurchan sixty-six sheep, twelve horses, and fifty goats.

Sir Ewen Cameron of Lochiel seems to have withdrawn all active support from the Macleans in 1678. According to the Ardgour MS. and other works he had solemnly promised to stand by them in their troubles. Argyll, however, succeeded in securing his non-interference by forgiving him a debt of 40,000 marks, which he had against him. Hence the saying came into existence, Chaill Eoghan a Dhia, ach chaill an t-Iarla chuid airgid, Ewen lost his God, but the Earl lost his money. Whatever may have been the nature of the transaction which took place between Argyll and Sir Ewen, it is certain that the latter never worked against the Macleans. He was always friendly to them. The probability is that he did all he could for them.

About the beginning of 1679, Argyll obtained a commission from the Privy Council to disarm and bring to obedience Lord Macdonell, Archibald Macdonald of Keppoch, Lachlan Maclean of

Torloisk, Lachlan Maclean of Brolas, John Maclean of Ardgour, and other persons who were suspected of popery or known to be rebels. The Macleans were Presbyterians, and Lord Macdonell probably an Episcopalian. Archibald of Keppoch was of course a Roman Catholic. But all the men named were rebels against Argyll, and consequently irreligious criminals in his eyes. On April 24th, he issued a command to them to deliver up to the Sheriff depute all the arms and ammunition in their possession. On May 24th, Donald Macdonald of Inveroy, Archibald Maclean, brother of Ardgour, John Maclean, brother of Torloisk, and Donald Gow Maclean of Sheba in Mull, acting according to Lord Macdonell's instructions, invaded the lands of Colin Campbell of Inveresrigane, and carried off sixteen horses, a hundred and six cows, and valuables of various kinds. About the beginning of June, the Macdonalds and Macleans invaded and plundered Glenshire, Brae Lochfine, and other Campbell lands.

On July 2d, 1679, Argyll invaded the Isle of Coll, and compelled Donald Maclean of Coll to surrender the castle of Breacachadh to him. According to the articles of capitulation, Donald and those who were with him agreed to deliver up all their arms and ammunition, to become obedient subjects and abstain from the committal of crimes, not to hinder the execution of the law, not to raise any forces, not to hold any convocations, and not to purchase arms without authority from Argyll.

On the 30th of the same month, Lachlan Maclean, son of the laird of Ardgour, surrendered to Argyll the castle of Kinlochaline on condition of being discharged from all criminal process. On the 11th of August, an agreement was entered into between Argyll and the Macleans, by which Lachlan Maclean of Brolas, John Maclean of Ardgour, John Maclean of Kinlochaline, Ewen Maclean, fiar of Ardgour, Hector Maclean, fiar of Kinlochaline, Allan Maclean of Inverscadale, and others, consented to dismiss all the prisoners taken by them. Argyll promised in return to drop all criminal processes against these men. At the same time, Lord Neil Campbell of Ardmaddy, Sir Ewen Cameron of Lochiel, and three others, received a commission empowering them to proceed against the Macleans with fire and sword should they make any further invasions of Argyll's lands. Argyll had now the castles of Breacachadh and Kinlochaline in his possession. He had also recovered those of his followers who had been prisoners in the hands of his enemies. He thus felt at greater liberty than ever to persecute and harass the Macleans. In November, 1679, Argyll, acting with shameless treachery, caused the Privy Council to grant a commission to John Campbell of Glenorchy, Lord Lorn, Lord Neil Campbell, Sir Hugh Campbell of Caddell, Sir Duncan Campbell of Auchinbreck, Sir James Campbell of Lawers, Colin Campbell of Ardkinglass, and others, to pursue and apprehend or slay Lachlan Maclean of Brolas and the other

Macleans who had refused to appear at court in Inverary on June 3d, 1675. On November 6th he obtained for himself a commission of fire and sword against John Maclean of Ardgour and Lachlan Maclean of Torloisk. Ardgour's crime consisted in taking violent possession of Ardnamurchan and Sunart, and plundering all the Macleans who had submitted to Argyll. With regard to Torloisk, the Earl states that he was "peaceable in 1674, but joined with Brolas in 1675 and became as disorderly as the rest of the Macleans." John Campbell of Glenorchy held unjustly the title of Earl of Caithness from 1677 to 1681. Consequently, he is described in the commission granted against Lachlan of Brolas and his associates, as Earl of Caithness. He was created Earl of Breadalbane in 1681, rejoiced over the massacre of Glencoe in 1692, and died in 1716.

The way in which Argyll fulfilled his written promises to the Macleans clearly shows what he was. He did not prosecute them for their plundering excursions into his lands, but he caused the Privy Council to grant their bitterest enemies a commission to hound them to death. He did not insert his own name in the commission, but he inserted his son's name in it, Glenorchy's name, and the names of a number of other persons who would act as his tools in carrying out his selfish and destructive purposes.

About the beginning of 1680, Lachlan Maclean of Brolas and Lachlan Maclean of Torloisk brought the matters in dispute between Argyll and themselves to the notice of King Charles a second time. The subject was considered by the Privy Council about the beginning of July. The Macleans strongly pled in favour of having Mull and the castle of Duart restored to them. Lauderdale used his utmost influence to have the matter "settled in the most advantageous method for Argyll." Both the King and the Duke of York yielded to him. The conclusion was that Argyll should have the whole of the Duart estates, and that £300 a year should be paid to Sir John out of Argyll's feu-duties. On July 10th, 1680, Charles II. wrote from Windsor Castle to the Privy Council of Scotland, proposing to purchase so much of Tiree as would make to "the laird of Maclean" £500 a year. On October 1st, 1681, Alexander Stewart, Earl of Moray and Secretary of State for Scotland, replied that the Council thought it not advisable to purchase a part of Tiree for the laird of Maclean. On October 19th, 1681, the King authorized the Scottish Council to draw yearly on Argyll £300 for the laird of Maclean, or Sir John. We may state that the Earl of Moray was a brother of Argyll's wife. He succeeded Lauderdale as Secretary of State in November, 1689.

Argyll had now possession of Duart, Morvern, and Tiree. He had no notion, however, of leaving the Macleans alone. In November, 1680, or thereabouts, he complained to the Privy Council, in Edinburgh, against them for garrisoning the rock and fortress of Cairnburgh and other illegal acts. The Council cited the men complained of, to appear before them to answer for their conduct. As they did not appear on the day appointed, they were denounced as rebels, and put to the horn. On the 22d of December, Argyll received a commission in which the Macleans were commanded to deliver to himself or any one having his order, the rock and fortress of Cairnburgh within fourteen days. The commission was executed on January 7th, 1681. The men who held Cairnburgh, and who were proclaimed rebels for holding it, were:—Lachlan Maclean of Brolas; Hector Og, his brother; John Maclean of Ardgour; Allan Maclean of Inverscadale; John Maclean of Kinlochaline; Lachlan Maclean of Torloisk; Donald Maclean of Kingerloch; Hector and John Macquarrie, uncles to Macquarrie of Ulva; Ewen Maclean, son of Kinlochaline; Charles Maclean of Ardnacross; Lachlan Mac Charles in Mornish; Allan Mac Charles in Mishnish; Donald Mac Charles in Aros; Hector and Ewen Mac Charles; Hector and Alexander Maclean, brothers of Kingerloch; Ewen Maclean of Carnae, and Hector, his son; Allan Maclean of Killintyn; and Ewen Maclean, late bailie of Tiree. Cairnburgh was either given up to Argyll or abandoned.

James, Duke of York, arrived in Scotland as Lord High Commissioner in November, 1679. He resided in the palace of Holyrood and lived in regal splendour. For some time he exerted himself to the utmost to conciliate the affections of all the influential men who came in contact with him. He interested himself especially in the Highland chiefs, and sought to adjust their difficulties, and remove their feuds. He returned to London in the course of three months, but remained there only a short time. Immediately after his return he began to show a spirit of intolerance, and a determination to have his own way both in civil and ecclesiastical matters. He hated the Covenanters and persecuted them with bitter cruelty. As the Earl of Argyll, who was an out-and-out Presbyterian, was opposed to his actions and purposes, he caused him to be arrested and thrown into prison. On December 12th, 1681, Argyll was tried for high treason and leasing-making, and pronounced guilty. Of treason he was certainly innocent, of leasing-making, or creating dissension between the King and his subjects, he was also innocent. As he expected to be condemned and executed, he fled from Edinburgh on December 20th. He was assisted in making his escape by his step-daughter, Sophia Lindsay, and also by Captain Campbell of Lochnell. He went from Edinburgh to London and thence to Holland. Immediately after his flight, sentence of attainder was pronounced against him. His titles, estates, and life were forfeited, and a large reward offered for his head. The whole of the proceedings against Argyll were utterly discreditable to the Duke of York and his followers. They were neither initiated nor carried on for the well-being of the state. However, if a man does wrong he may expect to suffer. Argyll dealt unjustly with the Macleans, and the Duke of York dealt unjustly with himself.

It is probable that after the forfeiture of Argyll the management of the Duart estates was left practically in the hands of Lachlan Maclean of Brolas and Lachlan Maclean of Torloisk. The Macleans would now be obedient subjects and pay the sums due the Government punctually.

Charles II. died on February 6, 1685, and was succeeded by his brother, James, Duke of York. The Duke of Monmouth, an illegitimate son of Charles II., and the Earl of Argyll were both exiles in Holland. They resolved to invade Britain and attempt to overthrow the despotic government of James. Monmouth landed at Lynne, in Dorsetshire, on June 11th, 1685. He was defeated at the battle of Sedgemoor on July 6th, captured on the 8th, and executed on Tower Hill on the 11th. Argyll landed at Campbellton, in Kintyre, about the 12th of May, 1685. He soon found himself at the head of 2,000 men, but he was unable to do anything. He was a commander only in name; he had to be guided in his movements by Sir John Cochrane, Sir Patrick Hume, and others who had come with him from Holland. With the consent of his advisers, he led his small army to Lennox, with the intention of marching to the Lowlands to call the Covenanters to arms. On arriving at

Kilpatrick, Argyll's followers, finding themselves in danger of being attacked and cut to pieces, dispersed and began to make their way back to their respective homes. Argyll and Major Fullarton crossed the Clyde and journeyed through Renfrewshire as far as Inchinnan. At this place a man named Riddel, and four others, seized Argyll and carried him off as a prisoner to Renfrew. He was immediately conveyed to Edinburgh. He was executed by the maiden on June 30th; not, however, for his rebellion, but for the treason for which he had been unjustly condemned in December, 1681. Argyll seems to have been greatly benefited by his misfortunes; he died like a brave man and a Christian.

The forces which had been raised to resist and attack the Earl of Argyll were placed under the command of the Marquis of Atholl. They were much more numerous than the followers of Argyll. Among them were the Camerons, the Macleans, and the Macdonalds. They were disbanded on the 21st of June. While Atholl's army was encamped at Aird Rannoch, Lochiel's men, mistaking in the night-time for Argyll's followers, a reconnoitering party sent out by Atholl, fired upon it and killed four or five men. Atholl resolved to place Lochiel under arrest. Lochiel withdrew his men to some distance from the main body of the army, and was joined by the Macleans, who promised to stand by him. As there was a possibility that the Macdonalds would follow the example of the Macleans, Atholl wisely concluded to leave Sir Ewen alone. Some time afterwards, however, he was mean enough to try to arrest him for the mistake committed by his men.

After the escape of the Earl of Argyll to Holland in 1681, the Marquis of Atholl was appointed Lord-Lieutenant of the county of Argyle. He held his court at Inverary, where he had 600 men under the command of Stewart of Ballechan, when Argyll returned in 1685. After the execution of Argyll, he allowed the lands of the Campbells to be plundered by his own retainers and others. Among those who took part in the work of spoliation were Struan Murray, Stewart of Ballechan, the Duke of Gordon's men, the Mackays of Strathnaver, the Stewarts of Appin, the Mackenzies of Lochalsh, the Macalisters of Tarbert, the Macphies of Islay, the Camerons of Lochaber, the Macdonalds of Keppoch, the Macdonalds of Glencoe, and the Macleans of Lochbuie, Torloisk, Brolas, Coll, and Ardgour. Lachlan Maclean of Torloisk besieged, captured, and destroyed the castle of Carnassary.

Lachlan Maclean of Brolas died in 1686, and Lachlan Maclean of Torloisk in 1687. On the death of the latter, Sir John Maclean took the management of the Duart estates into his own hands. He appointed John Macleod of Mishnish, Archibald Maclean of Ardtun, Lachlan Maclean of Calgary, and Allan Maclean, agents or factors for him. He visited London in 1688, and thence crossed over to France.

William I., Prince of Orange Nassau, and stadtholder of Holland, married Mary, daughter of Charles I., King of Britain, and had by her a son, who was also named William. William II. was born in 1650. On the 4th of November, 1677, he married Mary, eldest daughter of the Duke of York, afterwards James II. of England. In June, 1688, he received a letter from seven of the leading men in Britain, urging him to accept the rulership of the kingdom. On November 5th, he landed at Torbay in England, expelled his father-in-law from the throne, and compelled him to seek refuge in France. On February 13th, 1689, William and Mary were proclaimed King and Queen of England and Ireland. On the 11th of April, they were proclaimed King and Queen of Scotland.

Sir John Graham of Claverhouse was a man of energy and courage, a strong Episcopalian, and a zealous supporter of King James. He was an experienced warrior and possessed a good share of military skill. He persecuted the Covenanters with ardour and ferocity in 1679, and thus commended himself to King James. He was promoted to the rank of Major-General in 1688, and on the 12th of November in the same year, was created Viscount of Dundee. King James appointed him Commander-in-Chief of his forces in Scotland. Dundee went to the Highlands and succeeded in raising a small army.

King James sailed from Brest in France on the

7th of March, 1689, and landed at Kinsale in Ireland on the 11th. Among those who accompanied him were **Sir John Maclean of Duart and Sir Alexander Maclean of Otter.** On the 21st of March, King James commissioned Sir John to act as colonel of the Maclean regiment, and Hector Maclean of Lochbuie to act as lieutenant-colonel. On receiving his commission Sir John crossed over from Ireland to Mull. The Macleans welcomed their chief with great joy. They were all ready to fight under him, nominally against King William, but really against their hereditary foe, the Earl of Argyll. As hatred of tyranny led the Covenanters to join King William, so hatred of tyranny led the Macleans to join King James.

Early in May, Sir John Maclean sent Hector Maclean of Lochbuie with 300 men to join Dundee. As the Macleans were marching through Badenoch they were suddenly attacked by five troops of horse. They defeated their assailants, and slew the commander and several of those who were with him. A few of themselves were also killed. They joined Dundee on the day after their encounter with the troops. The place at which the skirmish took place was called Knockbreck. It was the first fight in Scotland in behalf of King James.

The Jacobite clans assembled in Lochaber on the 18th of May, but dispersed shortly afterwards. They met again in Lochaber in July, for the purpose of making an expedition into Atholl to save Blair Castle from falling into General Mackay's hands.

Their place of meeting was the lower end of Loch Lochy. They pitched their camp there on Saturday, July 21st, and left on Tuesday morning, July 24th. They marched through Glenroy, over the Drummond Hills—which lie between the upper vale of the Spey and Loch Laggan—and across the Hills of Drumuachter. They arrived in Blair Atholl on Saturday morning, July 27th. On the evening of that day the battle of Killiecrankie, or Rin Rory, was fought.

General Mackay advanced from Dunkeld with 3,000 foot and two troops of horse. He led his men through the Pass of Killiecrankie and arranged them on a narrow field beside the Garry. Dundee had about 2,500 men. He drew them up in battle array on an eminence which was only about a musket-shot from the Williamites. His men were arranged in the following order from right to left: the Macleans; 300 Irishmen under Colonel Cannon; the Macdonalds of Moydart; the Macdonells of Glengarry and the Grants of Glenmoriston; a small squadron of cavalry under Sir William Wallace; the Camerons under Sir Ewen of Lochiel; a battalion under Sir Alexander Maclean of Otter; and the Macdonalds of Sleat, Keppoch, and Glencoe. The battle began about half an hour before sunset. The Highlanders, while moving down the hill, received three successive volleys from Mackay's line. When they got near their enemies they fired at them, and then fell upon them with their swords. The battle lasted only a few minutes. The Highlanders gained a magnificent victory. Still it was a dear victory to them; about 800 of them were slain. Besides, they lost their commander, the only man who could keep them together and lead them to another victory. Of Mackay's men 2,000 were either killed or taken prisoners.

On the fall of Dundee, Colonel Cannon, who was next to him in rank, assumed the command of the army. He was utterly unfit for his new position. He attacked the Cameronians at Dunkeld on Wednesday, the 21st of August; but, after a stubborn fight of over four hours, was defeated with the loss of 300 men. The Highlanders retired from Dunkeld to Blair Atholl, and on the 24th of the month dispersed to their respective homes. Colonel Cannon and his Irishmen went to Mull with Sir John Maclean. According to the Ardgour MS., Sir George Rooke, one of King William's admirals, attacked the castle of Duart in 1689, but was unable to capture it.

King James appointed Major-General Buchan Commander-in-Chief of all his forces in Scotland. Colonel Cannon was next in command to him. Buchan arrived in Scotland in April, 1690. Only about 1200 men rallied to his standard. Of these, 200 were Macleans, commanded by Captain Allan Maclean, a near relative of Sir John, and Captain John Maclean, a brother of Sir Alexander Maclean of Otter. Sir Thomas Livingstone, at the head of a strong force of cavalry and some infantry, surprised General Buchan at Cromdale on the morning of May 1st, 1690, and easily defeated him. Four hundred of the Highlanders were either killed or taken prisoners. Buchan was an old soldier and a commander of some skill. On July 1st, 1690, James was defeated at the battle of the Boyne. King William was now full master of England, Scotland, and Ireland.

On the execution of the ninth Earl of Argyll in 1685, Archibald, his son and heir, fled to Holland. He returned with the Prince of Orange in 1688, and was allowed to take possession of all the titles and estates which had belonged to his father. He invaded Mull with a strong force about the beginning of October, 1690. According to one account he had 2,500 men; according to another account, he had only 1,600 foot and sixty horse. Sir John Maclean, accompanied by a few armed followers, took refuge in Cairnburgh. He seems to have left the castle of Duart in charge of Captain James Maclean, son of Archibald Maclean of Ardtun. The most of the Macleans surrendered their arms to Argyll, and took the oath of allegiance to King William. On October 22d, 1690, Argyll wrote the tutor of Torloisk, asking him to inform the lairds of Ardgour, Lochbuie, and Kinlochaline, and others of the name of Maclean, that unless they would immediately deliver up their arms under oath, and surrender their forts, he would not receive them under protection. About the same time he instructed John Campbell, bailie of Jura and governor of Aros, to fortify the old castle of Aros, and to seize the persons and goods of all in Mull, Coll, and Tiree, who continued in rebellion. He also instructed Colin Campbell of Braeglen to take possession of the castle of Moy.

In the spring of 1691, the Scottish Jacobites received a formal permission from the exiled King James to enter into negotiations with the Government for surrendering to it. Having obtained this permission, they applied to the Government, and obtained a cessation of hostilities until October 1st. On the 27th of August the Government issued a proclamation, promising an indemnity to all who had been in arms and who should take the oath of allegiance to the Government before January 1st, 1692. On March 31st, 1691, Sir John surrendered Cairnburgh and Duart Castles to the Government. On April 26th, he received an order from John, Earl of Tweeddale, Chancellor of Scotland, permitting himself and his two servants to travel from the place of his residence to any place in England or Flanders, to throw himself upon the King's mercy. He proceeded to London and was graciously received by William, who desired him to accompany him to his next campaign on the continent, and promised to do the best he could for him on his return. Sir John went back to Edinburgh to put matters in order before leaving for the continent. While in Edinburgh, Johnstone, the Secretary of State of Scotland, treated him very unkindly, and threatened to throw him into prison. He hastened back to London, but found that the King had gone over to the continent. He followed the King with the intention of joining him. When he landed on the continent he heard that King William had lost the battle of Steinkirk, which was fought on August 3d, 1692. He was also led to believe that there would be a counter-revolution in Britain in a very short time, and that King James would be restored. In his blind attachment to the Stewarts, he joined the exiled James at St. Germains instead of joining King William. This foolish step ruined his prospects. Had he followed King William he might possibly have recovered a part of his estate from the grasp of Argyll.

King William died on March 8th, 1702, and was succeeded by Anne, second daughter of King James. Shortly after her accession to the throne an indemnity was granted to all who had followed her father to France. Sir John Maclean returned to London about the beginning of 1704.

In September, 1703, Lord Lovat informed the Duke of Queensberry that the Duke of Atholl, the Duke of Hamilton, the Earl of Cromarty and others were engaged in a plot to dethrone Queen Anne and place her brother James, son and heir of James II., upon the throne. Sir John Maclean was immediately arrested on suspicion of being concerned in the plot referred to ; but as there was no proof against him he was set at liberty in a short time. The probability is that there was really no such plot. Lord Lovat was not incapable of inventing and spreading a false story. Sir John received from Queen Anne a pension of £500 sterling a year, which he enjoyed during her reign. He resided in London, but visited the Highlands occasionally.

It is proper to state that King William, after he had reduced the Highlands to obedience, allowed yearly pensions to the heads of the clans. The same plan was continued by the Government in Queen Anne's time. The sum allowed to each chief was about £360 sterling. The total spent annually in pensions among the chiefs was between £3,000 and £4,000.

On May 1st, 1707, Scotland and England were united under one legislature. In March, 1708, James, son of King James II., made an abortive attempt to enter Scotland, with twelve battalions of French soldiers, to incite an insurrection in his favour. On August 1st, 1714, Queen Anne died, and was succeeded by the Elector of Hanover, George I. of Britain. In January, 1715, the Parliament was dissolved, and writs issued for an election. When the Parliament met on the 17th of March, the Whigs, who had been out of office during the latter part of Queen Anne's reign, had a large majority on their side. The consequence was that the Tory ministry was dismissed, and a Whig ministry installed in its place. Among those who were deprived of their offices and emoluments was John Erskine, Earl of Mar, an accomplished courtier, and an able speaker, but a selfish politician.

At the time of Queen Anne's death, Sir John Maclean was at Achnacarry in Lochaber. When the governor of Fort William received the news of her death, he kept the matter to himself, and sent a kind invitation to the chief of the Macleans, John Cameron of Lochiel, and other Jacobites to come and dine with him. Lachlan Maclean of Grulin happened to notice that the governor's residence was surrounded by soldiers. He spoke to Sir John in Gaelic and made known the state of matters to him. The governor tried to arrest both Sir John and Lochiel, but they got out of the house and succeeded in making their escape.

In January, 1715, the following chiefs and chieftains signed a loyal address to King George :—Sir John Maclean, Macdonell of Glengarry, Mackenzie of Frazerdale, Cameron of Lochiel, Macleod of Contullich, Macdonald of Keppoch, Grant of Glenmoriston, Mackintosh of Mackintosh, Chisholm of Comar, Macpherson of Cluny, and Sir Donald Macdonald of Sleat. The address was written by Lord Grange, a brother of the Earl of Mar, but evidently composed by the latter. When Mar presented it to King George, he gruffly and foolishly refused to receive it. Mar at once departed for the Highlands to stir up a rebellion against the new Government. He had no further use for King George ; he wanted to see James, the son of King James, on the throne.

On August 26th, the Jacobites held a meeting at Braemar to consider what steps to take. After an eloquent speech from Mar, they agreed to return to their homes, raise their forces, and assemble at Aboyne on the 3d of September. They met on the day appointed. On the 6th of the month they unfurled the royal banner at Castletown, and proclaimed young James King, by the title of James VII. of Scotland, and James III. of England, Ireland, and their dependencies. During the night of September 8th, 100 of the Jacobite party tried to capture the castle of Edinburgh. Through their folly in allowing a woman to know their intention, their attempt failed. The garrison was prepared to meet them. Four of them, Captain Maclean, Alexander Ramsay, George Boswell, and a man named Lesley, were taken prisoners. The rest succeeded in making their escape.

The Earl of Mar acted as commander-in-chief of the Jacobites, and had his head-quarters at the city of Perth. He knew nothing at all about military matters, and lacked the ability to make a right use of the military skill of others. He was not only unfit to command an army, but utterly unfit to direct and control a large body of men in any capacity. He could intrigue, tell plausible stories, and make speeches; but he could really do nothing else.

About the 17th of September, 1715, a body of Highlanders, consisting of Macleans, Macdonalds from Moydart, and Camerons, attacked Fort William, and succeeded in taking two of the outworks and making prisoners of the men who defended them, twenty-six in number. Owing to the want of cannon they were unable to capture the fort itself. In October **Sir John Maclean** raised 300 men in Mull, Coll, Tiree, and Morvern, and was joined by young Ardgour with 100 men. On the 13th of the month he passed, with these 400 men, at the current of Ardgour, seven miles from Fort William, and on the following day, passing Callart, marched up through Glencoe to Glenorchy. The Macdonells of Glengarry, the Macdonalds of Moydart, the Campbells of Glenorchy, and others also assembled in Glenorchy. General Gordon, an experienced veteran, commanded them. He led them to Inverary, apparently to encourage those who were afraid of the power of Argyll, to rise up in arms. From Inverary he led his forces through Strathfillan towards Auchterarder. Among those who joined him were 400 of the Campbells of Breadalbane, under Glendaruel and Glenlyon.

John Campbell, second Duke of Argyll, possessed ability of a high order, and was a very excellent man. He distinguished himself highly as a general, statesman, and orator. Of all the Campbell chiefs he was the most renowned. He was born in 1678, and succeeded his father as Duke of Argyll in 1703. He took an active part in promoting the legislative union between Scotland and England, and was rewarded for his services, in 1704, by being created a peer of England by the title of Earl of Greenwich. He fought under Marlborough, and was raised to the rank of lieutenant-general in 1709. He was appointed Commander-in-Chief of the royal forces in Scotland in 1715. He had his head-quarters at Stirling.

On Thursday morning, November 10th, 1715, Mar led his forces out of Perth with the intention of proceeding to Stirling. He encamped at Auchterarder in the evening, but sent two squadrons of horse on to Dunblane. On Friday, the 11th, he was joined by General Gordon with the Macleans, Macdonalds, and other clans. On Saturday, the 12th, he led his army to Ardoch and thence to the bridge of Kinbuck. On the same day Argyll took possession of Dunblane. On the morning of Sunday, the 13th, the two armies met at Sheriffmuir. Mar had 8,400 men under him. He arranged his followers in two lines. The first line was drawn up in the following order:—a squadron of horse on the extreme right under the Master of Sinclair, son of Sinclair of Hermandston in Haddingtonshire; two squadrons of horse, under the Marquis of Huntly; the Macdonalds of Moydart; the Macdonells of Glengarry; the Macdonalds of Sleat; the Mackinnons; the Macdonalds of Glencoe; the Campbells of Breadalbane; the Macleans; the Camerons; the Stewarts of Appin; the men of Strathdon and Glenlivet, under Gordon of Glenbucket; and the Perthshire squadron of horse. This line was commanded by General Gordon. The second line was made up of two squadrons of horse, under the Earl Marischal; the Mackenzies; two battalions of Huntly's men; the Earl of Panmure's followers; the Marquis of Tullibardine's men; Lord Drummond's men; the Robertsons of Struan; and the Angus squadron of horse, under the Earl of Strathmore. Mar's reserve consisted of 400 horse. The second line was commanded by General Hamilton and Mar himself. The Duke of Argyll had 2,300 foot and 1,200 cavalry. Argyll's first line consisted of Evans's dragoons, the Scots Greys, a squadron of the Earl of Stair's dragoons, 1,800 foot, General Carpenter's dragoons, Ker's dragoons, and a squadron of Stair's dragoons. The second line was composed of two battalions of foot, with a squadron of dragoons on each wing. The Duke himself commanded the right wing, General Wightman the centre, and General Mitham the left wing. The battle began in the afternoon. It is said that Sir John Maclean addressed his clan as follows:—"Gentlemen, this is a day we have long wished to see. Yonder stands Maccallen Mor for King George; here stands Maclean for King James. God bless Maclean and King James. Charge, gentlemen." The Macdonalds of Moydart, the Macdonells of Glengarry, the Macdonalds of Sleat, the Campbells of Breadalbane, and the Macleans acted with great bravery, and routed Argyll's left wing in eight minutes. The Earl Marischal and Lord Drummond pursued the fugitives towards Dunblane.

Argyll defeated Mar's right wing, but met with stout opposition from the Perthshire and Angus horse. The victorious Highlanders of the right wing marched across the field of battle and drew up on an eminence, called the Stony Hill of Kippendavie. The Master of Stair and the Marquis of Atholl, through dissatisfaction with the Earl of Mar, took no active part in the battle. The Macgregors and the Macphersons watched it from a safe distance, but did not strike a blow. The Macdonalds of Keppoch also kept out of the fight. Mar retired to Ardoch, and Argyll to Dunblane. Of Argyll's men 290 were killed, 187 wounded, and 133 taken prisoners. According to the account given by the Jacobites, they had only sixty men killed and a few wounded. It is probable, however, that their losses in killed and wounded amounted at least to 400 men. Argyll took eighty-two prisoners with him to Stirling. Among the slain on the side of the Jacobites was the accomplished Ailein Muideartach. John Lyon, third Earl of Strathmore, was also killed. Of the Macleans only six men fell—Captain Allan Maclean of the Morvern family and five privates. Donald Maclean of Brolas, who was Sir John's lieutenant-colonel, was wounded.

On November 6th, Thomas Foster, a member of Parliament for the county of Northumberland, and the Earl of Derwentwater raised the standard of rebellion in England against King George. Mar, with great folly, sent a body of men under

Brigadier William Mackintosh of Borlum, to their assistance. The force under Borlum consisted of Mar's own regiment, the Mackintosh regiment, Lord Charles Murray's regiment, a part of the Earl of Strathmore's regiment, and others. Borlum arrived at Kelso on Saturday, October 22d. Here he found Alexander Gordon, fifth Viscount of Kenmure, and George Seton, fifth Earl of Wintoun, awaiting his arrival. The insurgents crossed the English border on November 1st, and marched to Brampton. Foster, who had been appointed by the Earl of Mar general of the Jacobite forces in England, now assumed the commandership, a position for which he did not possess a single qualification. He led his army to Preston, where he allowed it to be cooped up by his opponents. On Saturday, November 12th, General Wills attacked the Jacobites, but was repulsed. On the 13th he was joined by General Carpenter. On Monday morning, November 14th, Foster and his followers were compelled to surrender at discretion. The men taken prisoners numbered in all 1,468. Of these 1,005 were Scotsmen, and 463 Englishmen. Of the former, 143 were either noblemen or gentlemen, and of the latter, seventy-five.

On the 31st of January, 1716, Mar left Perth, and led his army towards Montrose, where he arrived on February 3d. On the 4th, Prince James, the Earl of Mar, the Earl of Milfort, Lord Drummond, and others went on board a small French vessel, and sailed to Waldham in French

Flanders. Prince James had been in Scotland only since the 22d of December. When he arrived he was accompanied only by six men.

General Gordon led the Jacobite army to Aberdeen, and there made known to them on the morning of February 6th that Prince James had set sail for France and that the insurrection was now at an end. With sad hearts they marched in the direction of Old Meldrum, and thence through Strathspey into Badenoch, where they quietly dispersed in various directions.

George I. treated the prisoners taken at Preston and other places, and indeed all the rebels whom he could find, with mean and savage vindictiveness. Major Nairne, Captain Philip Lockhart, Captain Shaftoe, and Ensign Nairne were tried before a court-martial and condemned for having deserted the King's army. They were shot on the 2d of December, 1715. The Earl of Derwentwater and Viscount Kenmure, both excellent men, were executed at Tower Hill on February 24th, 1716. Five prisoners were executed at Tyburn, and twenty-two in Lancashire. Seven hundred of the men taken at Preston, of whom the great majority were Highlanders, were by "the King's mercy" transported and sold as slaves to West India merchants. The Earl of Nottingham, Lord Alysford, Lord Finch, and Lord Guernsey were deprived of their offices because they were inclined to be somewhat merciful towards the men who had been in rebellion. The Duke of Argyll, the very man who had crushed the insurrection in Scotland, was punished. He was deprived of the command of the army in Scotland and General Carpenter appointed in his place. He committed no crime, but he was looked upon as being too humane towards his countrymen, as being unwilling to butcher them and sell them into slavery. If George I. was not equal in ferocity to his grandson, the Duke of Cumberland, he was certainly not far behind. The Earl of Wintoun, Foster, Brigadier Mackintosh, and a number of other persons succeeded in making their escape from the prisons in which they had been confined. It is probable that the jail-keepers were not as thirsty for their blood as their tyrannical Hanoverian King.

About forty persons were deprived of their estates for the rebellion of 1715. The estates were placed in the hands of trustees and ordered to be sold for the benefit of the public. They were purchased by a mercantile company in London, known as the York Building Company. They were all disposed of by the company in course of time. Some of them were bought in by friends of the lawful heirs and conveyed to them. Many of them, however, became the property of persons who had no hereditary claim to them.

Sir John Maclean caught cold on the night of his escape from Fort William, and never got over it. After the battle of Sheriffmuir he became unwell at Perth. He accompanied his men as far as Keith. Here he bade farewell to them, and retired to Gordon Castle in the vicinity of Fochabers, Elginshire. He died there of consumption on March 12th, 1716, in the forty-sixth year of his age. He was buried in the church of Raffin in Banffshire, in the burial-place of the Gordons of Buckie. He was the last of the powerful Lords of Duart.

Although Sir John Maclean held possession of the estate of Duart for some time, he never owned it. He was only ten years of age when it became the property of the crown in 1681. After the revolution in 1688, it was handed over to the Earl of Argyll. Sir John was absolutely landless when his clan loyally followed him, first to Killiecrankie, and afterwards to Sheriffmuir.

Sir John of Duart was a man of good ability, and was thoroughly honest and honourable in his ways. He was well educated, and spoke Gaelic, English, and French fluently. He was generous by nature, affable in his manners, brave and cool in battle, and fitted in every way to command the respect and love of his clan. He was probably the subject of more pathetic songs than any other Highland chief.

XX. Sir Eachann.

Sir Hector, only son of Sir John Maclean of Duart, was born at Calais in France on November 6th, 1703. He was taken to Scotland in 1707 and placed under the care of Donald Maclean, laird of Coll. He remained in Coll during eleven years.

He succeeded his father as chief of the Clan Gillean in 1716. He was sent to Edinburgh, to study at the university, in 1718. He made good progress in languages, philosophy, and mathematics. He went to France in 1721 to complete his education. One of the subjects to which he paid special attention there was civil law. He returned to Scotland in 1726. He went back to France in 1728. He lived sometimes at Boulogne and at other times in Paris. He had really no home.

Charles Stewart, son of Prince James, son of King James II., landed at Borodale in Moydart on July 25th, 1745. The Stewart standard was raised at Glenfinnan on the 19th of August. It was unfurled by William Murray, Marquis of Tullibardine, one of the men who had fought at Sheriffmuir in 1715. Prince James was acknowledged as king, and Charles proclaimed regent of the kingdoms of Scotland, England, France, and Ireland, and the dominions thereunto belonging. Prince Charles and his followers arrived at Blair Atholl on the 30th of August, and entered Perth on the 4th of September. He appointed Lord George Murray lieutenant-general of his forces.

Prince Charles defeated Sir John Cope at the battle of Prestonpans, or Gledsmuir, on Saturday the 21st of September. He invaded England with 4,500 men on the 8th of November, captured Carlisle on the 15th, entered Preston on the 26th and Manchester on the 28th, and arrived at Derby on the 4th of December. He was now within

127 miles of London, but had been joined only by 300 Englishmen. On the 6th of December he commenced a retreat towards Carlisle, and crossed the Esk back into Scotland on the 20th. He arrived in Glasgow on the 26th, and remained there a few days. On Thursday, the 17th of January, 1746, he defeated General Hawley at Falkirk. On Monday, the 14th of April, he pitched his camp on the flat moor of Drummossie, near Culloden, to await the approach of the Duke of Cumberland.

Sir Hector Maclean arrived in Edinburgh about the first of June, 1745, with the intention of joining Prince Charles. He lodged with a man named Blair. This man, in the expectation of obtaining a good reward for his political zeal, made known to the Government that Sir Hector was staying with him. On the 5th of June, Sir Hector was arrested and placed in confinement in Edinburgh Castle. Two men who were with him, Lachlan Maclean and George Bleau of Castlehill, were seized and imprisoned at the same time. The three of them were sent up to London.

John Campbell, son of John Campbell of Mamore, joined General Hawley with 1,000 men on the morning of the day on which the battle of Falkirk was fought. Shortly after his departure, Charles Maclean of Drimnin raised 500 Macleans and joined Prince Charles. The Maclachlans and themselves were formed into one regiment. Lachlan Maclachlan, chief of his clan, was appointed colonel, and Charles of Drimnin, lieutenant-colonel. The Maclachlans numbered about 300.

A party of Campbells invaded Morvern while the fighting men of that district were absent with Prince Charles, and committed disgraceful acts of barbarity. They plundered all the houses along the coast occupied either by Macleans or Camerons, stripped the women and children of their clothes, killed all the horses that came in their way, and burnt the byres and all the cattle in them.

Lord George Murray arrived at Drummossie Moor on Tuesday, the 15th of April. He objected at once to it as a place for encountering the Duke of Cumberland. He urged Prince Charles to leave it and pitch his camp on a hilly and boggy spot south of the water of Nairn. His reasons for proposing this course were: first, the necessity of fighting on a field in which Cumberland's cavalry could not act with advantage; secondly, the desirableness of giving the Macphersons, the Macgregors, the Mackinnons, the Macdonalds of Barrisdale, and the followers of the Earl of Cromarty time to arrive; and thirdly, the unfit condition of the men to engage, owing to their want of food. Prince Charles, instigated by his Irish and French officers, rejected Murray's advice. Murray then proposed a night march towards Nairn, where the Duke of Cumberland was encamped. The Prince hailed this proposal with great alacrity. But there were serious difficulties in the way. In the first place, it was neccessary to march ten miles and arrive at Nairn at two o'clock in the morning. In the second place, through the carelessness of those who had charge of the commissariat department, there was only one biscuit for each man in the camp. Indeed, the large majority of those who were expected to march to Nairn had not tasted any food for the last day and a half. Murray's intention was to surprise Cumberland's army before daylight. The plan of making a night march was resolved on about three o'clock in the afternoon. During the day a large number of half-starved men wandered off towards Inverness in search of food. The march to Nairn began at eight o'clock in the evening. Murray, at the head of the Atholl men, led the van, while the Duke of Perth had charge of the rear. The night was very dark, and the ground rough and hard to travel. The van arrived at Knockan Buie, or Yellow Knowe, two miles beyond Kilravock, about one o'clock in the morning. Lord Drummond and the Duke of Perth came to Murray and urged him to halt there for the rear. Their request was complied with. Murray had now marched ten miles, but he was still nearly four miles from Nairn. At two o'clock in the morning the rear was yet about a mile behind. As it was clearly impossible to get to Cumberland's camp in time to surprise it, he ordered a retreat. The Prince's army was back at Drummossie Moor about half-past five in the morning. The men were hungry, fatigued, sleepy, and dissatisfied. Murray again proposed to cross the river Nairn, and occupy a suitable place for battle, but Charles paid no attention to him. The Prince was a handsome, brave, and amiable man; but he was as stubborn as his grandfather, and just as full of absurd notions respecting the rights of kings. Murray was a loyal Jacobite, and as able a general as had ever led a Highland army, except Montrose; but he was blunt and honest and unwilling to flatter. Consequently, he was disliked by the Prince and his Frenchified followers.

On Wednesday, the 16th of April, 1746, about ten o'clock, the Jacobite forces were drawn up for battle on Drummossie, or Culloden Moor. The first line, reckoning from right to left, comprised the Atholl men, the Camerons, the Stewarts of Appin, the Frasers, the Mackintoshes and Macgillivrays, the Maclachlans and Macleans, the Farquharsons, John Roy Stewart's regiment, the Macdonalds of Moydart, the Macdonalds of Keppoch, and the Macdonells of Glengarry. Each wing was flanked by four field-pieces. There were also four field-pieces in the centre, between the Mackintoshes and Macgillivrays on the right and the Maclachlans and Macleans on the left. The second line consisted of Lord Lewis Gordon's regiment in column, Lord Ogilvie's, the Duke of Perth's, Lord John Drummond's French Royal Scots, the Irish Picquets, and Glenbucket's regiment in column. It was flanked on the right by Lord Elcho's horse guards and Fitzjames's horse, and on the left by

Lord Balmerino's horse guards. The reserve consisted of Strathallan's horse, Pitsligo's horse, and Lord Kilmarnock's foot guards, a body of cavalrymen who had no horses. There were only 250 horse in all. Murray commanded on the right of the first line, Lord John Drummond in the centre, and the Duke of Perth on the left. The second line was under the command of General Stapleton. The whole army amounted only to about 5,000. The most of these had nothing to eat during the last two days, except one biscuit. Some of them were nodding with sleep while they stood in the ranks. The Macdonalds and Macdonells were dissatisfied because they had not been placed on the right wing, and had made up their minds to take no part in the fight.

The Duke of Cumberland had 8,100 foot and 900 horse. His first line, reckoning from left to right, consisted of Barrel's regiment, Munro's, the Scots Fusiliers, Price's regiment, Cholmondley's regiment, the Scots Royals, and Pultney's regiment. It was flanked on the right by Ker's and Cobham's dragoons, and on the left by Kingston's dragoons. The second line consisted of Semple's regiment, Bligh's, Ligonier's, Fleming's, Howard's, and Bathereau's. Wolfe's regiment stood at right angles to the first and second lines, and at some distance away from them. Blakeney's dragoons formed the reserve. Each line was three deep. There were two pieces of cannon between every two regiments in the first line, three in the centre of the second line, and three on the flank of Semple's regiment. The first line was commanded by the Earl of Albemarle, the second by General Huske, and the reserve by Brigadier Mordaunt. The Campbells of Argyleshire had charge of the baggage, and as it did not contain any heiresses or titles to land they acted with scrupulous honesty.

The battle commenced about one o'clock, by a discharge of artillery. About the same time a shower of sleet from the north-east began to beat violently in the faces of the starving Highlanders. The Jacobites were cut down in large numbers by the cannon of the English, while their own artillery did little or no execution. About half-past one o'clock the Duke of Perth was ordered to advance with the left, but the Macdonalds and Macdonells refused to move. The Mackintoshes, who were near the centre of the first line, lost all patience and rushed forward to attack their foes. Murray immediately ordered a general charge and rode into the fight at the head of his men. In a few seconds the Atholl men, Camerons, Stewarts of Appin, Frasers, Mackintoshes and Macgillivrays, Maclachlans and Macleans, Farquharsons, and John Roy Stewart's men were all in motion. They were stormed at with musketry and grape-shot in front, and with a furious fire on their flank from Wolfe's regiment, but they pressed forward without flinching. They attacked the first line sword in hand and soon routed Barrel's regiment and Munro's. While advancing towards the second line they were cut down so thickly that they were forced to turn back. In the course of a few moments the whole Jacobite army gave way. The battle of Culloden was now over. It lasted only about forty minutes. About 1,200 of the Jacobites lay on the field, some dead, many only wounded. The English army had fifty killed and 259 wounded.

Lachlan Maclachlan, colonel of the united regiment of the Maclachlans and the Macleans, was killed by a cannon-ball at the beginning of the action. Charles Maclean of Drimnin, his lieutenant-colonel, then assumed the command, and led the regiment in the brilliant charge of the clans. As he was retreating, he missed his son Lachlan, and enquired of Allan, another of his sons, what had become of him. Allan, who was himself wounded, told him that he was afraid that Lachlan had been killed. His death shall not be unavenged, answered the grieved father, and immediately faced about. Allan began to beseech him not to go back. To the pleading Allan, his father said, Ailein, coma leat mise; ma's toil leat do bheatha thoir an aithre dhuit fhein, Allan, never mind me; if you value your life take care of yourself. The gallant but rash Charles went back, attacked two troopers, killed one, and wounded the other; but was in the course of a few minutes cut down by fresh foes. Allan escaped from the field, and got back to Drimnin.

The Duke of Cumberland murdered all the wounded men that he found on the field of Cul-

loden or in huts near it. He spent two days in
collecting and butchering them. He went to Fort
Augustus on the 23d of May, and made it his
head-quarters. He sent the most brutal of his
followers in detachments through the districts in
which the Jacobites lived. These men plundered
mansions and huts and then set fire to them.
They shot down the men as if they had been savage
wolves. They insulted, ravished, and abused the
women, stripped them of their clothes and rings,
and left themselves and their children to starve.
They collected horses, cattle, sheep, and goats in
thousands, drove them to Fort Augustus, sold
them to Whig speculators from England and the
Lowlands, and pocketed the proceeds as prize-
money. In all his butcheries, robberies, burnings,
and other atrocities, the Duke of Cumberland had
zealous assistants in General Hawley, Lieutenant-
Colonel Howard, Captain Caroline Scott, Major
Lockhart, and other varnished savages. The Government also acted in a very sanguinary manner
towards the rebels. They caused a large number
to be hanged by the neck for some time; to be
cut down while they were yet alive; to have their
bowels taken out and burnt before their faces; to
have their heads severed from their necks; and to
have their bodies divided into four quarters.
Hundreds of Highlanders were transported to the
West Indies and Carolina.

Sir Hector Maclean was set at liberty as a
French prisoner, in May, 1747. He left London

immediately and crossed over to France. He paid a visit to Rome in 1750. He had an attack of apoplexy in the month of July, but partly recovered from it. He had a second attack in November, and died shortly afterwards. He was buried in Rome.

Sir Hector was low in stature, and lame in one leg; but he was sturdy and active, and capable of bearing fatigue. His complexion was fair, his eyes large and piercing, and his manners and address polite and agreeable. He was a good Latin scholar, and spoke Gaelic, English, French, and Italian. He was well read and had a strong memory and clear judgment. The Ardgour MS. tells us that he was rather too generous. This statement is only a half-truth; he was unfortunately a little too fond of strong drink. He was never married.

CHAPTER X.

Genealogy of the Macleans of Duart.

I. Gillean of the battle-axe had three sons, Bristi, Gillebrìde, and Malise.

II. Malise had apparently two sons, Malcolm and Gilmory.

III. Malcolm married Rioghnach, or Reena, daughter of the Lord of Carrick, and had by her three sons, Donald, Neil, and John Dubh. Donald had four children, Malise, John, Beathag, and Aithbric. Neil had two sons, Diarmad and Malcolm.

IV. John Dubh had two sons, Lachlan Lùbanach and Hector Reaganach. The latter was the progenitor of the Macleans of Lochbuie.

V. Lachlan Lùbanach married Mary, daughter of John, first Lord of the Isles, and had by her seven children, John, Hector Roy, Lachlan, Neil, Somerled, Finvola, and Mary.

VI. Hector Roy, Eachann Ruadh nan Cath,

married a daughter of the Earl of Douglas, by whom he had Lachlan Bronnach.

VII. Lachlan Bronnach had a natural son named Donald by a daughter of Maceachern of Kingerloch. Lachlan married, first, Finvola, daughter of John Borb Macleod of Harris, and had by her two sons, Neil and John Garbh. He married, secondly, Janet, daughter of Alexander Stewart, Earl of Mar, and had by her three children, Lachlan Og, Finvola, and Ann. Donald was the progenitor of the Macleans of Ardgour. Neil was the progenitor of the Macleans of Lehir and Ross. Lachlan Og succeeded his father as chief of the clan. Finvola was married to Celestine of Lochalsh, by whom she had Alexander and two or three daughters, one of whom was married to Allan Cameron of Lochiel. Ann was married to Sir William Munro of Foulis. John Garbh was the progenitor of the Macleans of Coll.

VIII. Lachlan Og married a daughter of Gillespick Roy Campbell, son and heir of Lord Duncan Campbell of Lochow, and had by her two sons, Hector Odhar and Donald.

IX. Hector Odhar was slain by arrows at the battle of Flodden in 1513. He was succeeded in the chiefship by his son, Lachlan Cattanach.

X. Lachlan Cattanach married, first, Marion, daughter of John Maclean of Treshnish, and secondly, Elizabeth, daughter of Archibald Campbell, second Earl of Argyll. He had at least two sons by his first wife, Hector Mor and Allan.

He had a son named Patrick, but it is not certain who Patrick's mother was. According to a document of the year 1545, Patrick was a brother-german of Hector Mor, and was thus a son of Treshnish's daughter. According to the Ardgour MS., he was a natural son, his mother being a girl named Catherine Hay. As Patrick was not a Maclean name, we suspect that the Ardgour MS. is correct. Lachlan Cattanach was assassinated in Edinburgh by Sir John Campbell of Calder in the summer of 1523. Hector Mor succeeded his father in Duart. Allan—the famous Ailein nan Sop— was the progenitor of the Macleans of Gigha. Patrick was justiciar of the South Isles and bailie of Iona in 1545. He received from Queen Mary in August, 1547, a gift of the temporality of the bishopric of the Isles and the abbey of Iona, both of which he resigned in favour of the Rev. John Carsewell in 1567, on condition of receiving an annual pension.

XI. Hector Mor married Mary, daughter of Alexander Macdonald of Islay and the Glens, and had by her two sons and seven daughters, Hector Og, John Dubh, Marion, Mary, Catherine the elder, Julia, Una, Janet, and Catherine the younger. 1. Hector Og succeeded his father. 2. John Dubh was the progenitor of the Macleans of Morvern. 3. Marion was married to Norman Macleod, eleventh of Harris. 4. Mary was married to Donald Macdonald, sixth of Sleat. 5. Catherine the elder was a handsome, high-spirited, and accomplished woman. She was married, first, to Archibald, fourth Earl of Argyll, and, secondly, to Calvagh O' Donnell. It is said that she was married, thirdly, to Shane O' Neill. She was married, lastly, to John Stewart of Appin. Her first husband died in 1553. Her second husband was killed in 1565. Shane O' Neill was slain in 1567. Catherine was with him at the time, but may not have been married to him. She was living in 1576, and was then the wife of John Stewart of Appin. She had no children. 6. Allan Macdonald of Moydart married the eldest daughter of Alasdair Crotach Macleod of Dunvegan, and had at least one son by her, Allan Og. According to the Book of Clanranald, Allan paid a visit to Duart, fell in love with one of Hector Mor's clever girls, and carried her off to Castle Tirim. He lived with her as his wife and had two children by her, John of Strome and another son, probably Angus. Alasdair Crotach's daughter, Allan's lawful wife, found a home with Macdonald of Keppoch. It is a fact that one of Hector Mor's daughters ran off with Allan of Moydart. It is evident that Julia was the girl who committed this act of folly and sin. At any rate she is the only one whose husband is not mentioned in the Ardgour MS. 7. Una was married to Donald Cameron of Lochiel, but had no issue by him. 8. Janet was married to Angus Macdonald, seventh of Glengarry, by whom she had one son, Donald. 9. Catherine the younger was married to Archibald Campbell of

Craignish, by whom she had two sons, Dugald and Tearlach Mór, or Big Charles.

XII. Hector Og married Janet, daughter of Archibald Campbell, fourth Earl of Argyll, and had by her four children, Lachlan Mor, Mary, Janet, and Marion. Mary was married to Angus Macdonald of Islay, by whom she had three children, James, Angus Og, and Margaret. Janet was married, as his third wife, to Roderick Macleod, tenth of Lewis, and had two children, Torquil Dubh and Tormod, or Norman. Marion was married, first, to Hector Roy, sixth of Coll; and, secondly, to Charles Maclean of Inverscadale.

XIII. Lachlan Mor was born in 1557. He married Margaret, second daughter of William Cunningham, sixth Earl of Glencairn, and had by her six children, Hector Og, Lachlan Og, Allan, Gillean, Charles, and a daughter. He was slain at Gruinnart, on August 5th, 1598. 1. Hector Og succeeded his father. 2. Lachlan Og was the progenitor of the later Macleans of Torloisk. 3. Allan lived at Carnnacaillich in Morvern. He married a daughter of Allan Maclean of Ardtornish, and had at least one child, a daughter, who was married to Allan Macquarrie of Ulva. 4. Gillean is described in 1618 as Gillean Maclean of "Coull." He married a daughter of Allan of Ardtornish. 5. Charles seems to have lived in Mull. It is said that he married a daughter of Hector, eighth of Lochbuie. 6. Lachlan Mor's daughter was married to Hector Odhar, ninth of Lochbuie.

XIV. Hector Og married, first, Janet, second daughter of Colin Cam Mackenzie of Kintail, and had by her three children, Hector Mor, Lachlan, and Finvola. He married, secondly, Isabel, daughter of Archibald Acheson of Gosford, by whom he had two sons, Donald and John Dubh. Hector Mor succeeded his father. Lachlan succeeded Hector Mor. Donald was the progenitor of the Macleans of Brolas. John Dubh was the progenitor of the Macleans of Sweden. Finvola was married to John Garbh of Coll.

XV. Hector Mor married Margaret, eldest daughter of Sir Rory Mor Macleod of Dunvegan, but had no issue by her.

XVI. Lachlan married Mary, second daughter of Sir Rory Mor Macleod, and had by her five children, Hector Roy, Allan, Isabel, Mary, and Marion. He was created a baronet in 1631. He died in 1648. 1. Hector Roy succeeded his father. 2. Allan succeeded Hector Roy. 3. Isabel was married to Sir Ewen Cameron of Lochiel, and had seven children, John, Donald, Allan, Margaret, Ann, Catherine, and Janet. John succeeded his father as chief of the Clan Cameron. Donald died without issue. Allan died without male issue. Margaret was married to Alexander Drummond of Balhaldy; Ann, to Allan Maclean of Ardgour; Catherine, to William, third son of Sir Donald Macdonald, tenth of Sleat; and Janet, to John Grant, fourth of Glenmoriston. 4. Mary was married to Sir Lachlan Mor Mackinnon, by whom she had one son, John **Og**. 5. Marion seems to have died young.

XVII. Sir Hector Roy, second baronet, was killed at Inverkeithing, on July 20th, 1651.

XVIII. Sir Allan, third baronet, married Sheela, or Julia, third daughter of John Mor Macleod of Dunvegan, and had one child by her, John, his successor. He died in 1674.

XIX. **Sir** John, fourth baronet, married Mary, daughter of Sir Æneas Macpherson, by whom he had six children, Hector, Louisa, Isabel, Mary, Ann, and Beatrix. Hector succeeded his father in the chiefship. Ann was married to Hector Macquarrie of Ormaig, and had four children, John, Hector, Mary, and Margaret. Beatrix died at the age of fourteen, and is buried at Glendaruel. His wife predeceased Sir John. She was only thirty years of age at the time of her death. She is buried at Inchkenneth. Sir John died at Gordon Castle on March 12th, 1716.

XX. Sir Hector, fifth baronet, was the twentieth chief of the Clan Gillean. He was born at Calais in 1703 and died at Rome in 1750. He was succeeded in the chiefship by Allan, fourth Maclean of Brolas.

CHAPTER XI.

THE MACLEANS OF LOCHBUIE.

I. HECTOR REAGANACH, son of John, was the first Maclean of Lochbuie. He was a venturesome and daring warrior, and was noted for his sternness and determination. He received the lands of Lochbuie from John, first Lord of the Isles. According to tradition these lands were held in possession by a chieftain named Macfadyen. As Macfayden, however, was not in a position to contend with Hector Reaganach and his friends, he considered it the part of wisdom to leave Mull and seek a home somewhere else. Hector Reaganach was married twice. By his first wife he had at least one son, Terlach. By his second wife, Christina, daughter of Murdoch, son of Tormod Macleod of Harris, he had five sons, Murdoch Roy, Donald, Ewen, Thomas, and Malcolm. Terlach was the progenitor of the Macleans of Urchart. Murdoch Roy succeeded his father in

Lochbuie. The descendants of Terlach were known as Clann Thearlaich, or the children of Terlach, and the descendants of Murdoch as Sliochd Mhurchaidh Ruaidh, or the offspring of Murdoch Roy.

II. Murdoch Roy is said to have married a daughter of Roderick Macleod of Lewis. He had two sons, John and Terlach, and also a daughter, who became the wife of William Macleod of Harris.

III. John, son of Murdoch Roy, received a charter of Banvy, Corpach, and other lands in Lochiel, and also of Duror and Glencoe, from John of the Isles, in October, 1461.

IV. Hector, son of John, married Margaret Campbell, and had four children by her, John Og, Murdoch of Scallasdale, Margaret, and Christina. His wife was living in February, 1474. He witnessed a charter in 1478.

V. John Og received, in March, 1492, from John of the Isles and Alexander of Lochalsh, a charter of the office of bailiery of the south half of Tiree. In March, 1494, James IV. confirmed to him all his charters from the Lord of the Isles, and gave him some additional lands in Inverness-shire. In 1499 Lachlan Cattanach, John of Coll, and himself invaded Lochiel's lands, and carried off a large booty. He supported Donald Dubh in 1504. He quarrelled with Lachlan Cattanach in 1506, apparently about their conterminous lands in Morvern and Tiree. In 1507 the Government bound him " to keep the peace" towards Lachlan. In 1512 he attempted to enforce his claim to the lands of Lochiel, but failed. The feud between himself and Lachlan Cattanach was renewed about the same time, but did not last long. In March, 1517, he received remission for all his past offences. In June, 1522, he sold his claim to the lands of Lochiel and Duror, and to the office of bailiery of the south half of Tiree, to Sir John Campbell of Calder. In July, 1528, Calder transferred his title to the lands of Lochiel and Duror to his brother Colin, Earl of Argyll. It is probable that he transferred to his brother, at the same time, the office of bailiery of the south half of Tiree. In 1526, Ailein nan Sop invaded Lochbuie's lands and slew a number of his followers, among them John, his son. In 1529 John Og joined the Macleans of Duart and the Macdonalds in ravaging Roseneath, Craignish, and other Campbell lands.

John Og was born probably about the year 1470. He had two natural sons by the same woman, Murdoch Gearr and Charles. It is said that he married a daughter of Macdougall of Dunolly. He had two sons by his wife, John and Ewen. Murdoch Gearr and Charles were legitimated on September 13th, 1538. John left no issue. Ewen was known as Eoghan a chinn bhig, or Ewen of the little head. He was a distinguished warrior. He was married, and had an ill-tempered and penurious wife. He was killed in a fight with the Macleans of Duart some time before 1538. He was buried in Iona, where his tombstone is still pointed out.

According to the stories of superstition, Eòghan a chinn bhig is still going about in this world. He is always present when any of the Lochbuie family is in distress. He also very frequently attends the funerals of those who belong to that family. He wears his old cloak about him summer and winter, and always carries his trusty sword with him. He is still without his head. He rides a dun horse, the same horse on which he rode to Glen Cainnir, the place in which the battle in which he fell was fought. His horse has no equal in Arabia, or anywhere else. He travels over sea and land with equal facility. Ewen does not confine his wanderings to Scotland. He has been frequently in Ireland, Spain, and other countries. We are told that the cause of his restlessness is that "he fell fasting, his cross and worthless wife having given him no breakfast on the morning on which he left home for Glen Cainnir."

John Og died about the year 1539. His possessions at the time of his death included the lands of Lochbuie, and lands in Tiree, Morvern, Jura, and Scarba. He was succeeded by his eldest son, Murdoch Gearr.

VI. Murchadh Gearr, or Short Murdoch, was born about 1496. In January, 1538, he received from his father, Achalennan, Drimnin, and other lands in Morvern. On the death of his father, his uncle, Murdoch of Scallasdale, seized the estate and tried to keep possession of it. As Murdoch Gearr was only a legitimated son, Murdoch of

Scallasdale was supported by a strong party. Tradition gives the following account of their quarrel and their reconciliation:—When Murdoch of Scallasdale took possession of Lochbuie, Murdoch Gearr was compelled to seek refuge in Ireland. Having collected a number of resolute men in Antrim, he returned to Mull. He landed near Moy Castle after dark. He immediately called to see his old nurse. She told him that she would let loose the cattle, and that when the men who were in the castle came out to drive them back, he could rush with his men to the gate and secure possession of it. Murdoch approved of her plan, but said that it might endanger the life of her husband, who was keeper of the gate. As to that, she replied, Leig an t-earball leis a chraicionn, let the tail go with the hide. The plan proposed by the nurse was acted upon, and Murdoch Gearr became master of the castle of Lochbuie. Shortly afterwards he defeated Murdoch of Scallasdale at the battle of Grulin. After his defeat the latter led his forces to the glen east of Benbuy. During the night Murdoch Gearr entered his uncle's camp, and left his dirk sticking in the ground at his head. Overcome by a feeling of gratitude to his nephew for sparing his life, Murdoch of Scallasdale returned home and caused no further trouble to Murdoch Gearr. The battle of Grulin must have been fought about the year 1540. It is said that the Stewarts of Appin assisted Murdoch of Scallasdale, while the Macleans of Ross assisted Murdoch Gearr.

In June, 1542, Murdoch Gearr received a charter of all the lands which had belonged to his father. He supported Donald Dubh in 1543, and signed the petition addressed to Henry VIII. of England in 1545. In January, 1576, we find him complaining to the Privy Council that John, his son and heir-apparent, had used him very uncourteously, although he was then an old, decrepit man of fourscore years. He also states that John had acted badly towards Allan Maclachlan and Ewen Maclean. John was denounced a rebel. In 1576, Murdoch Gearr was willing to become surety for the good behaviour of John Dubh of Morvern, but Argyll refused to accept him. In 1578 we find John, his son, suing him for having spulzied him, and cast him into irons. It is pretty evident that Murdoch Gearr and his heir were on exceedingly bad terms. Probably John thought that his father should have dropped off at the age of seventy.

Murdoch Gearr married Ann, daughter of Sorley Buie Macdonald, and had five children by her, John Mor, Allan, Ewen, Lachlan, and Ann. He died in January, 1586. John Mor, his eldest son, succeeded him. Allan and Ewen are mentioned in 1579. Lachlan studied for the church. He was accused of trying to obtain the bishopric of the Isles and the abbacy of Iona for himself. He appeared before the Privy Council in May, 1567, denied the charges made against him, and renounced all claim to the bishopric and abbacy in favour of John Carsewell. It is probable that

Lachlan did not understand the art of keeping quiet and getting others to work for him as well as a man who seeks a better parish, or ecclesiastical promotion of any kind, should understand it. He was alive in 1579. Ann, Murdoch Gearr's daughter, was married to John Macnaughton of Dundarave.

VII. John Mor was one of the most expert swordsmen of his day. Tradition relates that a famous Italian swordsman visited Edinburgh, that he offered to fight any man in Scotland, and that John Mor accepted his challenge, defeated, and killed him. In June, 1581, John Mor, Hector, his son, and others attacked Peter Lymburner, burgess of Glasgow, while travelling in the Isle of Mull, robbed him of his pack of merchandise wares, which was worth 3,000 marks, and wounded him in several places. Lymburner lodged a complaint with the Privy Council. As John Mor and his accomplices did not appear before the Council, they were denounced rebels. In April, 1586, John Roy Maclean, a member of the family of Lochbuie, paid a visit to John Mor, but was seized by the latter, thrown into prison, and put in irons. John Auchinross, acting as procurator for John Roy, brought the matter to the notice of the Privy Council. On March 20th, 1588, the Council ordered John Mor to set his captive at liberty within six hours after the receipt of their charge, under pain of rebellion. John Mor married a daughter of James Macdonald of Islay, by whom he had apparently three sons, Hector, Murdoch, and John. He was succeeded by his eldest son, Hector.

VIII. Hector was born about 1555. He was the first of the Lochbuie chieftains who embraced the Protestant religion. He fought, in behalf of the Macdonalds of Islay, against the Macleans of Duart at the battle of Benvigory in 1598. He was taken prisoner by Allan Cameron of Lochiel, carried off to Lochaber, and kept in chains for six months. He was served heir to his grandfather, Murdoch Gearr, in November, 1609. He sold, about the same time, his claim to the lands of Lochiel to Archibald, seventh Earl of Argyll, for the small sum of 400 marks. His chief object was no doubt to take vengeance on Allan of Lochiel for having imprisoned him. He married Margaret, daughter of Archibald Campbell, second of Lochnell, and had by her four sons, Hector Odhar, Charles, Ewen, and Allan. He died about 1614.

IX. Hector Odhar received the lands of Lochbuie from his father in June, 1612. He was served heir to his great-grandfather, Murdoch Gearr, in July, 1615. In March, 1621, he came under obligation to the Government "not to shoot deer." Charles and Ewen, his brothers, and Allan "Anenach" Maclean, his servant, came under a similar obligation. He married the only daughter of Lachlan Mor of Duart, and had at least four children by her, Murdoch Mor, Lachlan Mor, Margaret, and Janet. Margaret was married to

Donald Macquarrie of Ormaig. Janet was married, in 1625, to Campbell of Kilmelfort. Hector Odhar died about 1628.

X. Murdoch Mor, son of Hector Odhar, received the estates from his father in July, 1625. In August, 1631, he came under obligation to the Rev. Martin Macgillivray, minister of the kirks of Killean and Kilfinichen, to pay his own yearly tithes and to compel his vassals and tenants also to pay their tithes; to make the inhabitants of the parishes referred to give due obedience to the discipline of the kirk; to cause them to repair to the kirks to hear the word of God and to participate in the holy sacraments; and also to prevent them from convening in any chapel or any other place within the bounds of Killean and Kilfinichen to hear the word of God or participate in the holy sacraments. If the religion to be maintained by Murdoch Mor was not creideamh a bhata bhuidhe, or the religion of the yellow stick, it was certainly something which bore a very close resemblance to it. Murdoch Mor joined Montrose, along with the Macleans of Duart, in June, 1645, and fought at the battle of Kilsyth. He was with Alister Mac Coll from September, 1645, until April, 1646, plundering Knapdale and Cowall, and other lands occupied by the Campbells. He was deprived of his estates in 1649, but received them afterwards. He married Juliana, fifth daughter of Sir Robert Campbell of Glenorchy. He died about 1662, and was succeeded by his brother, Lachlan Mor.

XI. Lachlan Mor took an active part in 1675 in supporting the Macleans of Duart against the rapacity of the Campbells of Argyll. He had a natural son named Allan. He married Margaret, daughter of Hector Maclean, second of Torloisk, and had four children by her, Murdoch Og, John, Hector, and Mary. Allan received from his father certain lands in life-rent. Murdoch Og married Anne, fourth daughter of Sir Hugh Campbell, sixth of Calder. He died without issue. John married Isabel, daughter of Macdougall of Dunolly, but had no issue. Hector succeeded his father. Mary was married to Ewen, ninth of Ardgour. Lachlan Mor died in 1701, and was interred in the burying-ground in Laggan.

XII. Hector, son of Lachlan Mor, received a charter of the lands of Lochbuie in March, 1670. On the night of March 31st, 1671, he was at Inverary, along with Archibald Campbell, fifth of Lochnell, Colonel Menzies, Maclachlan of Inchconnel, and others. All present were drinking, and at last began quarrelling. Lochbuie and Inchconnel threatened to kill Colonel Menzies, but were prevented from attacking him by some of those present. During the squabble the light went out. Colonel Menzies' servant fired at Lochbuie through the window, but missed him and killed Lochnell. On March 21st, 1689, Lochbuie was appointed lieutenant-colonel of the Maclean regiment, Sir John Maclean of Duart being colonel. In June, 1689, he defeated a body of cavalry, under Sir **Thomas** Livingston, at Knockbreck in Badenoch. **He** fought at the battle of Killiecrankie, which took place shortly afterwards. He was compelled to surrender the castle **of Moy to** the Earl of Argyll on October 22d, 1690. Argyll placed Colin Campbell of Braeglen, with twenty-four men, in charge of the castle.

Hector of Lochbuie married Margaret, second daughter of Colin Campbell, fifth of Lochnell, and had by her seven children, Murdoch, John, Allan, Lachlan, Margaret, Mary, and another daughter. 1. Murdoch succeeded his father in Lochbuie. 2. John received the lands of Pennygoun in life-rent from his father in 1705. 3. Allan received the lands of Garmony in life-rent in 1705. He married Julia, daughter of Lachlan Maclean of the Torloisk family, by whom he had John, Julia, and Finvola. John became laird of Lochbuie. Julia was married to James, son of Donald, third of Brolas; and Finvola, to John, son of Hector Og, son of Donald, first of Brolas. 4. Lachlan received the **lands** of Knockroy in life-rent in 1705. He married Flora, daughter of Lachlan Macquarrie, fourteenth of Ulva, by his wife Catherine, daughter of John Garbh of Coll. Lachlan had by his wife a son named Murdoch, who in course of time became laird **of** Lochbuie. Hector of Lochbuie died some time after 1717.

XIII. Murdoch, thirteenth of Lochbuie, received the estate from his father in 1705. He married

Anne, fourth daughter of Sir Hugh Campbell, sixth of Calder, and had by her four daughters, the eldest of whom became the wife of Donald Campbell of Airds. He was succeeded by his brother, John of Pennygoun.

XIV. John of Pennygoun married Isabel, daughter of Duncan Macdougall of Dunolly, by whom he had Lachlan and other children. He became laird of Lochbuie in 1727, and handed over the management of the estate to his son, Lachlan, in 1733.

Isabel Macdougall was a kind-hearted and brave woman, and was highly esteemed. Some time after the death of her husband, she went to reside on the farm of Drimnantighean, which she held for life by right of dowry. She lived in a small thatched cottage, and had a very pretty garden in front of it. She had six tenants on her farm, four brothers of the name of Livingston, and two Macdougalls. Her total rent from them was eight pounds per year, together with two pounds of tobacco. Her tenants treated her as if she were their mother, worked for her, and served her faithfully. She sued John, seventeenth of Lochbuie, in 1750, for certain moneys which she claimed from the estate. On one occasion she found Maclaine of Scallasdale and his men collecting kelp below her house. She seized a knife, waded out to the spot on which they were at work, cut the ropes used by them in gathering the kelp, and ordered them away. Scallasdale, influenced either by his knowledge of law or the fear of being scalped, promptly obeyed, and left the kelp alone. Isabel lived to a very great age, and spent the last years of her life at Dunolly. When she was dying she requested her friends to send for her tenants in Drimnantighean to carry her body to the grave. Her request was readily complied with by her attached tenants.

XV. Lachlan of Lochbuie married a daughter of Macdougall of Dunolly, by whom he had two children, Hector and Mary. He died on December 31st, 1744. Hector, his only son, succeeded him.

XVI. Hector obtained possession of the estate in June, 1742. He took no part in the rising of 1745. He died unmarried about 1759. He was succeeded by John, son of Allan of Garmony.

About 1750—the year in which Sir Hector Maclean died at Rome—the Macleans of Lochbuie began to distinguish themselves from the Macleans of Duart, and other descendants of Gilleain na Tuaighe, by writing their name Maclaine.

XVII. John Maclaine, Iain Mac Ailein Mhic Eachainn, was served heir male special to Hector Maclean of Lochbuie in February, 1751, and is described as "John McLean, son of Allan McLean of Garmony." He was served heir-general to his cousin, Lachlan Maclean of Lochbuie, in November, 1751, and is described as "John McLean of Lochbuy." He was somewhat rough in his ways, proud of his dignity as laird; but kind and very hospitable.

John of Lochbuie built a large and comfortable house near the old castle of Moy. It was forty feet long, twenty-eight feet wide within the walls, and eighteen feet high on the side walls. It was begun in May, 1750, and finished in 1752. Lochbuie arrested, in 1758, Hector, son of Maclean of Killean, and Allan Maclean of Kilmory, for certain misdemeanours, and confined them as prisoners in his castle for two days. On being set at liberty they sued him for damages. The result was that he was fined 500 marks Scots, and compelled to pay £180 sterling for damages and expenses. It seems that the men whom he imprisoned actually deserved some punishment. He had no right, however, to take the law in his own hands. He received a visit from Dr. Johnson and Boswell in October, 1773. John of Lochbuie found the estate burdened with debts, and certainly did nothing to lessen them. It is indeed evident that through erecting new buildings, exposing himself to prosecutions, and probably also through living beyond his means, he must have greatly increased them. He had a natural son named Gillean. He married Isabel, daughter of Donald Maclean, third of Brolas, and had three children by her, Archibald, Isabel, Catherine, and Margaret. Gillean was the progenitor of the Maclaines of Scallasdale.

XVIII. Archibald, son of John of Lochbuie, received the estate from his father in 1775, or thereabouts. He was a hot-headed, proud, and stubborn man, and was in the habit of using his tongue too freely. In 1776 he placed the estate under two trustees, and resolved to seek his fortune in America. The trustees appointed John Maclean of Grulin as factor under them. Archibald became a lieutenant in the old 84th, or Royal Highland Emigrant Regiment. In due time he was promoted to the rank of captain. About 1779 he quarrelled with his commander, Brigadier Allan Maclean of Torloisk, and brought several charges against him. Captain, or rather captain-lieutenant, Maclaine was tried by court-martial in Quebec, and suspended for six months. When the report of the trial was sent home to Britain, the sentence of suspension was changed to that of dismissal. In 1784 Captain Maclaine left Canada to lay his case personally before the King. He married Barbara Lowther in Boston, and took her with him. During the passage to the Old Country, he had a dispute with a fellow-passenger named Daniel Munro. Munro tried to avoid him, but Captain Maclaine kept up the quarrel day after day. At last he became so enraged against Munro that he started to his state-room for his sword, with the avowed intention of killing him. Munro hid behind the door, and ran his sword through young Lochbuie as the latter was passing by on his way back from his state-room. Munro was tried in Britain, but was acquitted. Captain Maclaine was killed on the 6th of August, 1784. His wife received about £800 from the estate. As Archibald predeceased his father, he was not a chieftain; he was merely a laird. He left his estate to Murdoch Maclaine, son of Lachlan of Knockroy. John of Lochbuie died in 1785.

XIX. Murdoch was born in 1730, and entered the army as an ensign in October, 1761. He went to America shortly after the breaking out of the Revolutionary War. He raised 100 men for the old 84th. He was appointed captain in that regiment in June, 1775. Shortly afterwards he was sent off with thirty recruits for the garrison at Halifax, Nova Scotia. The ship in which he sailed was attacked by an American privateer. He defeated his assailant, and inflicted on it a loss of eleven men killed and thirteen wounded. In 1778 he was sent from Halifax with dispatches to Sir William Howe. He was in South Carolina in 1782, with some companies of his regiment. He returned to Scotland in 1784. He was served heir to Captain Archibald Maclaine of Lochbuie in May, 1785. He sued the trustees of the Lochbuie estate in 1791, and compelled them to give an account of their management of its affairs. He built a new house for himself about the same time. He furnished 100 men for the Argyle Fencibles in 1793. He was appointed lieutenant-colonel of the Dumbarton Fencibles in 1794, and removed to the Argyle Fencibles in 1797. In the latter year those to whom he was indebted tried to get his estate sold, but did not succeed. The debt due by him at that time was £11,120.

Murdoch of Lochbuie married, in 1786, Jane,

daughter of Sir John Campbell of Airds and Ardnamurchan, and had by her eleven children. 1. Murdoch, the eldest son, succeeded his father. 2. John was a lieutenant in the 73d Highlanders, and was killed in an engagement with the natives of Ceylon in 1817. He was a very popular young man. 3. Jane was married to Captain Campbell. 4. Flora was married, first, to Dr. Allan Maclean; and, secondly, to Dr. Whitehead, of Ayr. 5. Margaret was married to Dugald Macdougall of Gallanach. 6. Phœbe was married to Colonel Donald Gregorson of Barrichboye. 7. Elizabeth was married to Donald Campbell of Achnacreig. 8. Harriet was married to John Stewart of Fasnacloich. 9. Catherine died unmarried. 10. Mary was married to John Gregorson of Ardtornish. 11. Jane-Jervis was married to Mr. Scott, of Ettrick Bank, Selkirkshire. Murdoch of Lochbuie died at Moy in July, 1804. He was a man of good qualities, and was highly respected.

XX. Murdoch of Lochbuie was born in 1791. He was for a few years a lieutenant in the 42d Royal Highlanders, and was present in some of the battles in which that regiment was engaged during the Peninsular War. He retired from the army in 1812. He married, in April, 1813, Christina, daughter of Donald Roy Maclean, of Kinloch, and had by her eleven children, Murdoch, Donald, John, Lillias, Jane, Allan, Elizabeth, Marion, Colquhoun, Alexander, and Margaret. He died in August, 1844. Murdoch, his eldest son, was an officer in the 91st Foot, or Argyleshire Regiment. He succeeded his father as chieftain of the Macleans of Lochbuie, but not in the estate. He died unmarried in 1850, and was succeeded in the chieftainship by his brother Donald. Alexander, the youngest son, married Marion-Palmer Sands, by whom he had one son, Alexander. Elizabeth, the third daughter, was married to Dr. Mackenzie.

XXI. Donald, twenty-first laird of Lochbuie, was born in 1816. He went to Batavia in Java, entered into business as a merchant, and amassed quite a fortune. He purchased the estate of Lochbuie from those who held it for debt, and thus fortunately saved it from passing out of the hands of the descendants of Hector Reaganach. All the Macleans and Maclaines on earth have reason to be thankful for Donald's energy and prosperity, and his success in getting possession of the lands of his forefathers. May they remain in the hands of his descendants as long as Scotland must have lairds. Donald made a number of valuable improvements on his estate, and was highly respected by his tenants. He was, like his ancestors before him from the time of Hector Odhar, a firm adherent of the Presbyterian Church.

Donald of Lochbuie married, in 1844, Emilie-Guillaumine, daughter of Charles-Antoine Vincent, and had by her four children, Murdoch-Gillian, Antoine, Emilie-Guillaumine, Rosa-Elizabeth, and Christina-Sarah. He died on October 12th, 1863.

He was succeeded by his elder son, Murdoch-Gillian. Emilie-Guillaumine, his eldest daughter, was married to Frederick Campbell.

XXII. Murdoch-Gillian Maclaine, twenty-second laird of Lochbuie, is the present chieftain of the Maclaines of Lochbuie. He was born in Batavia on September 1st, 1845, and came to Scotland with his father in 1853. He entered the 6th regiment of dragoon guards in 1864, and attained the rank of captain. He married, in June, 1869, Catherine-Marianna, youngest daughter of Salis Schwabe, of Glengyrth, Anglesey, and has seven children by her, Kathlein-Emilie, Mabel-Julia, Edith-Jane, Kenneth-Douglas-Lorn, and Ranald-Gillian. He belongs to the Episcopalian Church.

The Macleans of Scallasdale.

Murdoch, son of Hector, fourth of Lochbuie, was the first Maclean of Scallasdale. He married a daughter of Stewart of Appin. In 1785 there were four brothers in Mull who were descended from him in the male line. Their names were, John, Lachlan, Malcolm, and Hugh. John went to Glasgow, started in the cotton business, and built up quite an industry; but failed in the great financial crisis of 1825. Lachlan studied medicine, and settled in London. He married a Miss Goring. Hugh came to America, settled in Georgia, and became a successful planter. He had a daughter who became somewhat noted in the Civil War.

John, eldest son of the first of the four brothers, was born in Glasgow. He married Isabella Findlay, of Rothes, came to America, and settled in Ontario. William F. Maclean, eldest son of John, was born in Ancaster, Ontario, in 1854. He graduated at the University of Toronto in 1880, and in the same year established "The World," an independent Conservative journal, which is published in Toronto. He was elected to the House of Commons in May, 1892.

The Macleans of Uisken.

We find in 1656 Duncan Maclean, son of Patrick, son of John, described as servant to Murdoch Maclean of Lochbuie. This Duncan was in all probability the father of Angus Maclean of Assapol. Angus married Elizabeth, daughter of Duncan Campbell of Dunstaffnage, and had four children by her, Duncan, Marion, Catherine, and Mary. Duncan lived at Uisken in Mull. He married Mary, daughter of John Maclean of Grulin, by whom he had four sons, Alexander, John, Archibald, and Duncan. Duncan died in 1770. Alexander, the eldest of his sons, was lieutenant-colonel of the 3d West India regiment. According to his own account, he was of the race of the three Duncans and belonged to the family of Lochbuie. He left the sum of £20,000 for the support and education of boys of the name Maclean. John, second son of Duncan, was a captain in the army, and was killed in the Irish Rebellion. Archibald was a lieutenant in the 56th regiment. He was married, and had John-Ralph and other children. Duncan was a lieutenant in the army. John-Ralph Maclean is the only representative of the Uisken family now living.

The Maclaines of Scallasdale.

Gillean, son of John, seventeenth of Lochbuie, studied law, but settled in Scallasdale as tacksman. He married, in 1771, Maria, eldest daughter of Lachlan Macquarrie of Ulva, and had by her five sons and five daughters. 1. Allan, the eldest son, succeeded his father in Scallasdale. He married Marjory, daughter of Angus Gregorson of Ardtornish, by whom he had two sons, Gillean and Angus. Gillean was a merchant in Java. Angus was minister of Ardnamurchan from 1827 to 1841, and died at Ardrishaig in 1877. 2. Archibald will be noticed afterwards. 3. Murdoch was a captain in the 20th regiment, and was killed at the battle of Maida in 1806. He was a twin brother of Archibald. 4. John was a major in the 73d regiment, and was killed at Waterloo in 1815. 5. Hector was a lieutenant-colonel in the army. He married Martha, only child of William Osborne, of Knyeton, in the county of Gloucester, and had by her one child, William-Osborne. Hector died in 1847. William-Osborne, Hector's son, married Anna, daughter of John Thorburn of Murtle, in Aberdeenshire, by whom he had two sons, Hector and John-Thorburn. Hector was a lieutenant in the Royal Horse Artillery. He was taken prisoner at the battle of Maiward, kept for a month in Ayoub Khan's camp, and murdered a few minutes before General Roberts entered Candahar, on September 1st, 1880. John-Thorburn inherited through his mother the property of Murtle. He died without issue in 1892. 6. Alicia, eldest daughter of Gillean of Scallasdale, was married to John Wood, Edinburgh. 7. Julianna was married to Thomas Ross, by whom she had Mary, authoress of "Banners are waving o'er Morvern's dark heath." 8. Flora died unmarried. 9. Mary died unmarried. 10. Margaret-Ann was married to William Craig in Edinburgh.

Archibald Maclaine, second son of Gillean of Scallasdale, was born on January 13th, 1777. He entered the army in early life, and was a captain in the 94th regiment in 1810. In that year he greatly distinguished himself by his gallant defence of Fort Matagorda for fifty-five days, with only 155 men, against 8,000 men under Marshal Soult. For his services on this occasion he was knighted, and promoted to the rank of major in the 87th regiment. He was for some time lieutenant-colonel of the 7th West India regiment. He married, in 1823, Elizabeth Bridges. He died, without issue, in March, 1861. He was at the time of his death a lieutenant-general.

CHAPTER XII.

The Descendants of Terlach Mac Hector.

I. THE MACLEANS OF URCHART.

I. TERLACH MAC HECTOR, or Tearlach Mac Eachainn, was the progenitor of the Macleans of Urchart, Kingerloch, Dochgarroch, and Knock. He was the eldest son of Hector Reaganach, first Maclean of Lochbuie. It is said that he possessed Ardmeanach in Mull, Kilmalieu in Morvern, and Balmaccaan, or Baile-Mhic-Eachainn, and other lands in Glenurchart. He was constable of Urchart Castle from 1394 to 1411. Tradition affirms that the castle of Bona, Caisteal Spioradan, near the lower end of Lochness, was built by him. He seems to have married either a daughter of Ferchar Mackintosh, chief of the Mackintoshes, or of Ferchar Cumming of Altyre, probably a daughter of the former. He had a son named Ferchar.

II. Ferchar Mac Terlach seems to have predeceased his father. He left two children, Teriach and a daughter. The daughter was married to

Rory Macneil of Barra, by whom she had Gilleonan, and other children.

III. Terlach Mac Ferchar was a warlike and prominent man. He witnessed a charter in favour of his youthful nephew, Gilleonan Macneil, in 1427. He was a prisoner in Tantallon Castle in 1431, and had for companions the Lord of the Isles, Lachlan Bronnach of Duart, Torquil Macneill, and "Duncan Persoun," apparently Duncan Macpherson, chief of the Macphersons, and son-in-law of Ferchar Mackintosh. In 1439 Lachlan Bronnach, Terlach Mac Ferchar, and Hector Mac Terlach witnessed an obligation given by Alexander of the Isles to Alexander Sutherland of Dunbeath. It is evident that Terlach Mac Ferchar was a devoted follower of Lachlan Bronnach; and it is just possible that he derived some benefit in the way of getting lands, from the marriage of the latter with Mar's daughter. He had three sons, Hector Buie, Lachlan, and Donald. Lachlan was killed at the battle of Park in 1484. Donald had a daughter named Anna, who was prioress of Iona, and died in 1511.

IV. Hector Buie was chamberlain of Urchart in June, 1440. He became constable of Urchart Castle in 1454, and entertained John, Lord of the Isles, there in 1466.

In Hector Buie's time the Camerons and Kennedies of Lochaber were in the habit of making raids into Glenmoriston and Glenurchart, and carrying off the cattle. But Hector Buie was not a man to be trifled with; he entered Lochaber, plundered the country, and carried off Cameron of Glen-nevis and others as prisoners. Lochiel pursued him with a strong force, and succeeded in capturing several of his followers, among whom were two of his sons. On arriving at Castle Bona, Lochiel demanded the release of the prisoners in Hector Buie's hands, and at the same time threatened, in case of refusal, to hang the prisoners in his own hands. The end was that each of them hanged all the prisoners that he had taken. According to the "Memoirs of Lochiel," Hector Buie refused to exchange prisoners, and killed all the captives in his hands. Provoked by Hector's savage conduct, Lochiel retaliated by hanging in front of the castle, Hector's sons, and the other men whom he had captured. According to the "History of the Clan Terlach," Hector Buie—who had a much larger number of prisoners than his opponent—offered to make a fair exchange, but refused to comply in full with Lochiel's demands. Owing to this refusal the latter hanged Hector's two sons. Hector took immediate vengeance by putting all his prisoners to death.—It may be safely taken for granted that so far as moral qualities were concerned, Hector Buie and Lochiel stood on the same level; they were both, no doubt, capable of committing very cruel deeds. Tradition assures us that ever after the hangings and murders caused by them, the castle of Bona was haunted by noisy and troublesome ghosts. It seems that it became a very unpleasant place to live in.

The Macleans of Kingerloch.

It is asserted that Hector Buie married, first, a daughter of Allan Mac Rory of Moydart; secondly, Margaret, daughter of Malcolm Beg Mackintosh; and, thirdly, a daughter of Hugh Fraser, Lord Lovat. It is also said that he had six sons, Allan Dubh, Neil, Ewen, Terlach, Ferchar, and Alexander. Three of his sons survived him, Ewen, Terlach, and Ferchar. Ewen became laird of Kingerloch. Terlach and Ferchar appear as witnesses in 1498. Terlach was rector of Killindyke in the diocese of Lismore in 1542. Ferchar was Bishop of the Isles in 1529. He resigned his bishopric in 1544. It is said that he was killed at the battle of Pinkie in 1547. According to the "History of the Clan Terlach," he left six children: Roderick, Dean of the Isles; Donald, tacksman of Dochgarroch; James, priest of Glenurchart; Mary, prioress of Iona in 1548; and a daughter who was married to Rory Mor Mackenzie, first of Achilty.

II. The Macleans of Kingerloch.

1. Ewen, first Maclean of Kingerloch, must have been born between 1450 and 1455. He held possession of the Maclean lands in Urchart only for a few years. On July 1st, 1476, James III. deprived John, fourth Lord of the Isles, of the earldom of Ross, and placed the castle and lands of Urchart, and also the lands of Glenmoriston, in charge of George Gordon, second Earl of Huntly. Huntly appointed Hugh Rose of Kil-

ravock as his chamberlain, and also as constable of Urchart Castle. Ewen Maclean resolved to hold his lands by the sword, and was supported by the Clann Mhic Uidhein of Glenurchart, the Macdonalds of Glenmoriston, and Duncan Mackintosh, captain of the Clan Chattan. In March, 1479, Duncan Mackintosh and Hugh Rose agreed to submit to arbitration all matters in dispute between them. The arbitrators decided in favour of Rose, and decreed that he was entitled to possess in peace the lands which Ewen Maclean claimed. As Ewen had nothing to do with the appointment of the arbitrators he refused to be bound by their decision. He was deserted by the chief of the Mackintoshes, but was still supported by the Clann Mhic Uidhein and the Macdonalds of Glenmoriston. He had also a good friend in Lachlan Badenoch, second son of Malcolm Beg Mackintosh. In June, 1482, Hugh Rose was in so much trouble that he was glad to give up all connection with Urchart and Glenmoriston. Huntly appointed Sir Duncan Grant of Freuchie in his place. In 1509 Sir Duncan became proprietor both of Glenurchart and Glenmoriston. In the same year James IV. granted to Ewen Maclean a charter of Kilmalieu, Blaaich, and other lands. It is probable that the lands thus granted to him had belonged to his father. They were erected into the barony of Kingerloch in 1530.

Ewen of Kingerloch was evidently a resolute and active man. He supported Donald Dubh in

1513. He had apparently three sons, Hector, Allan Mor, and Ferchar. Allan Mor was put to death by Sir Duncan Grant in 1498. Ferchar was slain by one of Sir Duncan's followers about 1510. Ewen died some time after 1530. He was succeeded by Donald, who was probably his grandson, and a son of Hector.

II. Donald was laird of Kingerloch in 1545. He married Jean, daughter of Lachlan Beg Mackintosh by his wife, Jean, daughter of Sir Alexander Gordon of Lochinvar.

III. Hector, son of Donald, was laird of Kingerloch in 1609.

IV. Donald, son of Hector, appears as heir-apparent of Kingerloch in 1609.

V. Hector, son of Donald, joined Montrose in June, 1645. He fought at Kilsyth, and took part in plundering Knapdale, Cowall, and other Campbell lands. He was killed by the Camerons of Morvern about 1650. He was succeeded by his son, whose name was probably Lachlan.

VI. The sixth Maclean of Kingerloch had three sons, Donald, Hector, and Alexander. He died about 1675, and was succeeded by his eldest son, Donald. Hector, his youngest son, was killed at Dunkeld in 1689.

VII. Donald took an active part, in 1680, in supporting the Macleans of Duart against the Campbells. He had two sons, Lachlan and Allan. Lachlan succeeded his father. Allan married Una, daughter of John Maclean of Pennygoun. Donald died in May, 1726.

VIII. Lachlan of Kingerloch had three sons, Hugh, John, and Lachlan. Hugh succeeded his father. John entered the Black Watch as a lieutenant in 1739. He killed an officer named Mackenzie, in a duel, and had to leave the army. He was a captain in the Maclean battalion at the battle of Culloden, and fell bravely fighting for the hapless Stewarts. Lachlan settled at Rochester. Kingerloch died in 1756.

IX. Hugh of Kingerloch was a very intelligent man, and was well versed in the genealogy of his clan. He married Mary Stewart, and had nine children by her. 1. Donald, the eldest son, succeeded his father. 2. Murdoch was a captain in the 2d West India regiment, and was killed at St. Vincent. 3. Colin was a lieutenant in the 37th regiment, and was killed at the battle of Tournay in 1794. 4. James was a planter in Jamaica, and was killed in the war with the Caribs. 5. Hector succeeded Donald in Kingerloch. 6. Mary was married to the Rev. Donald Skinner, of Ardnamurchan, and had two sons: James, a doctor in Pictou, Nova Scotia; and Hugh, who kept a light-house in Cape Breton. 7. Margaret was married to Hugh Cameron. 8. Jane was married to John MacCormick. 9. The youngest daughter was married to Hugh Dunoon in Pictou. Hugh of Kingerloch died in March, 1784.

X. Donald of Kingerloch married Ann, daughter of Hugh Maclean of Ardgour. He died without issue.

XI. Hector, eleventh and last Maclean of Kingerloch, was a lieutenant in the Dumbartonshire Fencible regiment. He was served heir to his brother Donald in March, 1801. He found the estate in debt, and sold it. He came to Pictou, Nova Scotia, about 1812. He opened a store, but failed in a short time. He married Harriet-Elizabeth, daughter of Captain John Fraser of the 82d regiment, by whom he had four children. 1. Murdoch, his elder son, succeeded him as chieftain of the Macleans of Kingerloch. 2. Simon was a sea-captain. He married a Miss Noonan, and had by her three children, John, Fannie, and Christina. John died in prison in the Southern States at the time of the Civil War. Captain Simon Maclean died in Australia. 3. The elder daughter was married to George Mackay in Cape Breton. 4. The younger daughter was married to the Rev. Kenneth-John Mackenzie, of Pictou. Hector of Kingerloch died in Pictou town, and is buried in the old cemetery there.

XII. Murdoch, elder son of Hector of Kingerloch, was born in March, 1807. He was sheriff of the county of Guysborough, Nova Scotia, for a number of years. He married Elizabeth, daughter of the Hon. R. M. Cutler, and had by her eight children: Sophia, Elizabeth, Kenneth-John, Robert-Cutler, William-Murdoch, Charles-Shrieve, Norman, and Francis-George. He died in April, 1865. William-Murdoch, his third son, is married, and has six sons. Norman is married, and has three sons.

XIII. Kenneth-John, eldest son of Sheriff Maclean, died unmarried in 1873.

XIV. Robert-Cutler, second son of Sheriff Maclean, was born in 1846. He resides in Lynn, Massachusetts. He is married, and has three daughters. He is the present Mac-Mhic-Eachainn.

The Macleans of Rochester.

Lachlan, third son of Lachlan of Kingerloch, fought at Culloden in 1746. He escaped to Holland, but returned in 1747. He settled at Rochester, in Kent, England, and engaged in mercantile pursuits. He married a Miss Ferry in 1757, and had eight children by her, Charles, John, Lachlan, William, Elizabeth, Jane, Ann, and Sarah. 1. Charles died unmarried. 2. John was a navy agent. He was married, and had four children, John, Edward, Elizabeth, and Harriet. 3. Lachlan was an officer in the navy. He died in 1830, and left one daughter, Charlotte. 4. William was a surgeon in the Royal Marines. He was married and had two sons and three daughters. Lachlan, his eldest son, was a captain in the 6th regiment of Madras Native Infantry. William-Henry, the second son, was a clerk in the office of the Paymaster-General in London. He was married, and had four daughters. 5. Elizabeth, the eldest daughter, was married to William Maclean of Dochgarroch. Natural affection would have led Lachlan of Rochester to call his first son after his brother John. But Lachlan was a most loyal Jacobite, and therefore he called his first son after Prince Charles.

The Descendants of Captain John Maclean.

John Maclean belonged to the Kingerloch branch of the Macleans, and was born in 1753. He was captain of a vessel in the mercantile service of Anderson and Company, Edinburgh. He was presented by that firm, in 1794, with a large silver cup, for his gallantry in saving the vessel under his command from two French frigates which tried to capture it. He married, in 1795, Sibella, daughter of Alexander Maclean of Sollas, by whom he had eight children, Alexander-Anderson, Francis-Murray, Sibella, Johanna, Alexander, Susanna, John-Anderson, and Mary-Ann. He died in 1832. Alexander-Anderson, his eldest son, married, in 1837, Maria, daughter of Joseph Lightfoot, of Walworth, and had by her four sons, Henry, Joseph-John, Francis-William, and Septimus. Henry married, in 1864, Marion, daughter of James Abernethy, of Whiteness, by whom he had five children, Alexander, Harry-Abernethy, Francis-John, Edith-Marion, and Anne-Alice. Alexander was educated at Oxford. He resides in London, and is an artist by profession. Francis-William, third son of Alexander-Anderson, studied law, and is now Chief Justice of Bengal. He was knighted a few years ago. He is married, and has one son, Montague.

III. The Macleans of Dochgarroch.

I. Donald, son of Ferchar, son of Hector, son of Terlach, was the first Maclean of Dochgarroch. He settled there as tacksman in 1557. He received from the Bishop of the Isles a legal claim to the island of Raasay and a part of Troternish in Skye. As he was not able to obtain possession of these lands, his claim to them was of no use to him. He married, first, a daughter of the laird of Grant, and had by her four children, Alexander, John, Hector, and Elizabeth. He married, secondly, a Mackenzie woman, and had a son named Donald by her. Alexander succeeded his father in Dochgarroch. It is said that John was an officer under Gustavus Adolphus, and that he was killed at Altenburgh about the year 1632. Hector lived at Culcabok, and married, about 1621, Margaret, daughter of Paul Macpherson of Lonnie. Elizabeth was married to Walter Urquhart, sheriff of Cromarty. Donald of Dochgarroch died some time after 1606. According to the "History of the Clan Terlach," he was the second son of Bishop Ferchar, son of Hector Buie of Urchart.

II. Alexander of Dochgarroch was a man of good business capacity, and was in very prosperous circumstances. It is said that he was at the battle of Glenlivet in 1594. In 1609 he entered into a bond of manrent with Mackintosh, captain of the Clan Chattan. He purchased the lands of Dochgarroch and Dochnalurg from the Earls of Enzie and Huntly, and obtained a feu charter of them in May, 1623. It is said that he was married three times: first, to a daughter of Maclean of Kingerloch; secondly, to Margaret Grant, daughter of Grant of Glenmoriston; and, thirdly, to Annabella, daughter of Andrew Munro of Daan. He married his last wife in 1628. He had at least four sons and three daughters. 1. John, the eldest son, succeeded his father. 2. Charles settled in Culbokie. 3. David lived in Buntaite. He was a captain in Colonel Strachan's regiment, and was killed at Red Castle in a skirmish with some of Montrose's followers. He left a son named Hector, who had a son named Lachlan. Lachlan fought under Dundee at Killiecrankie in 1689. He settled some time afterwards at Broughty Ferry. 4. James, the fourth son, was born about 1630. He was a medical doctor, and was at one time provost of Inverness. He married Alice, daughter of Captain Kenneth Mackenzie, of Suddie. 5. Agnes, the eldest daughter, was married in 1614 to William Baillie, of the Dunain family. 6. Marion was married to William Baillie of Dochfour. 7. Janet was married, first, in 1625, to James Cumming of Dalshangie; and, secondly, to James Grant of Sheuglie.

III. John of Dochgarroch was known as Iain Mac Alasdair. He was born probably about 1600. He married, in 1629, Agnes, daughter of Thomas Fraser of Struy. It is said that he fought under Montrose in 1645, and at Inverkeithing in 1651.

He had by his wife six sons and three daughters.
1. Alexander, the eldest son, succeeded his father.
2. John lived in Leys in 1676. 3. Hector settled at Dochnalurg, and was killed at Killiecrankie. 4. Donald was a merchant burgess of Inverness. He was married and had at least one son, John. He died probably in 1693. John, his son, was served heir to him in May, 1694. 5. With regard to David, the fifth son, we have nothing to state. 6. Farquhar lived at Kinmylies, and was killed at Killiecrankie. 7. Elspet, the eldest daughter, was married, prior to 1657, to Angus Macqueen, in Inshes, Strathdearn. 8. Catherine was married, first, to Donald Munro of Culcabok; and, secondly, in 1669, to Duncan Macpherson in Daltochy of Ardclash. 9. Janet was married in 1665 to Malcolm, son of William Mackintosh of Holme. John Mac Alister died on October 8th, 1674.

IV. Alexander of Dochgarroch married, in November, 1656, Agnes, daughter of Alexander Chisholm of Comar, by whom he had two sons, John Og and Allan. He made his will on August 3d, 1671. He left his estate to his eldest son, and nominated John of Leys, his own brother, tutor to his son. He died in the following September. It is said that Allan, his second son, settled in Sutherlandshire.

V. John Og of Dochgarroch was only about fourteen years of age when his father died. He married, in 1682, Margaret, daughter of David Fowler, bailie of Inverness. He was an ardent

Jacobite. He appointed his brother Allan factor of his estate in October, 1688. He fought with his followers under Dundee at the battle of Killiecrankie in 1689. His loyalty to the Stewarts and to his chief, Sir John Maclean of Duart, led him into serious difficulties. He was declared an outlaw, and was thus under the necessity of hiding himself wherever he could find shelter, until the general amnesty of 1693 was passed. In 1694 his brother Allan handed back the management of the estate to him. John Og died in 1707, in the fiftieth year of his age. He left by his wife six sons and three daughters. 1. John, his eldest son, Iain Mac Iain Oig, succeeded him in Dochgarroch. 2. Alexander was a writer in Inverness. He was a greedy and dishonest man. He died at Borlum, leaving two sons, Robert and William. Robert was tacksman of Craigscorrie. He married a daughter of Fraser of Aigish, by whom he had Hugh and two daughters. Hugh married a daughter of the Rev. Malcolm Macnicol in Kiltarlity, and had three sons, Malcolm, Robert, and Peter; all of whom died unmarried. William, second son of Alexander, married a Miss Fraser, by whom he had two sons, Alexander and Hugh, and also three daughters. 3. David, third son of John Og, was a dyer by trade. He was a burgess of Inverness. He was married and had two sons, John, and Alexander of Lochgorm. John was married and left a son named Robert. Alexander of Lochgorm was the father of David Maclean, of West Branch, East River, Pictou. 4. Donald, fourth son of John Og, settled in Argyleshire. He married a daughter of Campbell of Airds, by whom he had Lachlan and others. Lachlan married Jane, daughter of Maclean of Kingerloch, by whom he had six children, Donald, Murdoch, Allan, Hector, Charles, and a daughter. Donald settled in Jamaica. Murdoch was a surgeon in the Royal Navy. Allan was married, and left one son, Charles. Hector was a jeweler in London. He married a Miss Miller, of Bungay in Suffolk, and had by her five children, Hector, Thomas, Sarah, Anne, and Mary. Hector was a purser in the Royal Navy. Thomas was a print-seller in London. Charles, fifth son of Donald, died in the military service of the East India Company. 5. With regard to Lachlan, fifth son of John Og, we have no information. 6. Ferchar, or Farquhar, the seventh son, was a man of roving habits. It is not known what became of him. 7. Janet, eldest daughter of John Og, was married in 1723 to William Mackintosh, son of Duncan, son of William of Borlum. She had one son, Alexander Mackintosh, a sea-captain. 8. Margaret was married in 1725 to William, son of John Grant of Corriemonie. 9. Annie was married to James Ross, a notary in Edinburgh, and had two children, Peter and Mary.

VI. John of Dochgarroch, Iain Mac Iain Oig, was noted for his strength and chivalrous disposition. Influenced by Sir John Maclean of Duart

and Lord Lovat, he joined the Earl of Mar in the
rising of 1715, and fought at the battle of Sheriffmuir. Before leaving home to join the Jacobite
army, he appointed his brother Alexander factor
of the estate. Shortly after his return from Sheriffmuir he found four Hessian soldiers plundering on
his lands. He attacked them, and killed one of
them with his sword. He remained in concealment
for some time. At last he surrendered himself to
the officers of the law in Inverness. He was put
on trial for killing the Hessian soldier, but as there
was no one mean enough to testify against him,
he was acquitted for want of evidence. He had a
good deal of trouble with his brother Alexander,
who tried to keep the management of the estate in
his own hands and get it for himself.

John of Dochgarroch married, in 1710, Christina, daughter of Alexander Dallas of Contray,
by whom he had three sons, John, Charles, and
William. He died in 1748. John, the eldest son,
died at a comparatively early age, and probably in
Jamaica. Charles succeeded his father in Dochgarroch. William joined the Black Watch as an
ensign in 1743. He married Mary, second daughter
of Lachlan Mackintosh, son of William of Borlum. In his contract of marriage, which is dated
November 6th, 1751, he is described as the "second
lawful son of the deceased John Maclean, late of
Dochgarroch." He was killed at the storming of
Guadaloupe in 1759. He left two sons, Lachlan
and John. Lachlan died young. John served in

the old 84th, and settled in America. As William was the second lawful son of John of Dochgarroch in 1751, it is evident that John, his eldest brother, had died before that date.

VII. Charles of Dochgarroch entered the Black Watch in 1743. He left the Episcopalian Church and became a Presbyterian. He had a lawsuit with the Duke of Gordon, by which he lost heavily. He married, in 1753, Marjory, second daughter of Angus Mackintosh of Drummond, by whom he had seven children, John, Phineas, Angus, William, Janet, Marjory, and Barbara. He died in 1778, in the sixty-first year of his age. 1. John, his eldest son, succeeded him in Dochgarroch. 2. Phineas died young. 3. Angus was a captain in the military service of the East India Company. He became administrator of his brother's estate in 1789. He died at Calicut in 1794. He was a very promising young man. 4. William succeeded his brother John in Dochgarroch. 5. Janet was born in 1756, and was married, in 1779, to Alexander Mackintosh, captain of a West India merchant ship. She had seven children, Charles, Phineas, William, Angus, Mary, Janet, and May. Angus made a good deal of money in Calcutta. He died at Forres without issue about the year 1856. May was married to Alexander Fraser, tacksman of Dochnalurg, by whom she had four children, Alexander, William, Charles, and Mary. Charles, her youngest son, is the accomplished and well-known antiquarian, Dr. Charles Fraser-Mackintosh

of Drummond. 6. Marjory, second daughter of
Charles of Dochgarroch, was married to Alexander
Lee, a merchant in Inverness. 7. Barbara died
in June, 1849, aged eighty-eight years.

VIII. John of Dochgarroch was educated at
the University of Aberdeen. He received an appointment in the civil service in the island of
Grenada in 1775. He had an attack of sunstroke
in 1777, which affected his brain to such an extent
that he became permanently insane. He returned
to Scotland shortly afterwards. He died on
October 7th, 1826.

IX. William, ninth and last Maclean of Dochgarroch, entered the 73d Foot, or old Macleod
Highlanders, as an ensign in 1779. He embarked
for Madras in 1780, along with others who had
been drafted from the regiment. The ship which
carried him was seized by a Spanish privateer and
taken to Cadiz. The soldiers were well treated by
the Spaniards, and in a short time exchanged as
prisoners of war and sent to Gibraltar. William
Maclean arrived in Madras in 1784. He returned
to Britain in 1788, and in the same year married
Elizabeth, daughter of Lachlan Maclean of
Rochester. He was appointed captain in the
Breadalbane Fencibles in 1790, and in 1794 captain
in the 83d regiment of the line. On the death of
his brother Angus in 1794, he became heir of
Dochgarroch. In 1796 he retired from the army
and took the management of the estate into his
hands. In 1826 he succeeded his brother John as
proprietor.

William of Dochgarroch was a careless and imprudent man, and got deeply into debt. In January, 1832, the estate was sold by the creditors, and purchased by Evan Baillie of Dochfour, who, it is said, had been looking upon it with a covetous eye for a long time. The price paid for it was £10,000. Allan Maclean, William's son, had a lease on the mansion at the time of the sale. As soon as the lease expired, which was in 1839, William had to leave the house of his forefathers. He died at Clach-na-harry, in a house which belonged to the canal engineer, on November 24th, 1841. He was eighty years of age. He left three sons, Allan, Charles-Maxwell, and William. Allan succeeded him in the representation of the Dochgarroch family. Charles-Maxwell was born in 1791, and joined the 72d in 1807. He was appointed lieutenant-colonel of the 3d West India regiment in 1850. He retired from active service in 1852, and settled at Woodside, Fortrose. He married, in 1823, Sarah-Amelia, daughter of Samuel Marshall, by whom he had one child, Charlotte-Amelia. He wrote a history of the Clan Terlach, a useful but exceedingly inaccurate work. He was a gentlemanly and honourable man. He died in December, 1864, and was buried with his forefathers in the Old Greyfriars churchyard in Inverness. William, third son of William of Dochgarroch, was for some time a clerk in the Royal Dock Yard at Sheerness. He was afterwards connected with the Imperial Fire Office,

Cornhill. He lived, during his later years, at Maize Hill, Greenwich Park. He married Elizabeth, only daughter of Dr. Thomas Henderson, in the island of Dominica, and had by her three children, William-Thomas-Henderson, Allan, and Marion. He died in October, 1841. His eldest son was for some time a subaltern in the 78th Highlanders.

X. Allan Maclean, eldest son of William of Dochgarroch, was born in 1790. He died unmarried, at the old house of Drummond, in 1876. He was succeeded as representative of the Macleans of Dochgarroch, by Allan, second son of his brother William.

XI. Allan married, in 1871, Marion, daughter of the Rev. Edward Guilie, vicar of St. Luke's, Jersey, by whom he has two sons and one daughter, Allan-Mackintosh, Hector, and Jessie. He is a life member of the Maclean Association, and lives at Brighton, England. His sons are both ministers of the Church of England.

THE MACLEANS OF CULBOKIE.

Charles, second son of Alexander, second of Dochgarroch, settled in Culbokie. He married, in 1625, a Miss Cumming, probably a daughter of Cumming of Dalshangie, and received a marriage portion of 1,000 marks with her. He had a large family. One of his grandsons in the male line had two sons, Simon of Kinmylies, and Charles. The latter was a draper in Inverness. His shop is referred to in one of Burt's Letters. He married Margaret Mackenzie.

1. Simon, or Sween, portioner of Kinmylies, was a writer in Inverness. He married Janet Baillie, and had at least two children, John and a daughter. He died on March 20th, 1754. His daughter was married to a Campbell, by whom she had two children, Donald and a daughter. Donald died in the West Indies at the age of forty, and left an estate which was worth about £15,000.

2. John was born in 1746. He married Margaret Patterson, by whom he had five children, Alexander, John, Donald, Finlay, and Jane. He lived in Inverness, and died in 1852, at the good old age of 106 years. He was known as the Centenarian. Alexander, his eldest son, was a sergeant in the army, and was wounded at Waterloo. Alexander settled in Limerick, and was married there. Finlay was a printer. He published his father's reminiscences, and also traditions related by him. He died in 1857. He was married and left a family.

3. Donald, third son of the Centenarian, came to Newfoundland in 1812, and to Cape Breton a year or two afterwards. He lived at Judique. He married Flora Macdonald, by whom he had five children, John, Donald, Allan, Mary, and Donald-Charles. He died in 1838. Allan lives in Halifax, Nova Scotia.

The Macleans of Kaffraria.

According to the "History of the Clan Terlach," David Maclean of Buntait, third son of Alexander, second of Dochgarroch, had a son named Hector, who had a son named Lachlan, who settled at Broughty Ferry in 1690. It is possible, but by no means certain, that this Lachlan was the grandfather of Murdoch Maclean, of the Aird, Aird Mhic Shimi, near Inverness.

Murdoch Maclean, of the Aird, was born probably about 1725. He married a Miss Mackenzie, by whom he had a son named Roderick. Roderick settled in Strathspey, and married a Miss Macbean. He had three sons, Alexander, John, and William. William was born about 1785. He entered the army in the 27th, or Enniskillen regiment, in 1805. He was appointed lieutenant in 1806, captain in 1820, and major in 1831. He married a Miss Grant, of Strathspey, by whom he had three children, John, Jessie, and Eliza. Jessie was married to Major Macpherson of the 27th regiment, and Eliza to Surgeon Mostyn of the same regiment. John, only son of Major William Maclean, was born at Enniskillen Castle on August 23d, 1810. He entered the army in the 27th regiment when quite young, and rose to the rank of lieutenant-colonel. He was for some time lieutenant-governor of Kaffraria, and afterwards governor of the colony of Natal. He spent the latter part of his life at East London in Cape

Colony. He had five children, William-Alexander, Allan-Cromdale, John-Kenneth, Ranald, and Annie-Matilda. William-Alexander, known as Lexy Maclean, captured a famous freebooter, Klaas Lucas, single-handed, and carried him into Cape Town. Allan was noted for his deeds of daring in the field. John married Jessie Macglashen, by whom he has five children. Ranald was born in 1851. He married Elizabeth-Jane Arnold, and has eight children, John-Kenneth, Ranald-Macpherson, William-Alexander, Allan-Cromdale, Clifford-Arnold, Grace-Annie, Lillian-Maud, and Clara. He resides in East London, Cape Colony. He is a captain in the Kaffrarian volunteers. He has been through six campaigns. He holds the Albert Medal of the first class and the Humane Society's Bronze Medal. Annie, only daughter of Major Maclean, was married to Captain Wilson of the 95th regiment.

According to Seannachie's History, Major William Maclean was the son of Roderick, son of Murdoch, and belonged to the Dochgarroch family. As this information was undoubtedly obtained from Major William himself, it may be regarded as correct.

THE MACLEANS OF PITMAIN AND WESTFIELD.

John of Leys, second son of John Mac Alister of Dochgarroch, fought under Dundee at Killiecrankie in 1689. It is said that he settled shortly afterwards in Strathdearn. He left a son who had

a son named John. John, grandson of John of
Leys, was born in 1725. He got a wadset from
the Duke of Gordon of the lands of Pitmain in
Badenoch. He married, first, Isabel, daughter of
James Fordyce, by whom he had Hugh, James,
and Grace. He married, secondly, Isabel, daughter
of Donald Macpherson of Kinlochlaggan, by
whom he had one daughter. He married, thirdly,
Margaret, daughter of John Macpherson of Invernahaven, by whom he had John, Alexander, and
Isabel. He married, fourthly, a daughter of Lewis
Macpherson of Dalraddie, and by her had Lewis,
Alexander, Christina, Una, Margaret, and Elizabeth. He died in 1808. James, second son of John
of Pitmain, was minister of Urquhart in Morayshire. He married, first, Elizabeth, daughter of
George Todd, by whom he had John, George,
and Hugh. He married, secondly, Elizabeth,
daughter of William Todd, by whom he had one
son, James. He died in 1840. John died at the
age of twenty-four. George became governor of
the Gold Coast, Africa, in 1829. He married
Letitia E. Landon. He died in 1847. Hugh
was a surgeon in the service of the East India
Company. He purchased Westfield in Elgin.
He married Isabel Gordon, by whom he had one
son, John-Alexander, who succeeded him in Westfield, and died without issue. James, fourth son
of the Rev. George Maclean, was a captain in the
Gold Coast corps. He married Barbara, daughter
of Harry Munro, of Seafield, by whom he had four

children, Hugh, James, George-Alexander, and Elizabeth. He died in 1877. James, his second son, succeeded his cousin in Westfield. James died in 1888 and was succeeded by his brother, George-Alexander, now of Westfield.

John, third son of John of Pitmain, entered the Royal Scots as an ensign on April 30th, 1794. On the following day he was promoted to a lieutenancy in the 92d regiment, or Gordon Highlanders. He fought a duel with Captain John Cameron of Fassiefern at Gibraltar in 1795. He became a captain in 1797. He was transferred to the 27th, or Enniskillen regiment, in 1804, and appointed major. He served in Holland, Egypt, and the Peninsula, and was wounded severely on four different occasions. He was created a K.C.B. in January, 1815. He was married and had one son, Alexander, who died without issue. Sir John died at Pitmain in 1860. He was at the time of his death a lieutenant-general. He left the greater part of his money to his nephew, Dr. Hugh Maclean of Westfield.

THE MACLEANS OF LOCHGORM.

I. Alexander Maclean of Lochgorm was the second son of David, third son of John Og, fifth of Dochgarroch. He married a Miss Macbean of the Kinchyle family, by whom he had two sons, David and Donald. Donald entered the army, and fought at the battle of Waterloo, and shortly afterwards retired with a pension. He spent his later years in Pictou, Nova Scotia. He was for some time crier of the court, and also held some other easy positions which suited an old pensioner. He died unmarried.

II. David, elder son of Alexander of Lochgorm, was for some time a sergeant in the old 73d, or Macleod Highlanders. He came to Pictou about 1784, and settled at the West Branch of the East River. He was a good scholar, and was quite a prominent man in the district in which he lived. He was a surveyor, a magistrate, and an elder in the Presbyterian Church. He married Isabel, daughter of Alexander Fraser, of Middle River, Pictou, and had ten children by her, Alexander, John, Donald, David, Catherine, William, Simon, Hugh, Margaret, and Marion. The sons were all big men. There was none of them under six feet in height. Donald was the tallest, being six feet eight inches in height. David himself was a big man. At any rate he was known as Daibhidh Mòr Mac Gilleain, or Big David Maclean. 1. Alexander, eldest son of David Maclean, settled on a portion of his father's farm. He married Mary Macdonald, by whom he had Hannah, Mary-Ann, John, David-Hugh, and Peter. David-Hugh married Mary Gray, by whom he had John, Enon, Mary, and Ella. 2. John, second son of David Maclean, settled on a part of his father's farm. He married Elizabeth Munro, by whom he had seven children, Isabella, Jessie, David, Henry, Alexander, Margaret, and

Thomas. Henry, John's second son, was engaged in business at Hopewell. He married Annie, daughter of John Gray, of Hopewell, and had by her six children, Jessie, Ella, Elizabeth, John-Brown, Alister, and Harry-Gray. Ella is married to the Rev. J. H. Hattie. John-Brown, now the Rev. J. B. Maclean, B.A., B.D., studied at Dalhousie University, Halifax, at the Presbyterian College, Halifax, and afterwards for one term in Edinburgh. He is settled at Upper Stewiacke, Nova Scotia. It is scarcely necessary to add that he belongs to the Presbyterian Church. Alister, second son of Henry Maclean, is a machinist. Harry-Gray, the third son, is a pattern-maker with the Robb Engineering Company, of Amherst, Nova Scotia. 3. Donald, third son of David Maclean, married Barbara Mackay, by whom he had five children, Isabella, Catherine, Simon, Daniel, and David. 4. David, fourth son of David Maclean, married Nancy Fraser, but had no issue. 5. William, the fifth son, married Marion Murray, by whom he had four sons, David, John, Alexander, and William. Simon and Hugh died unmarried. Margaret, his eldest daughter, was married to Alexander Maclean, of Maclennan's Brook, and had three sons and three daughters. Marion was married to Alexander Fraser, miller, near New Glasgow, and had five sons and five daughters. Catherine was married to John Maclean, Iain Ruadh, and had four sons and three daughters.

IV. The Macleans of Knock.

I. The Rev. Angus Maclean was rector of Morvern in 1626. He was the son of John, son of Angus, son of John, son of John, a priest, son of John, son of Charles Maclean of Glenurchart. He possessed Knock and Ulline in Morvern, Killean in Mull, and Scarinish in Tiree. He left two sons, John and Hector. He died in 1635. John, his elder son, seems to have died without issue.

II. Hector, second son of Angus, was born in 1605. He succeeded his father as minister of Morvern, and was appointed Bishop of Argyll in 1680. He married Jean, daughter of the Rev. Thomas Boyd, son of Bishop Andrew Boyd. He had six children, Andrew, Angus, Alexander, John, Janet, and another daughter. Angus was minister of Kilfinan and Cowall. Alexander was a prominent member of his clan. In 1686 he received the lands of Otter from James II., who had deprived Alexander Campbell of them. He was knighted shortly afterwards, and is known in history as Sir Alexander Maclean of Otter. He was severely wounded at Killiecrankie. He was taken to Duart Castle, and kept there until he got well. He entered the French service and was appointed lieutenant-colonel. He died at Aix-la-Chapelle. John, fourth son of Bishop Hector, was a lieutenant in the Earl of Portmore's regiment of Foot. He was killed at Kaizerswerth, probably about 1702.

III. Andrew, eldest son of Bishop Hector, possessed the lands of Knock; but owing to the depredations of the Camerons, was forced to sell them and remove to Mull. He was a captain in Dundee's army at Killiecrankie. He married Florence, daughter of Charles Maclean of Ardnacross, and had by her one son, Angus. He was the author of several Gaelic songs.

IV. Angus, son of Captain Andrew, was a major in the Spanish army. He married Grace, daughter of Colonel Gerald Fitzgerald, by whom he had three sons and a daughter. The sons were all in the Neapolitan service. Angus, the eldest of them, died in 1780.

CHAPTER XIII.

The Descendants of Donald of Ardgour.

I. THE MACLEANS OF ARDGOUR.

I. DONALD, son of Lachlan Bronnach, Dòmhnall Mac Lachainn Bhronnaich, was the first Maclean of Ardgour. He was a bold, resolute, and active man. About 1432 he received the lands of Ardgour from Alexander, third Lord of the Isles. It is said that the Lord of the Isles was at the time displeased with Macmaster, who had been in possession of these lands, but had no legal claim to them. Donald invaded Ardgour, attacked Macmaster, and slew himself and his sons. It is true that the Lord of the Isles and Lachlan Bronnach were very good friends, and had been companions for some time in Tantallon Castle. At the same time it is just possible that the influence of the Earl of Mar had something to do with getting Ardgour for Lachlan's son.

Donald of Ardgour was married to a daughter of Ewen Cameron of Lochiel, son of Donald

Dubh, and had three sons, Ewen, Neil Bàn, and John. He had also a natural son named Archibald. Ewen succeeded his father in Ardgour. Neil Bàn was the progenitor of the Macleans of Boreray. Archibald's descendants were known as Clann Eoghain an Fhraoich, or the children of Ewen of the heather.

II. Ewen of Ardgour was chamberlain of the house to John, fourth Lord of the Isles, in 1463. He was in possession of Ardgour at least from 1479 to 1495. He married a daughter of Thomas Chisholm of Comar, by whom he had five sons, Lachlan, Terlach, Allan, John Roy, and Hector. Lachlan succeeded his father in Ardgour. Terlach had one son, John. Allan married a daughter of Mac a Ghlasraich in the Braes of Lochaber, and had a son named John, who had a son named Allan. John was captain of Cairnburgh Castle. Hector was the first Maclean of Blaaich. It is from Ewen that the chieftains of the Macleans of Ardgour derive their patronymic of Mac-Mhic-Eoghain.

III. Lachlan of Ardgour was a young man of warlike character. He took an active part under Lachlan Cattanach of Duart, in 1513, in seizing the royal castles of Cairnburgh and Dunscàthaich. He supported Sir Donald Gallda of Lochalsh in 1517. He died without issue, and was succeeded by his nephew, Iain Mac Thearlaich, or John the son of Charles.

IV. John Mac Terlach was under age when he

succeeded to the estate. He supported Donald Dubh in 1545, and died about 1547. As he left no lawful heirs, his estate reverted to the crown. In March, 1549, the Government gave a charter of it—"the lands and barony of Ardgour"—to Hector Mor of Duart. Hector Mor conveyed it to Allan, son of John, son of Allan, third son of Ewen of Ardgour.

V. Allan of Ardgour handfasted with a daughter of Macdonald of Ardnamurchan, and had two sons by her, John of Inverscadale, and Hector. He had a natural son who was known as Iain Gleannach, or John of the Glens. He married, first, a daughter of Ewen Cameron of Lochiel, Ewen Mac Allan, by whom he had one son, Ewen. He married, secondly, a daughter of Macdonald of Moydart, and had two sons by her, Charles and Lachlan. John of Inverscadale, Iain an Ionair, was distinguished for his strength, bravery and activity. He was one of Sir Lachlan Mor's grandest warriors. Ewen became laird of Ardgour. Charles was the progenitor of the Macleans of Inverscadale. According to the Ardgour MS. the six sons of Allan were all men of great substance, while the most of them had a numerous issue.

VI. Ewen of Ardgour was known as Eoghan na h-Iteige, or Ewen of the feather, an appellation which indicated that he was quick and active in his movements or like a bird flying from place to place. He was laird of Ardgour in 1587. He married a daughter of Stewart of Appin, by whom he had two sons, Allan and John. He was killed in his boat, by the Macdonalds of Keppoch, at Sgeir-thir-Muir, a rock near the seashore opposite the farm of Coire-chaorachain in Lochaber. The Keppoch men mistook him for Cameron of Lochiel, against whom they had a bitter grudge. He was slain probably about the year 1590. Allan, his elder son, became laird of Ardgour. John had a son named Allan. This Allan was the father of John Maclean, the famous Mull poet, who was known as Iain Mac Ailein Mhic Iain Mhic Eoghain.

VII. Allan of Ardgour was a hostage in the hands of Angus Macdonald of Islay in 1587. He was only a young boy when his father was killed. His uncle Charles acted as tutor to him. Charles was a greedy and dishonest man, and succeeded by some crooked means in getting himself served heir male to the lands of Ardgour, in September, 1593. When Allan came to be of age, Charles refused to give up the estate to him. His mother's people then advised Allan to apply to the Earl of Argyll for assistance. Argyll agreed to obtain possession of the estate for him, on condition of holding it of himself as superior instead of holding it of the Crown. Allan accepted Argyll's terms. Charles was seized by a stratagem, by Stewart of Appin, and imprisoned on Stalker's Island—Eilein an Stalcaire—where he was detained for some time. Through the influence of Hector Og of

Duart, to whose aunt Charles was married, Allan agreed to give to Charles Inverscadale and certain other lands, on condition of his paying to him yearly the feu-duty which was to be given to Argyll. This duty consisted of twenty-five marks Scots, and a cuid oidhche, or night's entertainment. It was afterwards commuted to fifty marks Scots, or two pounds fifteen shillings and sixpence. Allan received Ardgour in November, 1618. He was served heir to John Mac Terlach Mac Ewen, son of the brother of his great-grandfather. He married Catherine, daughter of Allan Cameron of Lochiel, and had fourteen children by her: John Crùbach, his successor; Hector; Allan; Charles, whose son John settled at Anderton near Glasgow; Donald, who was killed at Inverkeithing; Lachlan Mor; Lachlan Og; Ewen the elder; Ewen the younger; Archibald; John Og; Mary, who was married to Charles Maclean of Ardnacross; Marion, who was married to John Maclean of Totaranald; and Christy. The Rev. John Maclean, D. D., minister of Gorbals, Glasgow, was the son of John Maclean, of Anderton. He married, in 1797, Ann Ballentine, and had by her John, James, John, Patrick, William, Robert, Alexander, Walter, Margaret, Euphemia, and Elizabeth. William was a merchant in Buenos Ayres. Robert was a merchant in Manchester.

VIII. John Crùbach, eighth Maclean of Ardgour, was a daring and active man. He was an ardent lover of the chase, and was always ready to draw the sword in support of his chief and king. He sprained his foot severely when he was quite young, and was ever afterwards lame. He was consequently known as Iain Crùbach, or Lame John. He was in possession of Ardgour in 1680. He received a crown charter of his lands from James II., on September 12th, 1688. He was married twice. By his first wife, a daughter of Campbell of Dunstaffnage, he had five sons: Ewen, Lachlan, Donald, Allan, and Archibald. By his second wife, Marion, daughter of Hector Maclean, second of Torloisk, and relict of Hector Roy of Coll, he had one son, John. He was ninety-two years of age at the time of his death. He was buried in Coll. Ewen, his eldest son, succeeded him in Ardgour. Lachlan was the progenitor of the later Macleans of Blaaich. Donald lived in Arighoulan.

IX. Ewen of Ardgour married Mary, daughter of Lachlan Maclean, eleventh of Lochbuie, and had by her five sons, Allan, Donald, Charles, John, and Lachlan. Allan succeeded his father. Donald married Janet, daughter of Lachlan Maclean of Calgary, by whom he had three sons, Ewen, John, and Lachlan. Lachlan, the youngest of Ardgour's sons, was a lieutenant in the Spanish service. He was killed at Madrid in a duel with a man named Cockpen.

X. Allan of Ardgour was born in 1668. He married Anne, second daughter of Sir Ewen Cameron of Lochiel, and had by her nine children:

Donald, Ewen, John, Archibald, Allan, James, Isabel, Margaret, and Mary. He was a very extravagant man and utterly mismanaged his affairs. He made over his estate to Donald, his eldest son, but Donald was as foolish and reckless as himself. Between them they sank the estate so deeply in debt that they brought it to the brink of ruin. Ewen, the second son, died at sea on his way home from Virginia. Allan died in Georgia. James was a lieutenant in the Montgomery Highlanders. He was killed at sea, in an engagement with a privateer, on June 1st, 1761. He was on the way to Minorca, and was in charge of a detachment of soldiers. Isabel was married to Donald of Brolas; Margaret, to Angus of Kinlochaline; and Mary, to John, son of Charles of Inverscadale.

XI. Donald of Ardgour predeceased his father, and was succeeded by Ewen, son of his brother John. John, third son of Allan of Ardgour, married Marjory, daughter of Allan Maclachlan of Corry, and had three children by her, Ewen, Hector, and Margaret. On the death of his brother Donald in 1731, he became heir to the estate. He died in Mull in March, 1739, and was buried at Kilmore in Quinish.

After the death of Donald of Ardgour, Hector Maclean of Coll, Donald Maclean of Torloisk, the Rev. John Maclean of Kilninian, and the Rev. Archibald Maclean of Kilvicewen, took the management of the estate into their own hands, and went to a good deal of trouble and expense in connection with it. They appointed Donald Cameron, of Strontian, factor under them. At the end of two or three years Donald pretended that he had some business to settle in Edinburgh. He went away, but never returned. It was believed, at the time, that he left Scotland. After his flight the management of the estate fell principally into the hands of John, third son of Allan of Ardgour. When John died, the Maclachlans of Corry tried to get control of the estate. Hector of Torloisk at once stepped in and prevented them from obtaining their object. Hector was a good Maclean, and a good lawyer, and knew what to do. He took charge of the estate and associated with him in the management of it the following persons:—Donald Campbell of Airds; John Campbell of Clahombie; James Maclean, sixth son of Allan of Ardgour; Lachlan Maclean, a merchant in Glasgow; and Dr. Hector Maclean of Grulin, who was then living in Glasgow. He placed Ewen, the youthful heir of Ardgour, in charge of Lachlan Maclean, the Glasgow merchant. He managed the affairs of the estate successfully, and was apparently the means of preserving it from passing out of the hands of the descendants of Donald Mac Lachlan Bronnach. John Maclean's widow went to Glasgow and resided there for a number of years. Lachlan Maclean acted in the kindest manner towards herself and her children. Hector, the second son, died young. Margaret also died at an early age. Allan of Ardgour died in November, 1756, at the ripe old age of eighty-eight years.

XII. Ewen of Ardgour was born about 1736. He was brought up in Glasgow. He was served heir to his uncle Donald in July, 1744. He married, in 1763, Elizabeth, daughter of Alexander Houston of Gordon Hill, by whom he had two children, Alexander and Anne. He was for some time a captain in the first regiment of Argyle Fencibles, which was raised in 1758. He died in 1768. He was succeeded by his son, Alexander. Anne, his daughter, was born in November, 1765, and died in Edinburgh in April, 1860. Several of the Ardgour family lived to a very old age.

XIII. Alexander, thirteenth of Ardgour, was born on April 16th, 1764. He entered the army as an ensign in 1780, and rose to the rank of major in the 8th regiment of Light Dragoons. He was appointed lieutenant-colonel in the third regiment of the local militia of Argyleshire in 1811. Like his ancestor, John Crùbach, he delighted in the chase. He was a magnificent horseman and was the most daring rider in the Caledonia Hunt. He married, in 1795, Margaret, daughter of John Hope, second Earl of Hopetoun, and had by her fourteen children. 1. Hugh, the eldest child, died in infancy. 2. John-Hugh was educated for the Scottish bar. He died at Rome in 1826. 3. Archibald was a captain in the navy. He died in Edinburgh in 1832. 4. Alexander became laird of Ardgour. 5. Henry-Dundas was senior major of the 95th regiment. He became owner of Lazenby Hall in Cumberland. He died without issue in 1863. 6. James-Charles was for some time barrack-master of Fort William, Bengal. He died at Calcutta in 1825. He was married and left two daughters. 7. Charles-Hope was educated at Balliol College, Oxford, and was called to the English bar in 1829. He took a deep and practical interest in his clan. He bore the expense of publishing Seannachie's "Account of the Clan Maclean" in 1838. He was married and had two daughters. He died in 1839. 8. Thomas was for some time assistant adjutant-general at Nagpore. 9. William was a commander in the Royal Navy. He married, in 1838, Elizabeth-Mary Charter, by whom he had three children, William-Gunston, Allan, and Frances-Margaret. 10. George was a colonel in the Royal Artillery. He married, in 1842, Amelia-Jane, daughter of Sir Colin Campbell, governor of Ceylon. 11. Robert died unmarried in 1835. 12. Peter was a colonel in the Royal Artillery. He married, in 1841, Elizabeth, daughter of Lieutenant-General Sir Henry Somerset, by whom he had seven children, Allan-Henry, John-Hugh, Henry-Eardley, Charles-Hope-Adrian, Margaret-Ann, Louisa-Charlotte, and Elizabeth-Frances. Alexander of Ardgour died at Ardgour House on September 8th, 1855. He was buried at Cille-Mhaodain.

XIV. Alexander of Ardgour was born in 1799. He entered the civil service of the East India

Company, and became collector of the Jaghire. He married, in 1833, Helen-Jane, eldest daughter of Major-General Sir John Dalrymple, by whom he had two sons, Alexander-Thomas and John-Dalrymple. Alexander-Thomas succeeded his father. John-Dalrymple lived at Lazenby Hall, Cumberland.

XV. Alexander-Thomas was born in Madras in 1835. He was educated at Harrow. He entered the civil service of the East India Company in Bengal in 1857, and rose to the position of judge of the high court of judicature at Fort William. He was married, in 1875, to Selina-Philippa, daughter of William S. Dicken, by whom he had four children, Alexander-John-Hew, Catherine-Helen-Dalrymple, Margaret, and Flora. He died a few years ago. He was succeeded by his only son.

XVI. Alexander-John-Hew was born in 1880. He is the sixteenth Maclean of Ardgour.

II. THE MACLEANS OF BORERAY.

I. Neil Bàn, second son of Donald, first laird of Ardgour, was the progenitor of the Macleans of Boreray. According to tradition, Patrick Roy Obeolan, lay abbot of Applecross, had three children, Norman, Austin Mor, and a daughter. Alexander, third Lord of the Isles, took the daughter to live with him, and had by her a son named Austin or Hugh. This son was brought up in Donald of Ardgour's family. He received the lands of Sleat and others from his father, and was the progenitor of the Macdonalds of Sleat. Neil Bàn Maclean married a daughter of Norman Obeolan. His wife and Hugh of Sleat were thus first cousins. Hugh was very much attached to Neil Bàn, the companion of his childhood, and gave him the lands of Boreray, Peinn Boreray, Claddach Carinish, Grimsay, Gearndu, Scotvein, Rhudu, Ardnastrùban, and Kallin. The conditions imposed were: first, that Neil Bàn and his successors should furnish Macdonald of Sleat with a certain number of fighting men whenever required; and, secondly, that each of the Macleans of Boreray, on taking up the succession, should deliver to his superior in the lands held by him fifteen cows and a bull. It is said that about the time of Sir Lachlan Mor of Duart, the Maclean who held Boreray refused to comply with the conditions, and was consequently deprived of his lands. They were leased, however, to his son, about 1612, at an annual rent of sixteen pounds three shillings and fourpence. The Macleans of Boreray were known as Sliochd Neill Bhàin, or the offspring of Neil Bàn.

II. John, son of Neil Bàn, was the second Maclean of Boreray.

III. The name of the third Maclean of Boreray we do not know.

IV. Alexander seems to have been the fourth Maclean of Boreray.

V. Ailein na Tuaighe was probably the dreaming Boreray of Sir Lachlan Mor's time.

VI. Donald of Boreray had three sons, Archibald, Neil Bàn, and Lachlan. Archibald was killed at Inverkeithing. Lachlan lived at Vallay.

VII. Neil Bàn married Ann, daughter of Alexander Mackenzie of Kilcoy, and had twelve children by her, John, Donald, Charles, Archibald, Murdoch, Allan, Ewen, Hector, Alexander, and three daughters. John succeeded his father in Boreray. Charles settled in Tiree. Archibald was tacksman of Kirkibost. Ewen had a son named John, who was a captain in the army or navy, and died at the siege of Carthagena. Hector settled in Tiree.

VIII. John was tacksman of Boreray when Martin visited the island in 1695. He married a daughter of Campbell of Strond, by whom he had four children, Archibald, John, Neil, and Ann. He died in 1723. 1. Archibald succeeded his father in Boreray. 2. Neil married a daughter of Lachlan Maclean of Vallay, and had three daughters by her. The eldest was married to Roderick, son of Macleod of Contullich. The second was married, as his second wife, to William Macdonald, tutor of Sleat. The third was married to Hugh Macdonald, the tutor's son. 3. John was minister of North Uist. He was married and left a son named John, who settled in Greenock. 4. Ann was married to John Macdonald of Castleton in the Isle of Skye.

IX. Archibald of Boreray was served heir to his father in 1723. He was married twice. By

his first wife, a daughter of Samuel Macdonald in
Sleat, he had Neil Bàn, John, and a daughter. By
his second wife, a daughter of John Macdonald of
Balkany, Bail'-a-Chanaich, he had Alexander,
Hector, and John. He was a man of intelligence
and good sense. He died in 1739. He was succeeded by his eldest son, Neil Bàn. Alexander
was a tenant in North Uist and had a son named
Archibald, who was in the year 1790 served heir
male to his grandfather, Archibald Maclean of
Boreray.

X. Neil Bàn married a daughter of William
Macdonald, tutor of Sleat, and had seven children
by her, Donald, John, Archibald, William, Allan,
Marion, and Margaret. John was a captain in the
army.

XI. Donald of Boreray married a daughter of
Campbell of Strond. He was in possession of the
estate in 1760, but his father was still living. He
was married to a daughter of Campbell of Strond.
He was succeeded apparently by Archibald, son of
Alexander, son of Archibald of Boreray.

XII. Archibald of Boreray had two children,
John, his successor, and Christina, who was married
to Macneil of Pabbay and Kyles, and had a son
named William.

XIII. John of Boreray was born in 1758. He
purchased the estate of Drimnin and went to live
on it. He married, in 1797, Jessie, daughter of
Donald Macleod of Bernera, and had eight children by her: Donald; John, who died young;

Archibald-Neil; Roderick-Norman, who was an officer in the Bengal army and died in 1845; William-Campbell; Alexandrina, who was married to Major-General Duncan Macpherson of the Bengal army; Marion who died in 1892; Margaret, who was married to the Rev. Dr. John Maclean, minister of Morvern; and Helen, who was married to Donald Macleod. He died on April 3d, 1821, and was buried at Ard-a-Mhorain in North Uist.

XIV. Donald of Boreray sold the lands of Drimnin a few years after his father's death. He sold his lease of Boreray, in 1865, to Sir John Campbell-Orde for £3,000. The lease was for "three lives and three nineteens." When Donald sold it there were twelve years of it to run. Donald died in North Devon, England, in 1874. He was married, but had no issue.

XV. Archibald-Neil, third son of John of Boreray, was a major-general in the Bombay army. He died in 1875.

XVI. William-Campbell, fifth son of John of Boreray, was born in 1811. He was a military surgeon in India for a long time. He married, in 1845, Louisa, daughter of John Macpherson, factor in Skye, and had by her several sons and daughters. He was appointed professor of military medicine at Netley School in England in 1860. He held the rank of surgeon-general, and was an LL.D., and a C.B. He printed for private circulation, in 1893, "Memoirs of a Long Life," a very interesting work. He died in 1898.

1. THE DESCENDANTS OF TERLACH MAC NEIL BÀN.

Charles, Tearlach Mac Neill Bhàin, third son of the second Neil Bàn of Boreray, settled in Tiree, and was in very comfortable circumstances. He married Florence, daughter of Neil of Drimnacross, and had nine children by her, Neil, Archibald, Lachlan, Donald, John, Catherine, Ann, Isabel, and Mary. Neil married Florence, daughter of Donald Maclean of Arighoulan, by whom he had Alexander, Lachlan, and daughters. Alexander was in the army and died in Holland. Lachlan was a captain in the military service of the East India Company. He settled at Craigebete in Mull. Lachlan, third son of Charles, was a captain in Colonel Lamby's regiment in Holland. He married Maria Fatmangle, by whom he had a daughter named Florentia. He died at the Brill in 1752. Catherine, eldest daughter of Charles, died unmarried. Ann was married to Hector Maclean; Isabel, to the Rev. John Maclean; and Mary, to John of Treshnish.

THE MACLEANS OF SCOUR.

Archibald, second son of Charles Mac Neil Bàn, graduated at the University of Glasgow in 1713, and became minister of Kilvicewen, or Kilfinichen, in Mull, in 1720. He was an amiable and excellent man. He married Susanna, daughter of Donald Campbell of Ardtun and Scamadale, by whom he had Charles, John, Neil, Florence, Margaret, Ann, and Barbara. Neil was for some time in the commissary department at Niagara. He was married, and left a daughter. Florence was married to Donald of Muck. Margaret was married in 1756 to the Rev. Neil Macleod of Kilfinichen, a brother of Donald Macleod of Swordale in Skye, and a nephew of the Rev. Norman Macleod of Morvern. She had four children, Alexander, Mary, Susanna, and Ann. Alexander studied for the ministry, settled in New York, and was the author of several works. Ann, third daughter of the Rev. Archibald Maclean, was married to Hugh Maclean of Langamuli. Barbara was married to Hugh Maclean, a lawyer in Glasgow.

Charles, eldest son of the Rev. Archibald Maclean, was a kind and pleasant man, and possessed of extraordinary strength. He was for some time in the army. He settled at Scour in Mull. He married Catherine, daughter of Lachlan Maclean, third of Muck, by whom he had three children, Archibald, Mary, and Isabel. Mary died unmarried. Isabel was married on May 20th, 1801, to the Rev. Edmund Macqueen, minister of Barra.

Archibald, second Maclean of Scour, was a mild and kind-hearted man. He was known as Gilleasbuig na Sgurra, or Archibald of Scour. He was for some time in the 71st regiment. He was appointed lieutenant-colonel in the 79th, or Cameron Highlanders, in 1801. He served in America, Holland, and Egypt. He was noted for his great strength. He was an officer of the most undaunted courage. He retired from the army in 1807. He died, unmarried, in 1817.

The Macleans of Princeton.

John, second son of the Rev. Archibald Maclean of Kilfinichen, was a doctor. He married, in April, 1756, Agnes Lang, of Glasgow, by whom he had five children, all of whom died young, except John. He was appointed surgeon in Fraser's Highlanders in 1757. He was present at the capture of Louisburg in 1758, and of Quebec in 1759. He is said to have been the third man who scaled the Heights of Abraham with General Wolfe. He returned to Scotland in 1762.

John, son of Dr. John Maclean, was born in Glasgow in 1771, and graduated at the University there as physician and surgeon in 1791. He studied chemistry for some time in Edinburgh, and surgery in Paris. He went to the United States in 1795, and was appointed professor of chemistry and natural philosphy in Princeton. He married Phœbe, daughter of Dr. Absalom Bainbridge, and a sister of Commodore Bainbridge. He had six children, John, William-Bainbridge, George-Mackintosh, Archibald, Mary, and Agnes. He died in 1814. He was a man of good ability and high character. **John,** his eldest son, was born in 1800. John studied for the ministry, and became president of Princeton College in 1853. He resigned in 1886, and was succeeded by Dr.

McCosh. He was the author of several valuable review articles and of a history of Princeton College. He was a benevolent, honourable, and amiable man. He died, unmarried, in 1886. Two of his brothers, William and Archibald, also died unmarried. They were both lawyers.

George-Mackintosh, third son of Professor John Maclean, studied medicine. He was for some time professor of chemistry and natural history in Hanover College, Indiana. He was married three times. By his first wife, Catherine O. Smith, he had one son, John. By his third wife, Caroline M. Fitch, he had three daughters, Mary-Agnes, Louisa-Bragdon, and Caroline-Fitch. He died in 1886. John, his only son, studied for the ministry. John died in 1870. He was married, and left a daughter named Phœbe.

THE MACLEANS OF KILMOLUAIG.

I. Donald, fourth son of Charles Mac Neil Bàn, was the only one of his father's sons that remained in Tiree. He was tacksman of Kilmoluaig. He married Isabel, daughter of John Campbell of the family of Dunstaffnage. He had six children, John, Charles, Archibald, Florence, Isabel, and Elizabeth. 1. John, his eldest son, was factor of the estate of Ardgour. John married Florence, daughter of John Maclean, son of Charles of Inverscadale, and had eight children, Charles, John, Donald, James, Hugh, Isabel, Ann, and Barbara. (1). Charles was a physician. He married Mary, daughter of Dr. Hector Campbell, of London, by whom he had six children, Hector, Charles, Frederick, Emma, Mary, and Adelaide. (2). John was collector of customs in the island of St. Domingo. He died in London in 1837. (3). Donald was a merchant in London. He married Jane, daughter of George Brown, and had eight children; John-George, Donald-James, William-Henry, Charles-Edward, Margaret-Ann, Jane, Anna, and Catherine. (4). James was a captain of dragoons in India. (5). Hugh was a merchant in New York. He died unmarried. (6). Isabel was married to John, son of Donald Maclean of Muck. (7). Ann was married to Lieutenant-General Skinner, and had six children, Thomas, John, James, Allan-Maclean, Anne, and Mary-Ann. 2. Charles, second son of Donald of Kilmoluaig, was a major in the 43d regiment. He died unmarried. 3. Archibald succeeded his father in Kilmoluaig. 4. Florence was married to Donald, son of Macdonald of Glencoe, and was the mother of Colonel Alexander Macdonald of the Royal Artillery. 5. Isabel was married to the Rev. John MacCubbin, minister in Galloway. 6. Elizabeth died unmarried.

II. Archibald, second of Kilmoluaig, married Catherine, daughter of Donald Campbell of Scamadale, and had five children; Donald, Charles, John, Annabella, and Mary. Donald and Charles died in the West Indies. John succeeded his father in Kilmoluaig.

III. John, third of Kilmoluaig, married Margaret, daughter of the Rev. Archibald MacColl, minister of Tiree, by whom he had at least one son, Donald.

IV. Donald, son of John of Kilmoluaig, went to New Zealand about 1840. He learned the Maori language, and could speak it as fluently as Gaelic. He was appointed local protector of the aborigines at Taraniki about 1844, and Native Administrator and Minister of Colonial Defence in 1869. He was created knight commander of the order of St. Michael and St. George in 1874. He married Susan-Douglas, daughter of Robert R. Strang, by whom he had one son, Robert-Douglas-Donald. He died in January, 1877.

The Hon. Sir Donald Maclean possessed administrative talent of a high order. He pursued a policy of fair dealing and kindness towards the natives, and wielded an immense influence over them. To his ability and sagacity, New Zealand was indebted to a large extent for its peace and prosperity in the early period of its history. Sir Donald was greatly lamented by the Maori tribes. His death was to them the loss of a great chief and kind father.

2. The Macleans of Heisker.

Archibald, fourth son of the second Neil Bàn of Boreray, was tacksman of Heisker and Kirkibost in North Uist. His son, Gilleasbuig Og, married, first, a daughter of Samuel Macdonald, and had by her two sons, Archibald, a coppersmith in Glasgow, and John. He married, secondly, a daughter of Ranald Macdonald of Ballishear, by whom he had Lachlan and two daughters. John, his second son, Iain Mac Ghilleasbuig Oig, resided for some time at Mingary in Mull. He married Catherine, daughter of the Rev. John Maclean. It is said that he had five sons, Archibald, Neil, Donald, John, and James. He left Mingary, and went back to North Uist. Archibald was tacksman of Heisker. He quarrelled with Macdonald of Vallay, and shortly afterwards emigrated to Canada. He was succeeded in Heisker by his brother, Captain James Maclean of Penmore. Neil, second son of John, son of Gilleasbuig Og, was born at Mingary in 1759. He was for some time a lieutenant in the 84th regiment. He settled at St. Andrews in the county of Stormont, Ontario, shortly after June, 1782. He was appointed lieutenant-colonel of the Stormont militia in 1812. He fought at the battle of Chrysler's Farm. He became a member of the Legislative Council of Upper Canada in 1815. He married, in 1784, a daughter of John Macdonald, of Leek, and had by her eight children, John, Archibald, Alexander, Catherine, James, Jessie, Isabel, and Ann. He died in 1832. John, his eldest son, was a sheriff. He was married and left three sons. Archibald was born in 1794, and began studying law in 1808. He joined the militia in 1812. He was dangerously wounded at the battle of Queenstown Heights and taken prisoner at the battle of Lundy's Lane. He was called to the bar in 1815. He was elected to the Legislative Assembly in 1820, and was for some time speaker. He was appointed to the bench in 1837, and became chief justice of Upper Canada in 1862. He married Joan Macpherson, and had by her, John, Archibald, Thomas, Neil, Duncan, Isabel, Mary, and Elizabeth. He was an honourable and amiable man, and a good judge. He died in 1865. He was a Tory in politics and a thorough Presbyterian in religion. Alexander, third son of Neil Maclean, was married and left two sons, Neil and Alexander.

3. The Macleans of Balliphetrish.

I. Hector, eighth son of the second Neil Bàn, settled at Balliphetrish in Tiree. He was apparently a merchant. He married Marion, daughter of John Macquarrie of Ulva. He had at least two sons, Neil and Ewen. Neil had a son named John. Ewen lived at Balliphetrish. The Ardgour MS. refers to him as "a worthy gentleman of the family of Boreray." He had two daughters: Catherine, who was married to Allan Maclean of Grishipol; and Mary, who was married to Hector Maclean, son of John Diurach.

John, son of Neil, son of Hector of Balliphetrish, was born in Tiree in August, 1707. He was an ensign in the Black Watch. He left Scotland on May 20th, 1757, and arrived in America on August 14th. He settled at Danbury,

Connecticut, and on October 12th, 1759, married Deborah, daughter of Samuel Adams, of Fairfield, Connecticut. He was a merchant, and prospered in his business. He joined the American army in the time of the Revolution, and acted as commissary for four or five years. When the British were approaching Danbury in 1777 he knew that his wife and children would be safe, but he was somewhat anxious about his whiskey. In order to preserve it, he put it in jars and hid the jars under his barn, and perhaps under the ground. The British burnt Danbury, but some of John Maclean's whiskey escaped. It seems that the jars were all destroyed except one. That lucky jar is still in existence; but to what use it is now put we do not know. In 1800 he was one of the heaviest taxpayers, and one of the wealthiest men in Danbury. He died on April 7th, 1805.

John Maclean and Deborah Adams had nine children; Mary, Anne, Deborah, Alexander, Lilly, John, Lany, Sally, and Hugh, or Ewen. Anne, was married to John Dodd, by whom she had Sally, Eliza, James, Frederick, and John. Deborah was married to Zadoc Starr, by whom she had Hugh, Flora, Sally, Amos, George, Clarissa, Mary, and Angeline. Lilly was married to William Chappell, by whom she had Julia, William-Ogden, Hannah, Mary, and Eliza. Lany was married to Samuel-Henley Philips, by whom she had William, Charles, Hannah-Amelia, and Thomas-Henley. Sally was married to Philo J.

Calhoun, by whom she had Nancy, Mary-Jane, Philo C., and Sarah. Hugh died at the age of nineteen.

Alexander, eldest son of John Maclean, was born in 1768. He married Laura Warner, by whom he had five children, Alexander, Mary, Laura, Deborah, and Hugh. Alexander was married twice. He had six children by his first wife; George, Sarah, Catherine-Amanda, Emiline, Julia, and Mary-Ellen; and two children by his second wife, William and John. Hugh, second son of Alexander, John's son, settled in Ohio. He was married and had nine children. Laura, daughter of Alexander, John's son, was married to John Hurlburt. Deborah was married to Cebra Lake.

John, second son of John Maclean, was born in 1773. He married, in 1797, Sally Chappell, by whom he had John-Adams and Sally. Sally was married to George Wade and had one son and three daughters. John-Adams was born in 1798. He was a medical doctor, and practised his profession at Norwalk, Connecticut, during sixty-three years. He married Elizabeth Jarvis, by whom he had one son, John-Wilson. He died in March, 1883. John-Wilson was like his father a doctor, and also lived at Norwalk. He served as a surgeon in the Northern army during the Civil War. He married Harriet Grumman, by whom he had two sons, Charles and Frederick. He died in April, 1897.

III. THE MACLEANS OF TRESHNISH.

Ewen, second Maclean of Ardgour, had five sons; Lachlan, Terlach, Allan, John, and Hector of Blaaich. Hector was the ancestor of the Macleans of Treshnish and the first Macleans of Blaaich.

I. John, fourth son of Ewen, second of Ardgour, was the first Maclean of Treshnish. He was known as Iain Ruadh, or John Roy. He was appointed hereditary constable of the fortress of Cairnburgh. He acted for some time as tutor to John Mac Terlach, fourth of Ardgour. He had two children, Donald and Marion. Donald succeeded his father in Treshnish. Marion was married to Lachlan Cattanach of Duart, and had at least two sons, Hector Mor and Ailein nan Sop.

II. Donald of Treshnish died without issue, and was succeeded by his cousin-german, Donald Dubh, son of Hector of Blaaich.

III. Donald Dubh was known as Dòmhnall Dubh a Chaisteil, or Black Donald of the Castle. He married, first, a daughter of Macmartin of Letterfinlay, by whom he had at least one son, Ewen. He married, secondly, a daughter of Clanranald, by whom he had at least three sons, Ewen Uaibhreach, John Odhar, and Lachlan Fionn. Besides the four sons mentioned he had also Lachlan and Donald, and several daughters. Donald Dubh was a bold and rough sort of man, but remarkably faithful to his chief. Ewen, his eldest son, succeeded him in Treshnish and in the constableship of Cairnburgh. Ewen Uaibhreach, or Ewen the Haughty, succeeded him in Blaaich. John Odhar held the lands of Achnadale in Lochaber. He was also bailie for Maclean of Duart of the lands of Garbhdhabhach. Lachlan Fionn, or Lachlan the Fair, was the first Maclean of Hynish in Tiree.

IV. Ewen of Treshnish was an active and prosperous man. He loved to distinguish himself and make a figure in the world. He married Ann Maclean of the family of Lethir, and had seven sons by her; Hector, Lachlan, Allan, John, Donald, Charles, and Archibald. He was buried in Icolmkill. Hector, his eldest son, succeeded him in Treshnish. Lachlan was an intelligent and prudent man, and acted for some time as bailie for Lachlan Og Maclean of Torloisk. Allan was a prominent warrior. He was killed in a skirmish with the Macdonalds at Sron-na-Cranalaich, near Lecklee. He was buried in Icolmkill.

V. Hector of Treshnish was an active man and a good manager. He was very well off. He is described in 1579 as Hector Mac Ewen Vic Donald Dow, captain of Cairnburgh. He obtained from Hector Og of Duart a charter of the lands of Treshnish, the half of the island of Gometra, and Gott, Vaal, and Hynish in Tiree. He married, first, Ann, daughter of Macquarrie of Ulva, and, secondly, Flora, daughter of Macneil of Barra. He had four sons; Donald, John, Neil, and Charles. Donald was by the first wife. He was a hostage in the hands of Angus Macdonald of Islay in 1587. He died shortly afterwards. Hector was succeeded by his second son, John.

VI. John of Treshnish married Margaret, daughter of Charles, son of Allan Og, son of Hector, son of Ailein nan Sop. He had a natural son, who was known as Iain a Ghanbhair. He had three sons by his wife; Ewen, Lachlan, and John Og. He was succeeded by his son Ewen.

VII. Ewen was a born warrior. Owing to a misunderstanding with his chief, he went to France about the year 1632. He spent ten years as a captain in the French service. He returned to Mull about 1642, and, having become reconciled to his chief, was sent to Ireland to command a company of Macleans in Sir Duncan Campbell's regiment. He returned to Scotland about twenty days before the battle of Inverlochy. He was present at that battle, and saved the life of an old companion, Campbell of Skipness, who was then fighting against him. Skipness was severely wounded. Ewen brought him to Cairnburgh, and thence went home with him to Skipness. He returned immediately to Montrose's army. He was a captain under his chief, Sir Lachlan of Duart. He was a great favourite with Montrose. While the latter, shortly after the battle of Alford, was marching towards Auchterader, he was annoyed by 300 horse sent in pursuit of him, under Sir John Urry. He ordered Ewen of Treshnish to select twenty good marksmen and check the cavalry. Ewen made his selection from the Macleans and the Camerons and placed his men behind rocks and bushes. They shot a number of their pursuers, and Urry deemed it prudent to retreat. Ewen was severely wounded at the battle of Inverkeithing, and died shortly afterwards.

Ewen of Treshnish married Catherine, daughter of Allan Maclean of Achnasaul, and had three sons by her. He was succeeded by Hector, the eldest of his sons.

VIII. Hector married Margaret, daughter of John Garbh, son of John Dubh of Morvern, and had one son by her, Ewen, his successor. He died in 1693.

IX. Ewen of Treshnish had two natural sons, John and Lachlan. He married Margaret, daughter of Neil Maclean of Drimnacross, and had by her two sons, Hector and John.

John, the eldest son of Ewen, was born about the year 1680. He became minister of Kilninian and Kilmore in Mull in 1702. He was a man of high character and a faithful minister. He went regularly through his parish, catechising and instructing his people. He married Isabel, daughter of Charles Mac Neil Bàn, by whom he had four children; Alexander, Ann, Mary, and Catherine. Alexander succeeded his father as minister of Kilninian. Ann was married, first, to John, son of Allan Maclean of Grishipol; and, secondly, to Hugh, son of Hector Maclean of Kilmorie.

Mary was married to Alexander, son of Donald Maclean of Calgary. Catherine was married to John, son of Archibald Og Maclean of Heisker. The Rev. John Maclean was an excellent poet. He died on March 12th, 1756. He was buried with his father at Kilninian. Alexander, son of the Rev. John Maclean, was born in 1722. He was licensed to preach in 1745, and became minister of Kilninian and Kilmore in 1750. He married, in 1750, Christy, daughter of Donald Maclean of Torloisk, by whom he had John, Donald, Lachlan, and two daughters. John was a captain in the American War, and was drowned near Halifax. Lachlan was a major-general in the army. He died in Halifax, Nova Scotia. Lachlan, second son of Ewen of Treshnish, married Jean, daughter of Donald Maclean of Calgary, by whom he had one son and several daughters. His only son was drowned while on his passage from Mull to Glasgow. Hector, third son of Ewen of Treshnish, was born in 1696. He became minister of Coll in 1733. He received a visit from Dr. Johnson in 1773. He married Janet, daughter of Hector Maclean, tacksman of Knock in Coll, by whom he had three children; Allan, Florence, and Margaret. Allan was a lieutenant in the army, and was lost at sea on his passage from New York to Scotland. Florence was married to Captain Lachlan Maclean, of the Coll family, and Margaret, to Alexander Maclean of Mingary. The Rev. Hector Maclean died in April, 1775. John, fourth son of Ewen of Treshnish, succeeded his father.

X. John of Treshnish married Mary, daughter of Charles Mac Neil Bàn, by whom he had Hugh, or Ewen, and several daughters. He was dispossessed of his estate by the managers of the Duke of Argyll, in 1738.

Treshnish was in possession of the Macleans for nearly three hundred years. Ewen, fourth of Treshnish, obtained a charter of his lands from Lachlan Mor of Duart. The charter was renewed by Hector Og, Lachlan Mor's son, the witnesses being Roderick Macleod of Harris and Roderick Macneil of Barra. When Ewen, seventh of Treshnish, was in France, his brother Lachlan gave the charter to Sir Lachlan of Duart for safe keeping. It was lost along with other papers which were in Sir Lachlan's possession. Owing to this loss, it was an easy matter for the Duke of Argyll to make himself the legal owner of Treshnish.

XI. Hugh, eleventh representative of the Macleans of Treshnish, was a lawyer by profession. He married Barbara, youngest daughter of the Rev. Archibald Maclean of Kilfinichen, and had by her five sons and two daughters.

THE FIRST MACLEANS OF BLAAICH.

I. Hector, fifth son of Ewen, second Maclean of Ardgour, was the first Maclean of Blaaich. He had three sons: Donald Dubh; Ewen, first

Maclean of Cornaig in Tiree; and Hector Odhar. According to the Ardgour MS. the descendants of Hector Odhar, Sliochd Eachainn Uidhir, were scattered over Mull and Tiree.

II. Donald Dubh, second of Blaaich and third of Treshnish, had six sons; Ewen of Treshnish, Ewen Uaibhreach of Blaaich, John Odhar of Achnadale, Lachlan Fionn of Hynish, Lachlan, and Donald.

III. Ewen Uaibhreach was succeeded in Blaaich by his son, Hector.

IV. Hector was succeeded by his son, Ewen.

V. Ewen, son of Hector, was the next Maclean of Blaaich.

VI. Hector, son of Ewen, was served heir to his father in 1615.

The Macleans of Achnadale.

John Odhar, third son of Donald Dubh of Treshnish, was the first Maclean of Achnadale. According to the Ardgour MS. the Macleans of "Keppernack" belonged to the Achnadale family. The first Maclean of Kepparnach had three sons, Alexander, William, and Lachlan. Alexander was a major in the army. He was killed in Germany in the year 1762. He was the subject of a very beautiful elegy by Rob Donn Mackay, or Calder, the celebrated Sutherlandshire bard. William was a lieutenant in Colonel Montgomerie's Highland regiment. Lachlan was a merchant in Barbadoes.

The Macleans of Hynish.

I. Lachlan Fionn, fourth son of Donald Dubh of Treshnish, was the first Maclean of Hynish in Tiree. He was a bold, active, and resolute man, and accumulated a good deal of wealth. He had nine sons, all of whom lived in Tiree.

II. Ewen, son of Lachlan Fionn, had a son named John.

III. John had a son named Donald.

IV. Donald, who was known as Donald Og, had two sons, Lachlan and Allan. Allan was the father of Charles, father of Donald Roy.

V. Lachlan, son of Donald Og, had a son named Charles.

VI. Charles, son of Lachlan, had three children; Lachlan, John, and Mary.

1. Lachlan had two sons, Charles and Archibald. Charles, the elder son of Lachlan Mac Terlach, had a son named Donald. Donald married Mary, daughter of Alexander Macfadyen, Alasdair Mac Neill Mhic Dhòmhnaill Mhic Dhùghaill, and had by her Charles and Archibald. Archibald, second son of Lachlan Mac Terlach, was known as Gilleasbuig Laidir, or Strong Archibald. He was a poet of fair ability. He married Flora Maclean, by whom he had John, Archibald, Alexander, James, and Hector. He died at Kilmoluaig.

2. John, second son of Charles, lived at Hoùh in Tiree. He was drowned near Mull at an early age. He was married and left one child,

Allan. Allan settled at Cnoc Mhic Dhùghaill in Caolas, Tiree. He married Margaret, daughter of Neil Macfadyen, Niall Mac Dhòmhnaill Mhic Dhùghaill, and had by her, Donald, Charles, John, Neil, and Mary. 1. Donald, Dòmhnall Cùbair, or Donald the Cooper, settled at Bailephuill in Tiree. He married Mary Macdonald, by whom he had Margaret, Mary, Marion, Catherine, Ann, Christy, Archibald, and John. Archibald died young. John succeeded his father in Bailephuill. He married Mary Sinclair, by whom he had Isabel, Mary, Catherine, Christy, Archibald, Dugald, and Donald. Margaret, the eldest of Dòmhnall Cùbair's family, was married to Neil Brown. Mary was married to Donald Maceachern; Catherine, to Colin Macmillan; and Christy, to John Macleod. Ann died unmarried. 2. Charles, second son of Allan, married Mary Lamont, by whom he had one son, Allan. He died in his boat at Tobermory about 1811. Allan, his son, married Mary Cameron and had two sons and a daughter. 3. John, third son of Allan, came to America. 4. Neil, fourth son of Allan, succeeded his father at Caolas. He married Marion Macdonald, by whom he had nine children; Margaret, Ann, Neil Og, Charles, Isabel, Catherine, Flora, Mary, and James. He died about 1847. Neil Og succeeded his father at Caolas. He married Flora Macfadyen, by whom he had five children; Christy, Neil, Mary-Ann, Alexander, and Marion. Charles, second son of Neil, married Ann Brown, by whom he had seven children; John,

Christy, Marion, Johanna, Catherine, Neil, and Hector. James, third son of Neil, lives in Glasgow, and is married. Margaret, eldest daughter of Neil, was married, in 1844, to Archibald Macdonald in Caolas. Ann was married to Lachlan Maclaine in Caolas. Neil Maclaine, vice-president of the Maclean Association, Glasgow, is her son. Isabel was married to Dugald Maclellan from Islay. Mary was married to Lachlan Maclean. 5. Mary, only daughter of Allan Maclean, was married to Roderick Macdonald in Caolas, and had by her eleven children; Allan, Lachlan, John, Alexander, Marion, Charles, Catherine, Margaret, Isabel, Duncan, and Lachlan. Roderick Macdonald died in 1883 at the advanced age of 103 years. He was a very kind and pleasant man. He visited Iona with us in August, 1869.

The Macleans of Glenbard.

John, third son of Allan Maclean—Ailein Mac Iain mhic Thearlaich mhic Lachain mhic Dhòmhnaill Oig mhic Iain mhic Eoghain mhic Lachainn Fhinn—was born at Cnoc Mhic Dhùghaill in Caolas, Tiree, on January 8th, 1787. He married in Glasgow, on July 19th, 1808, Isabel, daughter of Duncan Black in Lismore. He published his own poems, and some poems by other Gaelic bards, in 1818. He came to Nova Scotia in 1819, and settled at Bail'-a-Chnoic in Barney's River, Pictou County. He removed to Glenbard in Antigonish County in 1831. He died on January 26th, 1848. He was known in Scotland as Bàrd Thighearna Chola, or the Laird of Coll's Poet, and in America as Am Bàrd Mac-Gilleain, or the Bard Maclean. His poems were published in Clàrsach na Coille in 1881. His wife died in 1877. He had an intimate acquaintance with the poetry, legends, and history of the Macleans.

John Maclean and Isabel Black had six children; Christy, Charles, Archibald, John, Allan, and Elizabeth. Charles was born in Tiree in 1813. He succeeded his father in Glenbard, and died in 1880. He was never married. Archibald married Catherine Macphie, by whom he had three children; Isabel, Mary, and Christy-Ann. He was born in Tiree in 1815, and died on January 26th, 1899. He was with his father when the latter died. He died himself precisely fifty-one years afterwards. John, the poet's third son, was born at Bail'-a-Chnoic, or Balknock, in 1820. He married Margaret Robertson, by whom he had John, Alexander, Duncan, Isabel, Allan-Robert, Annie, Christy, and Charles-Sinclair. He succeeded his brother in Glenbard. He died on May 15th, 1897, and was succeeded in Glenbard by his second son, Alexander. Allan, the poet's fourth son, was born at Balknock in 1822. He married Rebecca Maclaughlan, by whom he had seven children; Rebecca, John, William, Charles, Anthony, Jane, and Isabel. He died in 1871. Christy, the eldest of the poet's family, was born in Tiree on December 25th, 1809.

She was married, as his second wife, in 1839, to John Sinclair from Strath-Halladale in Sutherlandshire, and had by him one child, Alexander-Maclean. She died on March 7th, 1887. Elizabeth, the youngest of the poet's family, was born at Balknock in 1826. She lives in Glenbard.

The Macleans of Inverscadale.

The Macleans of Inverscadale are descended from Charles, third lawful son of Allan, fifth Maclean of Ardgour.

I. Charles was tutor of Ardgour for some time. He is referred to as such in public documents in 1592 and 1601. He succeeded, through the influence of Hector Og of Duart, in procuring a hereditary right to the lands of Inverscadale, Arighoulan, Achaphubuill, and others. He married Marion, daughter of Hector Og of Duart, and relict of Hector Roy of Coll, and had two sons, Allan and Ewen. Allan succeeded his father in Inverscadale. Ewen, known as Ewen Dubh, obtained from his father a charter of Arighoulan and other lands.

II. Allan of Inverscadale was succeeded by his son, Ewen.

III. Ewen was succeeded by his son, Allan.

IV. Allan had two sons, Charles and Allan. Charles succeeded his father. Allan settled in Killean in Mull. He married Margaret, daughter of Lachlan Og, seventh son of Allan, seventh of Ardgour; and had two sons by her. Lachlan, the elder of the two, lived in Dublin. He was captain of a ship, and was in comfortable circumstances. He was shipwrecked on the south-west coast of Ireland. He got ashore, with most of his men, in the long-boat; but was murdered by the inhabitants, who carried off all the plunder which they could obtain.

V. Charles of Inverscadale was known as Tearlach Og. By his first wife, a daughter of Donald Cameron of Glendessary, he had Allan, his successor. By his second wife, a daughter of Archibald Maclean of Ardtun, he had John and others. John was known as Iain Mac Thearlaich Oig. He was a well-informed man and full of humour. He was the author of some excellent comic songs. He lived at Sorn in Mull. He married Mary, daughter of Allan, tenth of Ardgour, by whom he had two children, John and Florence. The latter was married to John Maclean of Kilmoluaig.

John, son of Iain Mac Thearlaich Oig, went to Jamaica in 1760 to obtain possession of an estate which had been left to him by the son of a paternal uncle. After his return he married Sibella, second daughter of Sir Allan Maclean of Brolas, and had two children by her, Allan and Mary-Ann. Allan was a captain in the 60th regiment, and died in the West Indies. Mary-Ann was married to Dr. Mackenzie Grieve.

VI. Allan of Inverscadale married Marjory, daughter of Allan Mac Ian Diurach, of the family of Torloisk, and had issue by her. He sold the reversion of the lands of Inverscadale to the Camerons, from whom they were purchased by Alexander, thirteenth of Ardgour.

The Later Macleans of Blaaich.

The later Macleans of Blaaich are descended from Lachlan, second son of John Crùbach of Ardgour. He seems to have been succeeded in Blaaich by his son, Allan. In March, 1758, we find William Maclean, lately a journeyman barber in Edinburgh, returned heir general to his grandfather, Allan Maclean of Blaaich.

Major-General Francis Maclean.

William Maclean, of the Ardgour family, was born in Mull, about 1660. He was an accomplished musician, and was appointed by James, Duke of York, master of the revels for Scotland. He had a son named William, who was a captain under the Duke of Marlborough. Captain William married a daughter of Sir Francis Kinloch, by whom he had two sons, Francis and James. The latter died in the West Indies in 1748. Francis entered the army, in the regiment in which his father served, at a very early age. He was a lieutenant in the Scottish brigade at the capture of Bergen-op-zoom in 1747. Allan, son of Maclean of Torloisk, was also a lieutenant in that brigade. Both were taken prisoners. When carried before General Lowendahl, that distinguished commander addressed them as follows:—"Gentlemen, consider yourselves on parole. If all had conducted themselves as you and your brave corps have done, I should not now be master of Bergen-op-zoom." Francis was appointed senior captain in the 2d battalion of the Black Watch in July, 1758. He was a lieutenant-colonel in 1762, and was in that year sent to Portugal to assist the Portuguese in their war with Spain. He was governor of Almeida for several years, and afterwards commander of the troops in Estramadura and Lisbon. He returned from Portugal in 1778, and was immediately sent to Nova Scotia to take charge of the forces in that province. He landed in Halifax on the 14th of August. He was accompanied by three regiments, one of them being the 74th, or Argyle Highlanders. In June, 1779, he went to Penobscot in Maine with 700 men, and began at once to erect a fort. Before he had completed his defences, a New England fleet arrived from Boston, having on board 2,500 men, under the command of General Lovell. The New Englanders landed on the 25th of July and began to lay siege to the newly erected fort. On the 13th of August Sir George Collier came to its relief with a fleet, attacked the besiegers, and destroyed their ships and transports. General Maclean received high praise for his gallant defence of Penobscot. He strengthened the fort, and placed it in charge of Lieutenant-Colonel Alexander Campbell of Menzie, with 600 men of the Argyle Highlanders. He returned to

Halifax on November 23d. He died on May 4th, 1781, and was buried on the morning of May 9th in the vault of St. Paul's Church, Halifax. He was a major-general, and in the sixty-fourth year of his age.

According to the Ardgour MS., General Francis Maclean was descended from Hector Odhar, third son of Hector, the first of the earlier Macleans of Blaaich. According to Seannachie's History, the General's grandfather, William Maclean, master of the revels, was a grandson of Lachlan, progenitor of the later Macleans of Blaaich.

CHAPTER XIV.

The Descendants of Neil of Lehir.

I. THE MACLEANS OF LEHIR.

I. NEIL, second son of Lachlan Bronnach of Duart, was the progenitor of the Macleans of Lehir, Ross, and Shuna. He was born probably about the year 1418. He received from his father the sixty marklands of Lehir in fee simple, to compensate him for the loss of Duart and the chiefship. His place of residence was called Baile Neill, Balneil, or Neil's Town. His estate was known as Leithir Baile Neill, or Lehir of Balneil. In course of time the name Baile Neill was changed to Torloisg, or Torloisgte, in English, Torloisk. The name of the estate was then changed to Leithir Thorloisg, or Lehir of Torloisk. Neil of Lehir was succeeded by his son, Neil.

II. Neil, second laird of Lehir, fought under Hector Odhar at the battle of Bloody Bay in 1484. Owing to the number of thumbs which he cut off as his opponents were trying to board his galley, he was afterwards known as Niall nan Ordag, or Neil of the thumbs. He was succeeded by his son, John.

III. John, third laird of Lehir, seems to have been known as John Dubh, and to have married a daughter of Malcolm Macneill of Gigha. He had apparently three sons, John Og, Malcolm, and Neil.

IV. John Og was slain by Ailein nan Sop about the year 1540. Allan seized the estate and kept possession of it. It was never given back to the lawful heirs.

The Macleans of Langamull.

Neil Maclean, son of Malcolm, Niall Mac Gillechaluim, was captain of Aros in 1592, and had a son named Malcolm. Hugh Maclean, Eoghan Mac Eachainn Mhic Eoghain Mhic Gillechaluim, was the representative of the Macleans of Lehir in 1762. Malcolm, his great-grandfather, was probably a grandson of Malcolm, son of the captain of Aros. At the same time all that we really know about his pedigree is that he was the son of Hector, son of Ewen, son of Malcolm. He married a daughter of Captain Allan Maclean. Lieutenant Hugh Maclean, of the Dutch service, was tenant of Langamull in 1762. He married Ann, daughter of the Rev. Archibald Maclean, minister of Ross and Brolas. He had at least two children, Lachlan and Archibald, who died young. His wife died in 1772. He died himself about

1775. In what relationship he stood to Hugh Maclean, the representative of the Lehir family in 1762, we do not know.

John Maclean of Langamull was known as Iain Mac Eoghain. As his father's name was Hugh, and as he succeeded Lieutenant Hugh in Langamull, the probability is that he was the son and heir of the latter. He may, however, have been a son of Hugh, the son of Hector, son of Ewen, son of Malcolm. He was, at all events, the acknowledged representative of the Macleans of Lehir. He was an intelligent man, an elder in the Church of Scotland, an ardent Jacobite, an excellent swordsman, and a composer and singer of Gaelic songs. He married Mary, daughter of Donald, son of Eachann Mac Iain Diuraich, and had by her nine children; Donald, Hugh, Alexander, Lachlan, Mary, Ann, Christy, Flora, and Margaret. Donald was a major in the Royal Scots. Donald married Catherine, daughter of Dr. Alexander Maclean of Pennycross. He died without issue in 1819. Hugh was a lieutenant in the 90th regiment, and died at Portsmouth. Alexander was a doctor, and died in India in 1821. Lachlan died young. Mary was married to Allan Maclean of Crossapol; Ann, to John Maclean of Tirouran; Christy, to Alexander Maclean of Kinnegharar; Flora, to Peter Macarthur; and Margaret, to Lieutenant Fraser. John of Langamull was drowned in February, 1810. His wife died in December, 1811.

II. THE MACLEANS OF ROSS.

The Macleans of Ross were descended from Neil of Ross, and were known as Sliochd a Chlaidhibh Iarainn, or the race of the iron sword. They were remarkably brave and warlike.

Neil of Ross was a great-grandson of Neil of Lehir, or Neil Mac Lachlan Bronnach, Niall Mac Lachainn Bhronnaich. He was probably the third son of John, third laird of Lehir. He settled in Ross some time after 1540. He had two sons, Donald and John Mor. Donald had at least three sons; Lachlan Odhar of Airdchraoishnish, Ewen of Ormsaig, and John Odhar.

1. LACHLAN ODHAR OF AIRDCHRAOISHNISH.

Lachlan Odhar was a distinguished warrior. He fought at the battle of Glenlivet in 1594, and at the battle of Benvigory in 1598. We find him described in 1616, as Lachlan Mac Donald Vic Neil, Lachainn Mac Dhòmhnaill mhic Neill. He lived at Airdchraoishnish in Mull. He was married and had a large family. It is said that five of his sons, Murdoch, Allan, Lachlan, Ewen, and John, were killed at Inverkeithing.

Tradition tells us that Allan Mac Eachann and Lachlan Odhar performed the horrible rite known as Taghairm nan Cat, or the invocation of the cats. They collected a number of cats and took them with them to a barn at Pennygoun in Mull. They began their invocation at the middle of the night between Friday and Saturday and continued it for four days, without tasting any food. Allan was the elder of the two, and acted as high priest. He stood at the door with a drawn sword, and gave the necessary directions. Lachlan's work consisted in putting a live cat on a spit, and roasting him to death before a huge peat fire. In the course of a day or two a black cat appeared and said to him, A Lachainn Uidhir mhic Dhòmhnaill mhic Neill is olc an diol sin air cait, Lachlan Odhar, son of Donald, son of Neil, that is a bad treatment of cats. Allan at once shouted to Lachlan, Ge b' e chi no chluinneas tu cùm an cat mu'n cuairt, whatever you see or hear keep the cat turning. As Lachlan took the advice given him, he had a large number of black cats before him in a short time. They joined their yells to those of the cat on the spit, and thus tried to frighten him and make him give up his work. They did not enter by the door, which was guarded by Allan. It is evident, then, that they were not real cats; they were demons in the guise of cats. On the fourth day Cluas Mhòr, or Big Ear, made his appearance. He was a cat of enormous size, and was black like all the other cats that came in. There was now a cat at the foot of each of the rafters of the barn. Cluas Mhòr threatened the performers with the severest punishment, but they paid no attention to him. Indeed they threatened to take hold of Cluas Mhòr himself and put him on the spit. When Cluas Mhòr saw their determination, he agreed to grant them their petitions. Allan asked for wealth; Lachlan asked for wealth and progeny; each of them received a promise of getting what he desired. It is said that the yells of the cat were at one time so terrific that they were heard distinctly in Morvern.

The word taghairm is derived from to-ghairm, and means a calling to, or invocation. The Irish form of it, which is the oldest, is toghairm. It was really a sacrifice to the devil, in order to bring him before one in a visible form. The purpose for which he was wanted was to get certain worldly benefits from him.

There is no ground for the supposition that Allan Mac Hector and Lachlan Odhar ever offered cats in sacrifice, or ever petitioned the evil one for blessings. It is certain that they never heard a cat talk. It is equally certain that they never saw demons in the shape of black cats. Allan Mac Eachann was evidently Allan Og, son of Hector, son of Ailein nan Sop. The Macleans in general looked upon him as an extremely wicked man, and were ready to believe any bad story about him. He seems to have lived among the Macleans of Lochbuie. We suspect that Lachlan Odhar and himself were not intimate friends. The probability is that they were enemies. They were both men of undoubted courage, and were probably the most daring fighters among the Macleans in the year 1600.

The Macleans of Monachuich.

Captain Allan Maclean of the 90th regiment was descended from Lachlan Odhar, and according to some persons, his actual representative. Captain Allan, resided at Monachuich, or the Cuckoo's Moor, which is half-way between Ardfinaig and the Sound of Iona. He seems to have been living in 1838. Donald Roy, who was either a brother or a son of Captain Allan, had two sons, Donald Bàn and Hector. The latter entered the army as a private and became an officer. He died unmarried. Donald Bàn settled in Glasgow and engaged in business as a tailor and clothier. He left a son who was also known as Donald Bàn. This Donald Bàn was a law clerk in Glasgow. He died at Partick about the year 1868. He was the last of the Monachuich family in the male line.

Lachlan Bàn of Bunessan.

Lachlan Bàn Maclean was a descendant of Lachainn Odhar. He lived at Bunessan in Mull, and was known as Lachainn Bàn Bhuneasain, or Lachlan Bàn of Bunessan. He kept the inn at Bunessan, and was at one time in very comfortable circumstances. He married Mary, daughter of Hector Maclean of Torren, by whom he had eight children; John, Hector, Allan, Charles, Sibella, Mary, Catherine, and Isabel. John, his eldest son, was for some time a dry-salter in Glasgow. He left Glasgow and took charge of the inn which had been kept by his father. He died unmarried about 1848. Hector, second son of Lachlan Bàn, was a captain in the 93d regiment. He married Ann, third daughter of the Rev. Neil Macleod of Kilfinichen in Mull, and had by her three children; Margaret-Burnett, Lachlan-Allan, and Mary-Sibella. After retiring from the army, Captain Maclean took up his residence at Carsaig in Mull. He removed to Campbellton about 1831. Margaret, his elder daughter, was married to George Grierson, teacher at Aberfeldy, and had six children. Mary-Sibella, his younger daughter, was born at Carsaig in November, 1821. She was married in August, 1851, to the Rev. Duncan B. Blair, D.D., minister of Barney's River and Blue Mountain in Pictou County, Nova Scotia. She had five children; Ewen, Thomas, Margaret, Lachlan, and John. She died on the 6th of June, 1882. She was a pious and friendly woman. Her husband died on June 4th, 1893. Dr. Blair was an excellent Gaelic scholar, and a good poet. Allan, third son of Lachlan Bàn, was a lieutenant in the 91st regiment. Charles, the fourth son, was a surgeon in the army. He was for some time inspector-general of hospitals. He died in Ireland. He was married, but had no issue.

Lachlan-Allan, son of Hector, son of Lachlan Bàn Maclean of Bunessan, came to America in 1842. He landed in New York, and went thence to Missouri. He fought in the United States army during the Mexican War. After the war he settled at Lexington, Missouri, as a surveyor. He fought in the Confederate army in the war between the Northern and Southern States. He was a captain under Major-General Sterling Price in July, 1862, and a major from October of that year to March, 1864. He was afterwards for a few months a major under Brigadier-General T. F. Drayton. On December 23d, 1864, he was stabbed and killed in his office at Lexington, Missouri, by Lieutenant-Colonel R. C. Wood.

Major Maclean married Eliza, daughter of Colonel Robert N. Smith, of Missouri, by whom he had one son, Nelson-Robert. Nelson was living in 1883 on a farm near Ellsworth in Kansas. He was married, and had one child, a daughter named Hope.

2. Ewen of Ormsaig.

Ewen, second son of Donald of Ross, had two sons, Allan and Hector. Allan is described in June, 1618, as "Allane McEwne in Ormesag." Allan had a grandson named Charles. Charles had a son named Donald. John, son of Donald, was known as Iain Mac Dhòmhnaill mhic Thearlaich. He was born in 1724. He was a doctor, and lived in Brolas. He married Christina, daughter of Captain Allan Maclean, son of Lachlan, second of Brolas. He had three children by his wife; Allan, Donald, and Marion. He died in March, 1808. His wife was born in 1718, and also died in March, 1808. Dr. Maclean was eighty-four years of age and his wife ninety. They were buried at Kilpatrick in Brolas. Donald, their younger son, was a lieutenant in the Cameron Highlanders. He died without issue about 1799.

Allan, **elder son of** Dr. Maclean, followed his father's profession. He was in 1800 lieutenant and surgeon in the 4th Fencible Infantry. He served for several years as surgeon in the Cameron Highlanders. On leaving the army he settled in Brolas. He was a very popular man. He is described in a well-known song as doctair ruadh nam blàth shùilean, or the red-haired doctor of the warm eyes. He married, when well advanced in years, Flora, daughter of Murdoch Maclaine of Lochbuie, a girl of about seventeen years of age, and had a large family by her. He died in October, 1827.

According to the inscription on the tombstone of Dr. John Maclean, he was "the eighth lineal descendant and the legal representative of Neil Maclean of Ross." It is apparently true enough that the doctor was the eighth lineal descendant of Neil of Ross. It does not follow, however, that he was the representative of the Macleans of Ross. He was simply the representative of Ewen, second son of Donald, son of Neil of Ross.

The Macleans of Killean.

Hector, second son of Ewen of Ormsaig, had a son named John, who had a son named Donald. Donald lived in Killean. He married Mary, daughter of Charles Maclean, son of John Garbh of Bunessan, and had by her John and others. John, second of Killean, married Catherine, daughter of Hector Maclean of Kilmory, and had by her five sons; Donald, Hector, Neil, John, and Lachlan. He was living in 1760. Donald, his eldest son, served as a volunteer in Majoribank's regiment, and died in Holland. Hector succeeded his father in Killean. Neil was a lieutenant in Lacell's regiment. John was an ensign in the old 84th. Lachlan followed the sea.

Hector of Killean was a lieutenant in the army. He married Janet, second daughter of Alexander Maclean of Shuna, by whom he had nine children; Donald, Dugald, Neil, John, Catherine, Jessie, Jane, Eleanor, and Anne. Neil, the third son, was lieutenant of the Leda frigate, and was a brave and skilful officer. On Sunday night, July 29th, 1804, he attempted, with the boats of the Leda, to cut out one of the French gunboats under Portel, near Boulogne. He got on board the gunboat with his men, killed the Frenchmen, about fifty in number, and took their vessel in tow. The tide having set in to the eastward, the Britons drifted down upon a brig full of soldiers. They boarded the brig in the face of a destructive fire, slew a number of the soldiers, but were finally overcome. When last seen, Lieutenant Maclean had his back against the mainmast of the brig. Though there were several bayonets in his body, he was cutting away with his sabre, and calling out "Victory," which was the rallying-word of his men. The captain of the forecastle killed upwards of seven Frenchmen before he fell. The men who boarded the brig were all slain, except fourteen, most of whom had been thrown overboard. A few weeks before he was killed at Boulogne the gallant Neil married Ann, daughter of Donald Maclean of Muck. He had no issue. John, fourth son of Hector of Killean, was an ensign in the 6th West India regiment, and was killed in action.

Donald, eldest son of Hector of Killean, was a lieutenant in the 74th regiment, or Argyle Highlanders. He came with his regiment to Halifax, Nova Scotia, in 1778, and was with it at Penobscot from 1779 to 1783, in which year the regiment was reduced. He retired on half pay. He received a grant of land from the Government in New Brunswick. He lost his house by fire and left New Brunswick. He spent several years in Danville, Vermont. He removed from the United States to Canada when the War of 1812 broke out. He received a grant of 2,600 acres on the St. Francis River, Quebec, and settled on it. The place in which he lived is now known as Maclean's Ferry. He married Susan Haney, daughter of a sea-captain in Castine, Maine, and had by her nine children; Catherine, Susan, Janet, Hector, Archibald, Eleanor, Betsey, Margaret, and John. He died in 1825. His wife was born in 1760. The Government granted her, in 1830, a pension of forty pounds a year. She died on May 19th, 1868, at the great age of 108 years and five months. Hector, eldest son of Lieutenant Maclean, married Lucretia Elkins, by whom he had John, Hector, Susanna, Catherine, Helen-Lucretia, and Samuel. Helen-Lucretia was married to Colonel Kimball, and resides in Washington. Archibald, second son of Lieutenant Maclean, married Hannah Lyster, and had by her, Donald, Archibald, Margaret, John, Alexander, Margaret - Reef, Susanna, Benjamin, and Elizabeth. John, third son of Lieutenant Maclean, was born in 1804. He ran the Maclean Ferry on the St. Francis River about sixty years. He married Deborah Harris, by whom he had Donald - Neil, John - Sinclair, and several daughters. He died in 1883. Donald-Neil died at the age of twenty-five. John-Sinclair resides at Martinville, Quebec. Catherine, eldest daughter of Lieutenant Maclean, was married to John Whicher. Susanna was married to Colonel James Morrill; Janet, to Ebenezer Morrill; Eleanor, to William Minneall; and Betsey, to Elisha Andrews.

The Macleans of Ardfinaig.

Dugald, second son of Hector of Killean, lived at Ardfinaig in Mull. He was for some time an officer in the Dumbarton Fencibles. He was afterwards captain in the Argyleshire regiment of Fencibles. He married Susanna, daughter of the Rev. Neil Macleod, minister of Kilfinichen and Kilvicewen, now Ross and Brolas, and had by her five children; Janet, Margaret, Hector-Neil, Susanna, and Donald-William. He was drowned near Crinan, on June 29th, 1818, while returning from Glasgow. His eldest daughter, Janet, died young. Margaret and Hector died unmarried. Susanna was born in 1808. She was married in 1837 to the Rev. Donald McVean, Free Church minister of Iona, and had seven children; Colin-Alexander, Annie-Catherine, Susan-Isabella, Mary-Helen, Dugald-Hector, Isabella-Merriman, and Archibald-Arthur. She died in 1883.

Colin-Alexander McVean is a prominent and well-known man. He was born in Iona, and is a civil engineer by profession. He was for some time surveyor-in-chief of Japan. He returned to Scotland in 1886, and settled at Kilfinichen in Mull. He married Mary-Wood Cowan, of Edinburgh, by whom he has four sons and five daughters. Donald, his eldest son, is a lieutenant in the 45th regiment.

Donald-William, second son of Captain Dugald Maclean of Ardfinaig, was born in 1819. He emigrated to Australia in 1839, and settled on a farm near the town of Inverell in New South Wales. He called his place of residence Killean. He married Catherine, youngest daughter of Finlay Macdonald, of Ellerston, New South Wales, and had by her seven children; Hector-Neil, Dugald-John, Francis-John, William-Pender, Neil-Finlay,

Susan-Catherine, and Archibald-Alexander. He was an energetic man, managed his affairs with prudence, and made a comfortable home for himself and his family. He died in 1875. Hector succeeded his father on the Killean farm. Susan and Archibald live with him. Dugald married Elizabeth, daughter of R. F. Fremlin. Francis married Caroline, daughter of James Cheadle. William came to America in 1894. He is a journalist by profession, and resides in Brooklyn, New York. He married Mary, daughter of the Hon. Otis Johnson, of Nassau, Bahama Islands. Neil married Emily, daughter of Alexander Currie. Dugald, Francis, and Neil have each of them sons with the good old clan names. It is a pleasure to see these names preserved. The Lachlans, Hectors, Allans, and Neils should not be forgotten.

3. John Odhar.

John, third son of Donald of Ross, was known as Iain Odhar. Donald, eldest son of John, had a son named Neil, who lived at Ballinahard. Neil was, in 1618, one of the principal followers of Hector Og of Duart. It is said that Donald and John Maclean, merchants in Blackburn, were descended from him.

III. The Macleans of Shuna.

According to the traditions of the Macleans of Shuna, as preserved in the Ardgour MS., they were descended from a younger son of Neil of

Ross. They also maintained that their ancestor was parson of Kilvicewen in Mull. On the assumption that their traditions respecting their origin are substantially correct, the Rev. Ewen Maclean must have been their ancestor. There was no other parson of Kilvicewen from whom they could have sprung. Ewen was not a son of Neil of Ross; he may, however, have been his grandson. The probability is that he was the son of John Mor, son of Neil of Ross. He was minister of Coll in 1621, of Killean in 1626, and of Kilvicewen at a later date. He married "Fionnaghal, nighean Ailein," Finvola the daughter of Allan, probably the daughter of Allan Mac Ian Duy. We find it stated in May, 1642, that "his widow intromitted with the stipend, according to custom, for herself and children."

I. Allan, first Maclean of Shuna, was born probably about the year 1625. If the Shuna tradition be correct, he must have been a son of Ewen Maclean, minister of Kilvicewen. On April 2d, 1679, he obtained from Lord Neil Campbell, a charter of the lands of Shuna in life-rent for himself and in fee for Donald, his eldest son. The charter was confirmed by the Earl of Argyll. Allan had at least three children, Donald, Archibald, and Ann. He died about 1706.

II. Donald, second Maclean of Shuna, had three sons. The eldest son, whose name was Archibald, died in 1698. The second son left a son named Alexander. The third son left a son named John. Donald was succeeded by his grandson, Alexander.

III. Alexander, third of Shuna, was, in March, 1731, served heir to his uncle Archibald. He was served "heir male of taillie and provision special in a redeemable annual rent of sixty pounds Scots over Shuna." In October, 1740, he received a precept of Clare Constat in his favour as heir to Donald Maclean, his grandfather. He was succeeded by John, son of the third son of Donald of Shuna.

IV. In September, 1765, John, fourth of Shuna, received a precept of Clare Constat as heir to Alexander Maclean of Shuna, his cousin-german. John married a daughter of Campbell of Ardlarach, by whom he had five children; Alexander, Samuel, and three daughters. Alexander succeeded his father in Shuna. Samuel married his first cousin, Jane, fourth daughter of Dugald Campbell of Ardlarach, and had two sons by her, Dugald and James, both of whom died in Jamaica, and without issue. One of Shuna's daughters was married to a Macaulay who lived in Greenock.

V. Alexander, fifth and last Maclean of Shuna, became laird of that island in March, 1787. He was the son of John, grandson of Donald, son of Allan, first of Shuna. He married the widow of Campbell of Sunderland, and had by her Mary-Ann and Janet. He was deeply in debt, and was under the necessity of placing his estate, on December 5th, 1796, in the hands of Alexander Keay, accountant in Edinburgh, as trustee for the creditors. In January, 1798, Major Alexander Macdonald of Lyndale took charge of it. Major Macdonald sold it in 1815 to James Yates, who in 1829 bequeathed it in trust to the provost and magistrates of Glasgow.

Alexander of Shuna spent his later years in Edinburgh. He was a good-looking man, and full of wit and humour. Mary-Ann, his elder daughter, was married, first, to a Captain Shaw of the British Army, and, secondly, to an Edinburgh lawyer named Handyside. Captain Shaw was killed in a duel by Maclean of Kilmory. Tradition throws the blame for the whole trouble upon the latter.

THE MACLEANS OF LAGGAN, ISLAY.

Allan, first Maclean of Shuna, had two sons, Donald and Archibald. The descendants of Donald, second of Shuna, are now extinct in the male line.

I. Archibald, second son of Allan of Shuna, settled in Islay.

II. Donald, Archibald's son, married Elizabeth Macnab, by whom he had two sons, Archibald and Allan. One of Allan's sons went to the Crimea, and rose to a good position in the Russian service. Donald died in 1711.

III. Archibald, Donald's eldest son, was born in 1699, and died in 1750. He was married, and left a son named John.

IV. John lived at Octofad in Islay. He was a capital scholar, and could converse freely in several languages. He had a powerful voice and could be heard on a calm day across Lochindaal. He married, first, Janet, daughter of Archibald Campbell of Jura, by whom he had Lachlan and other children. He married, secondly, either a daughter or very near relative of the Rev. John Murdoch, minister of Kilarrow and Kilmeny, and had by her Charles and Barbara. Charles was known as Tearlach Ghoirtein-taoid.

V. Lachlan married Lucy, daughter of James Campbell of Balinaby, by whom he had Donald, James, Alexander-Colin, Jessie, and another daughter. Donald and James died unmarried. The second daughter was the mother of Thomas Pattison, the poet and translator, and of Mrs. Archibald Robertson. Lachlan, died at a comparatively early age.

VI. Alexander-Colin, or Colin as he was invariably called, was a captain in the merchant service and also a ship-owner. He amassed a good deal of wealth. He gave up going to sea when he was about thirty-six years of age, and settled at Laggan in Islay. He received two medals from the Humane Society for rescuing shipwrecked crews on the Laggan Strand on two different occasions. He was the subject of a very pretty Gaelic song by John Maceachern, am Piobaire Cam, of Bowmore in Islay. The bard praises his fine looks, his gentlemanliness, and his skill with the gun and rod. Probably, inasmuch as he was a sea-captain, he thought it unnecessary to say that he was a thorough steersman. Captain Maclean was evidently a popular man. He married Margaret, daughter of Neil Macneill of Ardnacross in Mull, by whom he had five children ; Lachlan, Neil, Lucy-Campbell, Annabella-Gillies, and Flora-Ann. Lucy was married to Robert-Holmes Hunter, and Annabella to Robert Ballingal. Flora lives in Edinburgh. Captain Maclean died in 1861.

VII. Lachlan, eldest son of Captain Alexander-Colin Maclean, was born on the 24th of August, 1830. He spent a number of years in Java. He returned in 1870. On his return he rented Islay House in Islay, and resided there. He married Elizabeth, daughter of the Rev. Alexander Cameron of Kilchoman in Islay, and had by her Alexander-Colin, Alexander, Neil, Mary-Stiles, Lucy-Campbell, and Elizabeth-Nora. Lachlan died on August 9th, 1880. Mary is married to Percy Howard in London.

VIII. Alexander-Colin, eldest son of Lachlan Maclean, is a captain in the Cameron Highlanders. He married Dora, daughter of the late Sir Rivers Thomson, lieutenant-governor of Bengal, and has a son named Colin and two daughters.

Neil, second son of Captain Alexander-Colin Maclean of Laggan in Islay, was born on June 9th, 1836. He spent a number of years in Java with his brother Lachlan. He married, in 1871,

Elizabeth, daughter of Alexander Macneill of Borlands, fifth son of Neil Macneill of Ardnacross, and had by her six sons and two daughters; Colin, Alexander-Ellister, Lachlan, Godfrey, Neil-Gillean, **Loudon-Macneill**, Isabel-Agnes, and Elizabeth-Marjory. He purchased, about the year 1892, the property of Breda, near Alford in Aberdeenshire, and resides there. He is a thoroughly loyal Maclean—just as loyal as the Macleans of Ross used to be in the fighting days of old. His eldest son, Colin, is a lieutenant in the Black Watch.

CHAPTER XV.

The Descendants of John Garbh of Coll.

I. THE MACLEANS OF COLL.

I. John Garbh, third son of Lachlan Bronnach of Duart, was the first Maclean of Coll. He received a charter from Alexander, Lord of the Isles, of the twenty pound lands of Coll, the eighteen marklands of Quinish in Mull, and the six marklands of the Isle of Rum. He received some time afterwards a charter from Alexander of the Isles of the twenty pound lands of Lochiel in Lochaber. Both charters were confirmed by James II.

There is a tradition to the effect that Gilleonan Macneil of Barra claimed the island of Coll and tried to keep John Garbh from getting possession of it. The latter, having collected about fifty armed men, sailed from Mull and landed with his followers in Coll, at the place known as an Acarsaid Fhalaich. He marched in all haste to Grishipol, attacked Macneil, who had 120 men, and defeated him. Macneil and all his followers were slain. According to tradition Macneil was more than a match for John Garbh with the battle-axe, and was killed by one of the followers of the latter, who was known as An Gille Riabhach, or the Speckled Youth. Immediately after the battle of Grishipol, John Garbh sailed to Barra and took possession of that island. He kept it for a few years and then gave it up to the lawful heir.

John Garbh was a tall, powerful, and courageous man; possessed great shrewdness and determination; and was well fitted for the rough times in which he lived. He married Isabel, daughter of Fraser of Lovat, and had John, Lachlan, and other children. He became laird of Coll shortly after 1431. He was alive in 1469.

II. John, Iain Mac Iain Ghairbh, lived at Corpach in Lochaber, and was in possession of the twenty pound lands of Lochiel. The Camerons attacked and slew him, and destroyed all his charters. His wife and children were protected by the Macgillonies and sent to Coll. He was succeeded by his son, John Abrach.

The Macleans of Coll were so grateful to the Macgillonies for their kindness to the family of their slain chieftain that they caused the following inscription to be placed on a stone over the door of Breacachadh Castle:—" If any man of the Clan Gillonie shall appear before this castle, though he came at midnight with a man's head in his hand, he shall here find safety and protection against all but the King." In further token of their gratitude the Macleans of Coll were, for over two hundred years, in the habit of educating the representative of the man who saved John Abrach.

III. John Abrach received from James V. on December 1st, 1528, a charter of the lands of Coll, Quinish, and Rum. He received also from the King on the same day a charter of the three marklands of Achalennan, the forty shilling lands of Drimnin, and the twenty pound lands of Lochiel. In the spring of 1539 he presented a petition to the Privy Council, in which he states that his predecessors had peaceably enjoyed the lands of Lochiel for forty years, that his father was slain while living on these lands, and that afterwards Ewen Mac Allan unjustly took possession of them. He prays for relief. The Council appointed a commission on all the matters referred to. Whatever the action of the commission may have been, Ewen Mac Allan retained possession of Lochiel. John Abrach had at least two sons, John and Hector. He had his lands conveyed to John, the elder of the two, in September, 1542.

IV. John, fourth of Coll, Iain Mac Iain Abraich, joined Donald Dubh in the rebellion of 1545. He died without lawful issue about the beginning of 1558, and was succeeded by his brother, Hector.

V. Hector, Eachann Mac Iain Abraich, received a good education, and was known as An Cléireach Beag, or the Little Clerk. He was a man of genuine piety, and a good poet. Some of his poems were

written in Gaelic, and some in Latin. Two of his
Gaelic poems are still in existence, and are published in the Maclean Bards. Tradition relates
that on a certain occasion, about the year 1537, he
happened to make some uncomplimentary remarks
with regard to Ailein nan Sop's conduct. Allan,
deeply provoked by these remarks—which were
no doubt just—sailed to Coll with his fleet, seized
the pious but rash bard, and carried him off to
Tarbert Castle. Hector, in order to appease his
wrath, composed a song in praise of his captor.
Allan was so well pleased with the song that he
set his prisoner at liberty. He gave him, however, a friendly warning to be more guarded about
his tongue for the future. The song contains
nothing but the truth. It simply describes Allan's
good qualities—qualities which he undoubtedly
possessed.

Hector Mac Ian was married twice. By his
first wife, Meve, daughter of Alexander Macdonald
of Islay, he had at least one son and two daughters;
Hector Roy, Margaret, and Janet. By his second
wife, Finvola, daughter of Godfrey Mac Alister of
Loup, he had two sons; Allan and John. Hector
Roy, who was also known as Hector Og, succeeded his father. Allan was the progenitor of
the Macleans of Achnasaul. John was the progenitor of the Macleans of Grishipol. Hector
Mac Ian resigned his lands in favour of Hector
Roy in 1559. He was living in 1565.

VI. Hector Roy received, on June 25th, 1559,

a crown charter of the "twenty pound lands of Coll, the twelve pound lands of Quinish, the four pound lands of Rum, and the four pound lands of Achalennan and Drimnin." He married Marion, daughter of Hector Og of Duart, by whom he had Lachlan, his successor. He died in 1593.

VII. Lachlan of Coll was born about the year 1582. He spent the first fourteen years of his life with Lachlan Mor Mackintosh, captain of the Clan Chattan, whose wife was a daughter of Kenneth Mackenzie of Kintail. To Mackintosh and his family he formed a deep and lasting attachment. In July, 1617, he received from James I. of Britain a charter of all the lands which had belonged to his father. In August, 1617, he obtained from Andrew Knox, Bishop of the Isles, a charter of the three marklands of the Isle of Muck, on condition of paying to the Bishop and his successors in office sixteen bolls of barley per year. The charter granted by the Bishop was confirmed by King James in March, 1621. Lachlan had a good deal of trouble in connection with the Isle of Muck. Sir Donald Campbell of Ardnamurchan claimed it as a part of the estate of the Macdonalds of Ardnamurchan. Lachlan retained Muck, but was under the necessity of giving up Achalennan and Drimnin to Sir Donald. The Mac Ians were in possession of Muck, and endeavoured to keep possession. They annoyed Lachlan by their predatory acts. At last he arrested fourteen of their principal men and sent them as prisoners to

Inverary. Some of them were found guilty of gross crimes and put to death. Lachlan and Sir Rory Mor Macleod were very intimate friends. Two of Rory Mor's sons, Roderick of Talisker and Norman of Bernera, were brought up with him in their boyhood. It was through the mediation of Angus Macdonald of Islay and himself that the bitter feud, which raged in 1601 between the Macdonalds of Sleat and the Macleods of Dunvegan, was brought to an end.

Lachlan of Coll had a natural son named John. As John was brought up in the Lowlands he was known as Iain Gallda, or Lowland John. He received from his father the farm of Mingary in Mull, of which we find him in possession in November, 1627. Lachlan married Florence, daughter of Tormod Macleod of Dunvegan, and had six children by her; John Garbh, Hector, Neil, Catherine, and Janet. John of Mingary was killed in his boat by the Mac Ians of Ardnamurchan, in revenge for the execution of their relatives at Inverary. His body was pierced by sixteen arrows. John Garbh succeeded his father in Coll. Hector was the progenitor of the Macleans of Muck. Neil was the progenitor of the Macleans of Drimnacross. Catherine was married, in 1627, to John Balbh, chief of the Clan Fingon, or Mackinnons. She had a life interest in a part of Sornmor, a part of Sornbeg, a part of Lepennie, and a part of Knockcarrach in Mull. She was the mother of Sir Lachlan Mor Mackinnon. Janet, the second daughter of Lachlan of Coll, was married to the Rev. Farquhar Fraser, minister of Tiree. Lachlan died about the beginning of 1642. He was a man of ability and prudence, and possessed a good deal of influence in his time. He was a Presbyterian. He was probably the last laird of Coll who could not sign his name.

VIII. John Garbh of Coll was a man of intelligence and sound sense. He was also a religious man, and showed his faith by his works. He was temperate in all things, practised the virtues of benevolence and hospitality, and delighted in reading the Word of God. It is said that a certain man in Skye, who had a large debt against him, promised to forgive him the debt if he would spend a night drinking with him. He was urged by his friends to accept the offer, but refused. He was an excellent musician, and a skilful player on the harp. Two of his musical compositions, "An Caoineadh Rioghail" and "An Tom Murrain," are still known. Captain Witters, the English governor of Duart Castle in the time of Cromwell, paid him a visit, and in speaking of him afterwards said that he resembled King David very much, being a great reader of the Bible and a good player on the harp. It seems, however, that the resemblance went no farther; John Garbh was not so fond of war as King David; he was a man of peace.

John Garbh married, first, Florence, third

daughter of Sir Dugald Campbell of Auchinbreck by his wife, Mary, daughter of Sir Alexander Erskine of Gogar, son of John, fifth Earl of Mar; and, secondly, Florence, daughter of Hector Og of Duart, son of Sir Lachlan Mor. By his first wife he had six children; Hector Roy, John, Ewen, Florence, Janet, and Una. By his second wife he, had one child, Catherine. Hector Roy, his eldest son, succeeded him in Coll. John was the progenitor of the Macleans of Totaranald. Ewen, or Hugh, joined Montrose at Strathearn in 1646. He was killed at Inverkeithing in 1651. He was a very brave man. Florence was married to Donald, first Maclean of Brolas. Janet was married to Alexander Macdonald of Achdir. Una was married, first, to John Maclean of Kinlochaline; and, secondly, to Duncan Stewart of Ardshiel. Catherine was married to Lachlan Macquarrie of Ulva.

IX. Hector Roy received, in 1642, a charter of Coll, Rum, Muck, and two-thirds of Quinish. He was of a warlike nature. He fought at the battle of Inverlochy, in 1645, and probably at the battle of Inverkeithing, in 1651. He got deeply into debt, evidently through neglecting to pay his dues to the Government, and incurring expenses in arming his followers to fight for the Stewarts. On October 3d, 1655, it was found by a court held at Inverary, that George Campbell of Kinnochtrie had a claim of £5,380 Scots against him. On March 7th, 1656, Oliver Cromwell gave a charter of

Hector Roy's lands to George Campbell, to compensate the latter for the amount due him. In July, 1675, Colin Campbell, son and heir of George Campbell, surrendered the lands which had been granted to his father by Cromwell, to Charles II., who gave a charter of them to Sir Norman Macleod of Bernera. Sir Norman conveyed them either to Hector Roy or his heir.

Hector Roy married Marion, eldest daughter of Hector Maclean of Killean, afterwards second Maclean of Torloisk. The marriage contract was signed at Hogh in Tiree, on January 22d, 1641. The marriage took place shortly afterwards. Hector Roy had six children by his wife; Lachlan, Donald, Margaret, Catherine, Janet, and Una. Lachlan, his eldest son, succeeded him in Coll. Donald succeeded Lachlan's son. Catherine was married, first, to Allan Stewart of Appin, by whom she had a son who became laird of Appin. She was married, secondly, to Hector Maclean of Muck. Janet was married to Hector Maclean, son of Charles of Ardnacross. Una was married to John Maclean of Achnasaul. Hector Roy died in 1676. John Garbh, his father, died a few years afterwards.

X. Lachlan of Coll, Lachainn Mac Eachainn Ruaidh, raised a company of men on his estates for service in Holland, and was appointed captain in General Mackay's regiment. It is said that he acted with a good deal of severity in forcing the sons of his tenants to enter the army and go with him to Holland. He returned to Scotland on leave of absence in the summer of 1687. He was drowned in the water of the Lochy in Lochaber in the month of August. He was at the time on his way back to join his regiment. He was married to Marion, daughter of John Dubh Macdonald of Moydart, and had three children by her; John Garbh, Florence, and Catherine. John Garbh succeeded him in Coll. Florence was married to John Macleod of Talisker. Catherine was married to Norman Macleod of Grishornish, by whom she had Donald, Alexander, and Margaret. Donald was minister of Diurinish in Skye. He was a man of culture, and a poet of good ability.

XI. John Garbh of Coll was accidentally killed in Edinburgh while pursuing his studies. He was standing on the street looking at a riotous mob. A party of soldiers, acting under the direction of Captain Wallace, threw a grenade from the Abbey Church among those who were causing the disturbance. A splinter from it struck the young laird of Coll and killed him instantly. He was only about eighteen years of age. He was succeeded by his uncle, Donald.

XII. Donald, Dòmhnall Mac Eachainn Ruaidh, was born in 1656. He had charge of the Coll estates during the absence of his brother Lachlan in the army. On July 2d, 1679, we find him surrendering the castle of Breacachadh to Archibald, Earl of Argyll, on condition that neither himself nor any of those who were with him should be called to account for any of their past acts by the Privy Council. He became tutor of Coll in 1687, and laird of Coll a few years afterwards. He was a very popular man.

Donald of Coll had two sons named Hector. It is admitted that the first Hector was the eldest of his sons. It is also generally admitted that he was born out of wedlock. Donald married, first, Isabel, daughter of Sir Roderick Macleod of Talisker; and, secondly, Marion, daughter of Sir Norman Macleod of Bernera. By his first wife, and after his marriage with her, he had one son, Hector. By his second wife, he had five children; Lachlan, John, Hugh, Neil, and Catherine. Hector, eldest son of Donald, settled in Mull. Hector, second son of Donald, succeeded his father in Coll. Lachlan married Catherine, daughter of Donald Maclean of Brolas. He had several children by her, all of whom died young. He survived his brother Hector. Hugh succeeded his brother Hector in Coll. Neil was a merchant in Virginia. Catherine was married to Dr. Hector Maclean of Grulin. Donald of Coll died in April, 1729.

There is a tradition in Coll to the effect that Donald of Coll had Hector, his eldest son, by Isabel, daughter of Sir Roderick Macleod of Talisker. Some time after the birth of Hector he married Isabel, and had the second Hector by her. When Donald and his bride were leaving Talisker Sir Roderick told them that he would never see the inside of their roof. After his anger had cooled down he went to Coll to see his daughter. When Donald saw him coming he took a bunch of ripe barley and hung it to the roof of his house on the inside. After some conversation he asked his father-in-law if he had seen such barley as that anywhere. Sir Roderick looked up, and Donald at once exclaimed,—Chunnaic sibh an nis mullach an taighe ge b' oil leibh, you have now seen the roof of the house in spite of you. Of course this story may not be true. Some persons maintain that Donald of Coll was actually married three times; that his first wife was a daughter of John Macleod of Dunvegan; that he had Hector, his eldest son by her; and that for some reason or other he denied that he had been married to her, and disinherited Hector. Others again simply affirm that Hector was a natural son.

XIII. Hector of Coll, Eachann Mac Dhòmhnaill Mhic Eachainn Ruaidh, was a tall, handsome, and dignified-looking man. He was richly endowed with good sense, and managed his affairs with prudence. He found the estate heavily burdened with debts, but succeeded in paying them all, and also in laying some money by. He built a fine residence near the old castle, and lived in a style becoming his circumstances. He used all his influence to keep his own followers and other members of his clan from joining Prince Charles in 1745. On July 3d, 1753, he received from George II. a charter of the lands of Coll, Quinish, and Muck. He married, first, in 1715, Janet, fourth daughter of Alexander Campbell of Lochnell by his wife, Margaret, daughter of Stewart of Appin. He married, secondly, Jean, daughter of Donald Campbell of Airds. He had five daughters by his first wife; Isabel, Margaret, Mary, Una, and Sibella. Isabel was married in 1733 to Colin Campbell, eldest son of Colin Campbell of Ballimore. Margaret was married to Alexander Macdonald of Boisdale, and had two sons; Donald and Hector. Mary was married in 1745 to Captain John Macleod of Talisker. Una was married to Sir Allan Maclean of Brolas; and Sibella to Captain Allan Cameron of Glendessary. In his marriage contract with Lochnell's daughter, which was signed on September 14th, 1715, Hector is described as Hector Maclean of Coll, younger, eldest lawful son of Donald. He disposed of his estates in favour of his brother Hugh and his heirs male. He died in 1754. He was the last laird of Coll who kept a harper.

XIV. Hugh of Coll married Janet, daughter of Donald Macleod, third of Talisker, and had eight children by her; Donald, Alexander, Hector, Norman, Roderick, Allan, Hugh, and Marion. He was served heir of tailzie general to his brother Hector, in April, 1755. In February, 1756, he received from George II. a charter of the lands of Coll, Quinish, and Muck. He died on May 4th, 1786. 1. Donald, his eldest son, was an intelligent, well-educated, and promising young man. He was drowned in the Sound of Ulva on September 25th, 1774. 2. Alexander succeeded his father in Coll. 3. Hector was born in 1756. He entered the military service of the East India Company as an ensign in 1775. He was appointed captain in 1786, major in 1795, lieutenant-colonel in 1798, and major-general in 1811. He was created a K. C. B. in 1815. He was promoted to the rank of lieutenant-general in 1821. He spent the whole of his military life in India. He lived in London after retiring from active service. He died in 1849. 4. Norman was a major in the 78th regiment. He died of yellow fever in the island of Grenada. 5. Roderick was an officer in the army. He married Christina, daughter of Captain Allan Cameron of Glendessary, by whom he had one daughter, Marion. 6. Allan was a captain in the 36th regiment. He married Jean, daughter of Captain Allan Cameron of Glendessary. 7. Hugh was a captain in the 60th regiment. 8. Marion was married in 1783 to Alexander, son and heir of Colin Macdonald of Boisdale, by whom she had Hugh and other children.

XV. Alexander of Coll was born about the year 1754. He was known as Alasdair Ruadh, or Alexander Roy. He studied law for some time, with the intention of following it as a profession. On the sad death of his brother Donald in 1774 he abandoned his legal studies. He was for some time a captain in the Argyle Fencible regiment, which was embodied in Glasgow in April, 1778.

He was served heir to his father in May, 1790, and is described as Captain Alexander Maclean of Coll. He was appointed lieutenant-colonel in the Breadalbane Fencibles in 1794 or thereabouts. He seems to have gone to Ireland with the third battalion in 1795.

When Alexander of Coll was in the Argyle Fencibles, John Macdonald, of Hogh in Tiree, neglected to perform some duty, which had been entrusted to him, at a bridge. For this act of neglect Major Hugh Montgomery ordered that he should be whipped. Coll was at that time only a captain. As Macdonald was in his company, and as he had been acquainted with him from his youth, he went twice to the major and humbly pleaded with him to forgive Macdonald; but the major was inexorable. When the flogging was to begin Coll drew his sword and cut the cords with which the unfortunate soldier was tied to the whipping-post. Montgomery challenged Maclean to a duel with swords; the challenge was at once accepted. As there was some fear among the soldiers that Maclean might be killed, they sent word to Montgomery that if he should happen to kill Maclean, he would be instantly shot. Coll appeared on the ground; but Montgomery kept away. The duel was never fought.

One of Coll's tenants, who came to the island of Cape Breton, was one day telling his neighbour about the clearness of head and knowledge of law which the old laird possessed. Surely, said his neighbour, he did not know as much about law as Moses. Moses, was the reply, Moses never saw the day when he could split the law better than our own laird of Coll.

Alexander of Coll married Catherine, eldest daughter of Captain Allan Cameron of Glendessary, by whom he had one son and six daughters; Hugh, Janet, Sibella, Catherine, Maria, Marion, and Breadalbane. Hugh succeeded his father in Coll. Janet was married to the Honourable George Vere Hobart, second son of the Duke of Buckinghamshire. Both her husband and herself died a few years after their marriage. They left one child, a daughter named Vere-Louise-Catherine, who became the wife of Donald Cameron of Lochiel, and was the mother of the present Cameron of Lochiel. Sibella, second daughter of Alexander of Coll, died unmarried. Catherine was married to Major Donald Macleod of Talisker, who emigrated to Australia about the year 1821. She visited Britain in 1857, and died shortly after her return to Australia. She had a large family. Maria, fourth daughter of Alexander of Coll, was married to Alexander Hunter, Edinburgh. Marion and Breadalbane died unmarried. The latter was noted for her piety and charitable deeds.

Alasdair Ruadh was of an independent spirit, and somewhat quick-tempered. He was manly, obliging, and benevolent, and treated his tenants with thorough kindness. He was a chieftain of great popularity. He was, in 1818, laird of Coll,

Quinish, Rum, and Muck. He handed over his estates to Hugh, his eldest son, in 1828. He left Coll then and went to live in Quinish. He died on April 10th, 1835.

XVI. Hugh, sixteenth and last Maclean of Coll, was born in 1782. He served for some time in the Guards, and became a lieutenant-colonel. He purchased Ben More in Mull, and built the castle of Drimfin near Tobermory. He got into debt, and had to part with his estates, which were sold in April, 1856.

Hugh of Coll married, first, in 1814, Janet Dennistoun, by whom he had four daughters; Margaret, Catherine-Cameron, Elizabeth, and Isabella-Sibella. He married, secondly, in 1825, Jane Robertson, by whom he had six children; Juliet, Alexander, John-Hector-Norman, William, Hugh, and Jane-Albane. William died in India in 1867. Hugh was a captain in the army, and died in 1867. Margaret was married to James Hamilton of Barnes; Elizabeth, to Walter Griffith; Juliet, to Ashe Windham; and Jane-Albane, to George Dundas. Hugh of Coll lived in London during the latter part of his life. He died at Woodville in the house of his daughter Margaret in 1861. He was a kind-hearted man, and was well liked by his tenants.

XVII. Alexander, eldest son of Hugh of Coll, succeeded his father as representative of the descendants of John Garbh. He was tall and athletic, modest, and full of kindness. He emigrated to

South Africa in 1849. He died at Umgeni, near Durban, on Sunday afternoon, July 11th, 1875. He was in the forty-seventh year of his age. He was succeeded in the chieftainship of the Macleans of Coll by his brother, John-Hector-Norman.

XVIII. John Hector Norman Maclean was born in 1829. He entered the army in India in 1846, and rose to the rank of major-general. He married a daughter of Robert Rae, by whom he had three daughters; Emily-Agnes, Florence-Maude, and Isabel-Annie. On retiring from active service he returned from India, and took up his residence at Brighton in England. He died on the 29th of August, 1882.

II. THE MACLEANS OF ARNABOST.

Lachlan Maclean was born at Grimsary in the Isle of Coll, and died at Arnabost. He was the son of John, son of Donald, son of Rory, son of Hector, son of Neil, son of Malcolm, son of Lachlan, son of John Garbh, first of Coll. He married Catherine, daughter of John Campbell, by whom he had a son named John. John lived at Arnabost. He married Finvola, daughter of Hector Maclean, Eachann Mac Iain Mhic Thearlaich, and had seven children by her; Lachlan, Murdoch, John Og, Donald, Mary, Margaret, and Catherine. Murdoch was married, and had six sons; Donald, Alexander, Lachlan, Hugh, John, and Neil. He died at Sordidale in 1867. John Og came to Canada in 1846, and settled at

Melbourne above Montreal. He removed to the United States in 1869. He died at Wichita in Kansas, in 1892, and was eighty-eight years of age. He left a large family of sons and daughters. Donald, fourth son of Iain Mac Lachainn Mhic Iain, died unmarried. Mary, the eldest daughter, was married to Donald Macdonald, son of Ailein Muilleir, and was the mother of that worthy Highlander, the late D. T. Macdonald, of Red Jacket, Michigan.

Lachlan, eldest son of Iain Mac Lachainn Mhic Iain, was born at Arnabost, Coll, on June 2d, 1798, and was educated in his native island. He went to Glasgow about 1821 and engaged in the hosiery business. He was a scholarly and well-read man, and an admirable writer, both in Gaelic and English. He wrote a number of excellent articles for the "Teachdaire Gaidhealach" and "Cuairtear nan Gleann." He published "Adhamh agus Eubh," or Adam and Eve, in 1837, and "The History of the Keltic Language" in 1840. He composed a few short poems. He took an intense interest in his mother tongue, and was known as Lachainn na Gaidhlig, or Lachlan of the Gaelic. He was frank and genial in his manner, sociable by nature, and an exceedingly pleasant companion. He married Agnes Ashmore, by whom he had a son named Norman, and four daughters. He died at his residence, 49 Oxford Street, Glasgow, on November 22d, 1848, in the fifty-first year of his age. He was buried in the southern Necropolis.

The Maclean Association erected a handsome monument to his memory in 1896.

III. Neil Mor and Neil Og.

I. Neil Mor Maclean was a grandson of John Abrach. It is generally supposed that he was a natural son of John, fourth of Coll. According to the Rev. Neil Maclean, minister of Tiree, he was a son of Hector, fifth of Coll. He was distinguished for his strength, bravery, and manly character. He became military leader of the Macleans of Coll after the death of Hector Roy in 1593. Lachlan Mor of Duart sent an armed force to take possession of Coll. Neil Mor marched in great haste to meet the invaders. On his way to the encounter he found that the flag had been forgotten. An old warrior, known as Dòmhnall Mùgach, or Gloomy Donald, stepped forward, took off his bonnet, and pointing to his bald head exclaimed, This will do for a standard, and I promise that it will not go back a foot to-day. The two parties met at Struthan-nan-Ceann, or the streamlet of the heads; the invaders were defeated with great slaughter. Shortly afterwards Lachlan Mor sent a much larger force to Coll. The result was that he made himself master of that island. Neil Mor had to flee for his life. He resided at Drimnacross, but left Drimnacross and went to live at Cill-bheag. Lachlan Mor's men were seeking for an opportunity to kill him during three years. At last twenty-four of them came upon him by surprise in the middle of the night. He fled, but was overtaken at Clachan Dubh, and beaten to death in a most savage manner. The spot on which he was killed is still known as Dùnan Neill, or Neil's Hillock. His real murderer was Dughall Ruadh Mac Ailpein, Dugald Roy Mac Alpin. He was slain in the latter part of 1596 or the beginning of 1597. He was married, and left at least one son, Niall Og.

Lachlan, seventh of Coll, seized four of the men who formed the party that killed Niall Mor. He came upon them as they were playing shinty at Traigh Chalgari, the shore of Calgary in Mull. He took them to Coll, kept them in confinement for some time, and then hung them on a gibbet on the top of Cnoc a Chrochaire, or the Hangman's Hill. In 1896, or thereabouts, four skeletons were found at the spot on which the hanging took place. Some suppose that they were the skeletons of Niall Mor's murderers. We suspect, however, that they must have been of more recent origin. At the same time we must confess that we know nothing about the nature of the soil on Cnoc a Chrochaire, or the time it would take skeletons to decay in it. It is possible that the men who were put to death by Lachlan of Coll deserved their fate. But it is also possible that if they had not gone in pursuit of Niall Mor their lives might have been terminated sooner than they were. We certainly think that if the villain who gave the finishing blow to Niall Mor was one of them,

Lachlan of Coll cannot be blamed for sending him to the gallows.

II. Niall Og was only a young boy when his father was killed. Tradition states that immediately after his father's death he was taken to Coll, and carried thither in a creel by a Macquarrie. We must not deal with traditions as if they were acts of parliament. It would be folly to interpret them literally. They may be substantially true, yet at the same time contain a number of details which are purely ornamental. It may be taken for granted that Niall Og was taken to Coll shortly after his father's death. It is also likely enough that he was taken to Coll by a Macquarrie. We feel confident, however, that he must have been at least six or seven years of age, perhaps ten or eleven. We do not say that he was not carried in a creel; he may have been. And certainly, in a painting of the flight of Niall Og, we should rather see him in a big creel on Macquarrie's back than trotting along beside his protector.

Apart from tradition, we consider it certain that Niall Og was brought to Coll shortly after the death of his father. We consider it also certain that on coming of age he received a farm from the laird of Coll. From what we know of the manly character of the Macleans of Coll, we cannot for a moment believe that they would treat with indifference or neglect the son and heir of the hero of Struthan nan Ceann. They might cut off the head of an enemy without just cause, but they would not forget the good deeds of a valiant friend. There was a Neil Maclean in Gallanach, Coll, in 1617. He was a prominent man, and may possibly have been the same person as Niall Og.

THE MACLEANS OF CROSSAPOL.

I. Neil Maclean was tacksman of Crossapol in 1773. He was paying seven pounds a year of rent, and was in very comfortable circumstances. Neil was born probably about the year 1724. He married, about 1750, Julia Stewart, and had nine children by her; Donald, Margaret, Allan, Neil, Janet, Catherine, Flora, Una, and Ann. It is said that his wife was a grand-daughter of Hector Roy of Coll. She was born about 1734, and died about 1815. Donald, Neil's eldest son, studied for the ministry. Allan succeeded his father in Crossapol. Neil died young. Margaret was married to Charles Maclean of Gallanach. Janet was married to Captain Allan Macdonald of Darracha. Catherine died unmarried. Flora was married to Alexander Maclean, of Airleod, Coll, and had a son named Norman. Una was married to Allan, son of Malcolm Maclean. Ann was married, in 1796, to Neil Campbell of Treshnish and Sunipol, by whom she had Colin, Neil, Donald, John, Alexander, Archibald, and five daughters.

II. Allan Maclean of Crossapol was born in 1760. He married Mary, eldest daughter of John

Maclean of Langamull, by whom he had eight children; Neil, John, Donald, Catherine, Christina, Jessie, Julia, and Mary. He died in August, 1832, and was buried in the graveyard at Crossapol. Neil, eldest son of Allan, succeeded his father in Crossapol. John was born in 1810. He was a wine-merchant in London. He married, in 1831, Anne, daughter of Alexander Maclean of Kinnegharar, by whom he had two daughters, Catherine-Mary, and Christina-Julia. Catherine was married to Dr. William Lovejoy, New York; and Christina, to George Rose Innes, solicitor, London. John died in August, 1886. Donald was studying for the ministry. He died in March, 1834, in the twenty-second year of his age. Catherine, eldest daughter of Allan, was married to the Rev. Hugh Maclean, who went to America. She had ten sons. Christina was married to Hugh Maclean in Edinburgh. Janet was married to a Mr. Barron in Glasgow. Mary was married to the Rev. A. Fraser in Greenock.

III. Neil was the last Maclean of Crossapol. He was born in 1805, and died on January 10th, 1855. He was a thorough gentleman in every respect. He was never married.

The Descendants of the Rev. Donald Maclean.

I. Donald, eldest son of Neil Maclean of Crossapol, was born in 1752. He graduated at Aberdeen in 1773, and was licensed to preach in

1779. He acted for some time as chaplain to the Reay Fencibles. He became minister of Small Isles in 1787. He preached once a month in Rum, once a month in Muck, once a quarter in Canna, and the remainder of the time in Eigg, where he resided. He married, in 1777, Lillias, daughter of Alexander Maclean, of Gott, Tiree, and had five children by her; Margaret, Alexander, Neil, Hector, and Julia. He died in 1810. Neil, his second son, was born in 1784, and studied for the church. He became assistant minister of Coll in 1809, minister of Small Isles in 1811, and minister of Tiree and Coll in 1817. He married, in 1814, Isabella, daughter of Major Alexander Macdonald of Vallay, by whom he had five children; Donald, Harriet, Mary-Flora, Alexander, Lillias, and Isabel. Donald was a doctor, and died in Tiree. Alexander died in Australia. Lillias was married to William Mitchell, and Isabel to Alexander W. Cameron. The Rev. Neil Maclean died on August 26th, 1859. Hector, third son of the Rev. Donald Maclean, was minister of Lochalsh, and died in 1869.

II. Alexander, eldest son of the Rev. Donald Maclean, was born in 1782. He studied medicine, and became surgeon to the 64th Foot in 1813. He was present at the battle of Waterloo in 1815. He returned to Britain in 1817, and married at Plymouth, Ann-Maria, daughter of Captain Williams, R.N. He died on board of a ship, near Plymouth, on March 5th, 1818. His body was taken ashore and buried in Plymouth.

III. Alexander, only child of Dr. Maclean, was born on May 8th, 1818, two months after the death of his father. He joined the 94th regiment in India, in 1839, and was for eight years adjutant in it. He became captain in 1852. He married in February, 1857, Olivia-Louisa-Elizabeth, only daughter of the Rev. Samuel E. Day, vicar of the parish of St. Philip's and St. Jacob's, Bristol. In 1859 he was appointed staff officer of pensioners in Omagh, Tyrone County, Ireland. He retired from the army with the rank of lieutenant-colonel in July, 1878. After his retirement he resided at Bristol, England. He had by his wife five children; Alexander-William-Day, Mary-Olivia, Hector-Arthur-Coalson, Edith-Louisa-Maud, Louisa-Maud, and Henry-Donald-Neil. He died on November 11th, 1892. Hector, his second son, was born in Omagh, Ireland, on November 9th, 1861. He resides in London with his mother. He takes a deep interest in the history and genealogy of his clan, and is in every respect worthy of the good Maclean name which he bears. H. D. Neil was born at Clifton in June, 1872. He joined the King's Own Scottish Borderers at Mean Meer in India in April, 1893. He is a lieutenant, and was with his regiment in the Tirah expedition. Mary-Olivia was married, in 1884, to Captain William Holcombe Francis, of the 28th regiment. Edith died young. Louisa-Maud was married, in 1894, to Dr. Francis Henry Hawkins, of Reading.

IV. Alexander W. D. Maclean was born at

Bristol, on February 6th, 1858. He was educated at Clifton College, and prepared for the army at Sandhurst. He entered the 94th regiment, or Connaught Rangers, in 1878. He became a lieutenant in 1879, and was in the same year in the Zulu War. He was promoted to the rank of captain in 1883, and to that of major in 1893. He was for five years adjutant of the 3d battalion of his regiment at Castlebar in Ireland, and was highly esteemed by all classes. He married in July, 1889, Rose-Eaden-Abinger, daughter of Admiral William Fenwick. He is at the present time commandant at Kailana in India.

The origin of the Macleans of Crossapol is a matter of uncertainty, and has consequently occasioned a good deal of controversy. Unfortunately the Ardgour MS. makes no reference to them. We are thus left, to a very large extent, at the mercy of family traditions. According to one tradition, Neil Maclean, tacksman of Crossapol in 1773, was the son of Allan, son of Neil Og, son of the heroic Neil Mor. As Neil Mor was slain at least as early as the beginning of 1597, it is certain that the Neil of 1773 was not his great-grandson. According to another tradition, the Neil Maclean who was in Crossapol in 1773 was the son of Hector, son of Ewen, son of John Garbh, eighth of Coll. There are several difficulties in the way of accepting this view. There is no reference, either to the marriage or son of Ewen, John Garbh's son, in the Ardgour MS. He may, however, have been married; and whether he was married or not he may have left a son named Hector. As Ewen was killed at Inverkeithing in July, 1651, Hector, his son, must have been born at least as early as the spring of 1652. Now it is tolerably certain that the Neil who was tacksman of Crossapol in 1773 was not born earlier than 1724. Thus, then, if he was the son of Hector, son of Ewen, son of John Garbh of Coll, Hector must have been seventy-two years of age when his son Neil was born. Such, of course, may have been the case; but before believing that it was the case one would require some evidence. If the Neil of 1773 was really the son of Hector, we should expect to find one of his sons called Hector. As, however, the names of his children are all taken from the baptismal register, it may be assumed as a fact that he had no son named Hector. At the same time it is possible that his father's name was Hector. In support of the contention that the Neil of 1773 was the son of Hector, son of Ewen, son of John Garbh, we are told that there is a tradition in favour of it. The weak point about this argument is that there is another tradition which asserts that Neil was the son of Allan, son of Neil Og.

In July, 1642, Hector Maclean of the Isle of Muck, John Maclean in Crossapol, and others, witnessed a charter granted by John Garbh, eighth of Coll. It is evident that John Maclean in Crossapol was a man of good standing among the Macleans of Coll. He was in all probability tacksman of Crossapol, and is the first Maclean with whom we meet there. It is at least possible that this John —whoever he may have been—was the progenitor of the Macleans of Crossapol. He may have had a son named Neil, and Neil may have had a son who was known as Neil Og.

The Last Macleans of Giurdal.

John Maclean was born in Grishipol, Coll. He settled in the Isle of Rum, and was tenant of the farm of Giurdal. He married Mary, daughter of Allan Maclean of Grishipol, and had by her six children; Charles, Allan, Neil, Catherine, Ann, and Janet. Allan succeeded him in Giurdal.

According to the late Hugh Maclean of Ruel Cottage near Dunoon, Neil Og of Crossapol had two sons, Allan and Charles, and three daughters. Allan succeeded him in Crossapol, and had two sons, Neil and Lachlan. Neil was tacksman of Crossapol in 1773. Lachlan had three sons; Allan, Lachlan, and Hugh. He had also several daughters, one of whom was married to John Mackinnon in Grimsary, Coll. Charles, second son of Neil Og, had a son named John. John, Iain Mac Thearlaich, held the farm of Kinloch Scrisort in Rum. He married Rachel, daughter of Hector Campbell in Rum, and had by her four children; Allan, Charles, Margaret, and Flora. Allan succeeded his father in Kinloch Scrisort. Charles became tenant of Giurdal. He married a sister of Allan Maclean of Giurdal, and had by her three sons, Allan, Hector, and Alexander, all of whom emigrated to Cape Breton in 1826. Flora, second daughter of Iain Mac Thearlaich, was the grandmother of Hugh Maclean of Ruel Cottage.

Allan Maclean of Kinloch Scrisort, was factor of Rum and Muck. He married Margaret Macdonald, of the Isle of Eigg, and had by her five children; John, Donald, James, Mary, and Isabel. John died unmarried. Donald studied for the ministry. He was ordained, and settled in the parish of Small Isles, in 1818. He married, in 1822, Isabella, daughter of Charles Maclean of Gallanach, Coll. He died on board of a steamer between Greenock and Glasgow on October 6th, 1839. He left five children; Allan, Lachlan, Margaret, Breadalbane, and Maria. Allan remained in Scotland with his mother. Lachlan and the three girls went to Melbourne, Australia, about the year 1853. James, third son of Allan of Kinloch Scrisort, occupied the farm of Gallanach in Muck from 1826 to 1836. He married Mary, daughter of Eachann Ghiurdail, and had by her two sons, Hector and John. The whole family emigrated to Melbourne in 1838.

IV. THE MACLEANS OF ACHNASAUL.

I. Allan, second son of Hector, fifth of Coll, was the progenitor of the Macleans of Achnasaul. He married Anne, daughter of Macdonald of

Ardnamurchan, by whom he had three sons; Hector, Ranald, and Donald. He was with Sir Lachlan Mor at Gruinnart in 1598. He accompanied Lachlan Maclean of Coll to the Isle of Skye in 1601, when the latter was trying to effect a reconciliation between the Macleods and the Macdonalds. The descendants of Hector and Ranald settled in Ireland.

II. Donald, youngest son of Allan of Achnasaul, lived for some time in the island of Gunna, near Coll. Owing to a disagreement between the laird of Coll and himself, he was compelled to leave Gunna. He went to Skye, and took up his abode in Troternish. He was married, and had a son named Archibald.

III. Archibald married a daughter of Mackaskill of Rudh'-an-dùnain, and had two sons by her, Allan and Rory. In a fight with swords between Allan and one of the Macsweens of Skye, the latter was killed. Immediately afterwards Allan and his brother Roderick left Skye, and settled at Kilmory in the Isle of Rum. The descendants of the former were known as Sliochd Ailein Mhic Ghilleasbuig, and those of the latter as Sliochd Ruairidh Mhic Ghilleasbuig.

IV. Allan, son of Archibald, had two sons, Donald and Lachlan.

V. Donald, son of Allan, had four sons; Allan, John, Angus, and Neil. 1. Allan settled in Coll, where he had charge of the laird's galley, birlinn Thighearna Chola. He died unmarried at Tota-

ranald. 2. John succeeded his father in Kilmory.
3. Angus left a son named Rory, who was known as Rory Mor, and was ground officer in Muck. John, only son of Rory Mor, settled in Coll. He married Ann Maclean, by whom he had four sons; James, Hector, Neil, and John. James and Hector were drowned at Tràigh Ghortain in Coll, about the year 1828. John and Neil died shortly afterwards. 4. Neil obtained a croft in Totaranald in Coll. He was married, and had a large family of sons and daughters. All the sons, except Donald, emigrated to Cape Breton. Donald remained in Totaranald. He had four sons. Two of them emigrated to Cape Breton; and two, Donald and John, remained in Coll. Donald had two sons, Donald and Archibald. John was a carpenter, and was known as Iain Saor. He was married and had seven sons.

VI. John, second son of Donald, had three sons; Donald, Allan, and Archibald. Donald succeeded his father in Kilmory. Allan emigrated to Pictou, Nova Scotia. Archibald had two sons, Donald and John.

VII. Donald, eldest son of John, had thirteen children; John, Allan, Rory, Neil, Lachlan, Donald the elder, Hector, Donald the younger, Ewen, Mary, Catherine, Ann, and another daughter. Lachlan, Hector, and the two Donalds, died at an early age. Allan, the second son, lived at Kinloch in Rum. He had seven children; Hector, Peter, Donald, Kenneth, and three daughters. Hector,

Peter, Donald, and two of the daughters, emigrated to Upper Canada in 1852. Kenneth and the eldest daughter remained in Rum with their father. Kenneth was the last Maclean that lived in Rum. But he was not allowed to die there. He was removed to Perthshire. He died at Glenlyon in 1896. He was about seventy-eight years of age. Rory, third son of Donald, lived in Rothesay. He had five children; Neil, Donald, John, Allan, and Mary. Neil, fourth son of Donald, married Flora Macdonald, from Kilchoan, Ardnamurchan, and had three sons; Lachlan, Donald, and James. Lachlan, eldest son of Neil, lived in Oban. He married Ann Maclean, by whom he had five children; Donald, James, Archibald, and two daughters. Donald, second son of Neil, is tenant of the farm of Arileoid in Coll, for which he is paying a rent of £125 a year. He married, in 1860, Catherine, daughter of Donald MacColl in Lismore, and had by her eight children; Neil, Donald, Flora, James, Archibald, Hector, Lachlan, and Alexander. James, third son of Neil, is a plumber by trade, and resides in Greenock. He is well versed in the history of the Macleans. He married, in 1869, Margaret Macbride from Arran, by whom he has seven children; Flora, Mary, Kate, James, Alexander, Christy, and Margaret. Ewen, fifth son of Donald, was married and had two sons, Robert and Donald.

VIII. John, eldest son of Donald, had two sons, Donald and John. Donald had three sons;

Allan, Donald, and John. John, the younger son of John, son of Donald, came to Cape Breton in 1835.

The Descendants of Lachlan Maclean.

Lachlan Maclean, son of Allan, son of Archibald, son of Donald of Gunna, lived in Kilmory in the Isle of Rum, and was noted for his great strength. John, Lachlan's son, married a daughter of Donald Maclean, his uncle, and had by her John Mor and other children. John Mor was six feet four-and-one-half inches in height, and stout in proportion. He married, first, Marion, daughter of Murdoch Maclean, son of the Gobha Cru̇bach, and had by her four sons; John Og, Neil, Hector, and Murdoch Mor. He married, secondly, Christy, daughter of Neil Maclean, Niall Mac Thearlaich Mhic Iain Ghobha, and had by her six children; Mary, Christy, Flora, Marion, Margaret, and Donald. John Mor died in Kilmory at the age of fifty-five. The whole of his family, except Mary and Donald, came to Cape Breton in 1826. Mary, Mairi Mhór, was married to Charles Maclean. She died in Muck in May, 1838. Donald seems to have died young. John Og, eldest son of John Mor, married a Miss Macquarrie, by whom he had John, Marion, and other children. John was born in Rum in 1813. He married Margaret Macarthur, by whom he had Hector, John, Margaret, Donald, Hugh, Mary, and Allan. He died in 1897. Hector, his eldest son, was born at Port Hastings, Cape Breton, in 1843.

The Descendants of Rory Maclean.

Rory, second son of Archibald, son of Donald of Gunna, lived at Kilmory in Rum. John, son of Rory, was a blacksmith by trade, and was known as Iain Gobha, and, also, as an Gobha Crùbach. He was for some time in the army in Holland. He left two sons, Murdoch and Charles. Charles was in the army, and served for some time in America, under Sir Allan of Brolas. He had two sons, Neil and Donald, the latter of whom was reputed the swiftest man in Rum. Donald had a son named Angus, who had three sons, Donald, Gillespick Mor, and John. Donald, eldest son of Angus, left three daughters. Gillespick Mor was a cooper in Rothesay, and had five sons; Angus, Neil, John, Donald, and Archibald. Donald was a lawyer in Greenock. John, third son of Angus, settled in Eigg, and had two sons, Archibald and Lachlan.

Murdoch, elder son of John Gobha, had five sons, Rory, Lachlan, Neil, Hector, and Allan, all of whom came to Cape Breton, except Lachlan, who died in Rum. Lachlan left two sons, Donald and Allan. Both came to Cape Breton.

Rory, eldest son of Murdoch, married Ann Macisaac, by whom he had William, Murdoch, John, Neil, Charles, Allan, and Donald. Rory and all his sons, except Murdoch, left Rum for America in 1810. They were a night at Oban, attended a dance, and afterwards took part in a big fight with some militiamen who had unwisely provoked their wrath. Rory and his family spent two years in Prince Edward Island, and then removed to Broad Cove, Cape Breton. William was for some time in the army. He settled at Chimney Corner in Cape Breton. Murdoch was pressed into the navy, and served seven years in it. He came to Cape Breton some time after his father. He married Mary Macgregor, by whom he had three sons; Rory, Gregor, and Charles. John married Margaret Macdougall, by whom he had Murdoch, Duncan, Charles, John, Catherine, Ann, Mary, and Margaret. Mary was married to that excellent Highlander, Alexander Campbell, ex-M. P. P., Strathlorne, Cape Breton.

V. THE FIRST MACLEANS OF GRISHIPOL.

I. John, third son of Hector, fifth of Coll, was the first Maclean of Grishipol. He married Finvola, a daughter of the laird of Mackinnon, by whom he had a son named John.

II. John, second of Grishipol, married a daughter of Roderick Maclean, a merchant in Glasgow, and had by her four sons; Lachlan, John, Hugh, and Charles. John, the second son, graduated at the University of Edinburgh, in July, 1672, and became minister of Kilmorie in Kintyre in 1688. After the revolution he went to Ireland, and was for some time minister of Coleraine, and afterwards prebendary of Referchen. He was a man of extraordinary bodily strength. He was married twice. By his first wife, a daughter of Lachlan Macneill of Lossit, he had several daughters. By his second wife, a daughter of James Cubbage, he had three sons; John, Clotworthy, and James. John was minister of Clocher. He married Elizabeth, daughter of the Rev. Philip Matthews, by whom he had three sons; Lachlan, James, and Henry. Lachlan was a doctor, and a very clever man. He was for some time agent of the Nabob of Arcot. He was lost on his passage home to Britain. Clotworthy, second son of the Rev. John Maclean, was a doctor. James, the third son, was minister in Rachray. Charles, fourth son of Roderick of Grishipol, was the ancestor of Lachlan Maclean of Kilmore in Mull, whose son, John, was a wine-merchant in Glasgow in 1838.

III. Lachlan, third of Grishipol, Lachainn Mac Iain Mhic Iain, married Ann, daughter of Neil Maclean of Drimnacross, by whom he had four sons; Roderick, John, Hector, and Allan.

IV. Roderick, fourth of Grishipol, had a natural son named Neil. He married, first, Marion, daughter of John Macdonald of Moydart, and widow of Lachlan of Coll. He married, secondly, Marion, daughter of Donald Maclean of Arighoulan, by whom he had two sons, Lachlan and John. Neil had a son named John, who went to Jamaica. John, Roderick's third son, died young and unmarried.

V. Lachlan, son of Roderick of Grishipol, was

a captain in the military service of the East India Company. He married, first, a daughter of Hector Maclean, his uncle; and, secondly, a daughter of Alexander Maclean of Sollas in Uist. He had two sons and several daughters.

VI. THE MACLEANS OF MUCK.

I. Hector, second son of Lachlan, seventh of Coll, received the island of Muck from his father. He seems to have been educated for the ministry. He was a man of ability, and of noble appearance. He commanded under Sir Lachlan of Duart in Montrose's army, and distinguished himself very highly at the battle of Kilsyth.

The Mac Ians of Ardnamurchan were bitter enemies to Hector of Muck, because his father had brought some of them to justice for their misdeeds. They were also privately instigated by their enemy, Sir Donald Campbell of Ardnamurchan, to do all the harm they could to the Macleans of Coll, and thus bring themselves into trouble. Under the leadership of Mac Ian Gheir, a notorious thief and robber, a party of them landed at night in Muck, and began to drive away all the cattle they could find. Hector of Muck fired at them, but missed them. He was immediately surrounded and slain.

Hector of Muck was married to Julian, daughter of Allan of Ardtornish, and according to the Ardgour MS. had two sons by her, Hector and Hugh. It is certain that he had also a son named Lachlan. He was succeeded by Hector.

II. Hector, second of Muck, married a daughter of Hector Roy, ninth of Coll, and had by her three children ; Hector, Lachlan, and Julian. Hector married Marion, daughter of Lachlan Maclean of Calgary ; but both died at an early age, and without issue. Lachlan succeeded his father in Muck. Julian was married to Alexander Maclachlan, bailie of Tiree.

III. Lachlan of Muck was a captain under Sir John of Duart at Sheriffmuir in 1715. He married Mary, daughter of James Macdonald, of Balfinlay, and had four children by her ; Hector, Donald, Catherine, and Mary. Hector succeeded his father. Donald succeeded Hector. Catherine was married to Charles Maclean of Scour ; and Mary, to Alexander Maclean of Sollas.

IV. Hector, fourth of Muck, married Isabel, second daughter of Donald Macleod, third of Talisker, but died without issue.

V. Donald, fifth Maclean of Muck, was a very popular man. He held the farm of Cornaig in Coll, and was known as Fear Chòrnaig. He married, first, Flora, daughter of the Rev. Archibald Maclean, minister of Ross, by whom he had one son, Lachlan. His wife died on May 1st, 1756. He married, secondly, Florence, daughter of John Maclean of Treshnish, by whom he had one son and three daughters ; John, Florence, Mary, and Ann. John, his second son, was a captain in the army. He married Isabel, daughter of John Maclean, eldest son of Donald of Kilmoluaig in

Tiree, and had four sons by her; Donald, John, Alexander-Campbell, and James. Donald lived in Bermuda. He left one son and one daughter. John was a captain in the 43d regiment. He married a daughter of Grant of Red Castle, and had four sons. He lived for some time in New South Wales. Alexander-Campbell was a merchant in China. James was killed in the Crimea. Ann, youngest daughter of Donald of Muck, was married to Lieutenant Neil Maclean of the Leda frigate. Donald of Muck died in Edinburgh on August 31st, 1790. He was buried at Killinaig in Coll. He was the subject of a good elegy by Archibald Maclean of Tiree, the well-known Gilleasbuig Laidir.

VI. Lachlan, son of Donald Maclean of Muck, was for some time an officer in the 84th, or Royal Highland Emigrant regiment. He was appointed captain in the North Carolina Dragoons, and did good service under General Sir Henry Clinton, for which he received public thanks. He returned to Britain on half-pay in 1783, but re-entered the army in a short time. He was compelled by ill health to retire from active service, and to accept an official situation. He was for a short time lieutenant-colonel of the Breadalbane Fencibles. He lived in London during the latter part of his life. He held the rank of major in the army, and was deputy-lieutenant, or resident governor, of the Tower of London. He married Hannah-Barbara, daughter of Captain Cottnam, and had twelve children by her; Francis-John-Small, Donald, Charles, Lockhart, John, George, Hector, Elizabeth, Florianne, Mary-Gavinne, Henrietta, and Susan. He died in 1816 in the sixtieth year of his age. He is buried in London. Donald, his second son, was married, and had a son named Lachlan-Hector. Charles was married, and left one son, Lachlan. Lockhart was married, and left a son named Seymour. John was married, and left two sons, Henry-Grey and Lachlan. George died unmarried. Hector was first-lieutenant of the Crescent frigate, which was wrecked off the coast of Jutland. He lost his life while gallantly attempting to save the lives of those who had been wrecked along with him. Florianne was married to James Macleod of Raasay, with issue—John, James, Loudon, Francis, and Hannah-Elizabeth. John was the last Macleod of Raasay. Hannah-Elizabeth was married to Sir John Campbell of Ardnamurchan. Mary-Gavinne, third daughter of Lachlan, was the celebrated London beauty of 1816 and 1817. She was married to Captain William C. Clarke. She lost her health in the trying climate of India. She returned to Britain in 1828, and died in 1833. Henrietta was married to Major Poore.

VII. Francis John Small Maclean held an appointment in the ordnance department. He married Margaret, daughter of I. Hemp, of Herne Hill, Surrey, by whom he had one son, Archibald. He was killed in the island of Dominica, while assisting to suppress an insurrection of natives.

VIII. Archibald, eighth representative of the Macleans of Muck, entered the army as an ensign in the 68th Durham Light Infantry. He served in the army eight years; and then found it necessary to retire owing to impaired eyesight. He married Sarah-Elizabeth-Frances, daughter of Colonel Raynes of the 17th Dragoons, and had eleven children by her; Francis-Etherington, Herbert-Arthur, Fanny-Maria, Cottnam-Walter, Hector-Archibald, Charles-James, Septimius-Maitland, Isabel, Marion, Moira, and William. He died about 1883. Herbert, his second son, settled in Australia. He was married, and left sons and daughters. Fanny lives in London. Cottnam settled in Queensland. He married Ida Richardson, by whom he had two sons. Hector settled in New Zealand. He is married, and has several children. Charles-James resides in London. Septimius died young. Isabel, Marion, and Moira are married. William lives in London. He is married, and has a son and daughter.

IX. Francis Etherington Maclean is the present representative of the Macleans of Muck. He lives in Australia. He married Jessie Brown, and has several sons and daughters. If the Coll estates were still in possession of the descendants of John Garbh, Francis Etherington would be laird. He would have inherited the estates according to the charter granted to Hugh, fourteenth of Coll, in February, 1756.

The Descendants of Hugh Mac Hector.

Hugh, second son of Hector, first of Muck, married a daughter of the laird of Coll, by whom he had three sons; John, Hector, and Donald. John settled in Sandyneesher in Rum. He married Marion Macqueen, a sister of the Rev. Donald Macqueen, by whom he had a son named Hugh. Hugh married Flora, daughter of John Maclean, Iain Mac Thearlaich Mhic Neill Oig, and had six children by her; John, Hector, Hugh, John Og, Flora, and Marion. John married Mary, daughter of John Macaulay, and grand-daughter of the Rev. Angus Macaulay, and had by her four sons and two daughters; Hugh, John, Donald, Hector, Florence, and Marion. John left Rum about the year 1830. Hugh married Anne, daughter of John Cameron in Strathchur, Argyleshire, and had six children by her; John, James, Donald, Hugh, Mary, and Anne. He lived near Dunoon, Scotland, and died a few months ago.

The Descendants of Lachlan Mac Hector.

Lachlan, son of Hector, first of Muck, had a son named John. John married a Miss Campbell, and had by her Lachlan and Alexander. Lachlan was drowned at the age of twenty-two. Alexander married Eunice Mackinnon, by whom he had six children, Lachlan, Donald, Malcolm, Christy, Mary, and Catherine, all of whom emigrated to Cape Breton in 1826, except Catherine. Lachlan, known as Lachainn Mac Alasdair, was born in 1763. He was ground officer in Rum for about thirty years. He married Mary Mackay, by whom he had Donald Bàn and Marion. He came to Cape Breton in 1826, and settled in Strathlorne. Donald Bàn married Christy, daughter of John Mor Maclean, of Kilmory in Rum, and had twelve children by her; John, Lachlan, Alexander, Murdoch, Allan, Donald E., Hector, Neil, Marion, Isabella, and Christy. Donald E. is a loyal member of his clan. Donald Bàn died in 1874, aged eighty years.

THE MACLEANS OF HAREMERE HALL.

Alexander-Campbell, third son of Captain John Maclean, son of Donald of Muck, was a merchant in China, where he succeeded in amassing a large amount of wealth. He purchased Haremere Hall in the county of Sussex, England, where he lived during the latter part of his life. He married, in 1825, Mary Elizabeth Travers, of Fairfield, in Devonshire, England, and had six children by her; Henry-Travers, John-Lachlan, George-Francis, Alexander, Hector-Morgan, and Adelaide. His estate was sold after his death, and the proceeds divided among his surviving sons.

1. Henry-Travers, eldest son of Maclean of Haremere Hall, was a captain in the Indian army of Bombay. He married Marion, daughter of Captain Donald Maclean, son of Lachlan of Muck.

He died in 1863. He had a posthumous son, Henry-Travers, who resides in New Zealand.

2. John-Lachlan was a merchant in China. He married, in 1858, Mary, daughter of Henry Huttleston, of New Bedford, Massachusetts, by whom he had seven children; Lachlan-Percival, Cameron-Travers, Edmund-Henry, Hector-George, Mary, Annie, and Lilian.

3. George-Francis was a merchant in China. He married a daughter of J. W. Cole, by whom he had six children; Margaret-Gavinne, Emilie-Fordyce, Alexander-Henry-Herbert, Rosalie-Abbé, Lowry-Cole, and Adelaide-Travers. He died in 1885.

VII. THE MACLEANS OF DRIMNACROSS.

Neil, third son of Lachlan, seventh of Coll, lived on the farm of Drimnacross in Mull. He served under Sir Lachlan of Duart in the time of Montrose. He was at the battle of Inverkeithing in 1651, and was severely wounded. He married Florence, daughter of Allan Macdonald of Morar, by whom he had two sons and six daughters; Hector, Allan, Marion, Ann, a daughter whose name is not known, Florence, Margaret, and Janet. Marion was married to John Garbh, bailie of Ross. Ann was married to Lachlan Maclean of Grishipol. The third daughter was married to Hector Macquarrie of Ormaig. Florence was married to Charles Mac Neil Bàn in Tiree. Margaret was married, first, to Donald Maclean of Arighoulan; and, secondly, to Ewen Maclean of Treshnish. Janet was married to Charles Maclean, of the Gallanach family.

Hector, elder son of Neil of Drimnacross, occupied the farm of Torrestan in Coll. He married Florence, daughter of Lachlan Maclean of Calgary, by whom he had one son, Lachlan, his successor. Hector was a captain under Sir John of Duart at the battle of Killiecrankie in 1689. He was killed at Dunkeld shortly afterwards. Lachlan, second of Torrestan, served for some time as a volunteer in General Murray's regiment in Holland. He married Margaret, daughter of the Rev. Alexander Macdonald, minister of Sunart, by whom he had a daughter named Marjory. Marjory was married, in 1736, to the Rev. Donald Macqueen, minister of Small Isles, and had two sons, Allan and Edmund. Allan became minister of North Uist in 1770, and died in 1801. Edmund became minister of Barra in 1774, and died in 1812.

Allan, second son of Neil of Drimnacross, occupied the farm of Grishipol in Coll. He married Catherine, daughter of Ewen Maclean of Balliphetrish in Tiree, and had by her six children; Lachlan, John, Neil, Allan, Florence, and Mary. Lachlan was a merchant in Glasgow, and took a deep interest in his clan. He left a daughter named Catherine, who was married to Daniel Burrell of Annat Hill. John succeeded his father in Grishipol. Neil was a doctor. Allan was in the army. Both of them emigrated to Connecticut. Florence was married to Donald Maclean, of Calgary. Mary was married to John Maclean of Giurdal in Rum.

John, second of Grishipol, married Ann, daughter of the Rev. John Maclean, of Kilninian in Mull, and by her had John and Archibald, and two daughters. John was a merchant in Norfolk, Virginia. He was married and had one child, a daughter. Archibald settled in Germany.

The Macleans of Germany.

Archibald, second son of John of Grishipol, was a merchant in Dantzic. He married Mary Symson, by whom he had four sons; John, Lachlan, Archibald, and Henry. John lived in Dantzic. His present representative, whose name is also John, is an officer in the German army. Lachlan visited Coll about the year 1800, and died in 1831. His descendants live at Rodstock. Archibald, son of Archibald, or Archibald II., had two sons, Archibald and Hugh. Archibald III. had two sons, Archibald and Lachlan. Archibald IV. was born in 1842. He was premier-lieutenant of the Life Guards in the Franco-Prussian War. He received the Iron Cross for distinguished services. His son, Archibald V., visited Coll in 1896. The German Macleans have evidently retained the fighting propensities of their clan. It is pleasant to find that they have not forgotten the old Highland names.

The Descendants of Dr. Neil Maclean.

I. Dr. Neil Maclean, third son of Allan of Grishipol, emigrated to America in 1736, and settled at Wethersfield, Connecticut. He remained there about two years, and then removed to Hartford, where he had an extensive practice. He married, first, in 1737, Hannah Stillman, by whom he had Lachlan, Allan, John, and Neil. He married, secondly, in 1757, Hannah Knowles. He died in 1784. Allan, his second son, was a doctor by profession. He married Mary Sloan, by whom he had Catherine, Allan, Polly, Peggy, Elizabeth, and James. He died in 1829. Allan, his elder son, was a sea-captain, and resided at Savannah. John, third son of Dr. Neil, was a farmer, and lived at Windsor. He married Sarah Gardiner, by whom he had Dolly, John, James, Harry, Sally, and Betsey. Harry, his third son, lived at Bloomfield. He married Susanna Gillett, by whom he had Betsey, Henry, John, Daniel-Goodwin, Susanna, and Alexander-Dana. He died in 1844. Neil, fourth son of Dr. Neil, followed the sea. He was married, and left nine children.

II. Lachlan, eldest son of Dr. Neil Maclean, settled in Windsor, Connecticut. He married Lucy Humphrey, by whom he had Hector, Charles, Mary-Ann, Archibald, William, James, and Lucy. He removed with his family from Windsor to Whitestown, New York. He died in 1813.

Hector, his eldest son, was a sea-captain, and died in Lisbon, Portugal, on August 5th, 1800. By his wife, Dolly Bissell, he left two children, Esther and Henry. The former was married to Morris H. Tucker. Charles, second son of Lachlan, and Archibald, the third son, were married and left issue. William, the fourth son, was a printer by trade. He started the Whitestown Gazette in 1779, and the Cherry Valley Gazette in 1818. He married, first, Sukey Williams, by whom he had Albert, Adelaide, and Thomas. He married, secondly, Loise Gillette, by whom he had Amasa, Loise, Charles, Susan, Eliza, and William. Albert, his eldest son, married Rebecca Wilson, and left issue. Thomas died unmarried. Amasa married Louisa Elliston, by whom he had Joseph, Annie, and Sarah. Charles, fourth son of William, succeeded his father as publisher of the Cherry Valley Gazette. He married Mary Judd, by whom he had William-Oliver, Elizabeth, Charles-Dana, and John-Judd. William, fifth son of William, was a printer by trade, and lived at Cooperstown. He married Phœbe Webb, by whom he had one son, William-Melville.

The Descendants of Allan Maclean.

I. Allan, fourth son of Allan Maclean of Grishipol, was born at Kilbride in Coll on August 1st, 1715. He left Scotland on July 22d, 1740, and landed in Boston on the 17th of the following September. He opened a shop in Hartford shortly afterwards. He married, in 1744, Mary, daughter of James Loomis, and had by her Mary, Alexander, Jabez, and Susanna. He was a lieutenant and commissary in the British army in 1760. He settled on a farm at Vernon about 1763. He died in 1786.

II. Alexander, elder son of Allan, lived in Vernon. He married Johanna, daughter of Jonathan Smith, and had by her Hannah, Alexander, Francis, Allan, Mary, and Rosanna. He died in 1806. Hannah, his eldest daughter, was married to Elijah Fitch Reed, M. D., and had six children.

1. Alexander, eldest son of Alexander, was a farmer in Manchester, Connecticut. He married, first, Betsey Thrall, by whom he had Alexander, John, Betsey, Clarissa, Allan, Mary, and Charles. He had, by a second wife, a son named William. He was generally known as Deacon Maclean. He died in 1843. Alexander, his eldest son, married Mary Meakins, by whom he had Alexander, Edwin, George-Allan, and others. John, second son of Deacon Maclean, married, first, Sarah Bunce, by whom he had Caroline, Rosanna, Sarah, John-Dwight, Charlotte, and Maro. He married, secondly, Rhoda Woodford, and had by her one daughter, Almena. Allan, third son of Deacon Maclean, married Eliza Woodbridge, and had one son, Christopher. Charles, the fourth son, married Octa Strong, by whom he had William-Tyler, Jerusha, Octa, Charles-Noble, Emma, Clara, and George-Lincoln. William, fifth son of Deacon

Maclean, married, first, Mary T. Palmer, by whom he had Mary, William, Alfred, Clarence, and Arthur. He married, secondly, Helen Christian, and had by her Charles, John, Minnie, Frank, Edwin, Rosanna, Ernest, and Kate.

2. Francis, second son of Alexander, lived on the old homestead in Vernon, a farm of about 300 acres. He was a farmer, surveyor, and manufacturer. He was a member of the state legislature for several years. He was also lieutenant-colonel of a militia regiment. He married, first, Roxey Mackinney, by whom he had Otis, Lora, Francis, Mary, John, and Rosanna. He married, secondly, Sarah Barre Childs, with issue—Edward, Roxey, Sarah, Harriet, Maria, Mary, and John-Hall. He died in 1861.

3. Allan, third son of Alexander, was born in 1781. He studied for the ministry, and was settled over the Congregational Church at Simsbury, Connecticut, in August, 1809. He married, first, Sarah Pratt, with issue—Allan-Neal, Loyd, Charles-Backus, Sarah-Olmstead, and Dudley-Bestor. He married, secondly, Nancy Morgan. He was a tall, erect, and dignified-looking man. He was totally blind during the last twelve years of his life, but continued to preach. He died in March, 1861. He was pastor of the same church during the long period of fifty-one years and seven months.

Allan-Neal, eldest son of the Rev. Allan Maclean, married Emeline Barber, and by her had

Allan, Calvin-Barber, and Thomas-Neil. Loyd, second son of the Rev. Allan Maclean, died unmarried. Charles-Backus, the third son, was pastor of the Congregational Church at Collinsville, Connecticut. He married Mary D. Williams. He died at Wethersfield in 1873. Dudley-Bestor, fourth son of the Rev. Allan Maclean, lived in Simsbury. He married, in 1846, Mary Payne, by whom he had five children; Hannah-Bishop, Charles-Allan, John-Bunyan, Sally-Pratt, and George-Payne. John-Bunyan studied for the ministry. George-Payne is a lawyer in Hartford. Sally-Pratt was married to Franklin Lynde Greene. She is the authoress of "Cape Cod Folks," and other novels.

VIII. The Macleans of Totaranald.

I. John, second son of John Garbh, eighth of Coll, was the first Maclean of Totaranald. He was known as Iain Ruadh, or John Roy. He served under Sir Lachlan of Duart in Montrose's army. He was at Inverkeithing in 1651, and was severely wounded in the head. He was taken prisoner, and was kept in custody for a long time. He had a natural son named Ewen. He married Marion, daughter of Allan Maclean of Ardgour, and had by her Allan, Hector, Ann, Margaret, and Florence. Ewen was married and left issue. Allan succeeded his father in Totaranald. Hector had a son named Allan, who had a son named Hector, who had a son named Lachlan, who left a daughter who was married to Norman Maclean. It is highly probable that Lachainn Mac Mhic Iain, the poet, was a son of John of Totaranald.

II. Allan of Totaranald married Catherine, daughter of Roderick Macleod of Hamer, by whom he had two sons, Hector and Allan. Allan was drowned ere he had attained the age of manhood.

III. Hector, third of Totaranald, married Julian, daughter of Alexander Maclachlan, bailie of Tiree, by whom he had two sons, Allan and Roderick. Allan settled in Ireland, and may or may not have been married. Roderick settled in Ireland, and was married there.

The Macleans of Gallanach.

I. Hector, eldest son of Donald of Coll, was the progenitor of the Macleans of Gallanach. He lived in Mull. He was married and had two sons, Charles and Neil Bàn. His descendants were known as Sliochd Eachainn Mhic Dhòmhnaill, or the offspring of Hector the son of Donald. Neil Bàn resided at Balliscate, near Tobermory. He had a son named Charles, who settled in Coll, and had a son named John. John, Iain Mac Thearlaich, occupied the farm of Trialan. He had two children, Hector and Isabel. He died in 1760. His daughter was married to Donald Campbell. Hector had five children; John, Flora, Isabel, Ann, and Jane. He died in 1818. John, Iain Mac Eachainn Mhic Iain, had five sons; Hector,

Charles, John, Lachlan, and Alexander. He died in 1860. Hector, his eldest son, was for a long time a mason in Glasgow. He emigrated to Macomb, Illinois. Lachlan was a minister in Australia.

II. Charles, son of Hector, son of Donald of Coll, married Janet, youngest daughter of Neil Maclean of Drimnacross, and had by her a son named Lachlan. Charles fought at the battle of Culloden in 1746.

III. Lachlan, son of Charles, was born in 1730. In his younger days he engaged in business in the Lowlands, but returned to the Western Islands in the course of a few years, and settled at Gallanach in Coll. He married Susanna, daughter of John Maclean of Treshnish, by whom he had Charles and other children. He died in 1802.

IV. Charles, son of Lachlan, was born in 1760. He received a good education, and was a clear-headed and shrewd man. He kept a shop in Glasgow for a short time. He removed from Glasgow to Arinangour in Coll, where he also kept a shop. He entered into the kelp business and made a small fortune by it. He rented the farm of Gallanach in Coll, and was at the same time appointed factor of Coll. He purchased shortly afterwards the farm of Ardow in Mull. He married Margaret, daughter of Neil Maclean of Crossapol, by whom he had Lachlan, Margaret, Isabel, Sibella, and others. Margaret was married to a Mackinnon in Derrichuaig; Isabel, to the

Rev. Donald Maclean, minister of Small Isles; and Sibella, to John Campbell of Cornaig in Coll. Charles of Gallanach died in 1829, and was succeeded by his only son, Lachlan.

V. Lachlan of Gallanach was born on July 21st, 1789. He studied medicine. On leaving the university, he became manager of the Lochalsh estate. He took a lease of Talisker in Skye in 1817. He leased the whole island of Rum in 1825, and went to live there in the following year. He has been severely blamed for the evictions which took place from that island. He lost heavily through an expensive lawsuit and otherwise, and was reduced to poor circumstances. He left Rum in 1839, and went to Australia. He returned in 1843, and entered upon the practice of medicine at Tobermory. He married, in 1823, Isabella-Mary, daughter of Captain Donald Mackenzie of Hartfield, and had eleven children by her; Donald-Alexander, who went to Australia with his father, left Melbourne for the gold-diggings in 1846, and has never been heard of since; Alexander, who was a surgeon in the service of the East India Company; Charles-Smith; John-Mackenzie, who was a surgeon-major in the army; Lachlan-Roderick, who died young; Loudon-Francis, who is a civil engineer in India; Margaret, who was married to Colonel A. A. Macdonell, and whose son, Professor Arthur Macdonell of Oxford, is the author of an excellent Sanskrit-English dictionary; Jane-Mary, who died unmarried; Anne-Flora, who was married to Colonel John Anderson of the Royal Engineers; Elizabeth, who was married to the Rev. John Sharpe; and Sibella-Christina. Dr. Lachlan Maclean died in 1882, at the advanced age of ninety-three. His wife died at Oban in 1884. She was an excellent woman.

VI. Charles Smith Maclean, third son of Dr. Lachlan Maclean, was born in Rum on December 15th, 1836. He entered the army as an ensign in 1853. He saw a great deal of service in India, China, and Afghanistan. He was recommended for the Victoria Cross for his heroic conduct at Delhi on September 14th, 1857. He received two severe wounds at Agra on the 10th of October in the same year. In 1887 he was appointed agent to the Governor-General of India for Khurasan and Seistan, his residence being at Mashad. In 1888 he succeeded in inducing Ayub Khan to surrender to him. In 1889 he was appointed British consul-general for Khurasan and Seistan. In 1890-91 he laid out the boundary between Persia and Afghanistan in the district of Hashtadan. He erected the last pillar on May 24th, 1891. He returned to Europe in 1892. When leaving Persia he was presented with a sword of honour by His Majesty the Shah Nunorodeen. He resides at Newstead, Shanklin, Isle of Wight. He is a major-general in the army, a Companion of the Bath, and a Companion of the Order of the Indian Empire. He speaks, reads, and writes Gaelic, and is in every respect a man of whom his clan may well feel proud. Gu ma fada beo e is ceo de 'thaigh.

General Maclean married, in 1869, Margaret-Macqueen, daughter of Peter Bairnfather, of Dumbarrow, Forfarshire, by whom he had four sons and three daughters; Hector-Lachlan-Stewart; Isabel-Margaret-Sophia-Hastings; Maria-Penelope-Crighton; Donald-Charles-Hugh; Colin-Kenneth; Sheila-Loudon-Lindesay; and Alister-FitzHugh. Hector was born in a tent on the hill of Shekh, Budin, India, on September 13th, 1870. He was educated at Fettes College, Edinburgh, and Sandhurst. He entered the army in 1889, and was appointed lieutenant in the Queen's Own Corps of Guides at Marsdan in 1891. He took part in the Chitral campaign of 1895. He was appointed adjutant of the cavalry of the Guides in 1896. He was killed at Nawa Kila in the Upper Swat Valley, on August 17th, 1897. He was a brave soldier and a skilful officer. Donald, second son of General Maclean, entered the Royal Scots in 1895 and was appointed lieutenant in 1896.

CHAPTER XVI.

The Macleans of Gigha and Morvern.

THE MACLEANS OF GIGHA.

I. ALLAN, second son of Lachlan Cattanach of Duart, was a man of ability, courage, and intense energy. He got a strong fleet under his command, and made plundering expeditions to Ireland, the Lowlands, and parts of the Highlands. He received the name of Ailein nan Sop, or Allan of the straws, from the fact that he was in the habit of setting wisps of burning straw to the buildings in the districts invaded by him, and reducing them to ashes. He was one of the most celebrated plunderers that the Scottish Islands ever produced. About 1525 he plundered the lands of Lochbuie, and slew John, son of Lochbuie, and other persons. In 1535 Hector Mor, his brother, became security for his good behaviour towards Macdonald of Moydart. He attacked the Macneills of Gigha, slew their chief, and took possession of their lands. On July 28th, 1539, he received a "gift of the non-entry mails of Gigha, Comeravoch, Tarbert, and other lands, for all terms since the death of Malcolm Macneill, last possessor thereof, and until the entry of the rightful heir." Shortly afterwards he slew the laird of Lehir, seized his estate, and kept possession of it. He was an active supporter of Donald Dubh in 1545, and in 1546 offered to assist in making James Macdonald of Islay Lord of the Isles. The Earl of Argyll secured his non-interference by giving him the lands of Cille-Charmaig in Knapdale. It is said that it was through Sir James of Islay that he received Tarbert Castle and Gigha. It was probably owing to the favours bestowed upon him by Sir James that he was so ready to fight for him. He was not an ungrateful man; he would help those that would help him. He never interfered with his brother Hector or any of his followers. It is indeed probable that in his attacks upon the lairds of Lochbuie, Moydart, Coll, Gigha, and Lehir, he was encouraged by Hector. It seems that he was always friendly towards Murdoch Gearr, Lochbuie's natural son.

Ailein nan Sop plundered the Route in Ireland once, and the district of "Còrca" twice. He plundered the lands of the Colquhouns near Lochlomond. On a certain October night he made a raid into the district about Rothesay in Bute. He was accompanied by Murdoch Gearr. The sheriff collected a number of men to attack him, but Allan defeated his assailants and carried off a large drove of cattle. A few years before his death he gave up his predatory expeditions. His restless followers were displeased with his peaceful ways. On a certain day a large number of them were present at dinner in his castle. One of them was picking a rib of beef on which there was very little meat. He turned to the person who was sitting beside him and said, What a change has come over this house, when the bones are so bare! Allan heard the remark, and understood what was meant. Immediately after dinner he said to his men, Let every birlinn be ready for sea this evening, and we shall try to get a little meat for the winter. Allan, at the head of his fleet, left Tarbert, directed his course towards the Clyde, and sailed up that river as far as Erskine Ferry, near Renfrew. He landed there, collected a large number of cattle, and took them home with him. This was his greatest plundering expedition; it was also his last. It was known as Creach na h-Aisne, or the Foray of the rib. It derived its name, of course, from the rib which happened to be the innocent occasion of it. Allan died at peace with his church, on his bed in Tarbert Castle, in the year 1551, and was buried with his ancestors on the sacred Isle of Iona. He was probably about fifty-three years of age.

If any person is disposed to wonder that Ailein nan Sop was not sent to the gallows, let him consider these facts: first, that Allan was an accomplished warrior, that he had a strong fleet at his command, and that he had a large number

We know, however, that they contain several statements which are entirely contrary to facts. Treshnish's daughter was Lachlan Cattanach's first wife. We have never seen it affirmed that Hector Mor was a natural son; but Hector Mor and Allan had the same mother. We find Allan described in the Register of the Privy Seal, on August 3d, 1547, as "Allan McClane, brother-german of Hector McClane of Duart." As Allan was thus a son of Lachlan Cattanach by Lachlan's wife, it is outrageously unreasonable to think that he was born on a heap of straw. It is not at all probable that Allan was of so brutal a nature as to attempt to commit rape. As Allan's mother was Lachlan Cattanach's first wife, there can be no ground for thinking that she was ever married to the laird of Lehir. It has never been asserted that Lachlan divorced her. As the Macquarries were faithful followers of Hector Mor of Duart, it is not at all likely that Allan would go to Ulva with the intention of slaying their chief.

Ailein nan Sop, or Allan Maclean of Gigha, Tarbert, and Torloisk, left two natural sons, Hector and John, both of whom were legitimated on August 3d, 1547. He left also a natural daughter. Hector succeeded his father in his estates. John settled in Jura, and was known as Iain Diurach.

II. Hector, eldest son of Ailein nan Sop, was known as Eachann Mac Ailein, or Hector Mac

Allan. He received a gift of the non-entry mails of Gigha and certain lands in Kintyre and Islay on January 30th, 1552. He married Janet Campbell, daughter of Archibald, fourth Earl of Argyll, widow of Lachlan Og of Duart, and mother of Lachlan Mor, but had no children by her. He tried to get the estate of Duart for himself, and, evidently, to do away with Lachlan Mor and John Dubh of Morvern. He was beheaded in Coll by Lachlan Mor's orders in 1578. He left a natural son, Ailein Og.

III. Ailein Og, or Ailein Mac Eachainn, was legitimated on June 7th, 1573. He was thus in a position to succeed to his father's estate; and also to Duart, if Lachlan Mor and John Dubh of Morvern could be destroyed. He was a bitter enemy to both. He was a brave and cunning man. He left a natural son named Charles.

IV. Charles, son of Ailein Og, was legitimated on June 7th, 1573. He married Flora, daughter of Macneil of Barra, by whom he had at least one child, a daughter named Margaret. Hector, sixth of Treshnish, married his widow, as his second wife. John, seventh of Treshnish, married his daughter.

John Diurach.

John, second son of Ailein nan Sop, settled in Jura, and was the first Iain Diurach, or John of Jura. Two of his sons, John Og and Donald, were legitimated on June 7th, 1573. Donald was seized by Lachlan Mor of Duart, and imprisoned in Cairnburgh Castle in April, 1578. He was set at liberty through the interference of the Privy Council, in April, 1579, or shortly afterwards.

According to tradition, John Maclean, a native of Mull, fled to Jura on account of some unfriendly act committed against his chief. He was a strong, fierce, and lawless man, and had several sons who were in every way like himself. He hated taxes with a bitter hatred, and always refused to pay them. Iain Dubh Caimbeul, Black John Campbell, seized two of his horses for his taxes, and sold them in Inverary. He compelled John Dubh, however, at the point of the sword, to swear to him that he would pay him the price of the horses. John Dubh kept his oath, and never tried again to make John Diurach pay taxes.

The John Diurach who settled in Ballimartin was either John, son of Ailein nan Sop, or John Og, eldest son of John, son of Ailein nan Sop. He was thus either a son or grandson of the famous Allan. It is likely that he fled from Jura to Tiree in 1578.

THE MACLEANS OF MORVERN.

John Dubh, second son of Hector Mor of Duart, Iain Dubh Mac Eachainn Mhòir, was a man of ability and good sense. He received from his brother, Hector Og of Duart, in May, 1573, a tack of certain lands in Morvern and Islay, and was at the same time appointed bailie of Morvern

and other places. He fell in love with his first
cousin, Margaret, daughter of Hector, fifth of
Coll, but seems to have been unable to get the
dispensation required for a lawful marriage. He
got over this difficulty by handfasting with her.
He had at least one son by her, Donald Glas.
He married, first, Mary, daughter of John Gorm
Campbell of Lochnell, and relict of John Stewart
of Appin. He had one son by her, Allan of
Ardtornish. He married, secondly, Margaret,
daughter of Archibald Campbell of Ardintenny,
and had two sons by her, John Garbh and Charles.
John Dubh was put to death by Angus Macdonald
of Islay, in July, 1586. His descendants are
popularly known as the Macleans of Morvern.
Donald Glas, his eldest son, lost his life in the
explosion of the Florida in 1588.

I. THE DESCENDANTS OF ALLAN MAC IAN DUY.

Allan, eldest son of John Dubh, was known as
Ailein Mac Iain Duibh, or Allan Mac Ian Duy.
He succeeded his father as bailie of Morvern, and
is described as such in 1592. He lived at Ardtornish. He was at the battle of Glenlivet in 1594,
and was saved from falling into the hands of the
Gordons by the valiant Lachlan Odhar of Airdchraoishnish. He took part in the battle of
Benvigory in 1598. He was a man of ability and
influence, and was well-off. He married Una,
daughter of John Mac Ian of Ardnamurchan, and
had by her ten children; Hector of Kinlochaline,

Charles of Ardnacross, Donald Glas, Mary the elder, Mary the younger, Margaret, Janet, Julia, Christina, and Finvola. Donald Glas died without issue. Mary the elder was married to Gillean, son of Lachlan Mor; Mary the younger, to Allan, son of Lachlan Mor; Margaret, to Macneil of Barra; Janet, to Hector of Torloisk; Julia, to Hector of Muck; and Christina, to Maclean of Kingerloch.

The Macleans of Kinlochaline.

I. Hector, eldest son of Allan Mac Ian Duy, was the first Maclean of Kinlochaline, and the third chieftain of the Macleans of Morvern. He possessed those lands in Morvern of which his father and grandfather had been tacksmen and bailies. He also owned some lands in Mull and Tiree. He became laird of Kinlochaline some time after 1622. He commanded a company of men in Ireland in the rebellion of 1641. He married, first, Janet, daughter of Lachlan Og Maclean, first of Torloisk, and had two sons by her, John and Lachlan. He married, secondly, Margaret, daughter of Robert Campbell of Glenorchy, relict of John Cameron, and mother of the celebrated Sir Ewen Dubh of Lochiel. He had one son by his second wife. John, his eldest son, succeeded him in his possessions.

II. John was severely wounded at the battle of Inverkeithing in 1651. He married, first, Mary, daughter of John Campbell of Lochnell, by whom he had three children; Hector, Allan, and Janet. He married, secondly, Una, daughter of John Garbh, eighth of Coll, but had no issue by her. Janet was married to John Cameron of Glendessary.

III. Hector, son of John, married Janet, daughter of Hector Maclean, second of Torloisk, and had by her a son named Angus.

IV. Angus served for some time as a volunteer in General Murray's regiment in the Dutch service. He was a captain under Sir John of Duart at Sheriffmuir in 1715. He married, first, Janet, daughter of John Cameron of Glendessary. He had several children by her, but they all died young. He married, secondly, Ann, daughter of Ranald Macdonald of Kinloch-Moydart. He died on May 8th, 1735. He was succeeded in his estate by Charles Maclean of Drimnin.

The Macleans of Drimnin, Calgary, Grulin, and Other Places.

Charles, second son of Allan Mac Ian Duy, was tacksman of Ardnacross in Mull. He was invariably spoken of as Tearlach Mac Ailein, or Terlach Mac Allan. He purchased the lands of Drimnin from the Earl of Argyll, and gave them to his eldest son. He married Mary, daughter of Allan of Ardgour, and had by her nine children; Allan of Drimnin, Lachlan of Calgary, Allan of Grulin, Donald of Aros, Hector, Ewen, Ann, Finvola, and Mary. Ann was married to Alexander Macdonald of Kinloch-Moydart. Flora was married, first, to John Macquarrie of Laggan-Ulva, and, secondly, to Captain Andrew Maclean, the poet. Mary was married to Hugh Cameron. We meet with Terlach Mac Allan and all his sons, except Allan of Drimnin, in Cairnburgh Castle in December, 1680.

1. THE MACLEANS OF DRIMNIN.

I. Allan, eldest son of Terlach Mac Allan, or Charles Maclean of Ardnacross, was the first Maclean of Drimnin. He was an exceedingly handsome man. He married Mary, daughter of John Cameron of Callart, by whom he had three children; John, Donald, and Margaret. Allan of Drimnin died at the age of twenty-nine. John, his eldest son, succeeded him. Donald, his second son, married Florence, daughter of Lachlan Maclean of Calgary, by whom he had Lachlan and several daughters. Lachlan went to Ireland and settled at Mullach-Glas, near Dundalk. He married and left issue. Margaret, only daughter of Allan of Drimnin, was married to Allan Maclean, of the Torloisk family.

II. John, son of Allan, married Mary, daughter of John Crùbach of Ardgour, by whom he had Allan and Charles. He died, like his father, at the age of twenty-nine. He was succeeded by Allan, his elder son.

III. Allan died unmarried, and, like his father and grandfather, at the age of twenty-nine. He was succeeded by his brother Charles.

IV. Charles served for some time in the navy.

He was short in stature, but strongly built. He was hot-tempered and apt to commit rash acts. He struck the laird of Macleod with his fist, on the street in Edinburgh. He took hold of a schoolmaster, who was charged with lying by a mean shoemaker, put him across his knees, and thrashed him with the shoemaker's strap. He was the subject of several pieces of semi-sarcastic poetry by John Mac Allan, the famous Mull bard. He was kind and manly, and brave to rashness. He had a natural son named Lachlan. He married Isabel, daughter of John Cameron of Erracht, by whom he had Allan, John, Donald, Lachlan, and two or three daughters. He was killed at Culloden in 1746. Lachlan, his eldest son, was a captain under him at Culloden, and was also slain there. Lachlan was married, and left a son named Allan. Allan, second son of Charles, succeeded his father in Drimnin. John, the third son, married Margaret, daughter of Donald Campbell of Scamadale, by whom he had three sons; Donald, Charles, and Colin. He was lost in the Sound of Mull. Donald, his eldest son, was a doctor. It is said that he died in Nova Scotia, and left a numerous issue. It is also said that Charles died in Nova Scotia, that he was married, and left issue. Colin was a lieutenant in the army. He married Helen, daughter of Cameron of Callart, by whom he had one son and one daughter. He died in Jamaica. Donald, fourth son of Charles of Drimnin, was a surgeon in Colonel Montgomery's Highland regiment. He settled in New York. Lachlan, the fifth son, was a planter in Jamaica, and died there in 1764. Marjory, eldest daughter of Charles of Drimnin, was married to Donald Cameron of Erracht. The celebrated General Sir Allan Cameron of Erracht was her son.

V. Allan, fifth of Drimnin and sixth of Kinlochaline, was the eighth chieftain of the Macleans of Morvern. He was born in 1724. He was wounded in the battle of Culloden. He was served heir male special, in 1749, to John Maclean of Kinlochaline in Knock in Morvern, Killean in Mull, and Scarinish in Tiree. He married, first, Ann, daughter of Donald Maclean of Brolas, and had by her Charles, Una, and others. He married, secondly, Mary, daughter of Lachlan Maclean of Lochbuie, by whom he had Donald, John, Mary, Louisa, Catherine, and others. He was an excellent man, and was highly respected. He died in 1792. Charles, his eldest son, succeeded him. Donald succeeded Charles. John was a surgeon in the 79th Highlanders, and died at Martinique. Una was married to Ewen Cameron, of the family of Erracht. Mary was married to Dr. Hector Maclean, author of a small work on the plague. Louisa was married to a man named Wood. Catherine was married to Captain John Campbell, of the Royal Navy, and had seven children; Elizabeth, Allan, Mary, Margaret, Jane, Lillias-Grant, and Donald. Captain Campbell died in Charlottetown, Prince Edward Island. One of Allan of Drimnin's daughters was married to Captain Stewart, of the Royal Navy, and another to Ranald Macdonald of Glenturret, who was an officer in the 79th regiment.

VI. Charles of Drimnin and Kinlochaline, married Maria, eldest daughter of Sir Allan Maclean of Brolas. He received a third of Sir Allan's estate by his wife, and seems to have purchased the shares which belonged to her two sisters. He was a careless, imprudent, and extravagant man, and got deeply into debt. The final result was that, in 1798, or thereabouts, his estates were sold to pay his creditors.

VII. Donald, second son of Allan of Drimnin, was known as Dòmhnall Ruadh nan Drimnean, or Donald Roy of Drimnin. He was a writer to the signet in Edinburgh. He lived during the latter part of his life at Kinloch in Mull, and is generally referred to as Donald of Kinloch. He married Lillias, youngest daughter of Colquhoun Grant, a lawyer in Edinburgh, and had by her sixteen children; Christina, Allan, Colquhoun, Mary, Lillias, Ann, Hector, Margaret, Isabella, John, Charles, Jane, Alexander, Archibald, Andrew, and Fitzroy-Jeffreys-Grafton. Allan was a lieutenant in the 79th Highlanders, and was severely wounded at the battle of Toulouse, on April 10th, 1814. He died in 1818. Colquhoun was an officer in the Royal Navy. He died on the west coast of Africa in 1822. Hector was killed while capturing a slave dhow in the West Indies, in 1818. John died unmarried. Alexander died in 1818. Archibald was a writer to the signet in Edinburgh. Fitzroy was also a lawyer. Christina was married to Murdoch Maclean of Lochbuie; and Isabella, to Alexander Crawford.

VIII. Charles, fifth son of **Donald Roy of Kinloch**, was born in Edinburgh in 1806. He lost his eyesight at the age of sixteen, from a virulent form of Egyptian ophthalmy. He was, at the time, attending a college in London and preparing for entering the army. Being now unfitted for a military life, he entered the University of Edinburgh and studied for the ministry. He passed all his examinations successfully, but the General Assembly of the Church of Scotland refused to sanction his being inducted into a pastoral charge. He came to Canada in 1836, and purchased a farm at Seymour, Ontario. He married, in 1837, Jane-Jessie, daughter of Captain Campbell of Kintra, and had by her ten children; Lillias-Grant, Donald, Jane-Campbell, Colin-Campbell, Jane-Jarvis, William-Bruce, Sibella-Adelaide-Crawford, Archibald-Murdoch, Alexander-Campbell, and Charles. He was a man of high culture, and a good musician. He died at Kingston, Ontario, in 1872. Colin, his second son, was drowned at the age of fourteen. William died at the age of nineteen. Archibald is a doctor at Leadville, Colorado. He is married, and has a son and daughter. Alexander is a doctor at Salt

Lake City. He married Susan Maroner, by whom he has three children; Ailene, Donald, and Kenneth. Charles is a doctor at Hancock, Michigan. He is married, and has four sons and three daughters.

IX. Donald, eldest son of Charles Maclean, is a doctor in Detroit. He is married, and has two children, Donald and Annie. He is the present representative of John Dubh of Morvern.

Dr. Andrew Maclean.

Andrew, eighth son of Donald of Kinloch, was born in Edinburgh in 1812. He graduated as a medical doctor in 1832. He was appointed surgeon in the 64th Foot in 1833. He retired from the army as deputy inspector-general in 1878. He is still living, and resides in Church House, Kew, Surrey.

Dr. Maclean married, in 1838, Clara, daughter of Henry Holland Harrison, and had eleven children by her; Harry-Aubrey de Vere, Donald-Grant, Fitzroy-Beresford, Allan-Bruce, Charles-Gordon, Archibald-Douglas, Clara-Rosa, Alice-Lillias, Edith-Kathleen, Louisa-Flora, and Minnie-Margaret. Donald died in the twenty-second year of his age. Fitzroy studied medicine, and was appointed surgeon in the army in 1880. He is at the present date a surgeon-major. He married, in 1889, Mary Norris, daughter of the Rev. J. Erskine, of Wycliffe Rectory, Yorkshire. Allan is in the consular service. Archibald entered the Royal

Artillery as second lieutenant in 1882, but resigned his commission in 1889. He is married, and has one son. Clara resides with her parents. Alice is married to Surgeon-General C. D. Madden, C.B. Edith is married to Colonel C. W. Fothergill. Louisa was married to General Sir Duncan A. Cameron. Minnie died in Morocco.

Harry-Aubrey de Vere, eldest son of Deputy Surgeon-General Maclean, was born on June 15th, 1848. He entered the British army in 1869. He resigned his commission in 1876, and accepted an appointment as "Instructor in Drill and Discipline," in the army of the Sultan of Morocco. He holds the rank of kaid or chief. He is a fearless and energetic man, and has had a number of thrilling experiences and narrow escapes. He is an excellent horseman and a good marksman, and is always ready to run risks in the Sultan's service. He is very popular among the Moors.

Kaid Maclean has a Scottish piper, named John Macdonald Mortimer. With him six Moors are receiving instruction in playing, and are making good progress. All the pipes are decorated with ribbons of the Maclean tartan.

Kaid Maclean was married in 1875, and has one son, Andrew de Vere, and three daughters. His son was born in 1882, and is preparing for the army.

2. The Macleans of Calgary.

1. Lachlan, second son of Terlach Mac Allan, was tacksman of Calgary. He married, first,

Florence, daughter of Farquhar Fraser, dean of the Isles, by whom he had Donald and Florence. He married, secondly, Anne, daughter of John Maclean of Totaranald, by whom he had Charles, Allan, Peter, and Marion. He was succeeded by his eldest son, Donald. Florence was married, first, to Hector Maclean of Torrestan, and, secondly, to Donald, son of Allan Maclean of Drimnin.

II. Donald of Calgary married, first, Susanna, daughter of Duncan Campbell of Inverawe, by whom he had Charles, Alexander, and Allan. His wife died in 1715, aged thirty-one years. He married, secondly, Florence, daughter of Allan of Grishipol, with issue—Lachlan and Jean. Charles, his eldest son, died young. Alexander succeeded him in Calgary. Allan, his third son, was a lieutenant under Charles of Drimnin, and was killed at Culloden.

III. Alexander of Calgary married Mary, daughter of the Rev. John Maclean of Kilninian, and had by her Charles, Duncan, and Donald. Charles went to Jamaica. Duncan died in the navy. Donald was also in the navy. He settled in some part of America.

3. The Macleans of Grulin.

I. Allan, third son of Charles of Ardnacross, was the first Maclean of Grulin. He married Una, daughter of Donald Macquarrie of Ulva, by whom he had Lachlan, Charles, John, Margaret, and Janet. He died about 1720. Lachlan, his eldest son, succeeded him in Grulin. Charles lived in Killunaig, and John in Pennygoun. Margaret was married to Hector Maclean of Kilmory. Janet was married to John Dubh Campbell of Achaghuarain, by whom she had fourteen sons and three daughters, all of whom grew up. Mary, the eldest daughter, was married to Magnus Morison in Penmore; and Ellen, the second daughter, to Charles Macgregor in Ardmore.

II. Lachlan of Grulin was born about the year 1670. He received a good education, and was an intelligent, prudent, and highly-esteemed man. He was served heir to his father in March, 1721. He married, first, Janet, daughter of John Macleod, of Bernera, by whom he had Hector and Una. He married, secondly, Ann, daughter of John Campbell of Kirkton. He died about the year 1751. His daughter Una was married to Alexander Macgillivray of Pennyghael in Mull.

III. Hector, only son of Lachlan of Grulin, was a doctor by profession. He spent a few years in Flanders and Holland, apparently as a surgeon in the army. After his return he settled in Glasgow, and lived there for a number of years. He spent the latter part of his life at Erray, near Tobermory. He was a man of ability and literary culture, and took a deep interest in the history and poetry of his clan. He collected a large number of very valuable Gaelic poems. He married Catherine, only daughter of Donald Maclean of Coll, by whom he had one daughter,

Mary. Dr. Johnson spent a night at his house, and pronounced Mary the most accomplished lady that he had found in the Highlands. Dr. Maclean died about 1784. Mary died in 1826.

The Macleans of Killunaig.

Charles of Killunaig was the second son of Allan of Grulin. He studied law, but never followed it as a profession. He married Marion, daughter of John Maclean of Tarbert, by whom he had ten children; Allan, Hector, Donald, Allan Og, John, Alexander, Lachlan, Archibald, Isabel, and Anne. He died in the sixty-ninth year of his age. 1. Allan, his eldest son, was a lieutenant in the Dutch service. He married Isabel, daughter of Donald Campbell of Scamadale, by whom he had two sons, Charles and Allan. Charles was a lieutenant in the military service of the East India Company, and was killed in the war with Hyder Ali in 1754. Allan was a planter in Jamaica, and also died in 1754. 2. Hector resided at Torranbeg. 3. Donald lived at "the Queen's Ferry." He married Mary Mean, by whom he had James, John, Christopher, Mary, and Catherine. James was a merchant in Kingston, Jamaica. He married Mary-Ann, daughter of John Maclean in Kingston. John, second son of Donald, died unmarried. Christopher was married and had two sons. 4. Allan Og was a surgeon, and died at the age of twenty-four. 5. John was a planter in Jamaica, and resided at

Kingston. He married Marion, daughter of Fortunatus Duvaris, by whom he had Charles, Thomas, Mary-Ann, and another daughter. The two sons died unmarried. Mary-Ann was married, first, to James Maclean, Donald's son; and, secondly, to Dr. Alexander Grant. 6. Alexander was the first Maclean of Pennycross. 7. Lachlan was a lieutenant in the Black Watch, and was killed at Havana in 1762. 8. Archibald was in partnership with his brother John in Jamaica. He died unmarried.

HECTOR OF TORRANBEG.

Hector, second son of Charles Maclean of Killunaig, lived at Torranbeg in Mull. He married Julia, daughter of Allan Maclean of Suic, of the Lochbuie family, and had by her eight children; Allan, John, Alexander, Archibald, Ann, Mary, Catherine, and Alice. Ann was married to Alexander Mackinnon of Derryguaig; Mary, to Lachlan Bàn Maclean of Bunessan; Catherine, to Alexander Sinclair in Kintyre; and Alice, to Archibald Maclean of Pennycross. Allan, eldest son of Hector of Torranbeg, was a merchant in Kingston, Jamaica. John was tacksman of Grulin, and was served heir to his father in July, 1799. Alexander was lieutenant-colonel of the 2d West India regiment. Archibald was born in 1758. He was a captain in the New York volunteers. He was severely wounded at the battle of Eutaw Springs, September 8th, 1781.

He settled on the Nashwaak River in New Brunswick, Canada. He represented the county of York in the legislature for upwards of twenty years. He married, first, a Miss French, by whom he had Allan, Salome, and other daughters. He married, secondly, Susan Drummond, by whom he had Archibald and John. He died in 1829. Allan, his eldest son, was a lieutenant-colonel in the militia, and died in 1871. Salome, eldest daughter of Captain Archibald Maclean, was married to James S. Howard in Toronto.

The Macleans of Pennycross.

I. Alexander, sixth son of Charles Maclean of Killunaig, was a medical doctor. He lived in the Ross of Mull. He married, in 1760, Una, daughter of Alexander Macgillivray of Pennyghael, and had by her two children, Archibald and Catherine. He purchased the lands of Pennycross about 1798. He died in 1800. Catherine, his daughter, was married to Donald Maclean, of the Royal Scots.

II. Archibald, only son of Dr. Alexander Maclean, was born in 1761, and was served heir to his father in 1800. He was for some time major of the 3d regiment of the Argyleshire Fencibles. He was the writer of the Pennycross MS. He married Alice, daughter of Hector Maclean of Torranbeg, and had by her nine children; Alexander, Allan-Thomas, Charles-James, Mary, John, Julia, Hector, Lachlan, and Archibald-Donald. Alexander succeeded him in Pennycross. Allan-

Thomas, his second son, was born in May, 1793. He entered the army as cornet in the 13th Light Dragoons in 1809. He served in this regiment throughout the Peninsular War, and also at Waterloo, where he commanded it. He spent thirty-two years in India without returning home. He was appointed major-general in 1854, and lieutenant-general in 1861. He married, in 1843, Agnes Furlong, by whom he had three daughters; Agnes, Alice, and Margaret. The last named was married to Baron de Pollandt. Charles-James, third son of Archibald of Pennycross, entered the 79th Highlanders in 1813. He carried the colours at Quatre Bras and Waterloo. He was subsequently a lieutenant in the 31st Foot. He died at Calcutta in May, 1837. John, fourth son of Archibald of Pennycross, was a lieutenant in the 2d West India regiment. He died at Nassau, New Providence, in 1822. Hector, the fifth son, was in a mercantile establishment in London, and died in 1834. Lachlan, the sixth son, was a lieutenant in the Ceylon Rifles. He died at Colombo in 1830. Archibald-Donald, the seventh son, was deputy commissary-general in Bermuda.

III. Alexander, third of Pennycross, was born in 1791, and succeeded his father in 1830. He met with losses, borrowed money, and got deeply into debt. The fall in the price of kelp was to a large extent the cause of his difficulties. He married, in 1740, Charlotte-Brodie, daughter of John Maclean, of Elrick, and had by her two sons and three daughters; Archibald-John, Allan-Thomas-Lockhart, Alice, Charlotte, and Mary. He died on March 8th, 1876.

IV. Archibald-John, fourth and last Maclean of Pennycross, was born on March 6th, 1843. He was for some time engaged in mercantile pursuits. He was under the necessity of parting with his estate in 1888. He visited the United States and Canada in 1893, and spent a few days with us in Belfast. He is a good-hearted, cheerful, and pleasant man; and is, so far as is known to us, the present representative of the Macleans of Grulin. He married, first, in 1868, Isabella Alexandrina Simon, by whom he had eight children; Julian-Archibald, Charles-Alexander-Hugh, Isabel-Juliet, Norman-Henry, Allan-Fitzroy, Elsie-Una, Muriel, and Violet. His wife died in 1886. He married, secondly, in June, 1890, Clara-Isabel, daughter of W. H. Rudkin, of Woodside, Teignmouth. Charles A. H., his eldest son, is a lieutenant in the Sutherland Highlanders.

The Macleans of Pennygoun.

I. John, third son of Allan Maclean of Grulin, lived in Pennygoun. He married Isabel, daughter of Colin Campbell, of the family of Dunstaffnage, by whom he had five children; Donald, Allan, Una, Janet, and Catherine. Donald succeeded his father in Pennygoun. Allan came to America, and was killed at Casco Bay by the falling in of the roof of a storehouse. Una was married to

Allan, son of Maclean of Kingerloch. Janet was married to Duncan Macarthur; and Catherine, to Donald Macdonald.

II. Donald, second Maclean of Pennygoun, married Ann, natural daughter of Lachlan Maclean of Lochbuie, by whom he had Lachlan, John, Hector, Donald, Alexander, Ann, Mary, and Margaret. John entered the navy, and died in the East Indies. Hector was killed at the storming of Seringapatam, probably in 1799. He was the second man to mount the breach. Donald was a doctor, and lived at Achitenny. Alexander lived for some time at Kinnegharar in Mull. He married Christina, third daughter of John Maclean of Langamull, and had issue by her. He emigrated with his family to the Red River Settlement, now Manitoba, and was killed there. Mary, second daughter of Donald of Pennygoun, was married to David Fraser.

III. Lachlan, eldest son of Donald of Pennygoun, was a medical doctor. He lived for some time in the island of Jersey, and married there. He emigrated with his family to America, and settled near Nashville, in Tennessee. He left seven children; John, Joshua, Gabriel, Charles-Durell, Susan, Mary-Ann, and Isabel. John was a merchant and Joshua a doctor. Charles was editor and publisher of the Nashville Gazette. Susan was married to William Banks Anthony.

4. Donald, Fourth Son of Terlach Mac Allan.

Donald, fourth son of Terlach Mac Allan, lived at Aros. He married Catherine, second daughter of Donald Macquarrie of Ulva, by whom he had Alexander, Angus, Charles, and others. Alexander, the eldest son, was born in 1690. He was a major in the Spanish service. He was put to death at Madrid in 1739. He left three sons and a daughter. One of his sons was known as Don Andrew. The daughter, whose name was Zeiretta, was married to a Spanish nobleman of Arragon.

According to one account, Major Maclean was put to death for killing the colonel of his regiment in a duel. According to another account, the colonel and a subaltern named Lynch quarrelled near a monastery in Madrid, and began fighting with their swords. Major Maclean happened to come along at the time, and struck down the swords of both. Lynch took a treacherous advantage of the colonel, thrust his sword through him, and ran away. A crowd gathered immediately to the scene of the fight, and finding the major standing beside the slain colonel, concluded that he had killed him in a duel. Some of the occupants of the monastery saw everything that had taken place, and testified to the major's innocence. He was condemned, however, and put to death. The King of Spain took his wife and children under his own protection. It is a matter of little or no consequence which of the two versions is the correct one. We can readily believe that a fiery Highlander of the year 1739 would fight a duel with a Spanish colonel or any other man. We can also believe that he might get into trouble, when his own blood was cool, by trying to prevent others from fighting.

Angus, second son of Donald of Aros, married Ann, daughter of Allan Maclean, Ailein Mac Iain Diuraich, of the Torloisk family, and had one daughter by her. Charles, third son of Donald of Aros, married Jean Campbell, and had two children by her, Hector and Margaret. Hector married Marion, daughter of Donald Macquarrie of Ulva, and had a son named John, who settled in New York. Margaret was married to Alexander Macquarrie of Laggan in Ulva.

One of the daughters of Donald of Aros was married to Archibald Campbell, of the Lochnell family, by whom she had a numerous issue. The Rev. Archibald Mac Coll, who was born in 1746, and became minister of Tiree in 1780, was her grandson.

5. HECTOR, FIFTH SON OF TERLACH MAC ALLAN.

Hector, fifth son of Charles Maclean of Ardnacross, married Janet, daughter of Hector Roy, heir-apparent of John Garbh, eighth of Coll, and had by her four children; Lachlan, John, Donald, and Mary. Lachlan died young. John was for some time a lieutenant in the navy. He was a distinguished mathematician. He died unmarried at

Lynn in the county of Norfolk. Donald was married, but left no issue. Mary died unmarried.

6. EWEN, SIXTH SON OF TERLACH MAC ALLAN.

Ewen, or Hugh, sixth son of Terlach Mac Allan, or Charles Maclean of Ardnacross, married Marion, daughter of Archibald Maclean of Ardtun, of the Ardgour family, and left issue.

II. THE DESCENDANTS OF JOHN GARBH MAC IAN DUY.

John, third son of John Dubh of Morvern, was quite a prominent man in his day. We find him described as John Maclean, bailie of Ross, in 1592, as John Garbh Maclean in 1616, and as John Garbh of Bunessan in 1618. It is thus evident that he was known as John Garbh, that he was bailie of Ross, and that he resided at Bunessan. He married, first, Janet, second daughter of Hector, fifth Maclean of Coll; and, secondly, Mary, second daughter of Lachlan Og of Torloisk. He had six children; Charles, Hector, Donald, Margaret, Janet, and Catherine. Margaret was married to Hector Maclean of Treshnish; Janet, to Malcolm Macphie of Colonsay; and Catherine, to Ewen Maclean of Balliphetrish in Tiree.

Charles, eldest son of John Garbh of Bunessan, married Marion, daughter of Neil Maclean of Drimnacross, by whom he had four children; Allan, Hector, John, and Mary. Allan married Catherine Stewart, by whom he had three sons;

Hector, John, and Allan. Hector was killed in the Spanish service. John was killed in Flanders. Allan was killed at Sheriffmuir in 1715. He was a captain under Sir John of Duart. Hector, second son of John Garbh, lived in Assapol. He married Florence, daughter of Ewen Maclean of Treshnish, and had by her, John, Charles, Hugh, Janet, and Florence. John married Florence, daughter of Lachlan Maclean of Calgary, but had no issue. Charles married a daughter of Hector Macquarrie of Ormaig, by whom he had Lachlan, who was killed in Spain. According to the Ardgour MS., Hugh was married, but left no issue. Janet was married to Lachlan Maclean, of the Torloisk family, by whom she had a daughter named Julia, who became the wife of Allan Maclean of Garmony. Florence was married to John Macquarrie of Ulva. Lachlan, the last chief of Ulva's Isle, was her son. He was born in 1715, entered the army in 1778, and died in 1818. Donald, third son of John Garbh of Bunessan, seems to have died without issue.

III. The Descendants of Charles Mac Ian Duy.

Charles, fourth son of John Dubh of Morvern, married Julia, daughter of Neil Macgillivray of Glencannir, and had by her Lachlan of Achacreig, John Diurach, and others. Lachlan of Achacreig had a son named Donald, who was a merchant in Glasgow. Donald married a daughter of Peter

Macadam in Glasgow, by whom he had a son named Peter. Peter was major-commandant of Colonel Lamby's regiment, in Holland. He died in London in 1752. John Diurach, second son of Charles Mac Ian Duy, commanded the forlorn hope at the battle of Inverkeithing in 1651, and was one of the few Macleans who escaped from the dreadful carnage which took place. He received a number of severe wounds. He married Elizabeth, daughter of Charles Maclean of Hilis in Tiree, by whom he had Hector and other children. Hector, Eachann Mac Iain Diuraich, married Mary, daughter of Ewen Maclean of Balliphetrish in Tiree, and had three sons by her; Lachlan, John, and Donald. Lachlan served with distinction in the Scots Guards in Spain. He commanded a company of volunteers, under Brigadier Mackintosh, at Preston in 1715. He was taken prisoner there, but was liberated shortly afterwards. John was a captain under Charles of Drimnin at the battle of Culloden in 1746. He was killed in the ferocious massacre of the Gaidels by the Anglo-Saxons the day after the battle. Donald married, first, Ann, daughter of Charles Maclean of Killunaig, by whom he had one daughter, Mary. He married, secondly, Mary, daughter of John Maclean of Killean, by whom he had Lachlan, Mary, and another daughter. Lachlan lost his life in Major Paulson's expedition from Jamaica to the Spanish Main. Mary was married to John Maclean of Langamull.

CHAPTER XVII.

The Macleans of Torloisk, Sweden, and Brolas.

THE MACLEANS OF TORLOISK.

I. LACHLAN OG, second son of Lachlan Mor of Duart, was the progenitor of the Macleans of Torloisk. He was for a long time tenant of Ardnacross, and resided there. He received the lands of Torloisk from his brother, Hector Og of Duart. He married, first, Marion, daughter of Sir Duncan Campbell of Auchnambreck; secondly, Margaret, daughter of William Stewart, captain of Dumbarton; and, thirdly, Marion, daughter of Donald Macdonald of Moydart. He had by his first wife, Hector and several daughters. He had no issue by his second wife. By his third wife he had six sons; Lachlan Og, Ewen, Allan, Lachlan Cattanach, Neil, and John Diurach. He had also some daughters by her. He had six daughters in all; Janet, Mary, Catherine, Julia, Isabel, and Christina. Hector, his eldest son, succeeded him in Torloisk. Lachlan Og, his second son, died unmarried, but left a natural son named Donald. Ewen and Lachlan Cattanach were killed at Inverkeithing. Allan died in Harris. Neil married a daughter of Maclean of Lochbuie, by whom he had Lachlan and a daughter. Lachlan, Neil's son, was a lieutenant in the British army, and died in London. John Diurach, seventh son of Lachlan Og of Torloisk, married Janet, daughter of John Crùbach of Ardgour, and had by her Allan, and two or three daughters. Allan was married, and had two daughters: Marjory, who was married to Allan of Inverscadale; and Ann, who was married to Angus, son of Donald of Aros. Janet, eldest daughter of Lachlan Og, was married to Hector of Kinlochaline; Mary, to John Garbh Mac Ian Duy; Catherine, to John, son of Macneil of Barra; Julia, to Allan Maclean, of the Lochbuie family; Isabel, to the Rev. Martin Macgillivray of Pennyghael; and Christina, to Donald Macquarrie of Ulva, by whom she had six children; Allan of Ulva, Hector of Ormaig, Lachlan of Laggan, John of Ballighartan, Una, and Catherine.

II. Hector of Torloisk adhered to the party led by Argyll from 1647. He was placed in charge of Cairnburgh, which he garrisoned with thirty men for eighteen months. Sir Lachlan of Duart besieged Cairnburgh in 1648, but was unable to capture it. Hector was pardoned by the Act of Indemnity in 1661, but had to pay a fine of £4,000. We find him one of the commissioners for Argyleshire in 1667. He was married twice. By his first wife, Janet, daughter of Allan Mac Ian Duy, he had three daughters; Margaret, Marion, and Mary. By his second wife, Catherine, daughter of John Campbell of Lochnell, he had five children; Lachlan, Hector, John, Isabel, and Janet. Lachlan succeeded his father. Hector was murdered, near his own house at Torloisk, by the Maclachlans of Fiairt in Lismore, a notorious set of robbers, who were carrying off his cattle. John was the first Maclean of Tarbert. He married Catherine, daughter of Donald Campbell of Comguish, by whom he had Donald, John, and Marion. Donald succeeded his father in Tarbert. John was married and had issue. Marion, second daughter of Hector of Torloisk was married, first, to Hector Roy of Coll; and, secondly, to John Crùbach of Ardgour. Mary, the third daughter, was married to Duncan Campbell of Saundaick, and had by her two sons, John and Alexander. John was bailie of Jura, and governor of Aros Castle in 1690. Alexander was the ancestor of the Campbells of Glendaruel.

III. Lachlan of Torloisk was an able, high-spirited, and accomplished man. He gave valuable assistance to Donald of Brolas in managing the Duart estate during the minority of Sir John. He married Barbara, daughter of Sir Donald Macdonald, eighth of Sleat, by whom he had Hector, Alexander, and Janet. Hector, his elder son, died at the age of eighteen. Alexander succeeded him in Torloisk. Janet was married to Archibald Campbell of Inverawe.

IV. Alexander of Torloisk was born in 1686. He was a captain in the second battalion of the Scots Guards in Spain. He received a severe wound at the siege of Briguego in 1711, and died from its effects shortly afterwards. He was a very promising young man. He was succeeded in the estate by his cousin-german, Donald Maclean of Tarbert.

V. Donald of Torloisk was noted for his kindness and refinement of manners. He was major of the Maclean regiment at Sheriffmuir in 1715. He married Mary, daughter of Archibald Campbell of Sunderland, by whom he had Hector, Lachlan, Allan, Archibald, Mary, Ann, Alice, Christina, Betty, and Elizabeth. He died in August, 1748. Hector, his eldest son, succeeded him. Archibald, his fourth son, was a merchant in Laggan. He was a kind-hearted man, and was the author of several Gaelic songs. He died about 1800. He left a son named John, who had two sons, Lachlan and Archibald, both of whom died without issue. Ann, second daughter of Donald of Torloisk, was married to Donald Maclean of Raodel; and Alice, to Lachlan Macquarrie of Ulva. Elizabeth was married, first, to Lachlan Maclean of Garmony; and, secondly, to James Park of Jamaica. The Hon. Sir James Allan Park was her son. Allan, third son of Donald of Torloisk, was a lieutenant in the Dutch Brigade in 1747. He was severely wounded at Ticonderoga in 1758. He raised the 84th, or Royal Highland Emigrant regiment, in 1775, and was appointed lieutenant-colonel-commandant of the first battalion. He defeated Generals Arnold and Montgomery at Quebec on December 31st, 1775, and successfully defended that city against Arnold until the spring, when the latter was compelled to raise the siege and retire from Canada. He was promoted to the rank of brigadier-general. He returned to Britain in 1784. He married Janet, daughter of Donald of Brolas. He died in London in March, 1797. He was a man of intense energy, and a skilful officer. He certainly deserves a monument at Quebec.

VI. Hector of Torloisk studied law. We find him described in 1751 as a writer in Edinburgh. He died in Glasgow in May, 1765, and was succeeded by his brother, Lachlan.

VII. Lachlan followed the sea for a number of years. He was captain of the ship Mary, a merchantman which plied between London and Jamaica. He married Margaret, daughter of Richard Smith in Fifeshire, by whom he had one daughter, Marianne. He died in 1799, leaving the estate to his daughter.

Major-General William Maclean Douglas Clephane, of Carslogie, Fifeshire, married Marianne, daughter and heiress of Lachlan of Torloisk, and had by her three daughters; Margaret, Anna-Jane, and Wilmina-Marianne. He died in Grenada in

1803. Sir Walter Scott was appointed guardian of his children. Spencer Joshua Alwyne, afterwards Marquis of Northampton, married Margaret in 1815, and had by her Charles-Douglas, William, and four daughters. William succeeded his maternal grandmother in the estate of Torloisk. Anna-Jane, second daughter of General Clephane, died unmarried. Wilmina-Marianne was married, in 1831, to Wilhelm, Baron de Normann, of the diplomatic service of Prussia, and had one son, Wilhelm-Fredric-Carl-Helmuth. Her son, who succeeded his father as Baron de Normann, was murdered by the Chinese in Pekin.

The Descendants of Lachlan Og.

I. Lachlan Og, second son of Lachlan Og of Torloisk, had a son named Donald.

II. Donald married a daughter of the Rev. Martin Macgillivray of Pennyghael, and had three sons; Allan, Lachlan, and John. John was a lieutenant in the Darien expedition. He died in Flanders. He left no issue. Lachlan married Janet, daughter of Hector Maclean, of Assapol, and had two sons, Hector and Donald, both of whom died in Ireland.

III. Allan, eldest son of Donald Maclean, was a captain under Sir John of Duart at the battle of Killiecrankie in 1689 and at Sheriffmuir in 1715. He married Margaret, daughter of Allan Maclean, first of Drimnin, and had three children by her; Donald, John, and Florence. John died in Flanders. He left no issue.

IV. Donald, son of Captain Allan Maclean, lived in Raodel, and was regarded as one of the strongest men in Mull. He married Ann, daughter of Donald Maclean, fifth of Torloisk, and had by her, George, Hector, and Marion. George died unmarried in the East Indies. Marion was married to Hugh Maclean of Airdchraoishnish, son of John Maclean of Ardfergnish, and had a daughter named Flora. Flora was born at Gribun in August, 1784. She was married to Archibald, son of John, son of Lachlan Maclean, of Kirkipool in Tiree. She died at Greenhill, Tiree, in August, 1885, at the advanced age of 101 years.

V. Hector, son of Donald Maclean of Raodel, was known as Eachann Ruadh. He lived first in Mingary, and afterwards at Ensay, or Easadh. He married Ann, daughter of Donald Campbell, bailie of Tiree, by whom he had a son named George.

VI. George was for some time tenant of Hynish in Tiree, and was known as Deorsa Heinis. He was a very popular man. He married a daughter of Campbell of Barramholaich, by whom he had Sheela, Hector, Malcolm, George, Helen, and a son whose name we do not know. He died either in Australia or New Zealand.

The Macleans of Sweden.

I. John Dubh, fourth son of Hector Og of Duart, was for a short time an officer in the British navy. He was afterwards engaged in the diplomatic service of Charles I. He settled in Sweden about 1625, and changed his name to Mackeleer. He was admitted as a citizen and tradesman in Gottenburgh in 1639. He was a successful merchant, and became very wealthy. He was appointed a member of the town council of Gottenburgh in 1640. He was ennobled in 1649, and introduced at the Riddarhus, or house of knights, in 1652. He received a white flower as a coat of arms. He married, first, Lillias Hamilton, but had no children by her. He married, secondly, in 1629, Ann Gubbertz, daughter of a tradesman in Stockholm, and had nine children by her; Charles, Jacob, John, Gustaf, Peter, David, Maria, Catherine, and Eliza. He married, thirdly, Anna Thompson, but had no issue by her. He owned Gasewadholm in Holland, Hammaro in Hermland, and Hageby, Hokalla, and Rada in Westergothland.

Charles, eldest son of John Maclean, was a captain in the French army. Jacob was a colonel in the British army, and fought in behalf of Charles I. John was a judge. He married Ann Gordon, and had two sons, Gustaf and Charles, or Karl. Gustaf was born in 1641. He was, in 1676, colonel of Elfsborg's regiment. He married Sarah Carlberg. Peter was born in 1644. He was colonel in 1676, and afterwards commander at Stralsund. He married Sophia Van Plassen. David, the youngest of John Maclean's sons, laid aside the name Mackeleer and assumed his right name. He was a major in 1675, and rose afterwards to a higher rank in the army. He was governor of the province of Elfsborg in 1693. He was created Baron Maclean in 1708. He was married, and had five sons; Rutger, Gustaf, John-Adolf, Jacob, and Ludwig. Rutger was born in 1688. He was taken prisoner at Pultowa in 1709, and sent to Tobolsk. He rose to the rank of colonel. He died in 1748. John-Adolf was colonel of the Swedish Life Guards. He was married, and left a large family. Jacob died in 1771. Rutger of Swanholm and Gustaf of Strom, grandsons of Baron David Maclean, were introduced at the Riddarhus in 1784. Rutger was the fourth Baron Maclean of Sweden. He was living in 1798.

Maria, the eldest daughter of John Maclean, was married to General David Duncan; Catherine, to Colonel David Sinclair of Finnekumla; and Eliza, to Major Cailenkerheilm. The descendants of John Dubh seem to be now extinct in the male line, at least in Sweden.

THE MACLEANS OF BROLAS.

I. Donald, first Maclean of Brolas, Dòmhnall Mac Eachainn Oig, fought under Montrose in 1646 and at Inverkeithing in 1651. He was tutor to his nephew, Sir Allan of Duart, during the minority of the latter. He married Finvola, daughter of John Garbh, eighth of Coll, and had three sons by her; Lachlan, Hector Mor, and

Hector Og. 1. Lachlan succeeded his father.
2. Hector Mor died unmarried. 3. Hector Og married Janet, daughter of Macneil of Barra, by whom he had two sons, Donald and John. He was drowned while crossing the sea in a small open boat from Mull to Barra. Donald, his elder son, died young. John married Finvola, daughter of Allan Maclean of Garmony, by whom he had two sons, Donald and Hector. The latter was a merchant in Jamaica. He seems to have died without issue. Donald was, in 1760, a merchant in Glasgow. He was married twice. By his first wife, Mary, daughter of John Dickson, merchant, Glasgow, he had two children, Hector and Janet. By his second wife, Margaret, daughter of James Wall of Clonae in the county of Waterford, Ireland, he had one son, Fitzroy-Jeffreys-Grafton. He died between 1770 and 1775. Janet, his daughter, was married to General Allan Maclean, of the Torloisk family.

II. Lachlan, second Maclean of Brolas, was born in 1650. He was a man of good ability, sound sense, and unflinching fidelity to his chief and clan. He represented the county of Argyle in the Scottish Parliament during the commissionership of James, Duke of York, afterwards James II. He was tutor to Sir John of Duart, and managed the affairs of the estate in a most satisfactory manner. He married Isabel, daughter of Hector Maclean, second of Torloisk, and had by her two sons, Donald and Allan. Donald succeeded his father. Allan was a captain in the army. He died at Stirling in 1722. He was not married, but left one or two natural children.

III. Donald, third of Brolas, was born in 1671. He was left fatherless at the age of sixteen. He had many difficulties to contend with, but by prudent management overcame them all. He was for some time a lieutenant in the British army, and was, on one occasion, badly wounded by a trooper's sabre. He was lieutenant-colonel under Sir John of Duart at the battle of Sheriffmuir, and received two severe wounds on the head. He had two natural sons, James and Gillean. He married Isabel, daughter of Allan, tenth Maclean of Ardgour; and had by her four children; Allan, Catherine, Isabel, and Ann. He died on April 23d, 1725. James, his eldest son, married Julia, daughter of Allan Maclean of Garmony, and had at least one son, John. Gillean was a lieutenant in the army. He was in Guernsey in 1760. He was married and left issue. Allan succeeded his father as representative of the family of Brolas. Catherine was married to Lachlan Maclean of Coll. Isabel was married to John Maclean of Lochbuie. Ann was married to Allan Maclean of Drimnin.

John, son of James, son of Donald of Brolas, had five children; Allan, Dugald, Donald, Ann, and Mary-Julia. Allan, eldest son of John, worked at mining in Ayrshire. He had one son, Allan Og, and nine daughters. Allan Og had four sons;

Allan, Andrew, Alexander, and James. He came with his family to Pictou, Nova Scotia, and was engaged in coal mining. He removed to Pennsylvania in 1842. James, his fourth son, was born in Scotland in 1829. He was a doctor, and settled at St. Louis in Missouri. He amassed a large fortune by selling a patent medicine. He was a member of the 47th Congress. He died in 1866. Dugald, second son of John, was married and left issue. Donald, the third son, settled in Glasgow. Ann was married to a Maclellan who lived at Bowmore in Islay. Mary-Louisa was married, in 1822, to the Rev. John Sinclair, son of Peter Sinclair in Tiree. Mr. Sinclair came to Nova Scotia in 1838, and removed to Pennsylvania in 1852. We have seen it asserted that he was the author of Seannachie's history of the Macleans. He had nothing to do with that work.

The Last Five Chiefs of the Clan Gillean.

XXI. Sir Ailein Bhrolais.

Sir Allan of Brolas, sixth baronet, was born about the year 1710. He entered the army at an early age. He was for a short time a captain in the second battalion of Drumlanrig's regiment. When this battalion was disbanded in 1749, he returned to Mull. He was served heir male and of line to his grandfather, Lachlan Maclean of Brolas, in August, 1749. He married shortly afterwards, Una, daughter of Hector Maclean of

Coll. He succeeded Sir Hector, Sir John's son, in the chiefship of the Clan Gillean and in the baronetcy, in 1750. In January, 1757, he was appointed a captain in Montgomery's Highlanders. His company was raised by himself. It consisted of 100 men, all of whom it is said were natives of Mull. He sailed from Cork in Ireland in June, 1758, and landed at Charlestown in South Carolina. He took part in Brigadier Forbes's expedition against Fort du Quesne, now Pittsburg, in November of that year. He was with General Amherst in the expedition against Ticonderoga and Crown Point, in June, 1759. His wife died of a nervous fever on the 30th of May, 1760. He returned to Britain on leave of absence about the end of that year or early in 1761. He was appointed major in a regiment raised by Colonel Charles Fitzroy, afterwards Lord Southampton. He served in this regiment until the close of the Seven Years' War in 1763. As the regiment was then disbanded, Sir Allan returned to Mull. He was promoted to the rank of lieutenant-colonel some time afterwards. He leased the island of Inchkenneth, and went to live there. In October, 1773, he received a visit from Dr. Johnson and Boswell.

It seems that the Campbells took possession of Brolas in 1689. They claimed it as a part of the Duart estate. About 1770 Sir Allan commenced a lawsuit with John, fifth Duke of Argyll, for the recovery of Brolas. The suit was a tedious and expensive one, but Sir Allan won in the end.

Argyll was compelled in 1783 to restore the lands in dispute to their lawful owner. It was a source of great joy to the Macleans to see Sir Allan in possession of even a very small part of the lands which had belonged to his forefathers.

Sir Allan was a good-looking man, of a frank disposition and polished manners; and, like Highland chiefs in general, liberal and hospitable. He died on December 10th, 1783, and is buried at Inchkenneth. He was the last chief of the Macleans who lived in the Highlands, and probably the last of their chiefs who could address them in the melodious language of the poetic and warlike Gaidels. He is the subject of several excellent Gaelic songs. He was evidently greatly beloved by his clan. He had three children; Maria, Sibella, and Ann. Maria was married to Charles Maclean of Kinlochaline and Drimnin; and Sibella, to John Maclean of Inverscadale. Ann died unmarried.

XXII. Sir Hector Maclean.

Hector, son of Donald, son of John, son of Hector Og, third son of Donald of Brolas, succeeded Sir Allan in the chiefship. He was the seventh baronet of Morvern. He was for some time a lieutenant in the army, but spent the greater part of his life in retirement. Sir Hector died unmarried in 1818, and was succeeded by his brother, Fitzroy-Jeffreys-Grafton. As he did not live in Mull we have not given his name in Gaelic.

XXIII. Sir Fitzroy Jeffreys Grafton Maclean.

Fitzroy Jeffreys Grafton Maclean entered the army as an ensign in 1787. He went out to the West Indies in 1788, and saw a good deal of active service there. He was promoted to the rank of captain in 1793. He married, in 1794, the daughter and only child of Charles Kidd, and had by her two sons, Charles-Fitzroy and Donald. He received a medal for his gallant conduct at the capture of Guadaloupe in 1810, and was about the same time appointed major-general. He became a lieutenant-general in 1814. He returned to Britain in 1815, and spent the remainder of his days in London. He was raised to the rank of general in 1837. He died on July 5th, 1847. He was succeeded by his elder son, Charles-Fitzroy.

Donald, second son of General Maclean, was born in 1800. He graduated at Oxford in 1823 with the highest honours in classics. He was called to the bar at Lincoln's Inn in 1827, and in the same year married Harriet, daughter of General Frederick Maitland. He was elected in 1834 to the House of Commons, for Oxford, and represented that constituency until 1847. He was a Conservative in politics, and a strong friend of the Carlists in Spain. He died at Rome in 1874.

XXIV. Sir Charles Fitzroy Maclean.

Charles-Fitzroy was born in the West Indies in 1798. He was taken to Britain in 1806. He was educated at Eton College and the Royal Military College, Sandhurst. He entered the Scots Guards in 1816. He commanded the 81st regiment for some time, and was afterwards colonel of the 13th Light Dragoons. He was for a few years military secretary at Gibraltar. He was a good draughtsman, and took great delight in yachting and fishing. On retiring from his post at Gibraltar, he navigated his own vessel all over the Mediterranean as far as the Black Sea. He retired from military service in 1846. He was a true Highlander, and took a deep interest in the history of his clan. He was a tall, good-looking, and pleasant man, and was well liked. He married, in 1831, Emily-Eleanor, daughter of the Honourable and Reverend Jacob Marsham, D. D., Canon of Windsor, and had by her five children; Fitzroy-Donald, Emily-Frances-Harriet, Louisa-Marianne, Fanny-Henrietta, and Georgina-Marcia. Sir Charles-Fitzroy died at West Cliffe House, Folkestone, on December 27th, 1883. Fitzroy-Donald succeeded his father. Louisa was married in 1860 to the Hon. R. P. Neville, second son of the Earl of Abergavenny. Fanny was married in 1855 to Admiral Sir A. W. A. Hood. Georgina was married in 1868 to John A. Rolls, of The Hendre.

XXV. Sir Fitzroy Donald Maclean.

Fitzroy Donald Maclean was born on May 18th, 1835. He entered the 13th Light Dragoons, now the 13th Hussars, as a cornet, in August, 1852.

Sir Fitzroy Donald Maclean.

He was appointed lieutenant in 1854, captain in 1856, major in 1861, and lieutenant-colonel-commandant in 1871. He served in the same regiment —the 13th Hussars—over twenty-one years, and was with it wherever it was quartered or fighting. He was in Bulgaria and the Crimea in the war of 1854 and 1855. He went out to Bulgaria in the sailing transport Culloden, which landed the troops on board of it at Varna, but was afterwards wrecked in the Black Sea, and captured with all its crew by the Russians. He was with his regiment at the landing of Eupatoria, at the cavalry affair of Bulganak, at the battle of the Alma, and at the siege of Sebastopol. He received the Crimean medal from the Queen's own hand, on May 18th, 1855. He received two clasps and the Turkish War medal about the same time. He was aide-de-camp to Field Marshal Lord Seaton in 1859, and to General Sir George Brown in 1860. He was selected in 1865 to report on the French cavalry manœuvres at Chalons. While there he was frequently in conversation with the Emperor of the French. In 1880 he was appointed to the command of the West Kent Queen's Own Yeomanry Cavalry, and is now commander of the Kent Yeomanry Brigade. He became chief of the Clan Gillean in 1883. He received the decoration of the Order of the Bath in 1897. On the first of last March he was appointed president of the League of Mercy for the Hythe division of the county of Kent.

Sir Fitzroy has travelled extensively both in

Europe and America. He takes a deep and active interest in the history, traditions, and poetry of his clan, and also in the welfare of all his clansmen. He is a good linguist. We wish we could say that, like the Duke of Atholl, the Marquis of Tullibardine, and Sir Kenneth Mackenzie of Gairloch, he speaks the language in which Fingal fought and Ossian sung. He married, in 1872, Constance-Marianne, daughter of George Holland Ackers, Esq., of Moreton Hall, Cheshire, and has by her five children; Hector-Fitzroy, Charles-Lachlan, Fitzroy-Holland, George-John-Marsham, and Finovala-Marianne-Eleanor. Hector was born on February 17th, 1873. He is a lieutenant in the Scots Guards. Charles is a lieutenant in the Royal Navy. He took part in the Benin expedition in 1897. Fitzroy died in 1881. At the present time Sir Fitzroy and his three sons, Hector, Charles, and John, are the only representatives in the legitimate male line of Dòmhnall Mac Eachainn Oig, the first Maclean of Brolas. May his sons live to a good old age, and his grandsons be numerous and prosperous.

The Clan Maclean Association was instituted in Glasgow, Scotland, in 1892. It held its first annual gathering on the 28th of October in that year. There was a large number of Macleans present, probably a larger number than had been seen together since Charles of Drimnin led his heroic followers to Culloden. Addresses were delivered by Sir Fitzroy, who acted as chairman;

by that grand old man, Professor Blackie; and by the Rev. John Maclean, D.D., Glasgow. Annual meetings have been held regularly ever since. The Association has been of much service to the clan. It has helped to bring its scattered members together, to make them personally acquainted with each other, and to lead them to feel that they all belong to the same family. It has also helped to bring the Macleans to look upon themselves, not as a broken clan, but as a fully organized clan, and to take a real interest in the past history and present welfare of the clan, its branches, and its members.

In 1893 the Macleans of the United States and Canada, invited Sir Fitzroy, Lochbuie, Ardgour, Kingerloch, Dochgarroch, and Pennycross, to visit the World's Fair, in Chicago, and requested the privilege of having them as their guests during their stay. On Monday, June 12th, Sir Fitzroy and Pennycross arrived in Chicago. On Thursday, June 15th, they were entertained at a grand banquet. There were about ninety Macleans present, most of whom were accompanied by their wives.

Sir Fitzroy is the twenty-fifth chief of the Clan Gillean, and the tenth Baronet of Morvern. He is the son of Charles, son of Fitzroy, son of Donald, son of John, son of Hector Og, son of Donald of Brolas, son of Hector Og of Duart, son of Lachlan Mor of Duart, son of Hector Og of Duart, son of Hector Mor of Duart, son of Lachlan Cattanach of Duart, son of Hector Odhar of Duart, son of Lachlan Og of Duart, son of Lachlan Bronnach of Duart, son of Hector Roy of Duart, son of Lachlan Lùbanach of Duart, son of John Dubh, son of Malcolm, son of Malise, son of Gilleain na Tuaighe. He is thus the twenty-first in lineal descent from the founder of the clan of which he is the worthy and honoured CEANN-CINNIDH.

CHAPTER XVIII.

Untraced Families.

THERE are several prominent Macleans referred to in history, of whose origin we know nothing. There are also at the present day hundreds of true Macleans in the world who cannot trace themselves back step by step to the parent stock, or even tell to what branch of the clan they belong. There are many in this position simply because they neglected to write down the genealogical facts which they could easily have collected fifty years ago.

THE MACLEANS OF CUIDREACH.—Dr. Maclean settled in Skye, as physician to the Macdonalds of Sleat, about the year 1525. He was a native of Mull, and had probably studied medicine under the Beatons of Pennycross. His descendants were physicians in Skye during the period of 270 years. The last of them who lived in Skye, Dr. John Maclean, was born at Cuidreach in 1708. He was an excellent classical scholar. It is said

that he knew by heart Homer's Iliad and Virgil's
Æneid from beginning to end. He was celebrated
as a physician all over the Western Isles. He
held the farms of Uragag, and Shulista in 1733,
and acted as chamberlain to Lord Macdonald.
He died at Cuidreach on May 1st, 1793, and was
buried at Kilmuir in Troternish. He was married,
and had at least three sons; James, John, and
Malcolm. He had also a daughter named Mary.
James died young. John, known as Seocan, was
drowned on the coast of Uist. Malcolm was a
captain in one of the Highland regiments, and
served in America. He spent his latter days at
Aird-Mhic-Ceòlain in Skye. He was somewhat
eccentric. Mary, Dr. John's daughter, was married
to John Beaton, tenant of Achachorc in
Troternish.

It is said that Dr. Lachlan Maclean of Sudbury
was a son of Dr. John Maclean, but this may not
be a fact. Dr. Lachlan was at any rate a native
of Skye. He was for some time physician to the
Duke of Kent. He was elected member of parliament
for the borough of Arundel in 1768. He
retired from politics in 1771, and was knighted
some time afterwards. He was the author of several
works on medicine, copies of which are in the
British museum. He married Mary, daughter and
co-heiress of John Young, of The Priory, Suffolk,
and had three sons, Allan, John, and Hippisley,
and also two daughters. He died about 1840.
Allan was physician to the Essex and Colchester

Hospital. John died in 1822. Hippisley was born in 1808. He was vicar of Caistor in Lincolnshire from 1844 to 1886. He died at St. Alban's in 1895. Mary, second daughter of Sir Lachlan, was married to John Eaton, of Eaton Manor, Shrewsbury.

THE MACLEANS OF KILMORY.—Hector Maclean of Kilmory married, about 1690, Margaret, daughter of Allan Maclean of Grulin, and had at least two children, Hugh and Catherine. Hugh married Ann, daughter of the Rev. John Maclean of Kilninian, and widow of John, son of Allan of Grishipol. Hugh, son of Maclean of Kilmory, was a captain under Charles of Drimnin at Culloden. Allan of Kilmory died about the year 1759. Murdoch, son of Allan, was served heir to his father in July, 1761. Murdoch Hector Maclaine was appointed lieutenant-colonel of the 77th regiment in 1822. We find it stated that he was descended from the Macleans of Kilmory, and that he wrote a history of the Lochbuie family—the branch of the clan to which he belonged.

THE MACLAINES OF HOLLAND.—The Rev. Alexander Maclaine graduated at the University of Edinburgh in 1646, and was minister of Kilmaglas in 1655. He translated a number of the Psalms into Gaelic verse. According to Scott's Fasti Ecclesiæ Scoticanæ, he belonged to the Lochbuie branch of the clan. Archibald, son of Alexander, was licensed to preach in 1684, and in the following year became minister of Dunoon and Kilmun.

He accepted a call to Omagh in Ireland in 1699. He was married, and had four children; Daniel, Alexander, Thomas, and a daughter. Daniel became minister of Kilbride, Argyleshire, in 1704. Alexander was minister of Antrim, and Thomas minister of Monaghan. The daughter was married to the Rev. Thomas Milling, minister of the Scots church at The Hague. The Rev. Thomas Maclaine married Elizabeth, daughter of James Milling, and sister of the Rev. Robert Milling. He had two sons by her, Archibald and James. He died in 1740.

Archibald, son of the Rev. Thomas Maclaine, was born at Monaghan in 1722, and educated at the University of Glasgow. He went to Holland in 1746, and became assistant pastor to his maternal uncle, the Rev. Robert Milling. He acted for some time as preceptor to the Prince of Orange, afterwards King William I. He left The Hague in 1796, and settled at Bath in England. He translated Mosheim's History into English. He married Esther-Wilhelmina, daughter of the Rev. Charles Chaise, the French clergyman at The Hague, and had four children by her; Charles-Anthony, Henry, William-Nicholas, and Henrietta-Ann. He died in 1804. He was a man of deep piety and extensive learning. Henry, his second son, was a colonel in the Dutch army.

Charles-Anthony, eldest son of the Rev. Archibald Maclaine, studied law, and was recorder of the court at Brabant. He married Catherine

Spanjaard, by whom he had William and Mary. William settled in England, and had four children; Archibald, Charles, Catherine, and Mary. Archibald left a son named William, who resides in London.

Mary, daughter of Charles Anthony Maclaine, was married in 1812 to Pieter Pont, burgomaster of Modemblie, by whom she had three children; Frans-Maclaine, Archibald-Maclaine, and Mary. Frans-Maclaine had two sons; William-Maclaine and Archibald-Maclaine. Archibald-Maclaine, second son of Mary Maclean and Pieter Pont, was for some time a lieutenant in the Dutch navy. He married, in 1848, Johanna-Susanna-Cornelia-Maria Van Pabst Rutgers, and had by her Pieter-Maclaine, Willem-Maclaine, Archibald-Maclaine, and three daughters. Pieter resides at The Hague, and is a lawyer by profession. William is manager of a gold-mine at Totok in Celebes. Archibald is a lawyer, and resides in Batavia.

THE MACLEANS OF GOMETRA. — John Maclean belonged to the Lochbuie family. He had a son named Hector, who had a son named John. John, Iain Mac Eachainn, lived in Lag, and was succeeded there by his son Hector, who was succeeded by his son, Peter. Peter of Lag married Christy Lamont, by whom he had two sons, Hector and Duncan. Hector was for some time tenant of the farms of Achnasaul, Achnacreig, and Torosay. He removed to Kinnegharar in 1841. He married Flora, daughter of Donald Macarthur, tenant of Burg on the Torloisk estate, and had by her Donald, Peter, John, Margaret, Ann, Mary, and Flora. 1. Donald was born in 1814. He purchased the island of Gometra in 1857. He died in 1871. He was a very popular man. 2. Peter succeeded his brother in Gometra. He died in May, 1893. 3. John was tenant of Kinnegharar and Burg. He was a successful cattle-dealer. He died on February 24th, 1893. 4. Margaret, eldest daughter of Eachann Mac Phadruig, was married to Neil Morison of Aintuim, and was the mother of Coundullie Rankin Morison, the Mull antiquarian.

John Maclean, Iain Mac Dhòmhnaill Mhic Phadruig, married Flora Macleod, by whom he had Hector, John, Donald, and Neil. Hector married Catherine Macdonald, and had John, Roderick, and Peter. John is a merchant in Dervaig. Roderick is a merchant in Glasgow, and purchased the island of Gometra in 1893.

Iain Mac Eachainn.—John Maclaine, Iain Mac Eachainn Mhic Iain Mhic Dhòmhnaill Ghlais, lived at Dervaig, and belonged to the Lochbuie branch of the clan. He was the author of several pieces of Gaelic poetry. He married Flora, only daughter of Donald Mor Macquarrie in Ulva. Donald, his son, married Jessie, daughter of Captain John Cameron in Greenock, by whom he had six children; John, Donald, Sarah, Lachlan, Archibald, and Flora. Lachlan, his third son, is minister of Arisaig.

AONGHUS OG.—Angus Og Maclean was born in Coll, and belonged to the Boreray branch of the Macleans of Ardgour. His father's name was Angus. His mother was a Macfadyen. He had a son named Lachlan, who had a son named Neil. Neil had three sons; Lachlan, John, and Norman. Lachlan was a carpenter by trade, and was known as Lachainn Saor. He came to Nova Scotia, and settled in Keppoch, Antigonish County. He died in July, 1855, and left five sons; Neil, Archibald, Norman, John, and Alexander. The Rev. Lachlan A. Maclean, of Louisburg, Cape Breton, is a son of Alexander.

DONALD, ALEXANDER, AND JAMES MACLEAN.—Donald, Alexander, and James Maclean were brothers, and were born in North Uist. It is pretty certain that they belonged to the Boreray branch of the Ardgour family. Their parents were drowned while crossing from Uist to the mainland. Donald went to Jamaica, prospered in business, and sent for Alexander and James. He married Ann Susanna Rodon, by whom he had Lachlan, George-Rodon, and Ann. Alexander was born in 1767. He became proprietor of the Crawle River and Orange Hill estates in Jamaica. He returned to Scotland in 1819, and settled in Liberton. He married, in the same year, Mary Baigrie, by whom he had Catherine-Ann, Alexander, Donald, and John M. He died in 1839. His youngest son, John M., is the well-known member of parliament for Cardiff.

ALLAN MACLEAN IN ACHNACREIG.—Allan Maclean belonged to the Coll branch of the clan. He lived at Achnacreig, between Sorn and Dervaig, in Mull. Charles, his son, lived in the same place. Charles met Prince Charles when the latter arrived in Moydart in 1745. Having shaken hands with the Prince, he never afterwards gave his right hand to anyone. Allan, son of Charles, had a son named Hector. Hector lived at Cìllbheag, Kilveg, in or near Bellach Roy. Allan, son of Hector, lived at Cuinn, near Dervaig. Hector, son of Allan, resides at 5 Belgrave Street, Glasgow.

THE MACLEANS OF ALTANULL.—Lachlan Maclean was born in Rum, and belonged to the Coll branch of the clan. He came to Nova Scotia in October, 1781, and settled at Allta-'n-aoil, or Lime Brook, in Pictou County. He married Ann Macquarrie, by whom he had four children; David, Hector, Gormall, and Catherine. David married Margaret Mackenzie, by whom he had Lachlan, James, Duncan, Robert, and Alexander. Lachlan and Robert live at Lime Brook. James is minister of the Presbyterian Church at Great Village, Nova Scotia. Duncan was a doctor at Shubenacadie, Nova Scotia. He was skilful, kind, and self-sacrificing, and was highly esteemed. He made no money, but he did a great deal of good to his fellow-men. He died a year ago. Alexander lives in Pennsylvania. The Rev. James T. Maclean of Oakryn, Pennsylvania, is his son.

EÒGHAN MAC LACHAINN MHIC IAIN BHÀIN.—It is said that John Bàn was a son of Terlach Mac Allan Mac Ian Duy. He settled in Tiree, and had a son named Lachlan, who had a son named Ewen. Ewen, Eòghan Mac Lachainn Mhic Iain Bhàin, had two sons, Donald and Ewen. Donald had three sons; Lachlan, Charles, and John. 1. Lachlan had three sons; John, Hugh, and Donald. 2. Charles had six sons; John, Donald, Hugh, Hector, Alexander, and Dugald. Hugh, Hector, and Dugald came to Canada. Alexander lived at Ruaig, and had two sons, Donald and Hector. Hector is minister of Dalkeith, Scotland. 3. John was born in 1771. He was one of the tenants of Ruaig. He had three sons; Malcolm, Lachlan, and Donald. He died in 1861. Malcolm succeeded him in Ruaig, and was succeeded there by his son Allan. Lachlan was married, and had one daughter. Donald was born in 1817. He was a merchant and manufacturer in Glasgow. He had four sons; John, Andrew-Bruce, Archibald, and Malcolm. John came to Canada. Andrew-Bruce is a manufacturer of electric light cables at Craigpark, Glasgow. Archibald is an India-rubber merchant in Leeds. Malcolm is a manufacturer of electrical articles in London.

TEARLACH MAC LACHAINN MHIC EACHAINN.— Charles Maclean, Tearlach Mac Lachainn Mhic Eachainn, lived in Kilmoluaig. He married Ann Campbell, of Gortandonald, by whom he had Donald, Archibald, Lachlan, and Catherine. Donald married Mary Graham, and had by her, Alexander, Ann, Mary, and Margaret. Archibald died unmarried. Catherine was married to Archibald Maclean.

Lachlan, third son of Charles Maclean, occupied, during the latter part of his life, the farm of Grianail, or Greenhill, in Tiree. He married Catherine, daughter of Archibald Maclean, Gilleasbuig Mac Iain Mhic Lachainn, and had by her, Catherine, Archibald, Charles, Donald, Lachlan, Marion, and Donald-Archibald. Catherine, the eldest of his family, was married to John Macgavin, and Marion to Captain John Brodie. Archibald, eldest son of Lachlan Maclean, settled at Hawke's Bay, New Zealand. Charles, second son of Lachlan, is a farmer in Leicestershire, England. He married Jeanie Barr, and has six children; Robert, Lachlan, Charles, Mary, Katie-Jane, and Thomas. Donald, third son of Lachlan, settled at Hawke's Bay. He married Margaret Macfarlane, by whom he had Catherine, Lachlan, Margaret, and Elspeth. Donald-Archibald, fifth son of Lachlan, settled at Hawke's Bay. He married Elizabeth Macfarlane, and has one daughter, Catherine.

Lachlan, fourth son of Lachlan Maclean, was born at Crosh, Tiree, on May 28th, 1852. He left Tiree in April, 1868, to join the Glasgow office of the Leith, Hull, and Hamburg Steam Packet Company. He was transferred to Leith in 1871, and to London in 1874. He was appointed, in 1878, chief agent in South Africa for the Castle

Mail Packets Company. He married, in August, 1899, Margaret, daughter of John Cumming Crawford, of Edinburgh, and has one child, Sheila. He resides at Greenhill, Kenilworth, near Cape Town. He takes a thorough interest in his clan.

The Macleans of Grand Lake. — Archibald Maclean was a lieutenant in the Royal Navy. He settled in New York, and married there, on June 12th, 1780, Catherine Price. He came to St. John, New Brunswick, and received a grant of two lots of land in the city. He removed afterwards to Grand Lake, Queen's County, where he took up a large grant of land. John, his son, was born at Grand Lake in 1784. John was for a number of years judge of the court of common pleas. Lachlan, John's son, was a merchant in the city of St. John ; but was obliged to retire from business on account of ill health. He died at Mill Stream, King's County, in 1875. Hugh-Havelock, son of Lachlan, was born in Fredericton, on March, 22d, 1854. He was called to the bar in 1876, and is connected as solicitor or director with a number of wealthy companies. He takes a hereditary interest in military matters, and is lieutenant-colonel of the 62d St. John Fusiliers. He was lately in Britain as commandant of the Bisley Team from Canada. He is a good member of the great clan to which he belongs.

Iain Bàn Mac Ailein. — John Maclean, Iain Bàn Mac Ailein, was one of the tenants of the farm of Achadh-a-Chàirn on the north side of Loch-nan-

Ceall. He had three sons; Allan, Charles, and Lachlan. Allan, the eldest son, was for about sixty years a teacher in Iona, in connection with the Society for Propagating Christian Knowledge in the Highlands and Islands. Besides teaching, he expounded the Scriptures to the people, and also kept a Sabbath school for the children. He was a useful man, and was highly respected. Lachainn na Gaidhlig describes him as abbot of Iona. Charles, second son of John Bàn, was at one time a sergeant in the Breadalbane Fencibles. He was afterwards forester at Loch Sunart to the Duke of Argyll. He married Euphemia, daughter of Donald Campbell, by whom he had Neil, Ellen, Mary, Jessie, and others. Neil was born in 1796. He was educated at Iona and in the University of Glasgow. He was licensed to preach in 1822, and became minister of Ulva in 1826. He was translated to Halkirk in 1844. He married Clementina Clark, sister of Francis W. Clark of Ulva, and had six children; Charles, Neil, Francis, James A., Clementina, and Isabella. Charles was a minister, and died in Ceylon in 1897. Neil was mate of the steamship Tenasserim. He died at sea in 1878, and was buried in Malta. Francis was in the service of the Caledonian Insurance Company, Edinburgh, and died in 1885. James A. Maclean, youngest son of the Rev. Neil Maclean, is a lawyer and bank agent in Forfar.

GENERAL JOHN MACLEAN.—John Maclean was born in Mull in 1756. He served in the Revolutionary War under Washington, and was an officer of artillery in the War of 1812. He was the first commissary-general of the state of New York. He died in New York on February 28th, 1821. George W., son of General Maclean, graduated at the Military Academy at West Point in 1818. He had four sons; Henry-Clay, Malcolm, Donald, and Walter. Malcolm was born in 1848. He is a practising physician and surgeon in New York. He married the only daughter of Dr. George W. Jewett, by whom he has three children; Alfred, Donald, and Helen. Donald, third son of George W. Maclean, is a lawyer in New York. Walter is a lieutenant in the United States Navy.

The Macleans of Dysart.—George Maclean resided in Dysart, Fifeshire, and was known as George Mac Allan. He was married, and had two sons, George and William. George was licensed to preach in 1797, and became minister of Fogo in Berwickshire in 1814. He was returned heir to his father, " George Mac Allan, or Maclean," in 1818. He died in 1840. He was married and left issue. William, second son of George Mac Allan, was manager of the Dysart colliery. He married a daughter of John Brodie, by whom he had a son named George. George, son of William, was born at Dysart in 1795. He entered the commissariat department of the army in 1812. He was appointed commissary-general in 1849. He was knighted in 1854. He served in the Crimea from March, 1855, to the close of the war, when he was created a K. C. B. He married, first, a French lady, by whom he had one son. He married, secondly, Sarah M. Lord, of Nassau in the Bahamas, and had by her three sons and three daughters. He died about 1862.

Henry-John, eldest son of Sir George Maclean by his second wife, was born at Nassau in 1827, and entered the army in 1845. He served for nine years in the 11th North Devonshire regiment. He served for twenty-five years in the Rifle Brigade, and commanded one of its battalions. He was appointed, in 1878, to the head-quarter staff in Ireland. He was placed on the retired list, with the rank of major-general, in 1884. He was married twice, and had five sons and three daughters.

The Macleans of Plantation.—George Maclean was enrolled a burgess and guild brother of Glasgow in 1739. William, eldest son of George, was enrolled in 1782. William, eldest son of William, was born in Glasgow in 1783. He purchased, about 1830, the mansion and lands of Plantation, west of Glasgow. He married Mary Brown, by whom he had William and other children. He died in 1867. William, second of Plantation, was born in 1805. He paid strict attention to his business, but found time to compose upwards of 2,000 sacred melodies. He married Alice, daughter of the Rev. Robert Muter, D. D., by whom he had eight children; William, Jessie, Robert, Mary, Alice, Wilhelmina, Jane, and Charles-James. Jessie was married to William

Galbraith, of St. Rollox. She has composed several songs, and also some pieces of music. Alice was married to John Paterson Paton; Wilhelmina, to Henry Homan, a lawyer in Norway; and Jane, to Sheriff Hall of Ayrshire. William, eldest son of William, succeeded his father in Plantation. He is senior partner of the firm of Maclean, Fyfe, and Maclean, writers, in Glasgow. Robert, the second son, is an advocate in Edinburgh. Charles-James is, like his brother, a lawyer by profession. He is a partner in the firm of Maclean, Fife, and Maclean. He married Sara D. Holms, and has four children; William, Archibald-Campbell-Holms, Helen-Alice, and Hope-Sara.

GILBERT MACLEAN.—Gilbert Maclean emigrated from Scotland to Antrim in Ireland about 1770. He had a son named James, who had a son named Alexander. Alexander came to the United States about 1820, and engaged in the coal business. He settled on a large farm at Wilkes Barre, Pennsylvania, in 1848. He had six sons; James, Samuel-Swan, Leslie, George, William-Swan, and John. James continued the coal business, and died, quite a rich man, in 1863. Samuel-Swan was a lawyer, and represented the territory of Montana in Congress for two successive terms. Leslie went to California, thence to Australia, and died on his way back. George was receiver of public moneys for the district of Montana. William-Swan is a lawyer in the city of Wilkes Barre. John died in the Union army of camp fever.

CHARLES MCCLAIN was born in the north of Ireland in 1712. He came to America in early life, and settled in New Jersey. He removed about 1785 to Pennsylvania, and settled near Pittsburgh. He was for fifty years an elder in the Presbyterian Church. He died in 1807. D. G. McClain, of Denver, Colorado, is his great-grandson. The name Maclean was very commonly spelled McClain in 1700.

THE REV. ANDREW MACLEAN was born at Dalreach of Moy in 1821. He was descended from a Maclean who left Mull between 1715 and 1745, and settled in Strathdearn. He came to Canada in 1857, and became minister of a congregation at Crieff, Ontario. He married Catherine Cameron. He died in April, 1873. Lieutenant-Colonel John Bayne Maclean is his son. Colonel Maclean is president and managing editor of the Maclean Publishing Company, of Montreal and Toronto. He was elected president of the Clan Maclean Association of America in 1896. Like all loyal Macleans, whether they be rich or poor, he takes a real interest in the history of his forefathers.

EÓGHAN MÓR MAC THEARLAICH MHIC AN DOTAIR was born in Coll, and served for some time in the Black Watch. Lachlan, his son, was born about 1805, and came to Canada about 1822. He married Catherine Mackay, and settled at Lake Ainsley in Cape Breton. Captain Ewen Maclean in Charlottetown is his third son.

CHAPTER XIX.

The Chiefship of the Clan Gillean.

I. GENERAL FACTS WITH REGARD TO THE CHIEFSHIP OF CLANS.

A CLAN includes, first, those who claim descent from a common ancestor, and use the name of that ancestor as their surname. It includes, secondly, all who have joined it by adopting its name as their own. There are thus in all clans, clansmen by descent and clansmen by adoption. At the present day, however, it is, as a general rule, impossible to distinguish the one class from the other.

The man who stands at the head of a clan and represents the founder of it, is known in Gaelic as an ceann-cinnidh, the kenkinnie, or clan-head. The representative of a branch of a clan is known as an ceann-taighe, the kentie, or house-head. The word ceann-cinnidh is generally rendered into English by the term chief, and the word ceann-taighe by the term chieftain. In kentie, the

Anglicized form of ceann-taighe, the accent is on the last syllable; it is pronounced, not kenty, but ken-tie.

The English word chief is used in two distinct senses in connection with clans. It is used, first, as the equivalent of the word kenkinnie; and, secondly, in the sense of feudal superior, or landlord. In the latter sense Campbell of Breadalbane was chief of the Macintyres of Glennoe; in the former sense, he was not; the Macintyres had a kenkinnie of their own.

The kenkinnie was ruler, judge, and commander-in-chief of his clan. He protected the members of his clan in their rights, settled disputes between them, and punished evil-doers. He also led his followers to battle, and fought at their head. He had great influence, but he could not act as he pleased. He could neither make nor change laws without the consent of his people. He was of course largely under the control of his leading men. If he played the part of a tyrant, he would lose his head. It was thus absolutely necessary for him for his own safety and comfort to treat his followers in a kind and fatherly manner.

The law of primogeniture, as it exists in Britain at the present day, belongs entirely to the feudal system. It was utterly unknown to the clan system. It simply declared that the land-chief should be succeeded in his estate by his eldest lawful son, if he had sons; if not, by his daughters. Thus, it utterly ignored the existence of clans. It would be unreasonable, then, to regard it as a law fitted for regulating the succession to the headship of a clan.

There were two things required to constitute a person eligible for the chiefship. It was necessary, first, that he should be descended in the male line from the founder of the clan; and, secondly, that he should possess the intellectual and physical qualifications required for the performance of the duties required of him as chief.

A natural son, legitimated by an act of parliament, a letter of legitimation, or the marriage of his parents after his birth, was eligible for the chiefship of a clan as well as a son born in wedlock. Robert II. was chief of the Stewarts; Archibald the Grim, chief of the Douglases; and John of Killin was chief of the Mackenzies. Dugald Stewart was chieftain of the Stewarts of Appin; Aonghus na Feirte, chieftain of the Macdonalds of Keppoch; Donald Gallach, chieftain of the Macdonalds of Sleat; and John Muideartach, chieftain of the Clanranald.

There were three ways in which a person might become chief of his clan; by the general law of succession, through designation to the chiefship by the last chief, or by election. According to the general law, the eldest legitimate son succeeded his father, if he had the requisite qualifications for the chiefship. His fitness would, no doubt, be judged in the most favourable manner possible by those who were attached to his father. It was thus strongly probable that he would become chief.

Sometimes the chief of a clan passed by his eldest son, for prudential reasons, and settled the succession upon a younger son. John, first Lord of the Isles, appointed Donald, his third son, his heir-apparent. John Glas, the first Earl of Breadalbane, had two legitimate sons, Duncan Mor and John. He gave the estate to John, who was chieftain of the Campbells of Breadalbane from 1716 to 1752. Duncan Mor, who was equal to John in every respect, was married, and left two lawful sons, Patrick Mor and John.

When a clan elected a kenkinnie, the rule invariably followed by them was to select the best qualified person among the near relatives of the last chief. Of course they never selected a man who could not be traced back step by step in the male line to a former chief. As a general rule their choice fell upon a brother, uncle, or cousin of the last chief. A young and inexperienced person was never elected.

A clan had a right to depose a chief and to elect a more suitable person to fill his place. About the year 1405, Ferchar, ninth chief of the Mackintoshes, was deposed, and a near relative, Malcolm Beg, raised to the position of ruler of the clan. Ferchar had sons, who became the founders of several families. Malcolm Beg died in 1457, and left four sons. He was the progenitor of all the Mackintosh chiefs known to history from the time of his death to the present day. John Alàinn, chieftain of the Macdonalds of Keppoch, was deposed by his followers in 1505 or thereabouts, and his cousin-german, Donald Glas, chosen in his place. About 1515 the Clanranald murdered their chieftain, Dugald Mac Ranald, and placed themselves under the command of his uncle, Alexander Mac Allan. John Muideartach, Alexander's son, became laird of Moydart, and, under the name of captain, actual chieftain of the Clanranald. Allan, son and heir of the deposed Dugald, had to be satisfied with being laird of Morar.

In order to be chief of a clan it was always necessary that a person should be acknowledged as such by the majority of the clan. It was of no use for a man to call himself a chief unless he had followers enough to maintain him in that position. James, son of James II., called himself King of Britain, but in spite of his declarations the Georges remained kings. Theoretical claims are not of much value to a man unless he can obtain possession of that which he claims. James Stewart had no doubt very good claims to the British throne, but unfortunately for him the hated Brunswicker had more followers than he had. Probably it would have been as wise for him if he had never said anything about his claims.

II. THE CLAIMS OF THE MACLAINES OF LOCHBUIE TO THE CHIEFSHIP OF THE CLAN GILLEAN.

The Macleans of Ross knew perfectly well that their ancestor, Neil of Lehir, was the eldest of Lachlan Bronnach's lawful sons. But they knew also that Lachlan Og was acknowledged by the clan as their chief, and that his son, Hector Odhar, his grandson, Lachlan Cattanach, and his great-grandson, Hector Mor, were likewise acknowledged as chiefs. Instead of grumbling and complaining because they were not themselves chiefs they followed those who were chiefs, and proved on the battle-field that as men they were their equals in every respect. If they could not afford to purchase such polished swords as the chiefs had, they could make swords for themselves and cut down as many enemies with them as the chiefs could cut down with theirs. They were grand warriors and most loyal clansmen. The Macleans of Coll always asserted that their valiant ancestor, John Garbh, was an older son than Lachlan Og of Duart, but they never on that ground or any other claimed the chiefship of the clan. They were intelligent and well-informed men, and knew that they were only chieftains. They would never pretend to be what they were not.

The Macleans of Duart were in possession of the castle and lands of Duart, at least from 1366 to 1689. The Macleans of Lochbuie never, during that long period, claimed to be chiefs of the clan.

If they had on any occasion made such a claim, it is tolerably certain some old book, manuscript, or official document would contain a reference to it. They did not put forward their claim even for some time after Duart had ceased to be the property of Lachlan Lùbanach's descendants. They waited until Sir Hector Maclean, Sir John's only son, died in Rome in 1750. Then they said to themselves, The Campbells have taken their lands from our brethren, and we will take the chiefship from them; they are now too weak to defend themselves.

John, seventeenth of Lochbuie, obtained possession of the estate in 1751. It is not certain that he laboured under the delusion that he was chief of the Macleans, but it is quite possible that he did. Captain Archibald Maclaine, his son, addressed a memorial to the King, which commences thus:—"The subscriber is only son to a Maclaine of Lochbuie, a gentleman of as good family and connections as any in the Highlands of Scotland, and whose family has for the space of from eight to nine hundred years supported the character of what is called in that country a Highland chief, or the first man of his name." The memorial was written apparently about the year 1776. As the king had no special acquaintance with Highland history, it was probably safe enough to tell him him that there were Maclaine chiefs in the Highlands at least as early as the year 976, or about 234 years before Gilleain na Tuaighe was born.

A mural tablet in Laggan, Mull, contains the words, "In memory of Murdoch Maclaine, Esq., of Lochbuie, chief of his name." Murdoch died in 1844. The inscription was written some time after that date. The present Maclaine of Lochbuie became laird in 1863. He styles himself "Maclaine of Lochbuie, chief of the clan."

It will be noticed that Captain Archibald Maclaine, refers to his father, John Maclaine, merely as a chief, or the first man of his name. It will also be noticed that all that the writer of the inscription on the tablet claimed for Murdoch Maclaine was that he was chief of his name, or chief of the Maclaines. The present Maclaine of Lochbuie, according to his own statement, is much more than chief of his name; he is chief of the clan.

The Maclaines of Lochbuie maintain, in the first place, that Hector Reaganach of Lochbuie was older than Lachlan Lùbanach of Duart. They support this contention by asserting that there has always been a tradition in the Lochbuie family to that effect. It is a well-known fact that traditions are not always as old as they are supposed to be. The Ardgour MS. contains the following statement:—"It is known beyond all controversy that a tradition was handed down from father to son, from the very first eras of their settlement in Mull to the present day, that Gillean, progenitor of the Macleans, and Colin Fitzgerald, ancestor of the Mackenzies of Kintail, were brothers, and sons of the Earl of Kildare in Ireland." The tradition referred to was merely a false story started into existence about the year 1669. The tradition with regard to the seniority of Hector Reaganach, may also be a story of recent origin. If it could be shown that the second, third, fourth, fifth, or sixth Maclean of Lochbuie had held that Hector Reaganach was older than Lachlan Lùbanach, it is not likely that anyone would be disposed to call in question the correctness of his assertion. But it is impossible to show anything of the kind. So far as known to us, the tradition with regard to the seniority of Hector Reaganach cannot be proved to be older than 1750.

The Maclaines of Lochbuie maintain, in the second place, that inasmuch as Hector Reaganach was older than Lachlan Lùbanach, the present Maclaine of Lochbuie is chief of the Clan Gillean. As the assertion that Hector Reaganach was older than Lachlan Lùbanach cannot be shown to be a fact, it is utterly worthless as a ground of claim. Even if it were true, it would not follow that Hector Reaganach was chief of the Clan Gillean. According to the very tradition to which the Maclaines of Lochbuie attach so much importance, he was not. That tradition tells us that Lachlan was a wily character, and that he cheated his brother Hector out of the chiefship.

The validity of the claim of the Maclaines of Lochbuie to the chiefship of the Clan Gillean has never been acknowledged by any Scottish writer. Hugh Macdonald, of Sleat, who wrote about the year 1680, makes the following statements:— "Maclean fostered Donald Ballach, John Mor's eldest legitimate son. Finnon, the Green Abbot, a subtle and wicked counsellor, told John Mor that he had only a small portion of his father's estate, and that he should seize all the land south of the Point of Ardnamurchan. He brought over to his side the chief of the Macleans and Macleod of Harris." The person described as "Maclean" and "the chief of the Macleans," was Lachlan Bronnach of Duart. It is true that the Sleat historian asserts in one part of his work that Hector Reaganach was older than Lachlan Lùbanach. That opinion, however, never led him to think that the Macleans of Duart were not the chiefs of the Macleans. He knew perfectly well, whether they were descended from a younger son of John Dubh or not, that they stood at the head of the Clan Gillean. Douglas's Baronage was published in 1798. It contains the following statements with regard to the chiefship of the Macleans:—" It cannot be absolutely determined which of the two, Hector Reaganach and Lachlan Lùbanach, was the elder brother, the precedency being claimed by both; nor can it be discovered either from the private writs of their families or the public records. On the contrary, it appears that the whole clan, at different periods, have followed the heads of both families to the field and fought under their command." It is extremely absurd to assert that the precedency was claimed by both Hector Reaganach and Lachlan Lùbanach. Surely they must have known which of them held the more prominent position under the Lord of the Isles. There is not the slightest reason to suppose that they ever disputed about anything. They were evidently very affectionate brothers. It will be noticed that, according to the Baronage, it could not be absolutely determined which of the two brothers, Hector Reaganach or Lachlan Lùbanach, was the elder. If it could not be affirmed as a fact in 1798 that Hector Reaganach was older than Lachlan Lùbanach, how can it be affirmed as a fact to-day? The assertion that it appears that the Clan Gillean followed the leadership of the Macleans of Duart on some occasions and the leadership of the Macleans of Lochbuie on other occasions, is utterly groundless; it is actually false. There is nothing of the nature of evidence in existence to show that the Macleans of Duart ever followed, even for one day, the leadership of the Macleans of Lochbuie.

Gregory published his valuable history of the Western Islands and Highlands of Scotland in 1836. He writes as follows about the chiefship of the Macleans:—" Maclean of Duart has generally been considered as the chief of all the Macleans. The house of Lochbuie has always maintained that of the two brothers, Lachlan Lùbanach and Hector Reaganach, the latter was the senior; but this is a point on which there is no certain evidence."—For the assertion that the house of Lochbuie has always maintained that Hector Reaganach was older than Lachlan Lùbanach, there is not a particle of historic authority. Gregory could have no ground for it except the assertions of Murdoch of Lochbuie.

Skene published his Highlanders of Scotland in 1837. He makes the following reference to the chiefship of the Macleans:—"John Dubh had two sons, Lachlan and Hector. The descendants of these brothers have disputed among themselves the honour of the chieftainship of the Clan Gillean; but, although there are no data left from which to ascertain with any degree of certainty in which family the right lay, there seems little reason to doubt that the family of Duart was the principal branch of the clan. Both families produce tradition in support of their claims; but when we consider that upon the Lord of the Isles being compelled, when in the power of both the brothers, to give his daughter to one of them, Lachlan was selected, and that unvaried tradition asserts that his son commanded as lieutenant-general at the battle of Harlaw, it seems probable that Lachlan was the eldest brother, and consequently that the Macleans of Duart were chiefs of the Clan Gillean." The genealogy of the Macleans, which is given in the MS. of 1467, was not known to Gregory in 1836 or to Skene in 1837. It was not known to anyone until 1838. It was published by Skene in 1839. In the notes appended to it, that eminent historian makes the following statements:—" This genealogy of the Macleans agrees pretty exactly with the old genealogy of the clan preserved by the Beatons, their hereditary seannachies. It will be observed that it commences with Lachlan, the progenitor of the Duart family, and this proves the seniority of this branch over that of Lochbuie." We do not agree with Skene in thinking that the fact that the MS. of 1467 begins with Lachlan Lùbanach proves that Lachlan Lùbanach was older than Hector Reaganach. What it really proves is that Lachlan Lùbanach was chief of the Clan Gillean.

III. Proofs of the Chiefship of the Macleans of Duart.

As the Macleans of Duart and the Maclaines of Lochbuie trace themselves back to the same ancestor and call themselves by his name, they constitute only one clan. They have always looked upon themselves as one clan, and have always been looked upon by others as one clan.

The Macleans of Duart and the Maclaines of Lochbuie were feudally independent of one another. The former did not hold their lands of the latter; neither did the latter hold their lands of the former. Maclean of Duart was feudal chief of all the tenants on the Duart estates, whether they were Macleans or not. In the same way Maclean of Lochbuie and all other Maclean lairds who held crown charters, were feudal chiefs of the tenants on their respective estates.

We wish it to be distinctly understood that we do not lay it down as an historic fact that Lachlan Lùbanach was older than Hector Reaganach. So far as the chiefship of the Clan Gillean is concerned, it is a matter of perfect indifference which of the two brothers was the elder. It is only ignorance of the laws and history of the Scottish clans that would lead any person to affirm that if Hector Reaganach was older than Lachlan Lùbanach he must have been chief of the clan. The tradition to which the Maclaines of Lochbuie attach so much importance, does not assert that Hector Reaganach was chief of the Macleans. It tells us indeed that he was not—that his brother Lachlan cheated him out of the chiefship.

Among the proofs of the chiefship of the Macleans of Duart, are the following :—

1. The order in which the names of witnesses to charters is given, shows that the Macleans of Duart were first in rank among the Macleans.

The witnesses to a charter granted by Alexander, third Lord of the Isles, in February, 1443-4, were,—Lachlan M'Gilleon, Lord of Dowart; John Mac Murdoch McGilleon, Lord of Canlochbouye; John Mac Lachlan M'Gilleon, Lord of Coll; Wiland Chisholm and others. The witnesses to a charter granted by John, fourth Lord of the Isles, in August, 1449, were,—John Stewart, Lord of Lorn; Lachlan M'Gilleoin of Doward; John

Mac Murdoch M'Gilleoin of Fynschenys; John Mac Lachlan M'Gilleoin; William, Thane of Cawdor, and others. The witnesses to a charter granted by John of the Isles in April, 1463, were,—Donald of the Isles, Lord of Dunnowage and of the Glynns; Celestine of the Isles, of Lochalsh, and of Lochbryn; Lachlan M'Gilleon, Lord of Dowart; John Munro, Lord of Foulis; Lachlan Og M'Gilleon, son and heir of Lachlan McGilleon of Doward; Ranald Bàn of the Isles and others. The witnesses to a charter granted by John of the Isles in April, 1467, were,—Donald of the Isles; Lachlan McGilleoin, Lord of Doward; Alexander Mac Ian, Lord of Ardnamurchan; Lachlan Og McGilleoin, Master of Doward, and others. The witnesses to a charter granted by John, Lord of the Isles, in June, 1469, were,—Donald of the Isles; Celestine of Lochalsh; Lachlan M'Gilleoin, Lord of Doward; John M'Gilleoin of Lochboyg; Lachlan Og M'Gilleoin, Master of Doward; William M'Loyd of Glenelg; Roderick M'Leoid of Leoghas; Alexander Mac Ian of Ardnamurchan; John Mac Lachlan M'Gilleoin of Coll; and Thomas Monro, secretary to the Lord of the Isles and rector of Kilmanawik. The witnesses to a charter granted by John of the Isles in December, 1478, were,—Colin, Earl of Argyle; Lachlan MakGilleoin of Doward; Hector Mackgilleoin of Loichbowe; William Makloid of Glenelg; Rory Makloide of Lewis; Alexander M'Cane of Ardnamercho; and Malcolm Makneile of Geya.

The charters granted by the Lords of the Isles clearly prove two things: first, that the Macleans of Duart held the first or highest place among the Macleans; and, secondly, that the Macleans of Lochbuie were next in rank to them in the clan.

2. The order in which the names of the leading Islanders appear in a commission written by themselves in July, 1545, shows that Maclean of Duart was the most important man in his own clan. The names are given as follows:—Donald, Lord of the Isles and Earl of Ross; Hector Maclane, Lord of Doward; John Macallister, captain of Clanranald; Rory MacLeod of Lewis; Alexander MacLeod of Dunvegan; Murdoch Maclane of Lochbuy; Angus Maconill, brother of James Maconill; Allan Maclane of Torloisk; Archibald Maconill, captain of the Clan Huistein; Alexander Mackane of Ardnamurchan; John Maclain of Coll; Gilleonan MacNeill of Barray; Mackiynnan of Strathordill; John Macquarrie of Ulva; John Maclane of Ardgour; Alexander Rannoldson of Glengarrie; Angus Ranaldson of Knoydart; and Donald Maclane of Kingerloch.

3. The order in which the names of the barons and gentlemen of the Isles are given in the record of the court which was held at Icolmkill by Bishop Knox in 1609, shows that Maclean of Duart was the leading man among the Macleans. The names are given as follows:—Angus Macdonald of Dunnyveg; Hector Maclean of Dowart; Donald Gorm McDonald of Slait; Rory McCloyd of Harris;

Donald Mac Allan Vic Ian of Ilanteram; Lachlan McCleane of Coll; Lachlan McKynnoun of that ilk; Hector McCleane of Lochbowie; Lachlan and Allan McCleane, brothers-german to Hector McClane of Dowart; Gillespic McQuirie of Ullova; and Donald McFie in Collonsaye.

4. There are certain statements in the Register of the Privy Council which imply that Maclean of Duart was the principal man in his clan. On July 12th, 1616, it is stated that McClayne, McCleod of Harris, the captain of the Clanranald, McKynnoun, Lachlan McClayne, brother to McClayne, and the lairds of Coll and Lochbuy compeared before the Council. It seems that Hector of Duart was known to the Privy Council as Maclean, and Sir Lachlan of Strathordill as Mackinnon; but that Hector Maclean of Lochbuie was known to them merely as the laird of Lochbuie. It is pretty clear, then, that as there was only one "McKynnoun" in Scotland in 1616, so there was only one "McClayne."

5. According to the Highland genealogists, the Macleans of Duart were chiefs of the Clan Gillean. The MS. of 1467 gives the pedigree of the Macleans as follows:—Lachlan, son of John, grandson of Malise, son of Gillean. There is no reference to Hector Reaganach. In the genealogical tables published in Skene's Keltic Scotland, the pedigree of the chiefs of the Macleans is given thus:—Lachlan, son of Hector, son of Lachlan, son of John Dubh. We are also told that John Dubh

had two sons, Lachlan and Hector. It is not said that he had two sons, Hector and Lachlan. The pedigree in the MS. of 1467 begins with Lachlan Lùbanach. The pedigree in Skene's Keltic Scotland begins with Lachlan Bronnach. Macvurich gives the genealogy of the Macleans—not the Macleans of Duart, but the Macleans as a clan—in the Book of Clanranald, and begins it with Sir John of Duart.

6. The Highland bards must have known who the men were that were recognized as chiefs of clans. When we examine their productions we find that they speak of Maclean of Duart generally as Mac-Gilleain, or Maclean, sometimes as ceann-cinnidh Chloinn-Ghilleain, or the kenkinnie of the Macleans, and once or twice as ceannard Chloinn-Ghilleain, or the captain of the Macleans. They refer to Maclean of Lochbuie simply as Maclean of Lochbuie, as Murdoch of Moy, or as Lochbuie. It is thus evident that the old Highland bards believed that Maclean of Duart was the chief of the Macleans. It is equally evident that in the time of the old bards, Maclean of Duart was recognized throughout the whole Highlands as the chief of the Macleans.

7. In all the battles in which the Macleans took part as a clan, they were led by the Lords of Duart. Hector Roy of Duart commanded them at Harlaw; Hector Odhar of Duart commanded them at Bloody Bay and Hallidon Hill; Lachlan Mor of Duart commanded them at Glenlivet; Sir

Lachlan of Duart commanded them in the battles in which they took part in the time of Montrose; Sir Hector Roy of Duart commanded them at Inverkeithing; and Sir John of Duart commanded them at Killiecrankie and Sheriffmuir. The Macleans as a clan were never in one single instance led into battle by a Maclean of Lochbuie.

8. In a letter written by Charles II. to the Privy Council of Scotland on July 10th, 1680, he describes Sir John of Duart as "the laird of Maclean." Thus, according to King Charles, Sir John was chief of the Clan Gillean.

9. According to the acts of the parliaments of Scotland, Sir John Maclean of Duart was laird of Maclean. On May 13th, 1685, King James II. of Britain, with the advice and consent of parliament, appointed certain persons to be commissioners within the sheriffdom of Argyle, for ordering and uplifting the cess. Among those appointed were,—the Earl of Perth, the Marquis of Atholl, the Earl of Breadalbane, Campbell of Lochnell, the laird of Maclean, Lachlan Maclean of Brolas, Lachlan Maclean of Torloisk, Maclean of Ardgour, Maclean of Lochbuie, Macalister of Tarbert, Macdonald of Largie, the laird of Lamont, the laird of Macnaughton, Stewart of Appin, and John Campbell of Glendaruel. The laird of Brolas was convener. The person designated laird of Maclean, was Sir John Maclean of Duart. The words, laird of Maclean, and the words, chief of the Macleans, mean the same

thing. Thus, then, according to King James and the Scottish parliament, Sir John of Duart was the lawful chief of the Macleans, and their only chief.

10. According to the direct testimony of historians and other writers, the Macleans of Duart were the chiefs of the Clan Gillean. We have already seen that Hugh Macdonald, of Sleat, refers to Lachlan Bronnach as the chief of the Macleans. The author of Diurnal Occurrences in Scotland from 1652 to 1654, speaks of the Macleans as one of the greatest clans in Scotland, and states that it was their chief and divers of them who fought so stoutly at Inverkeithing. Thus, then, according to the testimony of a person who wrote in 1652, Hector Roy of Inverkeithing was chief of the Clan Gillean. Martin wrote his Description of the Western Isles of Scotland about 1695. In his account of Mull he makes the following statements :—" The castle of Duart was the seat of Sir John Maclean, head of the ancient family of the Macleans; the castle of Moy is the seat of Maclean of Lochbuie." To say that Sir John was the head of the family of the Macleans is precisely the same thing as to say that he was chief of the Clan Gillean. Dr. Johnson, who visited Mull in 1773, speaks of Sir Allan Maclean of Brolas as " the chieftain of the great clan of Maclean," and of Maclean of Lochbuie as "a very powerful laird." Boswell, who accompanied Dr. Johnson in his travels, speaks

of Sir Allan, in one place, as "the chief of his clan," and, in another place, as "the chief of the Macleans."

Sir Fitzroy Donald Maclean is the lawful heir male of Sir Allan of Brolas, Sir Lachlan of Duart, Hector Og of Duart, and Lachlan Mor of Duart, the mightiest chiefs the Macleans ever had. He is acknowledged as their chief by the Macleans of Duart, Ardgour, Ross, Coll, Kingerloch, Dochgarroch, and Morvern, and by some of the best men among the Maclaines of Lochbuie. We take for granted that some who loyally follow him as their chief really believe that Hector Reaganach was older than Lachlan Lùbanach. This belief, however, does not blind them to the historic fact that the Macleans of Duart were all along the head men or chiefs of the Macleans considered as one great clan. The truth is that, apart from the daring deeds performed by them under the leadership of the Lords of Duart, the Macleans have no historic position—no standing of any kind—as a portion of the Scottish nation from the battle of Harlaw in 1411 to the battle of Sheriffmuir in 1715. Surely the men under whom they distinguished themselves on one bloody field after another must have been their chiefs. If the lairds of Lochbuie were their chiefs, where were they when the Lords of Duart were leading the members of the clan, possibly to death, but certainly to fame as warriors?

ADDITIONS, REFERENCES, AND CORRECTIONS.

PAGE 9.—For "Ewen, Alexander, and Malcolm" read *Ewen, Alexander, and Lachlan;* and for "his brother Alexander" read *his son Alexander.*—According to Mr. A. Brown's Memorials of Argyleshire, the Chartulary of Cupar makes Alexander the son of Duncan. As we took for granted that this was really the case, we stated that Ewen was succeeded by his brother Alexander. We have lately learned from an article by that excellent Keltic scholar, Mr. Alexander Macbain, of Inverness, that the Duncan referred to in the Chartulary of Cupar was Duncan of Lornie, near Perth, not Duncan of Lorn in Argyleshire. There is thus no ground whatever for the assertion that Ewen of Lorn was succeeded by his brother Alexander. It is possible that Alexander was Ewen's nephew, but the probability is that he was his son.—*Transactions of the Gaelic Society of Inverness*, vol. xxi., p. 202.

PAGE 33.—The Ardgour MS. is a work of great value. It contains an account of the Macleans of Duart, Ardgour, Lehir and Ross, Coll, Morvern, Torloisk, and Brolas. It was written between 1762 and 1765. For our copy of it we are indebted to the kindness of the late Alexander Maclean, Esq., of Ardgour.

PAGE 36.—Old Dugald of Scone is referred to in Skene's Keltic Scotland, vol. iii., pp. 62, 343, 361, and 480.

PAGE 44.—For "Donlad" read *Donald*, and for "Bealachuain," *Bailechuain*.—The published portion of the history of the Clan Donald by the Sleat historian will be found in the *Collectanea de Rebus Albanicis*, a rare but very useful work.

PAGE 55.—Maoim Mor le Mac-Dhòmhnaill na h-Alba air Gallaibh Alba, agus Mac-Gille-eoin de mhuinntir Mhic-Dhomhnaill do mharbhadh e am frithghuin a mhaoim sin.—Great onset by Macdonald of Scotland on the Lowlanders of Scotland, and Maclean of Macdonald's people was slain in the heat of that onset.—*Annals of Loch Cé*, vol. ii., p. 137.

PAGE 57.—For the lands granted to Janet Stewart, see The Exchequer Rolls of Scotland, vol. vi., pp. 467, 519, and 654, and also p. 142 of the preface.

PAGE 61.—Apud Edinburgh, 3 Oct., 1496. Rex dedit legitimationem Lachlano Makgilleone, filio naturali Hectoris Macgilleone. Lachlan was thus legitimated on the 3d of October. On the 8th of the same month he received a charter of all the lands which had belonged to his father.

PAGE 68.—Among those slain at Flodden were the Bishop of the Isles, the Earl of Argyll, and "Mack Clene."—*Hall's Chronicle*, p. 563.

PAGE 75.—A.D., 1523.—Macgilleain, i.e., Lachainn Mor Mac Eachainn, do mharbhadh am foill leis an ridire Mac Mhic-Cailin am baile righ Alba *in hoc anno*.—Mac-Gillean, that is, Lachlan Mor, son of Hector, was killed in treachery by the knight, the son of Mac-Cailin, in the King of Albin's town in this year.—*Annals of Loch Cé*, vol. ii., p. 243.

It seems that Lachlan Cattanach was known in Ireland as Lachlan Mor. He was also known as Maclean. Hector Roy, who was killed at Harlaw in 1411, was likewise known in Ireland as Maclean.

PAGE. 95.—For "Tiree" in first line read *Tiree, Morvern, and other lands*. Hector Mor seems indeed to have received a remission for the rents of all his lands.—*Exchequer Rolls*, vol. xvi., p. 566.

ADDITIONS AND CORRECTIONS. 517

PAGE 111.—JOHN DUBH OF MORVERN,—

"REGISTER OF PRIVY COUNCIL.

"STIRLING CASTLE, 28th March, 1579.

"Complaint of John, Bishop of the Isles, as follows:— Although he is lawful Bishop of the Isles, 'be his Hienes and the ordour ressavit in the reformit Kirk of Scotland,' and has been in possession of the bishopric, uplifting 'the maillis and dewities of the samyn, be the space of diverse and sundrie yeiris, yet Johnne Dow McClayne, bailie of Morvarne, Murdo McClayne of Lochboy, Johnne McClayne, Allane McClayne, Ewin McClayne, and Master Lauchlane McClane, his sons, Gilleonane NcNeill of Barray, Rorie Oig, his son and heir, ... , his son, and Gilleonane, his brother, Lauchlane McClayne and Terloch McClayne sons to Donald Murynauch McClayne, Hector McClayne, and Tarloch McClayne, sons to Donald Crowdirnauch McClayne. Donald McClayne, Lauchlane Cam, his brother, Neill McAne VcNeill, Donald Barrach McAchin, Hectour McEwin VcDonald Dow, captain of Carnbulk, Johnne Rogach, his brother, Donald Goddach, his brother, Lauchlane McAne Dow, . . . McNaell of Ballenyntyne, Gillecallum McLauchlane Fyn and his brother, Terloch McAchin Row Our Roy McAchin, Fynnoun McKynnoun of Strathowardill, Lauchlane Oig, his son and apparent heir, Angus McConnell of Dunnaveg, Raunald, Donald Gorm, and Coll his brothers, Raunald McChoill, and Johnne McKane of the Randy, with their accomplices,' not onlie hes maid stop trubill, and impediment to the said Bischope, in uptaking of the maillis, fermes, teindis, proffettis, emolumentis, and dewiteis of the said bischoprik thir diverse yeiris bygane, and in a maner dispossest him thairfra, quhairthrow he gettis littill or na commoditie of the samyn, bot als hes stoppit, and still stoppis and makis impediment to him and his servandis to travell in the cuntrie for doing of thair lefull busines and executing of his office, swa that they, nor utheris our Soverane Lordis trew liegis, sic as merchandis, schipmers, and fischearis dar not resort to the saidis ylis for feir of thair lyvis and spuilyeing of thair guidis, without his Hienes and the Lordis of Secreit Counsale provide sum remeid."

This extract is valuable for its list of names. Professor Mackinnon, of Edinburgh, has kindly examined the original for us, and states that Ballenyntyne is clearly a mistake for Balemertyn, and that Our in Our Roy should perhaps be read Ewir or Ewin. Carnbulk stands for Carnaborg, or Cairnburg.

PAGE 169.—For "Moror" read *Morar*.

PAGE 185.—For "Glenroy, over" read *Glenroy, and over*.

PAGE 231.—For "General Carpenter's dragoons" read *one squadron of Carpenter's dragoons*.

PAGE 244.—For "aithre" read *aire*.

PAGE 248.—The sentence, "John Garbh was the progenitor of the Macleans of Coll," should have come in immediately after the words "Lehir and Ross."

PAGE 254.—"Hector Reaganach was married twice. By his first wife he had at least one son." Instead of these positive assertions we should have written, Hector Reaganach seems to have been married twice, and by his first wife to have had at least one son, Terlach.

According to the genealogical tables published in Skene's Keltic Scotland, Terlach was the third son of Hector Reaganach. The statements of the tables are as follows:—"John had two good sons, Lachlan and Hector. Hector had these sons; Murdoch, Donald, Charles, Ewen, Thomas and Malcolm. They were the sons of Christina, daughter of Macleod, namely, Murdoch, son of Tormod, son of Leod."

Among the reasons for thinking that Hector Reaganach was married twice are the following:—1. Tradition affirms that Terlach was the eldest son of Hector Reaganach. In a letter written on August 3d, 1786, by Hugh Maclean, laird of Kingerloch, to John Maclean of Grulin, we find this statement:—"From the tradition of your own family and others, it was currently affirmed that Charles, son to Hector, first of Lochbuie, was the oldest of several sons, but contented himself with the division of Ardmeanach, and left the rest to the other brothers to divide as they thought proper." The Ardgour MS. assures us that this tradition is true. 2. Douglas's Baronage contains the views held by the Maclaines of Lochbuie respecting their own origin when that work was written, and one of the statements made in it is this: "Hector Reaganach is said to have married a daughter of the Lord of the Isles." It is absolutely certain that Hector Reaganach married Christina, daughter of Murdoch Macleod. If then he married a daughter of the Lord of the Isles, it must have been as his first wife. Lieutenant-Colonel Charles M. Maclean tells us in his History of the Clan Tarlach that—"Tarlach, ancestor of the Clan Tarlach, was a son of Hector Reaganach by a daughter of the Lord of the Isles, and that Murdoch, progenitor of the Macleans of Lochbuie, was his son by a daughter of Macleod of Lewis." Of course Macleod of Lewis is a mistake for Murdoch Macleod, who was of the Harris family. 3. It is tolerably certain that John Og of Lochbuie was not born earlier than 1470. It is thus extremely probable that his great-grandfather, Murdoch of Lochbuie, was not born earlier than 1370. Now in a charter of the year 1427 we find as contemporaries, John Mac Murdoch Mac Hector and Terlach Mac Ferchar Mac Terlach Mac Hector, or John the grandson of Hector Reaganach and Terlach the great-grandson of Hector Reaganach. We also find that when the charter was granted, the daughter of Ferchar Mac Terlach Mac Hector was married, and had children. It is probable then that she was born as early as 1407. It is thus also probable that her grandfather, Terlach Mac Hector, was born as early as 1357—several years earlier than his brother Murdoch.

The argument from tradition in favour of the seniority of Terlach, taken by itself, is not sufficiently strong to counterbalance the statement in Skene's tables, and certainly the assertions of Douglas's Baronage and the History of the Clan Tarlach do not add much weight to it. Taken, however, in connection with the third argument advanced, it possesses some evidential value. The third argument, or the apparent teachings of historic facts, is really the one that leads us to think that Terlach of Urchart was actually older than Murdoch of Lochbuie. But whether he was or not, Murdoch was chieftain of the Macleans of Lochbuie. There can be no dispute about that point.

PAGE 256.—" Apud Linlithgow, 13 Sept., 1538. Rex dedit literas legitimationis Murdaco Makgilleoune et Karolo Makgilleoune bastardis, filiis naturalibus Johannis Makgilleoune de Lochboy, et eorum alteri."—*Register of the Great Seal*, vol. ii., p. 409.

PAGE 262.—A. D. 1651. Murdoch Maclean of Lochbuie and Lachlan Maclean of Calchellie complained to the Estates of Parliament against John Mac Alister Roy, alias Campbell, bailie of Colonsay; Neil Mac Alister Vic Phatrick, alias Campbell, of Torropafe in Islay; Malcolm Mac Ian Roy in Corranbeg, Creignish; Iver Ban Mac Iver of Ardlarich; and others, because in 1647 they went with guns, swords, bows, dorlochs, culverins, pistols, and other weapons, under silence and cloud of night, to the lands of Glengaristil belonging to Murdoch Maclean of Lochbuie, and most cruelly and barbarously murdered John Mac Gilliecalum Vic Donald Duy, John Mac Terlach Vic Alister, Donald Mac Angus Vic Ian, Donald Mac Gilliecalum Vic Donald, John Mac Neill Duy, tenants and servants to said Murdoch Maclean of Lochbuie, all being quietly and peaceably at their own houses. The said murderers were declared to be fugitives and rebels, and ordained to be put to the horn and all their moveable goods to be escheated.— *Acts of the Parliaments of Scotland*, vol. vii., p. 301.

PAGE 272.—For "Glengyrth" read *Glyngarth*.

PAGE 277.—For the obligation given by Alexander of the Isles, see *Thanes of Cawdor*, p. 15.

PAGE 279.—For the first three sentences read, *Hector Buie had six sons: Ewen, Allan, and Ferchar; Neil and Terlach; and Alexander. It is said that the mother of Ewen, Allan, and Ferchar was a daughter of Allan Mac Rory of Moydart. Mora, daughter of Malcolm Mackintosh, was the mother of*

Neil and Terlach. Margaret, daughter *of Hugh Fraser, Lord Lovat, was the mother of Alexander.* **Three of Hector Buie's sons, Ewen,** Ferchar, and Terlach, **survived him.**

PAGE 280.—For " In the same year," &c., read, *On January 6th, 1510, James IV. gave to Ewen Maclean a charter of Kilmalieu, Blaaich, and other lands, all of which had been formerly held by him under the Lord of the Isles. It is certain that the lands thus granted to him had belonged to his father.*—*Reg. Mag. Sig., Lib. XV., No. 71.*

PAGE 307.—HANDFASTING. In his History of the Macleans, Seannachie makes the following statements:—"John, fourth laird of Ardgour, had two sons by a daughter of Mac Ian of Ardnamurchan, whom he had taken upon the prospect of marriage if she pleased him. At the expiration of two years— the period of her noviciate—he sent her home to her father, but the children by her were reputed lawful children, because their mother was taken upon a prospect of marriage."

The assertion that the children by Mac Ian's daughter were reputed lawful children is not true. John of Inverscadale, the elder of the two sons, was a man of ability and prominence; but there was no attempt to make him chieftain of the Macleans of Ardgour. Had he been a lawful son he would certainly have been appointed chieftain.

According to the lowest conception which can be formed of marriage as a divine institution, it is necessary that a man and woman should take each other as husband and wife until God shall separate them by death. In the handfasting ceremony a man merely stood up before witnesses, took a woman by the hand, and declared that he accepted her as his wife for a year and a day or perhaps a longer period. It is clear that there is nothing of the nature of marriage in this ceremony. It is equally clear that the children of handfasting persons were simply illegitimate.

The Ardgour MS. contains the following statements:— "Allan, fourth laird of Ardgour, had two sons by a daughter of Mac Ian of Ardnamurchan, whom he had taken upon a prospect of marriage. After living with him for a year or two, he sent her home to her friends, but the children were reputed as good as lawfully begotten, because their mother was taken upon a prospect of marriage." These statements are correct; but Seannachie in copying them changed their meaning. What the writer of the Ardgour MS. meant was, not that the children were reputed lawful children, but that they held as good a social position as lawful children, which was undoubtedly the case. There were really two classes of natural children; those acknowledged by their fathers as their children, and those who were ignored by their fathers. A child acknowledged by his father as his, provided for and protected by him, was in a very different position from a child who had no father to care for him. It may be regarded as a fact that all the natural children referred to in this work were children who had been treated by their fathers as if they had been born in wedlock. We may state that in Seannachie's History a natural son is invariably described as " another son."

PAGE 309.—For " Anderton" read *Anderston*.

PAGE 310.—Marion, daughter of John Crùbach, was married to Lachlan Macquarrie of Ulva, by whom she had John, whose son Lachlan was born in 1715.

PAGE 320.—The Rev. Archibald Maclean was born in 1679. He died on March 10th, 1755.

PAGE 337.—For "Hodh" read *Hogh*.

PAGE 342.—Extracts from letters by John Maclean, Inverscadale—John, son of Ian Mac Thearlaich Oig.

"ST. ANDREWS, 20th March, 1797.

"One of the chiefs of our clan married a daughter of Macdonald of the Isles, whose arms were blended with ours and used by the clan till lately. On searching the Heralds' Office, it was found that those I use were the proper ones; namely, a mountain called Kernaburg—the stronghold of the clan in times of danger, and very difficult of access—in one quarter; a hand and cross crosslet in another; a galley or lymphad in the third; and two hawk's or griffin's heads and a salmon in the fourth, with a Lochaber axe between branches of laurel and cypress as a crest. The different families of the clan have little or no distinction. Excepting the family of Lochbuie, they all, since the above discovery, at least such as chose to be at the expense of new seals, have assumed them. The lairds of Lochbuie, indeed, have of late taken it into their heads to dispute the chiefship, and have chosen sea dogs or seals for their supporters, animals as awkward and clumsy as their pretensions, as the honour of the chiefship by universal consent was vested in the Duart branch from the earliest settlement of the clan in Scotland.

"The motto was originally *Vincere vel mori*, but as some other clans had the same, Sir John or Sir Hector—I forget which—changed it to *Altera merces*, which is of pretty much the same import, alluding to the crest, cypress and laurel, emblems of death and victory. The full arms with supporters have for motto, *Virtus et durissima terit*, alluding to the digestive power of the ostrich's stomach, said, whether true or false, to overcome the hardest substances, even iron.

"At the battle of Largs in 1263, Gillean made such slaughter among the Danes with his battle-axe as drew the attention of the King and his generals. After the battle the King took great notice of him and gave him lands and armorial bearings, insisting he should have a Lochaber axe as his crest, to commemorate the noble use he made of it that day.

"At the battle of Flodden in 1513, where James IV. was killed, one of our chiefs and 500 of his clan fell fighting around that brave though rash prince. Sir Hector, one of the first warriors of the age, was killed at Inverkeithing with 750 Macleans. Of 1000 fine fellows who followed their chief 250 only got off, most of them wounded. In point of numbers we have scarcely got the better of this yet."

PAGE 364.—Lachlan Maclean and Lucy Campbell, his wife, had five children; Donald, James, Alexander-Colin, Jessie, and Bethia. The second daughter, Bethia, was married to Peter

Pattison, by whom she had Thomas and Mary-Hamilton. Mary was married to Archibald Robertson.

PAGE 366.—In the last circular anent this history it was stated that the Chief of the Clan had offered to take ten copies more, and Lieutenant-Colonel H. H. McLean five copies more, if necessary. It should have been stated that Mr. Maclean of Breda had also offered to take five copies more.

PAGE 372.—For " Knockcarrach " read *Knockcorrach*.

PAGES 384 and 395.—For "Grimsary" read *Grimisary*.

PAGE 389.—For "Airleod" read *Arileod*.

PAGE 414, line 12.—For "Catherine," &c., read *Catherine, Allan, Helena, Polly*, &c.

PAGE 416.—Dr. E. F. Reed and Hannah Maclean, his wife, had seven children; Julia, Ebenezer-Fitch, Maro-Maclean, Mary-Eliza, Harriet-Smith, Julius-Alexander, and Rosanna. Julius married Caroline Blood, by whom he had Anna, Rosanna, and Mary. Anna was married to Henry M. Wilkinson.

PAGE 443, line 8.—For "Deputy Surgeon-General" read *Deputy Inspector-General*.

PAGE 468.—For "Mary-Louisa" read *Mary-Julia*. Seannachie's History was written by Neil Maclean.

PAGE 468.—For "BHRÓLAIS" read BHRÒLAIS.

PAGE 474, line 10.—For "and has by her five children," &c., read *and had by her five children; Hector-Fitzroy, Charles-Lachlan, Fitzroy-Holland, John-Marsham, and Finvola-Marianne-Eleanor*.

PAGE 484, line 29.—Alexander Maclean married Lydia Catherine Rice, by whom he had James T., Annie M., Armenia E., and Alice A.

PAGE 487, line 2.—For "1899" read *1889*.

PAGE 488, lines 22 and 28.—For "James A." read *J. A.*

PAGE 503, line 10.—For "absolutely be determined" read *be absolutely determined*.

PAGE 513, line 7.—For "chiefs" read *chief*.

LIST OF SUBSCRIBERS.

SCOTLAND.

The Clan Maclean Association, Glasgow (**20** copies)
Prof. Magnus Maclean, D.Sc., 51 Kersland Terrace, Glasgow
John Maclean, 68 Mitchell Street, Glasgow
Mrs. A. H. Maclean, 3 Kirklee Gardens, Glasgow
Andrew Bruce Maclean, Craigpark, Denniston, Glasgow
Peter Maclean, 5 Cecil Street, Ibrox, Glasgow
Neil Maclaine, 2 Rutland Crescent, Glasgow
Sir Andrew Maclean, Viewfield House, Partick, **Glasgow**
John Maclean, 4 Buchanan Street, Partick, Glasgow
John Maclean, 35 Thornwood Terrace, Partick, Glasgow
Hugh Maclean, 32 Gardner Street, Partick, Glasgow
Angus Maclean, 6 Lorne Street, Glasgow
James B. Maclean, 52 West Nile Street, Glasgow
Lachlan Maclean, 56 Paterson Street, S.S., Glasgow
Neil Maclean, 56 Paterson Street, S.S., Glasgow
William Maclean, 345 St. Vincent Street, Glasgow
William Maclean of Plantation, 115 St. Vincent Street, Glasgow
Charles J. Maclean, 115 St. Vincent Street, **Glasgow**
Walter Maclean, 2 Bothwell Circus, Glasgow
Peter Maclean, 76 Elderslie Street, Glasgow
William Maclean, 25 Wellington Street, Glasgow
Hugh Maclean, 122 Union Street, Glasgow
Hector Maclean, 84 Paisley Road West, Glasgow
Hector Maclean, 5 Belgrave Street, Glasgow
Alexander Maclean, 42 Blackburn Street, Glasgow
R. Maclean, 69 Main Street, Anderston, Glasgow
Roderick Maclean 58 Sandyford Street, Glasgow
John Maclean, 23 Kensington Terrace, Ibrox, Glasgow (2 **copies**)
Malcolm Maclean, 42 York Street, Glasgow
Hugh Maclean, 14 Selborne Terrace, Woodlands Road, Glasgow
Allan Maclaine, 1085 Pollokshaws Road, Glasgow
Hugh Maclean, 74 Ardgowan Street, Glasgow
Malcolm B. Maclean, 59 Cambridge Drive, Glasgow
Rev. E. D. Fingland, 9 Fitzroy Place, Glasgow
Neil C. Colquhoun, 64 Couper Street, Glasgow

LIST OF SUBSCRIBERS.

Mrs. Donald, 13 Gloucester Street, Glasgow
Duncan Macfarlane, 7 May Terrace, Mount Florida, Glasgow
The University Library, Glasgow
The Faculty of Procurators' Library, Glasgow
The Mitchell Library, Glasgow
Neil Maclean of Breda, Alford, Aberdeenshire (10 copies)
Rev. Lachlan Maclean Watt, M.A., B.D., Turiff, Aberdeenshire
J. A. Maclean, Forfar, Forfarshire (3 copies)
A. R. Maclean Murray, Grove House, Brechin, Forfarshire
James A. Maclean, Linden Lodge, Strawberry Bank, Dundee
Neil Maclean, 4 Windsor Terrace, Stranraer, Wigtownshire
C. A. Maclean, Writer, Wigtown, Wigtownshire
Rev. John Maclean, Minister of Grandtully, Aberfeldy, **Perthshire**
Duncan Maclean, 4 Rose Terrace, Perth
Rev. Daniel Maclean, Bellvue, Alloa, **Clackmannanshire**
William **Gordon** Maclean, Lindenlee, **Trinity Road, Edinburgh**
Robert Maclean, Advocate, 19 Queen **Street, Edinburgh**
The Advocates' Library, Edinburgh
University Library, Edinburgh
Rev. **A.** G. Maclean, The Rectory, Selkirk
James S. Maclean, Myrtle Cottage, Alexandria, Dumbartonshire
Robert M. MacFarlane, 2 Strathleven Place, Dumbartonshire
R. Maclean, Merchant, Bridge of Weir, Renfrewshire
A. Scott Maclean, M. I. M. E., 31 Bank Street, Greenock (2 copies)
James Maclean, 7 Ardgowan Street, Greenock
Donald Maclean, Rhives, Golspie, Sutherlandshire
Duncan Maclean, 14 Strath, Gairloch, Ross-shire
Murdo Maclean, Commission Agent, Stornoway, Lewis
John Maclean, Merchant, Point Street, Stornoway
Charles Maclean, Milton, South Uist, Inverness-shire
Rev. D. Maclean, Duirinish, Skye
Rev. John Maclean, Bracadale, Skye
Rev. D. Maclean, Tomatin, Inverness-shire
Ewen Maclean, 106 Church Street, Inverness
William Mackay, Solicitor, Inverness
Nigel Banks Mackenzie, Fort-William, Lochaber
Mrs. Maclean of Ardgour, Ardgour, Argyleshire
Angus McLean, Contractor, Tobermory, Mull
Peter Maclean, M.D., Glenview, Dervaig, Mull
C. R. Morison, Aintuim, Dervaig, Mull
C. A. McVean, Kilfinichen, Mull
Archibald Maclean, Arileod, Coll
John Lorne Stewart of Coll, Coll
Rev. Dugald Maclean, Hylipol, Tiree

ENGLAND.

The Chief of the Clan Gillean, **15** Hyde Park Terrace, London (10 copies)
Hector Fitzroy Maclean, **15** Hyde **Park** Terrace, London (3 copies)
R. M. Maclean, Royal Colonial Institute, London (3 copies)
Malcolm Maclean, Elmdale, Palmer's Green, London (4 copies)
Charles Maclean, M.D., 159 Cromwell Road, South Kensington, London
C. Fraser-Mackintosh of **Drummond**, LL.D., F.S.A. Scot., 18 Pont Street, London, S.W.

LIST OF SUBSCRIBERS.

Major Alex. W. D. Maclean, 50 Bessborough Street, London, S.W.
Hector A. C. Maclean, 50 Bessborough Street, London, S.W.
Lieut. H. D. Neil Maclean, 50 Bessborough Street, London, S.W.
Mrs. O. L. E. Maclean, 50 Bessborough Street, London, S.W.
Lord Alwyne Compton, M.P., 7 Balfour Place, London, W.
Ewen J. Maclean, M.D., 51 Linden Gardens, Bayswater, London, W.
J. G. Maclean, 21 Cadogan Garden, London, S.W.
David Maclean, 5 Kensington Court, London, W. (2 copies)
Thomas Maclean, 7 Haymarket, London, N.
Miss Georgiana Flora Maclean, 13 Fopstone Road, Earle's Court, London, W.
Miss Isabella S. Maclean, 60 Central Hill, Upper Norwood, London
Miss F. M. Maclean, 54 Belvedere Road, Norwood, London, S.E.
Miss Lucy Maclean, 63 Fitzjohns Avenue, Hampstead, London.
Miss Margaret Maclean, 63 Fitzjohns Avenue
Miss Nora Maclean, 63 Fitzjohns Avenue
Mrs. S. Percy Howard, 25 Sussex Gardens, London, W.
Baroness De Pallandt, 36 Bryanston Street, London
Lady Hood of Avalon, 19 Queen's Gate Place, London
Rev. Arthur J. Maclean, Isthmean Club, Piccadilly, London
James Maclean, M.D., 97 Fitzwilliam Street, Sheffield
William Maclean, Grandtully, West Hartlepool (2 copies)
Miss Emily F. H. Maclean, West Cliffe House, Folkestone (2 copies)
Capt. William Maclean, Superintendent Sailors' Home, Southampton
Allan Maclean, M.D., Weymouth, Dorset
Allan Maclean, 47 Hove Park, Hove, Brighton
Rev. Allan M. Maclean, 47 Hove Park, Hove, Brighton
Rev. Hector Maclean, 47 Hove Park, Hove, Brighton
John Robert Maclean of Aston Hall, Shifnal, Shropshire (2 copies)
George W. Maclean, 3 Jesmond Villas, Newcastle-on-Tyne
Major-General C. S. Maclean, Shanklin, Isle of Wight
James Maclean, Old Wittington, N. Chesterfield
The Honourable Mrs. Nevill, Birling Manor, Maidstone
Mrs. Francis, Woodhurst Shorne, near Gravesend
The Marquis of Northampton, Castle Ashby, Northampton
J. Campbell Maclean, M.D., Swindon House, Swindon, Wilts
Mrs. Hamilton-Dundas, Duddingstoun, Torquay
T. B. Maclean, Gresham Rectory, Norwich
Mrs. D. H. Maclean, Stobery, Wells, Somerset
Lady Llangattock, The Hendre, Monmouth (2 copies)
Donald Maclean, Albion Chambers, Cardiff
John Mackay, C.E., Reay House, Hereford

NORWAY, GERMANY, AND HOLLAND.

W. M. Homan, Oscars Gade, Christiania
Archibald Maclean, 25 Koninggraetzer Strasse, Berlin
Dr. P. Maclaine Pont, Copes 72, The Hague
Miss M. W. Maclaine Pont, Zetten, Gelderland

ASIA, AFRICA, AND AUSTRALASIA.

Lieut. A. H. Maclean, 93d Highlanders, Shahjahanpur, N.W.P., India
Lieut. Charles A. H. Maclean, 93d Highlanders, Shahjahanpur, N.W.P., India

LIST OF SUBSCRIBERS.

Surgeon-Major Fitzroy B. Maclean, Campbellpore, Punjaub
W. Maclaine Pont. Totok, Manado, Dutch East India
Kaid Maclean, C.M.G., Fez, Morocco
Lachlan Maclean, Greenhill, Kenilworth, Cape Town (10 copies)
Hon. R. D. Douglas Maclean, Napier, Hawke's Bay, New Zealand, (2 copies)
P. S. Maclean, Barrister and Solicitor, Napier, New Zealand
A. A. Maclean, Inverell, New South Wales
John E. B. Maclean, Munbilla, Queensland
Capt. Alex. McLean, Geelong Street, E. Brisbane, Queensland

UNITED STATES.

Malcolm Maclean, M.D., 29 East 126th Street, New York (2 copies)
Donald Maclean, Counsellor-at-Law, 27 William Street, New York, (2 copies)
George Hammond Maclean, 126 West 57th Street, New York (2 copies)
Frank B. Maclean, 1829 Washington Avenue, New York
Rev. J. L. Campbell, D.D., 20 East 120th Street, New York
W. Pender Maclean, 476 Lexington Avenue, New York.
Hon. J. R. Maclean, 1500 First Street, Washington, D.C.
Mrs. Helen L. McL. Kimball, office of Comptroller of the Currency, Washington, D.C.
Mrs. George Mackintosh Maclean, 73 Alexander Street, Princeton, New Jersey
Mrs. C. F. Kroeh, 328 Central Avenue, Orange, New Jersey
Thomas Neil Maclean, M.D., Elizabeth, New Jersey
Mrs. John A. Buckingham, Watertown, Connecticut (2 copies)
Hon. George P. Maclean, Simsbury, Connecticut
Mrs. Mary D. Maclean, Wethersfield, Connecticut
Mrs. Theodore S. Ferry, Bethel, Connecticut
John McLean, Danbury, Connecticut (2 copies)
Mrs. Henry W. Wilkinson, 168 Bowen St., Providence, R.I. (2 copies)
R. E. Maclean, Escanaba, Michigan (3 copies)
Rev. J. T Maclean, M A., Oakryn, Penn. (4 copies)
W. S. McLean, Wilkes Barre, Penn. (2 copies)
David M. McLean, Chicago, Ill.
Alexander Campbell Maclean, M.D., Salt Lake City, Utah
G. D. McClain, 1537 Washington Avenue, Denver, Colorado
Robert A. McLean, M.D., 305 Kearney St., San Francisco, California

CANADA.

Alexander Campbell, Strathlorne, Cape Breton
Donald E. Maclean, Strathlorne, Cape Breton
A. G. McLean, Sydney, Cape Breton
Rev. Lachlan A. Maclean, B.A., Louisburg, Cape Breton
Allan Maclean, 28 Cornwallis Street, Halifax, N.S.
A. H. Mackay, LL.D., Superintendent of Education, Halifax, N.S.
A. K. Maclean, Barrister and Solicitor, Lunenburg, N.S.
Mrs. Hector Maclean, Bridgetown, Annapolis, N.S.
James A. Maclean, Q.C., Bridgewater, N.S.
Rev. J. B. Maclean, Upper Stewiacke. N.S. (2 copies)
Henry Gray Maclean, Amherst, N.S.
Alister Maclean, Amherst, N.S.
Rev. James Maclean, Great Village, N.S.

List of Subscribers.

Rev. A. Maclean, D.D., Hopewell, Pictou, N.S.
Rev. Andrew Macgillivray, Dunmaglass, Antigonish, N.S.
Alexander Maclean, Glenbard, Antigonish, N.S.
Hon. D. Farquharson, Premier of Prince Edward Island, Charlottetown, P.E.I.
Hon. James R. Maclean, Charlottetown, P.E.I.
J. J. Davies, Hotel Davies, Charlottetown, P.E.I. (3 copies)
Capt. Alexander Cameron, Charlottetown, P.E.I.
Capt. Ewen Maclean, Charlottetown, P.E.I.
Tormoid Mac-Leoid, Charlottetown, P.E.I.
Malcolm Macleod, Q.C., Charlottetown, P.E.I.
J. D. Macleod, Charlottetown, P.E.I.
D. A. Mackinnon, M.L.A., Charlottetown, P.E.I.
Mrs. John F. Whear, Charlottetown, P.E.I.
Rev. J. C. Maclean, St. George's, P.E.I.
Rev. Malcolm Campbell, Strathalbyn, P.E.I.
Lieut.-Col. H. H. McLean, St. John, N.B. (10 copies)
Rev. D. Henderson, Chatham, N.B.
Lieut.-Col. John Bayne Maclean, Montreal (7 copies)
David McLean, City Hall, Montreal, Quebec
Capt. Hugh C. Maclean, 20 Front Street, Toronto, Ontario
W. F. Maclean, M.P., 610 Jarvis Street, Toronto, Ontario
Allan Maclean Howard, 192 Carlton Street, Toronto, Ontario
Malcolm Maclean, Postmaster, Walkerton, Ontario

THE MACLEAN BARDS.

"THE OLD MACLEAN BARDS" was published in 1898. It is the first volume of "The Maclean Bards," and contains the extant productions of all the Maclean poets who flourished between 1525 and 1775. It is sold at the low price of two shillings and sixpence, and is thus within the reach of the poorest persons who may desire to have a copy of it. Towards defraying the expenses of publishing it, the following contributions were given :—

Sir Andrew Maclean, Partick, Glasgow	$ 5.10
The Clan Maclean Association, Glasgow	5.10
Prof. Magnus Maclean, Glasgow	5.00
William Maclean, 115 St. Vincent Street, Glasgow	1.82
C. J. Maclean, 115 St. Vincent Street, Glasgow	1.82
Walter Maclean, 2 Bothwell Circus, Glasgow	1.82
James B. Maclean, 56 West Nile Street, Glasgow	1.22
John Maclean, 68 Mitchell Street, Glasgow	1.22
Robert M. MacFarlane, 2 Strathleven Place, Dumbartonshire	2.43
Thomas Maclean, B. L. Bank, Alexandria	1.22
Neil Maclean of Breda, Aberdeenshire	25.00
J. A. Maclean, Forfar	9.75
James A. Maclean, Dundee	5.10
Rev. John Maclean, Aberfeldy, Perthshire	1.22
Neil Maclaine, Stranraer	1.22
K. A. Maclean, Muir of Ord	1.22
C. R. Morison, Aintuim, Mull	2.43
THE CHIEF OF THE CLAN GILLEAN	25.00
Miss E. F. H. Maclean, West Cliffe House, Folkestone	7.31
H. A. C. Maclean, 50 Bessborough Street, London	4.87
William Maclean, West Hartlepool	3.10
Mrs. Hamilton-Dundas, Duddingstoun	2.55
Edmund Eaton, Burwash, Sussex	1.34
Lachlan Maclean, Kenilworth, Cape Town	10.21

Prof. J. P. MacLean, Greenville, Ohio	$ 5.00
D. T. Macdonald, Red Jacket, Michigan	5.00
Mrs. H. L. McL. Kimball, Washington, D.C.	2.00
Lieut.-Col. H. H. McLean, St. John, N.B.	10.00
Lieut.-Col. John Bayne Maclean, Montreal	5.00
Rev. A. Maclean, D.D., Hopewell, N.S.	5.00
Hector Maclean, Bridgetown, N.S.	5.00
Rev. Roderick Maclean, Valleyfield, P.E.I	5.00

※ ※ ※

"THE MACLEAN BARDS FROM 1775 TO 1900," or Vol. II. of "The Maclean Bards," is ready for publication. It contains poems by all the Maclean poets and song-writers who have written in Gaelic during the last one hundred and twenty-five years. The following sums have been received towards defraying the cost of publishing it:—

THE CHIEF OF THE CLAN GILLEAN	$14.60
Neil Maclean of Breda, Aberdeenshire	14.60
Major-General C. S. Maclean, Isle of Wight	4.87
Hector Maclean, Bridgetown, N.S.	5.00
Rev. Andrew Macgillivray, Dunmaglass, N.S.	5.00

It would take an additional sum of about one hundred dollars to make the work what it ought to be. The printer should have the copy in his hands in December. The book would then appear early in 1900.

Supplementary List of Subscribers.

Charles Lachlan Maclean, Lieut. R.N., 15 Hyde Park Terrace, London.

John Marsham Maclean, Lieut. R.A., 15 Hyde Park Terrace, London.

Alexander Maclean, H.M.S. "Re Adelaide," Chatham.

Andrew Bruce Maclean, Craigpark, Dennistoun, Glasgow *(additional 4 copies)*.

George A. Maclean, Hythe Hill, Elgin *(2 copies)*.

John Maclean, 43 Paisley Road West, Glasgow.

Ronald John Maclean, 113 Springburn Road, Glasgow.

George W Maclean, 3 Jesmond Villas, Newcastle-on-Tyne

John A. Maclean, Mariano Railway, Havana, Cuba. *(additional)*.

D. G. Macdonald, Point Prison, P.E.I.

James Paton, Charlottetown, P.E.I.

H. Travers Maclean, Supreme Court Library, Auckland, New Zealand.

Charles James Maclean, 14 Winchester Road, South Hampstead, London, N.W.

Angus Maclean, 1 Buchanan Street, Partick.

A. G. Robertson, Lismore, New South Wales.

www.ingramcontent.com/pod-product-compliance
Lightning Source LLC
Chambersburg PA
CBHW030300010526
44108CB00038B/693